Visual Perception

VISUAL PERCEPTION

TOM N. CORNSWEET

Stanford Research Institute

Academic Press   New York and London

Academic Press, Inc.
111 Fifth Avenue, New York, New York 10003

United Kingdom Edition published by
Academic Press, Inc. (London) Ltd.
Berkeley Square House, London W1X 6BA

Library of Congress Catalog Card Number: 71-107570

Printed in the United States of America

Contents

Preface

This book grew out of courses that I have taught at Yale University and the University of California, Berkeley. It is aimed at bright undergraduate and graduate students, regardless of their academic backgrounds. Although the text leans heavily upon physical and physiological concepts, I have tried to include explanations of the relevant physics and physiology, so that readers with limited backgrounds in these areas will not be handicapped.

I have covered what I believe are the fundamental topics underlying the entire, broad field of visual perception. This material can serve both as a factual background for further topics in perception, and also, I hope, as a set of paradigms for approaches to additional topics in vision and other sensory modalities. The areas discussed most extensively are those related to the perception of brightness and color. These topics are considered in depth, and I have tried to discuss both aspects of perception that are well understood and problems that have not yet been solved.

I consider that a perceptual phenomenon has a scientific explanation if it can be shown to be a particular instance of a more general perceptual property or law, or if its physiological correlates are understood. In this light, I have restricted the coverage to only two kinds of topics, those for which there is a widely accepted explanation at the present time, and those for which I can imagine one or more plausible explanations that may not yet have been adequately tested. Thus, I have excluded many topics (for example, the influence of motivation upon perception) because my own capacity for inventing coherent and complete explanations is simply not sufficient to handle them, and others because I do not know enough about them to explain them plausibly (for example, the perception of movement).

Because each section of this book is built upon the material that has preceded it, the text should be read in the order presented. I would also urge the reader not to skip any of the material; if he is already familiar with a given topic (for example, the physics of light, Chapter III), he should skim those pages, not skip them, since there may well be material there that *is* new to him (for example, the material on the optics of the eye in Chapter III).

This is not a reference work; rather, it is aimed at developing an *understanding* of visual perception. For this reason, the number of references is limited. I have tried to select those references on each topic that seemed most likely to lead the interested reader to a more complete listing of the relevant literature. (Many of the references that are included are given in the figure captions.) There is a listing of some secondary sources at the end of the book that provide more complete documentation.

There are brief problem sets following some chapters. These problems are an integral part of the text, in that many of them require the reader to consider aspects of the topics that are not directly covered in the text itself. I have furnished answers to only a small proportion of the problems, because I have found that easy access to answers often short-circuits even the most earnest student's thinking.

Acknowledgments

Several people have provided invaluable help in the preparation of this book. John Krauskopf and Michael Katcher have given me extremely useful comments on the entire manuscript, and Donald H. Kelly, Hewitt D. Crane, and John Foley have been very helpful with certain sections of the book. All of the illustrations except the simpler graphs have been beautifully prepared by Peter Howland.

I also wish to thank all of my students. They will readily recognize their large contributions to this book.

Visual Perception

1 ◇◇◇ INTRODUCTION

AT every instant, the amount of information available to us is immeasurably great. Electromagnetic radiation of all wavelengths and combinations of wavelengths—radio waves, light waves, and X rays—shower us all the time. Our environment is saturated with sounds, changes in air pressure and temperature, and changes in the chemical composition of the air. No real system, physical or biological, could possibly register and make use of all of this vast array of combinations of the physical conditions in the environment. The information that is actually registered or acted upon by a real organism is always a very small fraction of that which could be used by an imaginary perfect system. All organisms select part of the information in their environment to register or act upon, and the rest of that information is lost to them. The factors that determine the way in which this selection is performed are properties of the organism itself. They are the ways in which the organism interacts with the physical properties of its environment.

In this book, the nature of our perceptual system will be discussed in terms of the kinds of information that we are able to assimilate from the world. This selection of information is governed by the structure of our receptors and the neural circuits that are connected to them. The topic defined by these considerations consists of the relationships between the physical variables in the environment and the physiological properties of the sensory systems of an organism. Our knowledge of these relationships is based in part on physiological studies, but it is also based in large part on a certain class of perceptual studies in which a subject is presented with stimuli, and in certain carefully prescribed ways, is asked what he sees. This book will discuss data gathered both in physiological and perceptual experiments.

The study of the relationship between information assimilation and the physiology of the visual system is only a part of the topic called visual perception. We use language and other symbols to refer to our experiences. We say that a light is bright or red. The relationships between these symbols and their corresponding physical and physiological variables are also in the domain of perception, but, while they are closely related to information processing, they must be treated separately, and will be so treated here.

INFORMATION The term *information* will be used in its common-sense meaning in this book, and it is important to clarify just what the common-sense meaning of that term is. If you acquire some information, that means that you know something that you did not know before. For example, suppose that a red bulb is on. (It could be on or off.) If your eyes are built in such a way that they can interact with the energy sent out by the bulb, and if your eyes are open and pointed at the bulb, and if there is nothing opaque between you and it, you will be able to acquire the bit of information that the light is on (instead of the alternative, off). This particular bit of information thus would allow you to make the correct choice between two alternatives, light on and light off. You will also acquire many other bits of information related to the color, the shape, etc. of the bulb.

In general, visual information is transmitted to us by light energy, or more accurately, by differences in light energy (in this example, the difference between the energy when the bulb is on versus that when it is off), but it is useful to distinguish between the energy and the information itself. For example, you might acquire the information that the bulb is on even if you are blind. Someone else might tell you. In that case, the information was carried to you by sound energy, but it is exactly the same information. A more relevant example is this: When the light from the bulb is absorbed by your visual receptors, the energy that carries the bit of information that the bulb is on (instead of off) is changed from light to chemical energy, but the bit of information itself is unchanged.

If the red light is on but the subject's eyes are closed, we may say that the information is present in the environment, but it is not assimilated by his system. Now suppose his eyes are open. How can we find out whether or not his system loses the information that the bulb is on? We must have some means of measuring the transmission of information through the subject's system.

We have been assuming that *we* know whether or not the bulb is on. Say that we know it is on because we can see it. (You may wish to call this the *definition* of the fact that the bulb is on.) If we want to know whether or not the subject's system is capable of retaining or acting upon that information (i.e., whether or not he sees this particular kind of light), we must engage in a somewhat complicated procedure. Suppose we just ask him if he sees the light, and he says "yes." That response tells us nothing positive about his response to the light. It only tells us about his response to the question. He might be lying, or he might not really understand the question. (For instance, if he had been blind from birth, he might well use the word "see" to refer to something when he is able to imagine it.) To determine whether or not his system really retains the information about the *light*, we must give him a series of trials such that, in some of them the bulb is on and in the remainder the bulb is off, recording his response to each trial. We then look at the correlation between the presence or absence of the light and his responses, and if that correlation is great enough, we can conclude that his system does not lose the information carried by the rays from the bulb. (There are obviously several restrictions we must impose on the procedure, making sure that no information other than the light itself is available to the subject. For instance, the bulb should not make a noise audible to the subject.)

The measurement just described tells us whether or not the subject's system in its entirety, including his eyes, brain, vocal cords, toes, etc., is capable of retaining and acting upon information about the presence or absence of the light. If we want to be more specific about which parts of his system are involved in the process, we must do additional experiments. One class of such experiments involves cutting off things like toes. If he can demonstrate that he still retains the information after the removal of his toes, we know that toes are not necessary. If the removed toes themselves respond in a way correlated with the presence or absence of the light, we can conclude that they are sufficient for the process.

A second class of experiments involves the measurement of responses within the system. For example, we might place electrodes on the nerves leading from the eyes to the brain, and determine whether or not the electrical responses recorded there correlate with the presence or absence of the light. If there is a correlation, then we may say that the information is present at that point in the nervous system.

The discussion above has been quite general, and, in some ways, loose. It is intended primarily as an introduction to the use of the word *information* in the context of perceptual studies, because this concept will be used extensively throughout the remainder of the book. The collection of phenomena that we call visual perception will be discussed in terms of information processing, and the physiological correlates of this processing will be analyzed where it is possible to do so.

The likelihood that an animal will survive depends upon his ability to use information from his environment. That is, he must be able to sense the occurrence of various conditions (the lion in the grass) and also to respond appropriately (faint). The ideal animal would be able to sense every aspect of the infinite array of information present in the environment and respond appropriately. However, there is obviously no advantage in being able to sense information for which the appropriate response is impossible, or for which there is no useful response. Furthermore, there is no survival value in having the capability for sensing some form of information that is never present in the environment. If we assume that the processes of evolution result in the selection of mechanisms advantageous for survival and the elimination of useless mechanisms, then it follows that the range of stimuli to which our sensory systems respond will be limited by the nature of the interaction between the environment and our *response* capabilities. In other words, our sensory systems select and transmit, from the infinite array of information impinging upon us, those aspects of the information that are useful, and lose the remaining information.

Our sensory capacities are not only limited by the factors just discussed, however. Each of us is of a finite size, and evolution still has a long way to go. Thus, there are many kinds of information that would be useful, but we are simply not big enough to contain the systems needed for detecting them or responding to them. (While we wait for evolution to provide us with ionizing radiation receptors, we build devices like Geiger counters. The results of this kind of technology may be considered either to hinder evolution or to be a part of it.) There appears to be a very real order to the kinds of selections of information that have been forced upon our sensory systems by this size limitation, and we are making rapid progress in understanding the nature of these selections and the mechanisms that make them. That is the heart of the content of this book.

II ◇◇◇ THE EXPERIMENT OF HECHT, SCHLAER, AND PIRENNE

IN 1942, Hecht, Schlaer, and Pirenne reported an experiment of extraordinary significance.[1] They presented flashes of light to normal human subjects, and determined the lowest possible intensity of that light that the subjects could see. The results were extremely surprising, and led immediately to many strong conclusions about the structure of the visual system and the nature of perceptual processes.

Their experiment is also very useful in a different way. The considerations that Hecht et al. had to entertain in order to design and perform the experiment form a useful outline of a large part of our knowledge of perceptual phenomena and of their underlying physiological pro-

[1]The articles and books referred to in the text are listed in the bibliography at the end of the book.

6

cesses. These considerations, and the results of the experiment, will be described briefly in this chapter and elaborated in succeeding chapters.

THE GENERAL DESIGN OF THE EXPERIMENT An apparatus was built that permitted the experimenters to present a subject with flashes of light at a particular location in his visual field. The intensity, color, size, and duration of these flashes could be controlled very accurately. The location, color, size, and duration were then set at particular values (chosen by the criteria to be discussed below), and a series of flashes was presented at varying intensities.[2]

Each time a flash was given, the subject said whether or not he saw it, and the intensity at which he said he saw the flash on 60% of the trials was defined as the threshold intensity.

The immediate goal of the experiment was to find the lowest possible intensity that permitted the subject to see the flashes, and it was already well known that the color of the light, its location on the eye, its timing, and its size all influenced this threshold level. It was also known that the state of the subject's eye critically affected his threshold. Therefore, Hecht et al. chose the values for each of these aspects of the experiment that yielded the lowest possible threshold.

THE STATE OF THE SUBJECT—DARK ADAPTATION It was already well known, at the time that Hecht et al. performed their experiment, that a subject is more sensitive to dim flashes of light if he has been in the dark for a period of time than if he has just come in out of the light. It is a common experience to be almost blind when first entering a movie theater, but to be able to see quite a lot after 5 or 10 minutes. This phenomenon is dark adaptation.

[2]The names and classes of photometric units (units describing amounts of light) have grown over the years into an unbelievably confusing jumble. There are few among even the most scholarly who can tell you how many nits (sic) there are in an apostilb, or even whether or not there are any. (There are either $1/\pi$ or $1.018/\pi$, depending upon whether in the book I am referring to, cd stands for candle or candela; or maybe there are $1.10/\pi$ if the apostilbs are in German [Hefner] units.) Worse yet, a few words that have useful and unambiguous meanings to the typical speaker of English have been assigned specific definitions, so that it is now improper to use those terms to refer to what they used to refer to. The difficulties involved in correctly using photometric units are further compounded in a book of this kind because the meanings of most units depend upon certain optical and perceptual concepts and facts with which the reader is not yet acquainted.

The term "intensity" is improperly used throughout this book. Technically, it applies only to point sources of light; it is not proper, for example, to say anything about the intensity of light falling on a surface, or the intensity of the stimulus (unless it happens to be a point source). Nevertheless, it is probably better, pedagogically, to use the word "intensity" improperly. When used in this book, it means just what you think it means.

The curve in Fig. 2.1 is the result of a study of this phenomenon. The subject was first exposed to a bright light for a few minutes, then the light was extinguished, and his sensitivity to brief flashes of light was measured, under conditions similar to Hecht's experiment, as a function of time after the offset of the bright light. Notice that his sensitivity increases rapidly at first, and then more slowly for 30 or 40 min. Dark adaptation is virtually complete after about 40 min in the dark. Because of this, Hecht *et al.* dark-adapted their subjects for at least 40 min before they began to take their data.

At the time that Hecht *et al.* performed their experiment, some of the physiological properties of the visual system related to dark adaptation were understood. In order for a subject to see that a lighted test spot is in fact lighted, some of the light from the spot must interact with some part of his system. In almost all light-sensing elements, whether they are in a human eye, a photographic film, or a satellite tracker, this interaction is the absorption of light by some of the molecules of material in the sensor. The molecules that absorb light in the receptors of the eye are called visual pigment molecules. When any one of these molecules absorbs light, it changes its state, and, if enough molecules change their state, these changes are signaled to the rest of the subject's system, and he says he sees the light. After a visual pigment molecule has been in this new state for a very short time, it is almost incapable of absorbing more light. Therefore, if a subject were shown a flash

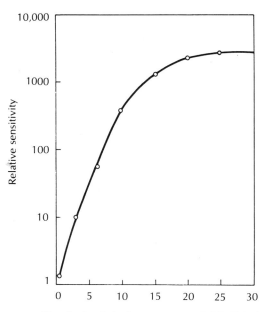

Fig. 2.1 **Change in human visual sensitivity as a function of time in the dark after exposure to a bright light.** [*After Kohlrausch (1931), curve for green light.*]

Time in the dark after exposure to bright light (min)

of light so intense that it changed the state of virtually all of his visual pigment molecules, he would subsequently be very insensitive to a second flash (since his eyes would contain very few molecules capable of absorbing the light from the new flash).

However, if a molecule has absorbed some light and is in its insensitive state, it will have a tendency to regenerate to its original, sensitive, state if it is in the presence of the various other chemicals in the eye. For the kind of visual pigment relevant here, the strength of this tendency is such that any single molecule in the insensitive state will have a 50% probability of regenerating in a period of about 5 min. The regeneration of each molecule is independent of the states of the other molecules. Thus, if all the molecules were in the insensitive state at the beginning of a period in the dark, about half of them would be regenerated after 5 min in the dark, 75% after 10 min (that is 50% plus half of the remaining 50%), 87.5% after 15 min, etc. Obviously, as the number of molecules that are in the sensitive state increases, the subject's sensitivity, as it is shown in Fig. 2.1, will increase.

For a long time, this physiological property of the visual system was accepted (in a more formal and quantitative form) as a complete explanation of the perceptual phenomenon called dark adaptation. In fact, almost every textbook in psychology and in visual perception written before the 1960's (and too many written since then) offer this explanation. However, it is now firmly established that this explanation is inadequate as it is stated above. Several modifications of the theory, and some altogether different explanations of dark adaptation, have recently been proposed. These will be discussed and evaluated in Chapter V. At the time of this writing, however, there is no entirely satisfactory physiological explanation of dark adaptation.

LOCATION OF THE TEST FLASH IN THE VISUAL FIELD

Suppose that a subject is in a room that is entirely dark except for a single small point of light (say a flashlight bulb), and he closes one eye and fixates the light with the other eye. A top view of the subject's eye and the fixation point is shown in Fig. 2.2. Light from the fixation point radiates in all directions, and some of it enters his eye, where it is refracted by the surfaces and forms an image of the fixation point on the back of the eyeball. (These processes, and all the others discussed in this chapter, will be explained in more detail in the succeeding chapters.) In other words, there will be a small spot of light at a particular location on the back of the subject's eye. The location of that image is determined by the location of the fixation point and the shape of the eyeball. For the time being, it is sufficient to understand that a straight

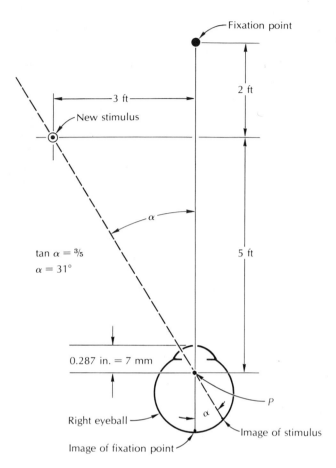

Fixation point

New stimulus

3 ft

2 ft

α

$\tan \alpha = ^3/_5$

$\alpha = 31°$

5 ft

0.287 in. = 7 mm

P

α

Right eyeball

Image of stimulus

Image of fixation point

Fig. 2.2 **Top view of the right eye of a subject looking at a fixation point. The new stimulus is presented at 31° of visual angle to the left of the fixation point.**

line drawn from the fixation point through a particular point, P, within the eye, will intersect the back of the eye in the center of the image of the fixation point, as indicated in Fig. 2.2. Now suppose a second bright point is introduced into the room, as indicated by the point labeled "new stimulus" in Fig. 2.2, but the subject keeps looking at the original fixation point. Some of the light from the new stimulus will also enter his eye, and an image of the new stimulus will be formed as in Fig. 2.2, in a location determined by the line between the new stimulus and the point, P. (The location of P in the eye is determined by the structure of some of the parts of the eyeball, and therefore does not vary as the location of the stimulus is changed.)

Now it would be useful to develop a scale for defining the location of the new stimulus with respect to the fixation point. From Fig. 2.2, it is obvious that the position of the new stimulus could be completely defined with respect to the fixation point by stating that, "It is 3 ft to the left of the subject's line of sight at a distance from him such that a line drawn through the new stimulus and perpendicular to the line of sight intersects the line of sight 5 ft from the subject." However, that description contains more information than we really need, if we are interested in vision, rather than in the apparatus itself, for the following reason: So far as the subject is concerned, the new stimulus might be anywhere along the dashed line in Fig. 2.2. (Remember that only one eye is open in this example.) The only information he has about the apparatus is what is on the back of his eye, and if the new stimulus were moved to any new position along the dashed line, its location on the back of his eyeball would not change.[3] Therefore, there is no point in describing the location of the new stimulus as completely as it was described above. It is sufficient to locate the stimulus by locating the dashed line with respect to the fixation point, and this may be done simply by stating the size of the angle between the dashed line and the line of sight. This angle, called the visual angle, is the angle whose tangent is 3 ft/5 ft, that is, 31°. Note also, from Fig. 2.2, that the angle formed by the lines connecting the point P with the images of the fixation point and the new stimulus is this same visual angle.

Lining the back of the eyeball, where the images are formed, is a surface called the retina, which contains millions of very tiny cells, some of which are rod-shaped, and are called rods. The curve in Fig. 2.3

[3]It is true that, under most conditions, the sharpness of focus of the new stimulus might change as it is moved along the dashed line, but for the purposes of this discussion we are concerned only with the location of the center of the image. Focusing will be discussed later.

Fig. 2.3 **Rod receptor cell density as a function of the horizontal location across the retina of the right eye. (The "blindspot," a region where there are no visual receptors, will be discussed later.)** [After Pirenne (1967), p. 32.]

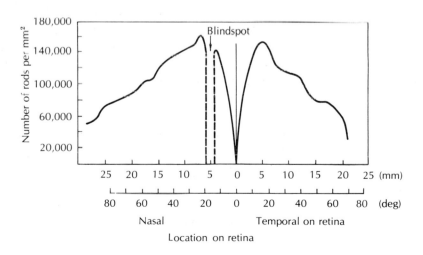

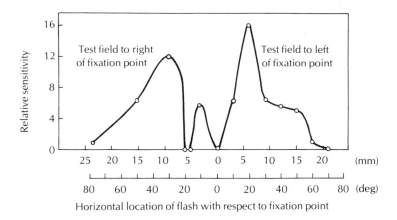

shows the distribution of these rods across the retina. The horizontal axis in this figure has two scales. One is simply the distance, in millimeters (mm), between an anatomically defined point in the retina called the fovea, and the region where the density of rods is measured. It is known, from data to be discussed later, that, when a subject is instructed to fixate a point, he moves his eyes until, in each eye, the image of the point falls on the fovea. Therefore, the millimeter scale in Fig. 2.3 corresponds simply to the other horizontal scale, visual angle, the fovea being located at zero angle with respect to the line of sight. (The distance from the point P to the retina, in Fig. 2.2, is approximately 17 mm. This is the factor required to convert millimeters on the retina into visual angles.)

The rods are the cells that respond to very dim light. Therefore, Hecht *et al.* reasoned that the light constituting their stimulus should fall 20° to the right of the subject's fovea (temporal retina for the right eye), where the rods are most tightly packed together. To accomplish this, they presented the subject with a dim point of light to look at, and their test stimulus was flashed 20° to the left of the fixation point.

There is a common experience that is closely related to the reasoning of Hecht, *et al.* If you look directly at an object, you can see its fine details much better than you can if you are not looking right at it. However, if the object is simply a very dim spot of light in an otherwise dark field, for example, a star, and if your eyes are dark-adapted, then you are more likely to see it if you look a little to the side then if you look directly at it. You can see a star "out of the corner of your eye" that might be too dim to be seen when you look directly at it. Hecht *et al.* assumed that this perceptual phenomenon was at least partly attributable to the increased rod density farther from the fovea, as plotted in Fig. 2.3, and thus chose to put their test stimulus 20° from the fovea.

The relationship between the sensitivity to dim light and the location of the stimulus on the retina has been studied more recently, and the results that are plotted in Fig. 2.4 generally verify the supposition that the sensitivity follows the rod density.

SIZE OF THE TEST FLASH—SPATIAL SUMMATION Next, Hecht et al. had to decide how large the flash should be. That is, over how large an area on the back of the subject's eye should the light be spread? There are perceptual data in the literature that provide an answer to this question, and these data are presented in Fig. 2.5. In this figure, the labeling of the axes requires some explanation.

The vertical axis is labeled "threshold (log mean relative number of quanta required for 60% seeing)." A beam of light may be described as a stream of packets of energy, each of which is called a quantum. Whenever light is absorbed by anything (e.g., the rods in the eye), the resulting events can be described as though the light consisted of these elementary packets, each packet being either wholly absorbed or not absorbed at all. (There is no such thing as the absorption of half a quantum.) Similar events occur when light is being generated. That is, a source of light emits a stream of quanta, and cannot emit half a quantum.

The intensity of a light is usually measured by causing the light to be absorbed by some detector. Therefore, the intensity may be measured in terms of the number of quanta per unit of time that are absorbed by the detector. The data in Fig. 2.5 are thresholds for short flashes of fixed duration. The total number of quanta in each flash is a measure of the flash intensity.

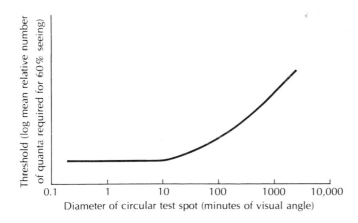

Fig. 2.5 **Total light required for seeing a flash as a function of the size of the test spot.** [After Barlow (1958), test flash duration 0.0085 sec, dark background.]

There are many ways by which the *threshold* for a flash of light may be measured. The method used for collecting the data in Fig. 2.5 (also used by Hecht *et al.*) involves, in essence, the following procedure: The subject is presented with a series of flashes of different intensities, that is, different numbers of quanta, and, after each flash, he signals whether or not he saw it. If there were some intensity above which flashes were always seen and below which they were never seen, that intensity would be called the threshold intensity. However, that is not the case. At very low intensities, the flashes are almost never seen, and at very high intensities they are almost always seen, but between those levels, there is a range of intensities for which the likelihood of seeing the flash gradually and smoothly changes from low to high.

The result of a typical set of measurements is shown in Fig. 2.6. There is no "threshold" in the common sense meaning of that term; thus, the intensity that will be called the threshold must be chosen arbitrarily. In the experiment represented in Fig. 2.5 and in the Hecht *et al.* experiment, the threshold intensity was defined as that intensity at which the subject reported that he saw the flash 60% of the times that it was delivered at that intensity; this threshold is indicated on Fig. 2.6. Thus, the vertical axis in Fig. 2.5 indicates the threshold, measured by the number of quanta required in a short flash in order that the subject see the flash 60% of the time, for each area represented along the horizontal axis.

Note that the threshold and sensitivity are inversely related. That is, a high threshold means low sensitivity (many quanta are required for seeing), and vice versa. Thus the vertical axes in Figs. 2.4 and 2.5 are inverted with respect to each other.

The horizontal axis on Fig. 2.5 is the area of the (disk-shaped) test flash, in units of visual angle. [One degree equals 60 minutes (60') of arc.] (See Appendix I for a table of the sizes of common objects in units of visual angle.)

The curve in this plot indicates that, so long as the test spot diameter

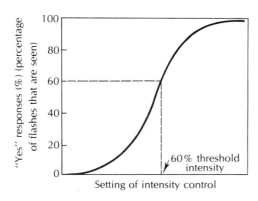

Fig. 2.6 **Typical result of a set of measurements to determine the threshold intensity of a flash. The percentage of flashes that are seen increases gradually as the intensity is increased. The threshold intensity must be arbitrarily chosen.**

is smaller than about 10 minutes (10′) of arc (the size of a thumb tack about 10 ft away), the threshold is the same. In other words, if the subject could just see a flash containing 1000 quanta spread over a disk 10′ in diameter, he would also just see a flash containing 1000 quanta spread over a disk only 1′ in diameter. The intensity per unit area at threshold would thus be greater for smaller test spots, but the total number of quanta is constant. For test spots larger than 10′ in diameter, the curve slopes upward—as the area increases, the threshold number of quanta also increases.

Hecht *et al.* might therefore have chosen any test spot diameter equal to or smaller than about 10′ in order to achieve the lowest possible threshold. They chose a diameter of 10′ probably because it is difficult to build an apparatus that can present smaller spots. (For example, pieces of dust in the apparatus are more likely to impair the viewing of a small spot than of a larger spot.)

The data in Figs. 2.4 and 2.5 are called psychophysical data, because they show the relationship between some physical characteristic of the stimulus and the corresponding psychological, or perceptual, events.

The physiological properties of the visual system that underlie the psychophysical data in Fig. 2.5 are not easy to present in simple graphical form. They will be discussed briefly here, and examined more thoroughly in Chapter VI. Figure 2.7 is a photomicrograph of a cross section through the back of the human eye. Light entering the eye passes through some neural tissue and part of the light is absorbed by the visual pigment in the receptors, where it is converted into neural signals. Those signals undergo a series of transformations as they travel (upward in the figure) toward the optic nerve. Physiological and anatomical studies have shown that each of the optic nerve fibers leading from this part of the eye (20° from the fovea) is connected, through intervening neurons, with a large number of rods; the signals from all or most of the rods in a given area feed to the same optic nerve fiber, where their effects are summated. At least 300 rods are connected to each optic nerve fiber in this region of the human retina. Figure 2.8 shows a schematic view of the rods and their neural connections. Each large circle represents one of the "summation" areas. Now suppose that the subject is presented with two flashes of light, each delivering ten quanta to one summation area, but in one flash, the quanta are spread out over a larger area than in the other. The absorptions of quanta are represented by solidly colored receptors for the small flash and by shaded receptors for the larger one. The effects on the optic nerve fiber will be exactly the same for these two flashes, since the optic nerve fiber "sees" the sum of the signals from all the rods

Fig. 2.7 **Cross section through the back of the human retina, stained with haematoxylin and eosin. Magnification approximately** × **150.** [*From Polyak (1957) Copyright©️ 1957 by the University of Chicago Press*]

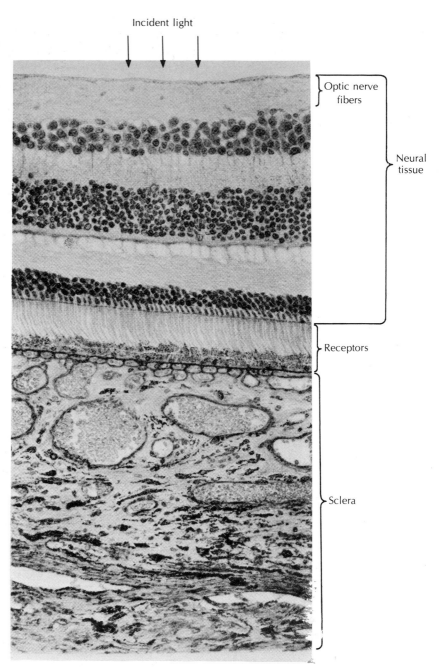

Incident light

Optic nerve fibers

Neural tissue

Receptors

Sclera

within the summation area, that is, ten signals. This process is called *spatial summation*.

So long as most of the quanta in a flash are absorbed by rods all within one summation area, the size of the flash does not matter. This consideration leads to the expectation that the curve in Fig. 2.5 will be horizontal for small areas. That is, the threshold number of quanta should be the same for all areas equal to or smaller than one summation area.

It is very difficult to obtain and interpret physiological information about the human retina, and as a consequence, there are no good quantitative physiological or anatomical estimates of the sizes of the summation areas in the human retina. However, the data in Fig. 2.5 suggest that the areas in this region of the dark-adapted eye are at least 10' in diameter.[4] Although quantitative data are absent, physiological

[4]The actual size of the summation area cannot be deduced from the data in Fig. 2.5 unless the extent of the overlapping of summation areas is known. (It is not known.) (See problem 2.3 at the end of this chapter.)

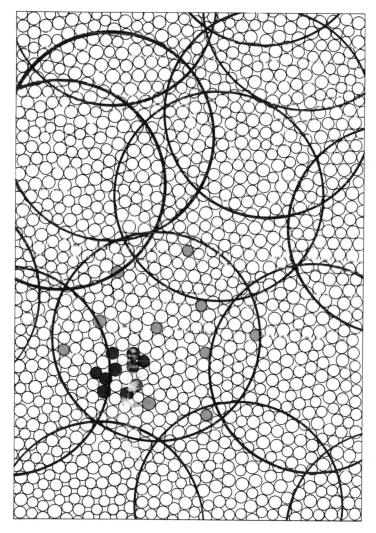

Fig. 2.8 Semischematic representation of the summation areas of the dark-adapted human retina, 20° from the fixation area (the fovea). Each small circle represents the end view of a rod, and each large circle represents the area over which the excitations in all the rods it contains summate. The summation areas overlap, but the actual extent of overlapping in the eye is not known.

and anatomical evidence does indicate that many rods converge on each optic nerve fiber, and this seems to explain, qualitatively, the fact that the curve in Fig. 2.5 is horizontal for some distance.

DURATION OF THE TEST FLASH— TEMPORAL SUMMATION

The psychophysical data in Fig. 2.9 were collected by dark-adapting the subject for 40 min and then presenting him with flashes of a test spot 2′ in diameter and 15° to the side of the fixation point. The duration of the flashes was the independent variable. This curve looks strikingly similar to the curve in Fig. 2.5, in which the test spot *area* was the independent variable. So long as the flash is shorter than about 0.1 sec [100 milliseconds (msec)], its duration has no effect on the threshold, no matter how short it is (even a millionth of a second). When the duration is longer than about 100 milliseconds (msec), more light is required for a threshold flash. Knowing this relation, Hecht *et al.* could have chosen any test flash duration shorter than 100 msec, and they arbitrarily chose a duration of 1 msec.

The physiological correlates of the data in Fig. 2.9 are very poorly understood, and research is actively being carried out on this problem. However, it is appropriate here to point out the relationship between these data and those in Fig. 2.5. *Spatial* summation may be said to occur over areas smaller than 10′ in diameter (20° away from the fovea), in that the effects of quanta absorbed anywhere within such an area are added together by the visual system. Put another way, the spatial distribution of the quanta has no effect on the threshold so long as the distribution extends over less than about 10′. From Fig. 2.9, it

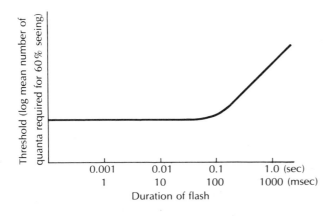

Fig. 2.9 **Total light required for seeing a flash as a function of the duration of the flash.** [*From Graham and Margaria (1935), 2′ curve.*]

can be seen that the temporal distribution of quanta has no effect on the threshold, so long as it extends over less than about 100 msec. All the quanta can be delivered in 1 microsecond (μsec) or they can be spread out evenly over 100,000 microseconds (μsec) and they still produce the same effect on the visual system. Although it is not shown explicitly in this figure, it is also true that the same effect will result if half of the quanta are delivered in a 1-μsec flash and the other half in another 1-μsec flash 100,000 μsec later. This means that the effect of each single absorption of a quantum must somehow last for at least 100 msec, so that it can add to the effects of any other quanta that are absorbed within 100 msec. This process is called *temporal summation*.

COLOR OF THE TEST FLASH – THE SPECTRAL SENSITIV- ITY CURVE Hecht *et al.* now had to select a color for the test spot. It is often convenient to consider a beam of light as consisting of a stream of quanta — individual packets of energy. Light was described that way earlier in this book. On the other hand, if light is passed through a very small hole in an opaque surface, it spreads out widely on the other side of the hole and this and many other optical phenomena can be most easily explained by saying that the beam of light, or the quanta in the beam, have wave properties. That is, a beam of light behaves, in some ways, like the waves on the surface of a pool of water. Quantitative measures of this aspect of the behavior of light may be interpreted by ascribing particular wavelengths to the quanta in a light beam.

When a beam of light from the sun or from an ordinary light bulb is passed through a slit and a prism, and allowed to fall on a screen, a spectrum of colors can be seen on the screen (provided that the light is intense enough and the observer has normal color vision), as diagrammed in Fig. 2.10. Now suppose that the screen has a narrow slit opening in it, and any light that passes through the slit falls on a device that measures the wavelength, as in Fig. 2.10. As the slit is moved along the spectrum, the measured wavelengths will be as plotted in the figure. Several conclusions can be drawn from this demonstration. First, light from the bulb contains quanta of many wavelengths (and since the light looks white if the prism is not in the path, this mixture of wavelengths looks white). Second, the prism interacts differentially with the quanta of different wavelengths, bending the paths of the quanta of shorter wavelength more strongly. Third, since repetitions of this demonstration give the same results,

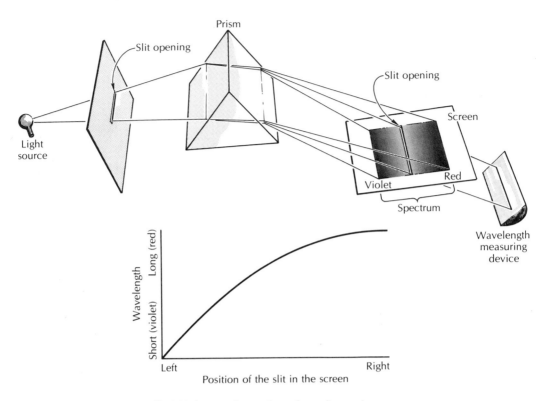

Fig. 2.10 **A means of separating and spreading out the wavelengths of light emitted from a light bulb.**

there is a fixed relationship between the wavelength of the light and the color that the observer reports (again, provided that the light is intense enough and the observer has normal color vision). Fourth, this device can be used to obtain light of any desired wavelength in the visible spectrum.

Now let us perform a psychophysical experiment in which flashes of light of different wavelengths are presented to a completely dark-adapted subject (for example, by putting his eye where the wavelength measuring device used to be), and his threshold for seeing the flash is measured at each wavelength. The results of such an experiment are shown in Fig. 2.11. (The subject was completely dark-adapted, the flash was presented peripheral to the fixation point, the test spot was small, and the flash was short.) The plot, called a spectral sensitivity curve, indicates that when the light is chosen from the middle of the spectrum, relatively fewer quanta are required for him to see it than if it is chosen from either end of the spectrum, and he is maximally sensitive to quanta of about 510 nanometers wavelength. [One nanometer (abbreviated nm), or millimicron, is 10^{-9} meters.] Therefore, Hecht et al. used test flashes whose wavelength was 510 nanometers (nm).

(You may wonder why Hecht et al. bothered to perform their experiment if the data in Fig. 2.11 were already available. There are several reasons that they went ahead. First, many of the earlier experiments were not sufficiently precise for the exact determination they wished to make. Second, none of the previous experiments optimized all of the experimental conditions. Third, all of the graphs presented thus far, have, on their vertical axes, *relative* number of quanta, or some similar relative measure. The determination of the *absolute* number of quanta at threshold is very much more difficult than a determination of the relative numbers under different conditions, and none of the previous experiments had been designed or performed with provision for such precise absolute measurement.)

Fig. 2.11 **Relative number of quanta required to see a short flash to the dark-adapted retina, peripheral to the fixation point, as a function of the wavelength of the quanta. The unit of length applied to wavelengths of light is the nanometer. One nanometer is 1/1,000,000,000 m (i.e., 10^{-9} m). The threshold may be expressed either in relative terms, as on the right, or as logarithms of relative units, as on the left. Note that the logarithmic units are merely the exponents of ten. That is, the numbers on the left are simply the numbers of zeros contained in the corresponding numbers on the right. The curve is called the** *spectral sensitivity curve* **of the rods.** [*From Wald (1945), rod curve, corrected from energy to quantal units.*]

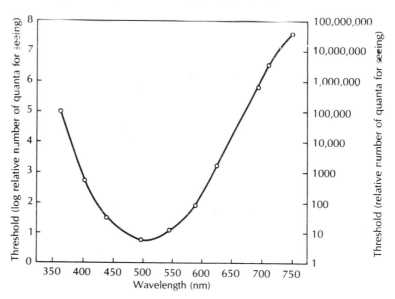

The title of this section is "The color of the test flash—. . .," but the discussion has centered around the choice of a *wavelength* for the flash. The word *color* was used because it is a familiar one, but it is not a good one in this context. The word *color* refers to a perceptual phenomenon that is closely associated with the physical property of light called wavelength; in general, particular wavelengths give rise to the experiences of (or if you prefer, reports of) particular colors. However, this relationship does not always obtain, and under the particular conditions of the Hecht experiment, it does not hold at all. As a consequence of some of the properties of the eye, to be discussed in detail in later chapters, a dark-adapted observer looking at very dim lights will see no colors at all over most of the spectrum of wavelengths. He will describe all of the stimuli (except those at the very long-wavelength end of the spectrum) as colorless or grey. Light of the wavelength that Hecht *et al.* used in their test flash looks bluish-green when it is intense, but under their conditions, the subject saw only colorless flashes.

The spectral sensitivity curve in Fig. 2.11 has nothing whatever to do with color vision. It does show that the sensitivity of the dark-adapted subject varies with the wavelength of the test light, but the data are determined only by whether or not the subject *saw* the flash. He is never even asked whether he saw any color in the test flashes.

The lack of color at low illuminations is easy to observe. On a moonlit night, the flowers in a garden can be easily seen, but they are colorless. The physical properties of the flowers have hardly changed, but the intensity of light is too low to bring into operation the color-sensing apparatus in our visual systems.

The physiological correlates of the dark-adapted spectral sensitivity curve are quite well understood. If the subject sees the light in the test flash, then one or more of the quanta must have been absorbed by the visual pigment in his rods. The structure of each pigment molecule is such that, as a quantum passes through it, the quantum has a certain probability of being caught by the molecule. This probability can be imagined as depending upon the fit between the sites on the molecule and the wavelength or energy of the quanta. All of the visual pigment molecules in human rods have the same structure, and that structure fits or resonates best with quanta whose wavelength is about 510 nm. Quanta at 510 nm are most likely to be captured by the pigment, and quanta of other wavelengths are less likely to be captured. If each quantum in a flash is more likely to be captured, fewer quanta must be put into the eye in order that any particular number are captured. Therefore, if it is assumed that a certain number of quanta must be captured by the visual system in order for the subject to see the flash, then the visual threshold would be expected to be lowest at 510 nm.

THE EXPERIMENT The subject was dark adapted, one eye was covered, and he was care-
ITSELF fully positioned in the apparatus where he looked at a very dim red fixation point with his uncovered eye. The fixation point was just bright enough to see, but not bright enough to interfere with his seeing the test spot when it was flashed 20° away. When the subject was ready, he pressed a key that opened a shutter, delivering a flash having the properties described in the preceding sections. He then signaled whether or not he had seen the flash. This procedure was repeated over and over for many different test-flash intensities. Several subjects were run in this way.

The results for one subject are shown in Fig. 2.12. The other subjects' results were similar. The horizontal scale in this figure is in arbitrary intensity units. The scale on the device that controlled the test-flash intensity was arbitrarily labeled, say on a scale from 0 to 100. On this scale, a setting of 5 will yield an intensity that will be reported as seen 60% of the time. In order to determine how many quanta are contained in this threshold test flash, the intensity control knob might be set at 5, the shutter fired, and the number of quanta arriving at the eye measured with some quantum counting device.

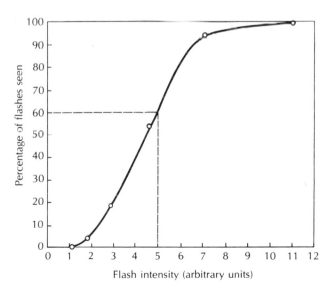

Fig. 2.12 "Frequency of seeing" curve. The data from one subject in the Hecht *et al.* **experiment.** [*From Hecht et al. (1942), subject S.S.*]

If Hecht *et al.* had tried to follow that procedure, (and they may have), they would have found that the number of quanta was so small that it simply could not be measured with the devices that were available to them. In other words, the eye is considerably more sensitive than any physical device that existed at the time. The way in which Hecht *et al.* solved this problem and arrived at a correct intensity calibration will be explained in the next chapter, where those aspects of the physics of light that are important in visual perception will be discussed. From their intensity calibrations, they determined that the flash contained an average of about 90 quanta when the intensity knob was set at 5, that is, at the 60% threshold level.

THE INTERPRETA-
TION OF RESULTS
Hecht *et al.* determined that the monocular human visual system, under optimal conditions, can detect a flash 60% of the time when it contains about 90 quanta. Thus the eye is remarkably sensitive compared with most physical light-detecting devices. However, that finding is probably the least interesting and least important of their conclusions.

Under their conditions, it is the rods themselves that are the primary receivers of light. That is, any light lost before it gets to the rods cannot affect the subject; he cannot assimilate any visual information about the light if it is not absorbed by the visual pigment in his rods. Therefore, Hecht *et al.* went on to estimate the actual number of quanta absorbed by the visual pigment in the rods during a threshold test flash.

Consider a group of quanta heading for the eye. About 3% of them will be reflected from the front surface of the eye, the cornea. (In the Hecht *et al.* experiment, the light was focused in such a way that none of it struck the subject's iris.) About half of the remaining quanta are absorbed by pigment in the media that fill the eyeball itself. Thus, about 48% of the quanta incident on the eye actually arrive in the region of the rods.

If the back of the human eye 20° from the fovea is examined under a microscope, it will be evident that the rods, seen end on, are spaced approximately as shown in Fig. 2.13. Because of this spacing, some of the quanta that get to the rod surface fall between rods and are lost to the visual system. Even if a quantum does finally enter a rod, it is not necessarily absorbed by a visual pigment molecule. The percentage of incident quanta absorbed depends upon the fit between the quanta and the pigment molecules, and also upon the density of pigment in the rods. From independent observations, Hecht *et al.* estimated that at a wavelength of 510 nm, no more than 20% of the quanta incident on the retina are actually absorbed by the visual pigment in the rods.

Taking all these losses into account, it may be concluded that a subject will report seeing a flash, under optimal conditions, when only about nine or ten quanta are absorbed by the visual pigment. That is an extraordinarily small amount of energy. A typical lighted flashlight bulb radiates about 2×10^{15} quanta every millisecond (two million million million million million).

Hecht et al. were able to carry their conclusions even further. In the average threshold flash about ten quanta are absorbed, but they are spread out over an area of the retina 10' in diameter, (about the size of the retinal patch in Fig. 2.13). They estimated that such an area contains about 500 rods. If ten quanta are distributed randomly over an area containing 500 rods, the chances that two quanta will be absorbed by the same rod are very small. Therefore, they concluded that a visual effect will be produced if about ten rods, all within an area 10' in diameter, each absorb a single quantum during the 1-msec flash. This means that a single quantum must be sufficient to activate a rod, and that the effects of the activation of about ten rods all near each other are somehow added up by the visual system.

Since the time that Hecht et al. performed their experiment, some of their estimates of the parameters have been superseded (e.g., it is now estimated that the area stimulated contains only about 350 rods), but none of the new estimates are sufficiently different to require a substantial alteration in their conclusions. Other workers have made similar measurements in somewhat different ways, and some have concluded that the total number of quanta absorbed by visual pigment at threshold is only two, rather than ten (Bouman, 1955). However, the

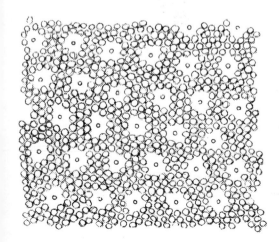

Fig. 2.13   **Spacing of the rods, seen end on, results in the loss of about half of the incident quanta. The small circles in this drawing are receptors of a different kind (cones), which are evidently inoperative at threshold intensities in the dark-adapted eye.**
[From Schultz (1866), periphery.]

principal finding of Hecht *et al.*, that a single quantum is sufficient to activate a rod, is firmly established.

Hecht *et al.* drew still another conclusion of fundamental importance from their study. Why is it true that, as the intensity of the flash is increased, the proportion of "yes" responses increases *gradually*? Why does it not simply jump from zero, when the apparatus is set to deliver fewer than ten quanta, to 100% when more than ten quanta are absorbed? Put another way, why is it that, with the apparatus set to give a constant intensity, say at the threshold level, the subject sometimes sees the flash and sometimes does not? It is easy to "explain" this observation by simply saying that the subject is human, after all, and is thus variable. Hecht *et al.* demonstrated that, in fact, a large part of the variability is a consequence of the physics of the light itself, and that when this source of variation is taken into account, the subject's judgments are remarkably consistent. This conclusion requires considerable explanation, and is of such fundamental significance to the understanding of visual perception that it will be covered at length in Chapter IV.

PROBLEMS   2.1   (a) What is the visual angle subtended by a bull's-eye 1 in. in diameter, 50 yd away?

Answer: 1'56".

(b) What are the visual angles subtended by the side of a barn (40 × 100 ft) 50 ft away?

2.2   (a) What is the visual angle subtended by an image on the retina that is 1 mm long?

(b) How big (in millimeters) is the retinal image of the bull's-eye in problem 2.1a?

Answer: 0.009 mm.

2.3   (a) What is the diameter of the area of total spatial summation, given that the curve in Fig. 2.5 begins to go up at 10' and that the summation areas overlap to such an extent that each point on the retina is part of two different summation areas, on the average? (If you wish to simplify this problem conceptually, assume that the summation areas are all square.)

(b) What is the diameter if, on the average, each point is part of three different areas?

2.4   From the data in Fig. 2.11, calculate and plot the relative probability of absorption of a quantum by the visual pigment versus wavelength.

III ◇◇◇ THE PHYSICS OF LIGHT

A DEFINITION OF **THE** information that we have about the visual world, and our percep-
"SEEING" tions of objects and visual events in the world, depend only indirectly
upon the state of that world. They depend directly upon the nature of
the images formed on the backs of our eyeballs, and these images are
different in many important ways from the world itself. It is certainly
true that the state of the observer plays a fundamental role in determining the things he sees, and that role will be discussed at length in this
book, but the relationship between our perceptions and the world itself depends first of all upon the nature of our retinal images. If information about some aspect of an object is not contained in the retinal
image of it, the information cannot be recovered or regenerated by
later parts of the system.

Put more precisely, if two physically different objects produce identical retinal images, it is impossible for an observer visually to tell them

27

apart. He might discover that they are different by feeling them, but then his discrimination is based on something not relevant to a discussion of visual perception. He might say, after feeling the difference between the objects, "Now I see that they are different." Even if he insists that he is using the word "see" in its usual sense, it is clear that he is not referring to the properties of his visual perception. After having felt the two objects, he may insist that they *really look* different to him, and, of course, such a claim cannot be refuted. That claim does *not* mean that the two objects transmit different *visual* information, and what it does mean is unclear.

It is possible and very useful to establish a definition of "seeing" that is not subject to such ambiguity. This definition can be illustrated by performing the following experiment: The observer who maintains that he sees the difference between the two objects after he has felt their difference, is shown the two objects and allowed to feel them. Then, in a series of trials, he is shown the objects without being permitted to feel them, but the positions of the objects are switched in a random sequence on successive trials, and he is asked to say which object is which on each trial. If the correlation between the positions of the objects and his responses is not significantly greater than it might be expected to be by chance, then there is no evidence that he "sees" the difference, according to *our* definition of "seeing."

He might, under those circumstances, say that he cannot see the difference any more anyway, since he is not allowed to feel the objects. We could then perform a modification of the experiment, in which he is allowed to feel the objects on each trial just before and after he looks at them, but, although he is unaware of it, the positions of the objects are reversed randomly from trial to trial just during the time he is looking at them, and restored to their original positions before he feels them. Under those conditions, he would still say that he sees the difference, but the correlation between his reports and the positions of the objects during the time he is seeing them will be close to zero, and we may conclude, using our definition of "seeing," that he cannot see the difference.

It is necessary to consider the somewhat belabored argument above in order to avoid confusions that might otherwise arise in this book. This argument illustrates a definition of "seeing" that probably ought to be formalized as follows: An observer will be said to *see* a property of the external world if it can be demonstrated that he is assimilating the information that the property is present, through the interaction between his anatomy and the light carrying that information.

There is infinitely more information in the world than our systems can assimilate, and a good part of the study of visual perception can really be described as a study of the kinds of information that are *lost* to us. A substantial part of this loss is a consequence of the interaction between the nature of light itself and the nature of our visual systems, and for this reason, a knowledge of certain aspects of the physics of light is essential for an understanding of visual perception. This chapter will discuss the physics of light as it is relevant to perception.

LIGHT SOURCES An ordinary incandescent bulb consists of a coil of wire, usually tungsten wire, suspended in a glass envelope from which most of the oxygen has been removed and replaced by an inert gas. The two ends of the filament are brought out through connections in the base of the bulb, so that when a voltage is applied between the connections, an electric current will flow through the filament. When current flows through any wire, the wire heats up, and if enough current flows, the filament will get so hot that it begins to glow, that is, to radiate light. (If wire is made very hot in the presence of oxygen, it will burn up. It is for this reason that the oxygen in the bulb is replaced with an inert gas.)

When any material is heated, electrons jump among locations in the material and some of these jumps result in the radiation of quanta. If a single electron jumps from one location to a new one at a lower energy level, the difference in energy between the original and the new levels will be radiated as a single quantum of what is called electromagnetic radiation. (The nature of these energy levels is beyond the scope of this discussion.) Thus the energy radiated by a heated material is emitted in the form of discrete quanta, each corresponding to the abrupt change of energy of an electron. In any solid body that is hot, a continuum of energy levels is present, so that any given quantum might have any energy level within that continuum. It is also true that the characteristics of a quantum defining its wavelength are strictly related to its energy. This relationship is an inverse one; that is, a quantum of twice the energy will have half the wavelength.

Now suppose the quanta radiated from the filament of a light bulb were allowed to fall for a while on a device that registered each quantum and measured its wavelength. Since the energy levels in the filament are continuous, quanta of every wavelength within that continuum have finite probabilities of being radiated, and therefore if the device is exposed for a long enough time, it will record quanta of all wavelengths in the continuum. The expected result of such a long exposure is shown in Fig. 3.1. Consider, first, the curve labeled

2750°K. This is the spectral emission curve for a tungsten filament at a temperature of 2750°K, a typical temperature for a domestic light bulb. The curve is continuous, in that there are quanta at every wavelength.

If the exposure of the detector had been extremely short, only a few quanta would have been recorded, and the "curve" in that case would simply be a few points, each corresponding to a different quantum. The continuous curve plotted in Fig. 3.1 would only be expected after an exposure of infinite duration, and the scale on the vertical axis is really the relative probability of occurrence of each of the wavelengths on the horizontal axis. However, quanta are emitted from a light bulb at such a high rate that, in practice, the data would conform very closely to this curve even for an exposure of only a fraction of a second.

The other curve in Fig. 3.1 represents the comparable data when the filament temperature is raised to 3500°K (the temperature of a bright photoflood lamp). The peak of the spectral emission curve of any material is shifted toward shorter wavelengths when the temperature is increased, and the rate of emission of quanta increases at all wavelengths.

Not all sources of radiation deliver continuous spectra. Many light sources consist of gases excited by electrical energy. For example, in a

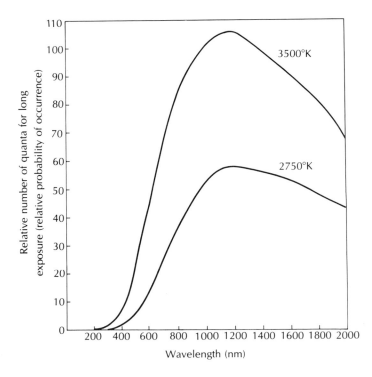

Fig. 3.1 **Spectral emission curves for tungsten at 2750°K, a typical household lamp temperature and 3500°K, the temperature of a very bright photoflood lamp.**

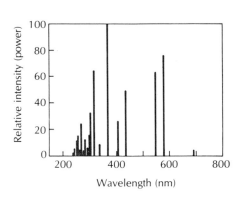

Fig. 3.2 **Emission spectrum of a typical mercury arc lamp at a pressure of one atmosphere. The spikes represent energy gaps in mercury atoms.**

mercury arc lamp (see Fig. 3.2), the electrons primarily jump between orbits around the atomic nuclei of mercury, and these orbits exist at only a small number of discrete energy levels. When the mercury is replaced with a different gas, the emitted wavelengths will be different because the energy levels of the electron orbits for the two kinds of atoms are different.

The curve in Fig. 3.3a is the emission spectrum of a relatively new kind of light source called a solid state, electroluminescent source, or light-emitting diode. When an electric current is passed through this unit, electric charges jump among energy levels within the crystal structure of the diode, emitting quanta within a relatively narrow band of wavelengths.

The source that provides light of the most narrow wavelength band is the laser. The emission spectrum in Fig. 3.3b is not a good represen tation of the light from a properly adjusted laser because the line on the graph is too wide. However, a line correctly representing laser light on this horizontal scale would be too narrow to print.

LENSES AND REFRACTION All quanta of electromagnetic radiation, regardless of their wavelengths, travel in straight lines and at the same velocity (186,000 miles per second) through empty space. However, their velocities are reduced when they pass through any medium, the reduction in velocity depending upon the nature of the medium and the wavelengths of the quanta. The velocity of light in air is so close to its velocity in a vacuum that the effect of air on light may be ignored for the present purposes. The velocity of a quantum in water or glass, however, may be reduced by one third or more.

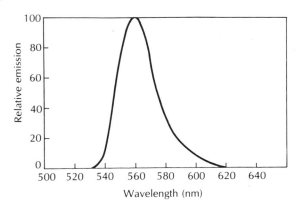

(a)

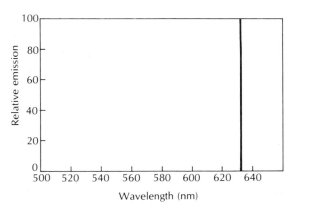

(b)

Fig. 3.3 **Emission spectra of relatively new sources. (a) The spectrum of a gallium phosphide electroluminescent crystal. Note that the horizontal scale is expanded as compared with those in the preceding figures. (b) The spectrum of a helium-neon laser.**

Consider a single quantum following the path labeled 1 in Fig. 3.4. As the quantum enters the glass, it continues in its original path at a reduced velocity. (There is a probability of about 0.04 that the quantum will be reflected from the surface and travel back along its incoming path. For the present discussion, only those quanta that are not reflected will be considered.) However, if a quantum is incident on the glass at an angle other than perpendicular to the surface, as indicated by the path labeled 2, its direction of motion will be changed when it enters the glass. The amount of this change in direction depends upon the angle of incidence (angle *ABN*) of the quantum and its change in velocity as it enters the glass. The angle *CBN* in Fig. 3.4 is called the angle of refraction, and the process by which the glass bends the path of the quantum is called refraction. (Note that the quantum in path 1 has an angle of incidence of zero, and it will then necessarily have an angle of refraction of zero as well.) The theoretical considerations from which the laws of refraction may be deduced are not necessary for the understanding of visual processes, at least at the level of this book. It is sufficient to understand that the refraction of the path of a quantum depends both upon its angle of incidence and upon its change in velocity (which in turn depends upon the kind of refracting material and the wavelength of the quantum).

Optical systems, in general, obey what is called the "law of reversibility." In the present example, this means that, if a quantum originated inside the glass and traveled toward the surface along, say, path *CB*, its path upon emerging from the glass would be *BA*. In that instance, the only change required in the diagram would be that the labels for the two angles should be reversed. That is, the angle that was formerly called the angle of incidence would now be called the angle of refraction and vice versa.

Image Formation   Consider the quantum path labeled *A* in Fig. 3.5. The path is refracted when it enters the glass, and bent again as the quantum leaves the glass.

Now consider *B*. The angles of the surfaces of the glass have been chosen so that this path of a quantum will be bent just far enough that it will intersect the path *A* at point *I*. The glass in path *C* is similarly chosen. Here the two surfaces of the glass are perpendicular to the line from the source to *I*, so that the angles of refraction are zero.

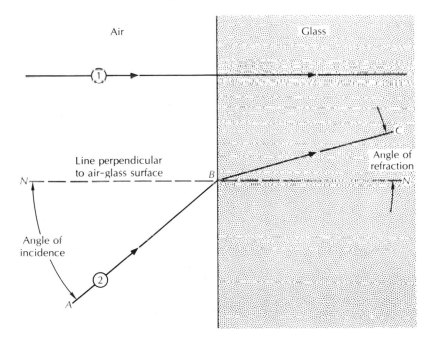

Fig. 3.4 **Paths traveled by light incident upon an air-glass interface.**

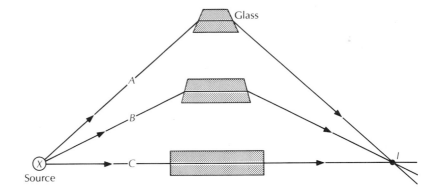

Fig. 3.5 **Three pieces of glass with faces angled so that the three light paths, A, B, and C all intersect at point I.**

This process of putting more and more pieces of glass into the path, each with its surface angles properly chosen, can be continued indefinitely, and the end result of such a series is a single smooth piece of glass, as in Fig. 3.6. The surfaces of this piece of glass, or lens, are such that any quantum emitted by the source, S, that strikes the lens will be refracted just enough to pass through point I, regardless of where it happens to hit the lens. If a screen were placed in the plane of I, the pattern inset at the bottom of this figure would be seen. The outer regions of the screen would be lighted evenly by the quanta that did not hit the lens, and within this area would be a dark disk with a bright point centered in it. The bright point is called the *image of the source*. By the principle of reversibility, if the source were placed at I, the lens would form an image of the source at point S.

The line through the center of the lens, the broken line in Fig. 3.6, is called the optic axis of the lens. The source in this figure lies on the optic axis of the lens. If a source lies on the optic axis of any lens, it will necessarily be true that, if an image of the source is formed at all, that image will also lie on the optic axis. The reason for this should be evident from an examination of Fig. 3.6. A quantum that leaves the source and travels along the optic axis will meet the surfaces of the glass with an angle of incidence of zero. Therefore, its angle of refraction will also be zero—it will not be deflected. All quanta that happen to be radiated along the optic axis will pass through the lens completely undeflected. Then, since the image is the point upon which *all* the quanta that pass through the lens converge, the image must fall on the optic axis of the lens.

The source and its image are redrawn as S_1 and I_1, respectively, in Fig. 3.7. Now suppose a second source, S_2, is introduced, about the same distance from the lens as S_1. Consider the behavior of a quantum radiated from S_2 along the path indicated. It will be deflected very slightly upon entering the glass, but if the lens is symmetric, it will be deflected through the same angle in the opposite direction upon leaving the glass, and its paths entering and leaving the lens will therefore be parallel. The actual net deflection of the path is very small, so long as the lens is thin relative to the other distances involved, and may be ignored for the moment. This particular path is unique. There is no other path for which the quanta leaving S_2 are undeflected. This path intersects the optic axis (which is the only path of zero deflection for a source at S_1) at a point inside the lens, and the one undeflected path from *any* source (for example, S_3) will always pass through this same point.

When the surfaces of a lens are so designed that they form an image of S_1, they will also form images of any other sources about the same distance away from the lens, and the images will all be formed at about the same distance on the other side of the lens. Thus, the images of S_2 and S_3 *must* be located where they are shown in the diagram. Given the fact that a path through the center of a lens is undeflected, and given the location of any one source and its image, the image of any other source in the same plane is determined.[1]

[1]There are small errors in most of this discussion. For example, for any real, simple lens, the images of off-axis sources are formed at slightly different distances from the lens, depending upon their off-axis angles. This discussion will be confined to first-order approximations except where more exact descriptions are relevant to visual perception.

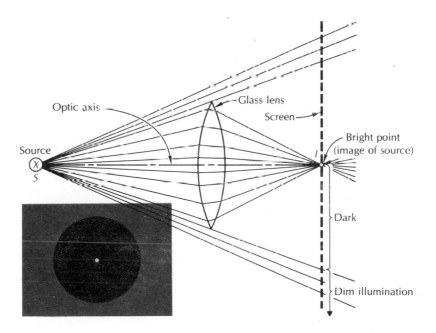

Fig. 3.6 **A lens forming an image** *I*, **of a light source,** *S*. **The inset at the bottom represents the distribution of light falling on the screen, as seen when viewed along the direction of the optic axis.**

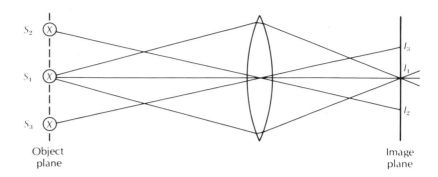

Fig. 3.7 **A lens forming an image of a set of three sources, all equally distant from the lens. The plane containing the sources is called the object plane (the set of sources can be called an object) and the plane containing the images is called the image plane.**

Ordinarily, point sources of light are not of much interest. We are usually concerned with images of illuminated or luminous objects. For optical purposes, however, any object may be considered as a collection of point sources of light, whether the object is glowing or is reflecting light from some other source. Therefore, the principles just discussed may be used to locate the image of any planar object, as is illustrated in Fig. 3.8. If the location of the image of the end of the thumb is known, images of the other points may be found by simple geometry.

The plane perpendicular to the optic axis of a lens that contains the object is called the *object plane*. The parallel plane that contains the image is called the *image plane*.

Focal Length

The diagram in Fig. 3.6 is redrawn in Fig. 3.9a. Suppose, now, that the source is moved farther away from the lens, as in Fig. 3.9b. The new angles that the paths form with the lens surfaces will be such that the image will be formed closer to the lens. If the point source is moved a very long distance away, the paths of quanta radiated from it that strike the lens will be essentially parallel, and the image will be formed even closer to the lens. Let us call the distance between the object and the lens d_o and the distance between the image and the lens d_i. The diagram in Fig. 3.9c represents the special case of the source of infinity. The distance d_i, in this special case, is called the focal length of the lens, and is a very useful parameter of the lens.

To find the focal length of any lens, simply hold it up in the path of some light from an object fairly far away (say a tree through a win-

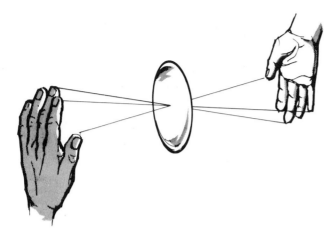

Fig. 3.8   A lens forming an image of an object. Each straight line is the path of the undeviated ray from a point in the object, through the optical center of the lens, to the corresponding point in the image.

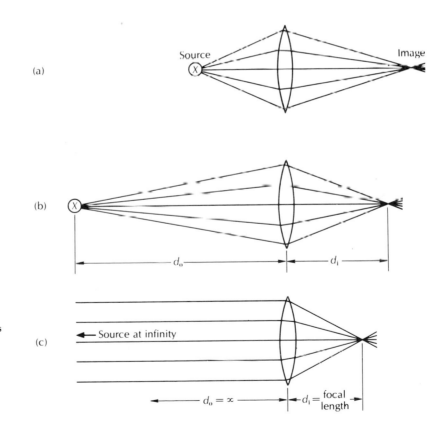

(a)

Source

Image

(b)

d_o

d_i

Fig. 3.9 A lens forming an image of a point source. As the source moves away from the lens, the image moves closer. In (c), the source is at infinity and the image is at the focal distance of the lens.

(c)

← Source at infinity

$d_o = \infty$

$d_i = \dfrac{focal}{length}$

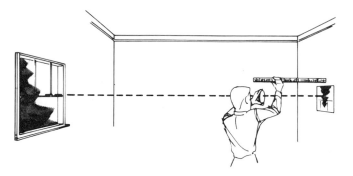

Fig. 3.10 The focal length of a lens is the distance between the lens and
the image it forms of a distant object. In this sketch, the lens has been
moved back and forth until the image of the tree is in sharp focus on the
wall. The distance between the lens and the wall is then the focal length
of the lens.

dow), and measure the distance from the lens to the image of the object, as shown in Fig. 3.10.

The focal length of a lens may be used to find the image or object distance, or to find the sizes of images or objects. The relationship between the focal length and the distances of images and objects from the lens is as follows:

$$\frac{1}{F} = \frac{1}{d_o} + \frac{1}{d_i} \tag{1}$$

or the equivalent:

$$F = \frac{d_o \cdot d_i}{d_o + d_i} \tag{2}$$

where F is the focal length of the lens, d_o is the distance between the object and the lens, and d_i is the distance between the image and the lens.

Consider, first, the special case illustrated in Fig. 3.9c. The source is an infinite distance from the lens. Therefore:

$$\frac{1}{F} = \frac{1}{d_o} + \frac{1}{d_i}$$

$$\frac{1}{F} = \frac{1}{\infty} + \frac{1}{d_i}$$

$$F = d_i$$

That is, the image will lie at a distance from the lens equal to the focal length of the lens. For the converse special case, when the source is in the focal plane of a lens:

$$d_o = F$$

Therefore,

$$\frac{1}{F} = \frac{1}{F} + \frac{1}{d_i}$$

$$\frac{1}{d_i} = 0$$

$$d_i = \infty$$

That is, the image will be formed at infinity.

Another special case that is very useful is the one for which the source is just two focal lengths from the lens. Then:

$$d_o = 2F$$

$$\frac{1}{F} = \frac{1}{2F} + \frac{1}{d_i}$$

$$d_i = 2F$$

That is, the image will be formed in a plane just two focal lengths on the other side of the lens.

Figure 3.11a is a diagrammatic cross section of the human eye and Fig. 3.11b is a simplified optical representation of the eye. This optical system is slightly different in two respects from the ones discussed thus far. First, once the quanta enter the optical media, they do not pass back into air again. Quanta entering the cornea are refracted by its surface, then refracted more by the body called the lens, and finally form an image of the source at the retina. The combination of corneal and lens surfaces all may be considered as a single lens that forms an image of an object on the retina.[2]

The eye's optical system differs from a simple lens in one other way. The lens in the eye is flexible, at least in young people, and it is attached to the eyeball by muscles that can change the curvatures of its surfaces, thus changing the refractive power of the eye as a whole.

[2]The refractive power of a lens depends, in part, upon the amount by which the velocity of light changes when entering the medium of the lens. The speed of light in water is much slower than in air, and therefore, when the eye is immersed in water, the refractive power of the cornea is greatly reduced. That is why objects appear so badly out of focus when you open your eyes under water. Some of the diving ducks have a mechanism that overcomes this difficulty very simply. Their eyelids are transparent, and have lenses built into them. When these ducks dive, they close their lids, adding more refractive power. The combination of the refractive powers of the eyes and the lids is great enough to form images in the planes of their retinas under water.

Fig. 3.11 **(a) Diagram of a cross section of the human eye; (b) simplified optical representation of the eye looking at a tree.**

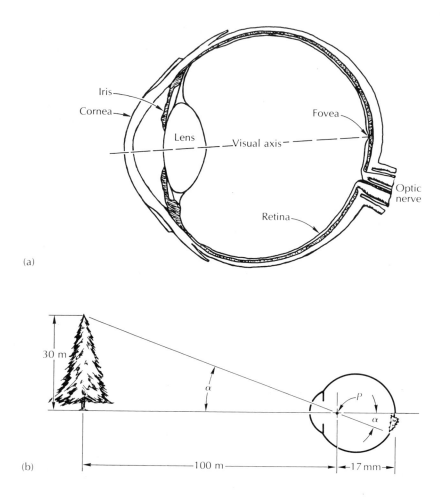

Reexamination of Figs. 3.5 and 3.6 will indicate that if the surfaces of a lens were curved less strongly, the paths of the quanta would be bent through smaller angles, and the image would be formed farther from the lens. Now suppose that an object in space is in a position such that its image is formed 1 mm in front of the retina. The lens of the eye and its associated muscles and nervous system are so constructed that the curvatures of the lens surfaces will "automatically" be reduced, decreasing the total refractive power of the eye until the image is in focus in the plane of the retina.

The shapes of many people's eyeballs are such that their lenses cannot bring an image into sharp focus on the retina. For example, in some eyes, the distance between the cornea and the retina is so great that the image of a distant object is formed in front of the retina, and the distribution of light that falls on the retina is blurred. If the object is moved closer to the eye, the image moves farther from the cornea until, at some close distance, it is in sharp focus on the retina. Such people are called myopic, or near-sighted, since the only things they can see sharply are nearby objects.

Just as frequently, an individual's eyes will be too short, with respect the refractive power of his corneas and lenses, so that, if he were to relax the muscles that change the shape of the lenses, the images of distant objects would be formed behind his retinas. This condition is called hyperopia. A young hyperope, when he wants to look at an object a long distance away, will activate the muscles that allow his lenses to bulge more strongly, thus increasing the refractive power of his eyes until the images are in focus on his retinas. In this way, he can see distant objects clearly. However, as a person ages, his lenses stiffen, and their curvatures cannot be changed as much. Thus, as a hyperope grows older, he can no longer see distant objects clearly.

If an object is sharply focused on an observer's retinas and then it is moved closer to him, the retinal images will blur, and, in order to make them sharp again, he must increase the curvatures of his lenses. Therefore, anyone who has normal vision or is a hyperope when young cannot read print as he grows older, unless he uses reading glasses, which are simply lenses that add to the refractive power of his eyes.

There is a point in the center of any lens such that quanta passing through that point will not be deflected in their paths, and that point is useful in locating images, as was shown in Fig. 3.7. In the human eye, this point is located about 17 mm in front of the retina. (Its distance varies from 17 down to about 14 mm as the refractive power of the lens in the eye increases from its minimum to its maximum. When the normal eye is focused on an object farther than about 10 ft away, the lens exhibits its lowest refractive power, and when focused on a very near object, it is most strongly refractive.) With this information, it is easy to calculate the size of the retinal image of any object. In Fig. 3.11, the observer is looking at a tree 30 m (about 97 ft) high and 100 m away. His lens will have adjusted its curvature until the image is in the plane of the retina. Then the images of the top and the bottom of the tree can be located on the retina simply by drawing the paths of no deflection, that is, through point P, from each of those points to the retina. The following simple geometrical relationship holds:

$$30/100 = \text{size of image (mm)}/17,$$
$$\text{size} = 30 \times 17/100 = 5.1 \text{ mm}.$$

In general,

$$\frac{d_o}{d_i} = \frac{S_o}{S_i}$$

where d_o and d_i are the distances from the center of a lens to the object and image, respectively, and S_o and S_i are the sizes of the object and image, respectively.

In Chapter II, it was explained that visual angle is often a convenient measure of the size of a visual stimulus. In the present example, the visual angle, labeled α in Fig. 3.11, is:

$$\alpha = \arctan(30/100) = 16°27'.$$

Conversely, if the size of the object were given in visual angle instead of length and distance, the size of the retinal image would be

$$\frac{\text{size of image (mm)}}{17} = \tan \alpha,$$

$$\text{size} = 17 \times 0.30 = 5.1 \text{ mm.}$$

Hecht *et al.* used as their test spot, a disk of light of diameter 10′. The image of the test spot thus extended over:

$$\frac{S_i}{17 \text{ mm}} = \tan 10',$$

$$S_i = 17 \times 0.00291 = 0.0495 \text{ mm on the retina.}$$

THE INTENSITY OF AN IMAGE

The Effect of Pupil Size

Suppose that an image of a point source of light is formed on a human retina, as in Fig. 3.12a. The total number of quanta per second that fall on the retina is obviously directly proportional to the intensity of the source, that is, the number of quanta per second radiated by the source. It is also directly proportional to the area of the pupil, the hole in the iris through which the quanta must pass in order to strike the retina. If the pupil of the eye were to double in diameter, and thus quadruple in area, four times as many of the quanta radiated from the source would be able to pass through to the retina, and the image would be four times as intense.

Now consider the case illustrated in Fig. 3.12b, where two point sources are imaged on the retina. The intensity of each of the images will depend upon the intensity of the corresponding source and upon the area of the pupil. If the pupil enlarges, both images will become

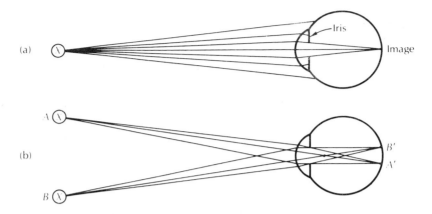

Fig. 3.12 **The intensity of the retinal image of a source of light is directly proportional to the area of the pupil, that is, the area through which light can enter the eye. Changes in pupil diameter change the intensity of the retinal image, but do not change its size.**

more intense, but note that the distance between the two images will not change.

Now suppose that the entire line between the two sources in Fig. 3.12b were filled with point sources. That is, suppose that the source were really a line of length *AB*. Then, when the pupil changes size, the brightness of the image of the line will change but the length will not. In general, the size of the retinal image is unaffected by changes in pupil size, but the intensity of the image is directly proportional to the pupil area.

The Effect of Object Distance The inverse-square law of light intensity is a familiar law, and knowledge of it frequently leads to a misconception about the intensities of images. The inverse-square law states that the intensity of light falling on a surface, in units such as quanta per second per square millimeter of the surface, is inversely proportional to the square of the distance between the source and the surface. The reason for this law is easily seen by examining Fig. 3.13. When a surface is at distance *S* from the source, a part of the quanta radiating (in all directions) from the source will strike each square millimeter of the surface. If the surface is then moved twice as far away, all of the quanta that would have struck the square with sides 1 mm long will now fall evenly on a square with sides 2 mm long. That is, they will be distributed over an area four times as great. Conversely, the number of quanta falling on a 1 mm square at distance 2*S* will be ¼ of the number falling on the same square at distance *S*. In general, the number of quanta falling on a given area will vary inversely with the square of the distance between a point source and the area.

Knowledge of this law often leads to the mistaken conclusion that

Fig. 3.13 **The inverse-
square law of light intensity. The amount of light
falling on the 1-mm square
is reduced by a factor of
four when the square is
moved twice as far from
the point source of light.**

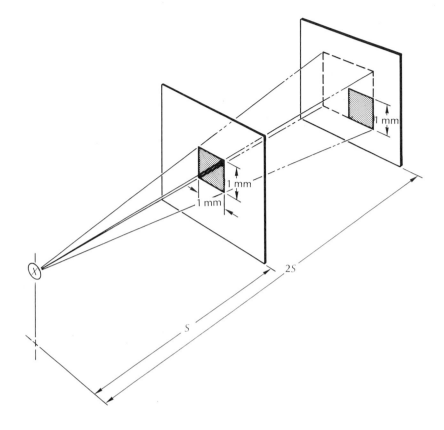

the intensity of an *image* of a source will be inversely proportional to
the distance between the source and the lens (e.g., that the intensity of
the retinal image of an object decreases when the object moves farther
away).

The diagram in Fig. 3.14a shows a square source of light and a lens
that forms an image of the source. In Fig. 3.14b, the source has been
moved twice as far from the lens, and we wish to determine what has
happened to the intensity of the image. *Each point* on the source radiates light, some of which falls on the lens and is then made to converge to an image of that point in the image plane. When the source is
moved twice as far away, the quanta radiated from each point that
actually pass through the lens will be reduced by a factor of four, (by
the inverse square law, since the lens aperture is a fixed size, and acts
just as the square millimeter did in Fig. 3.13). Thus when the source is
moved twice as far from the lens, the image of each point on the
source will be reduced in intensity by fourfold. However, when the
source is moved farther away, the entire image is reduced in *size*. That
is, the distance between the images of any two points on the source is

reduced, and, in any square millimeter of area in the image plane, there will be images of *more* source points. Thus, while the image of each point is less intense, the total number of quanta per second per square millimeter in the image plane will not be reduced by as much as fourfold.

When the distance between the lens and the source is more than about ten times the focal length of the lens, the *length and width* of the image will essentially be inversely proportional to the distance of the source.[3] Therefore, the *area* of the image will be inversely proportional to the square of the distance from the source. Then, as the source moves farther away, the intensity of the image of each point will be reduced, but the images of the points will come closer together by exactly the same factor, and the intensity of the image will not change.

The effective focal length of the human eye is about 17 mm. Therefore, so long as an object is more than about 170 mm, or 7 in. away, the intensity of its retinal image will not change as the distance between the object and the eye changes.

DEPTH OF FOCUS The solid lines in Fig. 3.15 represent a point source of light imaged in front of the retina, and thus out of focus in the plane of the retina. The

[3]When $d_o \geq 10F$, d_i approximately equals F and increases in d_o do not change d_i appreciably. Since $s_i/s_o = d_i/d_o$, and since s_o and d_i are constant, s_i, the linear size of the image, is inversely proportional to d_o.

(a)

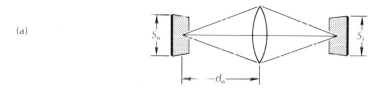

(b)

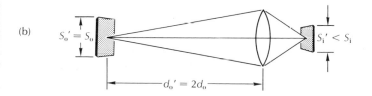

Fig. 3.14 **The relationship between the size of the image and the distance of the object. As the object is moved farther away, the image becomes smaller. This effect tends to cancel the effect of the inverse-square law.**

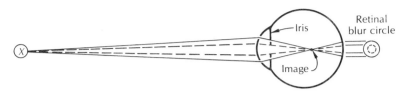

Fig. 3.15 A "blur circle" is formed on the retina when the image of a point is formed in front of (or behind) the retina. The diameter of the blur circle depends upon how far the image is from the retina and how large the pupil is.

distribution of light on the retina itself will be circular, as indicated in the figure, and this distribution is called a blur circle. For a given degree of defocusing, that is, for a given distance between the image and the retina, the diameter of the blur circle is directly proportional to the diameter of the pupil. Thus when the pupil contracts to half its diameter, the blur circle is reduced to half its diameter, as shown by the dashed lines in Fig. 3.15. If the pupil diameter is halved, the image can be about twice as far from the retina and still yield the same size of blur circle. That is, the smaller the pupil, the greater is the permissible distance between the retina and the image for any given amount of blurring.

Now if two sources at different distances from the eye are imaged by the optics of the eye, the images will lie at different distances from the retina. Therefore, if the pupil size is reduced, the range in space which will be imaged on the retina within any given sharpness will be increased, and the eye is said to have a greater depth of focus. In general, the depth of focus increases as the pupil size decreases.

This phenomenon is familiar to photographers. Between the taking of the first and second photographs in Fig. 3.16, the iris in the camera was closed down (and the exposure duration was increased to compensate for the reduction in the intensity of the image). While the camera is focused exactly for only one distance in the photographs, that is, while objects at only one particular distance from the camera lens are in exact focus in the plane of the film, the depth of acceptable focus is greater in the picture taken through the smaller aperture.

THE STIMULUS IN Given the preceding information about optics, it is possible to under-
THE HECHT stand the apparatus used by Hecht *et al.* in their experiment. This ap-
EXPERIMENT paratus will be explained in some detail for two reasons. First, such a
discussion will clarify the application of the principles of optics both in

man-made apparatus and in the eye itself. Second, their apparatus is typical of the optical systems used in a great many experiments in visual perception; an understanding of it is necessary for the interpretation of the results of their experiment and others like it.

The Hecht *et al.* optical system is diagrammed in Fig. 3.17. (This

Fig. 3.16 **Two photographs of the same scene taken through iris openings of different sizes. The camera is focused on the same plane in both photographs. However, objects closer and farther from the plane of best focus are more blurred in the photograph taken through the larger opening.**

diagram has been simplified slightly, but the basic elements are present.) It looks like a fairly complicated system, but the principles it employs are really not hard to understand.

The Monochromator   The source is an incandescent lamp whose filament is a vertical metal ribbon. Since the diagram is a top view, the ribbon runs perpendicular to the paper. Some of the light from this source passes through a lens, L_1, which forms an image of the source in the plane of a narrow slit, called the entrance slit for reasons that will become apparent. The image of the filament is wider than the entrance slit, and the only purpose that this slit serves is to narrow the effective size of the image. The light then passes through another lens, L_2, placed exactly at its focal length away from the entrance slit. Therefore, the light emerging from L_2 will be parallel (see Fig. 3.9c and remember the principle of reversibility). This parallel light then passes through a prism.

The angle through which a path is bent by a prism depends upon the angle of incidence and also upon the change in velocity that the quanta undergo when they enter and leave the prism. In a vacuum, and to a very close approximation, in air, the velocities of all quanta of electromagnetic radiation are equal. However, when light is slowed down upon entering the glass prism, short wavelength quanta are slowed more than longer ones. Therefore, as the quanta pass through the prism in this device, the paths of quanta of shorter wavelength will be bent more strongly than those of the longer wavelengths. This is illustrated, for just three wavelengths, in the inset to Fig. 3.17.

The quanta that leave the prism pass through another lens, L_3. If the prism were not in the path (and lens L_3 were moved up to be in line with the light), L_3 would form an image of the entrance slit at a distance from L_3 that equaled the focal length of L_3 (see Fig. 3.9c). When the prism is in the path, L_3 will form a whole set of images of the entrance slit, one for each wavelength contained in the incoming light, and these images will be spread out along a line, in order of their wavelength. That is, a spectrum will be formed. The exit slit is simply another narrow slit that lets light through from only a narrow band of this spectrum, and in the Hecht *et al.* experiment, the slit was placed where it would pass quanta of wavelengths centered around 510 nm, as in the inset to Fig. 3.17. (Since the source radiates a continuum of wavelengths, the region of the exit slit will also contain overlapping images of the wavelengths neighboring 510 nm, and the transmitted light will therefore consist of a *band* of wavelengths, centered at 510 nm. The narrower the exit slit, the smaller the range of wavelengths of quanta that pass through it.)

This entire device, then, takes light of many wavelengths at its input (the entrance slit) and has as its output light containing only a narrow band of wavelengths. For this reason it is called a monochromator.

The Filters Quanta emerging from the monochromator pass through a set of filters. These are the devices that permit adjustment of the intensity of the stimulus. Filters used for adjusting the intensity of a visual stimulus can be made by a simple and familiar process. Photographic film is exposed to a controlled amount of light and then developed. If more light falls on the film during the exposure, it will be darker when developed. Thus, by exposing a set of films to various amounts of light, a set of filters of systematically varying darkness can be made, and when these filters are placed in the path of light, the intensity of the stimulus will be changed accordingly.

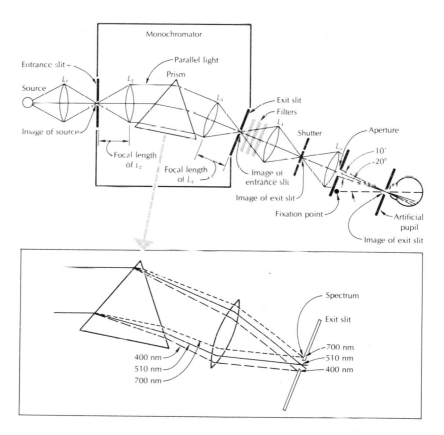

Fig. 3.17 **Diagram of the apparatus used by Hecht** *et al.* **It is explained in the text.**

The process by which a developed film "filters" the light is relatively simple. The unexposed film is a transparent sheet coated with a chemical whose molecules change their state if they absorb a quantum of light. Consider a single molecule of this chemical. When the exposing light is incident on the film, this molecule may or may not be struck by a quantum, and if it is struck, it may or may not absorb the quantum. If it does absorb a quantum, it changes state. The more quanta there are in the exposing light, the higher is the probability that any one molecule will absorb a quantum and change its state. The entire film is covered with billions of molecules, and thus when more quanta are in the exposing light, more of those molecules will change their state.

Next, the film is developed. That is, it is placed in a series of baths containing chemicals that react with the chemicals in the film in the following way: Any molecule from the film coating that is in its original state will be washed away, but any molecule that had absorbed a quantum and changed its state will be reduced to a new granule that is opaque, that is, which absorbs or reflects any new quantum incident on it. Thus, after development, the film is coated with a more or less dense layer of opaque granules. If the exposure was of extremely high intensity, the granules will be so close together that the film as a whole will be virtually opaque. On the other hand, if only a few quanta were absorbed during the exposure, the film will be mostly transparent except for a few opaque granules here and there.

Suppose the intensity of the exposure had been just enough to cover half of the area of the film with opaque granules. Then, if the developed film were placed in a beam of light, half of the quanta would be absorbed or reflected from the film, and the remaining half would be transmitted. Such a filter is said to have a transmittance of 50%.

If you look at two filters, one of which has a transmittance of, say, 50% and the other 1% (that is, 99% of its surface is occluded by opaque particles), the one with 1% transmittance will obviously look darker, and the opaque particles will be more densely distributed. A filter of lower transmittance has a greater density. Filters are usually labeled not by their transmittance, but by their density, in units that are very convenient in some ways and very confusing in others. These density units are so extensively used in studies of visual perception that it is necessary to explain them.

Density is defined as follows:

$$\text{density} = \log_{10}(1/T),$$

where T is the proportion of light transmitted.

It follows that:

$$T = \frac{1}{10^d}$$

where d is the density of the filter.

An easier way of remembering this is to note that the density d is the logarithm (base 10) of the transmittance, with the sign changed. For example, suppose the transmittance of a filter is 1%, that is, the proportion transmitted is 1/100.

$$\frac{1}{100} = 10^{-2}$$

Then the log of the transmittance is -2.0 and the density is 2.0. A filter of density 1 transmits $1/10^1 = 10\%$ of the light, density 2 transmits $1/10^2 = 1\%$, 3 transmits 0.1%, etc. A filter that transmits about 50% of the light has a density of 0.3. A table of densities and corresponding transmittances is included in Appendix II.

When a beam of light is passed through a combination of filters, the density of the combination is simply the sum of the densities of the components. For example, suppose that a 1 0 and a 2.0 density filter are both placed in a beam of light, the light first passing through the 1.0 and then the 2.0 filter. The 1.0 filter transmits 1/10 of the incident light, and the 2.0 density filter transmits 1/100 of *that* light. The combination of the two filters thus transmits 1/1000 of the light, and this is the equivalent of a single filter of density 3.0. (Obviously, if the light passed through the combination of filters in the other direction, hitting the 2.0 filter first, the result would be the same.)

The filters just described are called neutral density filters. The "neutral" is to distinguish them from colored filters. Neutral filters transmit all visible wavelengths about equally, and look grey, while colored filters look colored because they transmit different wavelengths differently. (Colored filters will be discussed Chapter VIII.)[4]

The Shutter   The light that passes through the exit slit and the filters in Fig. 3.17 encounters lens L_4, which forms an image of the exit slit in the plane of a shutter. Almost all shutters are one or another form of an opaque sur-

---

[4]Hecht et al. used neutral density filters in their experiment. Since the stimuli they used were monochromatic, it really would not have mattered whether or not the filters they used were neutral, so long as the filters absorbed the light in known amounts. However, sets of neutral density filters with carefully calibrated densities were and are readily available.

face that moves into and out of the light path. The narrower the beam of light in the plane of the shutter, the more quickly the shutter can cut off or let through the light. Therefore, when short exposures are required, the shutter is usually placed in a narrow part of the path. Theoretically, the shutter could just as well have been placed in the plane of the source or the entrance or exit slits, but that is hard to achieve mechanically. Therefore, lens L_4 is used to form a mechanically available narrow place in the beam. That is the only function of lens L_4.

The Stimulating Field Light passing the shutter enters lens L_5, which converges the light again, forming another image of the exit slit in the plane of a small hole called the artificial pupil. The subject's eye is placed directly behind this pupil, and the light, after being refracted by the optics of his eye, strikes the retina. The artificial pupil is present for the following reason. In the Hecht apparatus, the image of the exit slit was a strip of light 2.4 mm wide and over 10 mm long. The natural pupil of the human eye is no more than about 8 or 9 mm in diameter at its largest, and its diameter may change from time to time, even in the dark. (The diameter of the pupil is affected not only by the intensity of light striking the retina, but also by the system that controls lens curvature, by the angle between the lines of sight of the two eyes, and by the emotional state of the subject.) If there were no artificial pupil, and if the subject's pupil diameter were to change, the amount of light passing through the pupil would change, and the intensity of the light at the retina would consequently change. To circumvent this source of variance, an artificial pupil, smaller than the smallest sized natural pupil (2 mm diameter), is placed immediately in front of the natural pupil.

Before a test flash occurs, the subject looks at the dim red fixation point. This means that he does two relevant things. He moves his eyeball so that the image of the fixation point falls on his fovea, and he adjusts the refractive power of the lens of his eye until the fixation point is sharply focused on his retina. Now, if the shutter is briefly opened, the light in the *stimulus path* will fall on a region 20° from the fovea. In addition, since the aperture between L_5 and the eye is the same distance from his eye as is the fixation point, an image of that aperture will also be sharply focused on the retina. (In fact, when the artificial pupil is as small as 2 mm in diameter, the depth of focus is so great that the images of the fixation point and the aperture will remain relatively sharp despite large changes in the power of the lens in the eye.) The aperture is filled with light, and acts as a disk-shaped source.

Thus, the fact that an image of the aperture is formed on the retina means that a disk of light will be formed on the retina. The diameter of that disk can be adjusted to be 10′ by choosing the appropriate aperture diameter.

The experiment proceeded in the following way: After the subject was dark-adapted, he looked at the fixation point, and when he was ready to make a judgment, he pressed a switch that opened the shutter for 1 msec. He then reported whether or not he had seen the flash. Between flashes, the experimenter changed the density of the filters in the stimulus path, and in this way, over a large number of trials, determined how often the subject could see the flash for each of a series of intensities.

Several times during the course of the experiment, the physical intensities of the stimuli were measured. Since they were too small to measure directly, Hecht et al. measured the intensity of the light when no filters were in place, and when the aperture and the artificial pupil were removed. Since they knew the sizes of the aperture and pupil, they were able to correct those measures by the appropriate factors. They calibrated the filters separately by measuring, in relatively strong lights, the percentage of light transmitted by each. The percentage of incident light that a filter transmits is independent of the amount of light falling on it. Therefore, since the experimenters now knew the unfiltered intensity and also the transmittances of the filters, they could determine the actual stimulus intensities delivered to the eye when the various filters were in the stimulus path

COLLIMATED LIGHT   When a point source of light is placed in the focal plane of a lens, the paths of quanta emerging from the other side of the lens are parallel, and in this case it can be said that an image of the source will be formed at infinity. Conversely, if parallel light falls on a lens, an image of the source will be formed at the focal distance from the lens. Light traveling in parallel paths is called *collimated light*.

In the nondefective human eye, when the muscles controlling the lens are relaxed, the focal length of the combination of cornea and lens equals the distance from the optical center of the lens to the retina. Therefore, when collimated light falls on such an eye, an image of the source will be focused on the retina. For example, stars are, for all practical purposes, infinitely distant, and they are sharply in focus on a normal observer's retinas when his lens muscles are relaxed. But objects need not *actually* be far away in order for their retinal images to

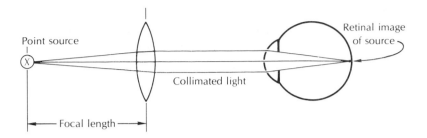

Fig. 3.18 **When the eye is focused for infinity, a nearby source can be sharply imaged on the retina if it is placed in the focal plane of a lens.**

be in focus when the eye is focused at infinity. All that is required is that the paths of rays from the object be parallel. The lens in Fig. 3.18 is at its focal distance from the source, the light between the lens and the eye is therefore collimated, and the image of the source will be sharply in focus on the subject's retina when his eye is focused at infinity. Although the source is actually close to the subject, it is optically an infinite distance from him.

The diagram in Fig. 3.18 is relatively simple. The source is a point on the optic axis of the lens and the eye. Generally, sources are off axis, and the diagram in Fig. 3.19 illustrates this more general case. To locate the retinal image of point A, the first step is to draw a straight line from point A through the center of the lens, the line labeled AC in the diagram. This is the only path from A through the lens that undergoes no bending, and can thus be drawn immediately. Since it is given that A is a focal length away from the lens, then all rays from A that emerge from the lens will be parallel, and because the path AC establishes the direction of these rays, all other paths from A between the lens and the eye must be drawn parallel to AC.

The line labeled AD is the path of some of the quanta from A, but these are not of interest, since they do not enter the pupil. One path of particular interest is the one already discussed that passes through the optical center of the eye, P, and is thus undeflected by the eye. The intersection of that path with the retina establishes the position of the retinal image of A. The other paths of interest from A are the paths labeled AE and AF, which are the outer limits of the paths of light from A that finally enter into forming the retinal image of A; this set of paths has been shaded in the diagram. The intensity of the retinal image of A is determined by the intensity of the light radiating from point A and the size of the shaded cone of light whose apex is A.

To determine the size of the image of an object extending from A to B, the location of B' on the retina must be established. This is accomplished by drawing the path from B through the center of the eye, just as was done to locate the image of A.

It follows from the geometry of this diagram that the size of the retinal image depends upon the focal length of the lens according to the following relationship:

$$\frac{S_i}{S_o} = \frac{FL_{eye}}{FL_{lens}}$$

Therefore, the shorter the focal length of the lens, the larger will be the retinal image of the object. This is exactly the process that occurs when we look through a magnifying glass. The object is placed in the focal plane of the magnifier, and the magnification of the retinal image of the object is greater when the lens is stronger, that is, when its focal length is shorter.

Two other features of this diagram should be noted. First, although the light between the lens and the eye is still said to be collimated, it is *not* all parallel. The paths from *any one point* on the object are parallel and this satisfies the definition of "collimation," but the paths from different points are not parallel to each other. This fact is closely related to the second notable feature of the diagram. If the eye were moved farther and farther away from the lens, the size of the retinal image of any part of the object would remain unchanged. (This can be deduced from the diagram, and is indicated by the fact that the equation above, for determining the size of the retinal image, does not contain any term for the distance between the lens and the eye.) But when the eye is moved farther away, less and less of the object can be seen, because the paths from the more extreme parts of the object that go through the lens will simply not enter the eye. It is a useful exercise to prove this by redrawing Fig. 3.19 with the eye twice as far from the lens. This effect is also easily observable with a magnifying lens. If the eye is very close to the lens, a large field of view is visible through the lens. As the eye is moved farther away, but the lens is kept at its focal distance from the object, less and less of the object is visible through the lens, but the part that *is* visible will retain the same magnification.

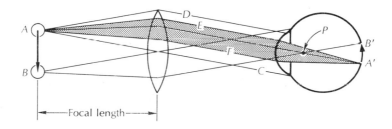

SOURCES OF IM-
PERFECTION OF THE
RETINAL IMAGE
From the discussion of geometrical optics given so far, it might be expected that the retinal image of an object would be a perfect replica of the object itself, changed only in size, intensity, and location in space. The hypothetical image derived from the geometry of perfect lenses is sometimes called the geometrical image. It is a useful concept because it usually provides a good approximation to the real image. However, in any real optical system, the image is a degraded version of the ideal image, and some of the factors that contribute to this degradation have important effects upon retinal images. Those factors will be discussed here.

Chromatic Aberration
It was mentioned earlier that the amount by which the path of a quantum is bent at a refracting surface depends upon the angle of incidence but also upon the change in velocity that the quantum undergoes upon crossing the surface. In a vacuum, quanta of all wavelengths travel at the same velocity, but when they enter any medium, such as glass or the media of the eye, the amount by which their velocities are reduced depends upon their wavelengths. This is the effect by which a prism can produce a spectrum, as in Fig. 3.17.

For the same reason, the refractive power of a *lens* will be different for different wavelengths of light. Thus, if a source that radiates many wavelengths is imaged by the optics of the eye, a series of images will be formed at different distances from the cornea, one for each wavelength. If the retina is in the plane of any one of these images, the rest of them will be out of focus in that plane, and will produce blur. This is called chromatic aberration.

Chromatic aberration is fairly strong in the human eye, and it must be taken into account if one is interested in the nature of retinal images. Nevertheless, for reasons that are not presently understood, measurements of visual acuity are scarcely affected when chromatic aberration is eliminated (Luria and Schwartz, 1960). Thus, chromatic aberration is mentioned here because it ought to affect visual perception, but present evidence indicates that it does not.

Spherical Aberration
The surfaces of the lens drawn in Fig. 3.6 are shaped so that all rays from the source converge to a point on the other side of the lens. While such a shape can be found for a point source and any given object distance, focal length, lens material, and wavelength of light, a slightly different shape is required if any of those parameters changes. Spherical surfaces are relatively easy to make, and since they are reasonably

close to the ideal surface, almost all manufactured lenses have spherical surfaces. However, because the sphere is not precisely the correct surface, the image formed will be degraded, and that degradation is called spherical aberration.

This term is also used, somewhat imprecisely, to refer to an important form of aberration in the human eye. None of the optically effective surfaces in the eye is perfectly spherical, and the refractive power of the media within the lens of the eye is greater at the center of the lens than at its edges. The particular shapes of the surfaces and the distribution of media are such that, for most eyes, the rays from a point source at infinity do not all meet in a perfect point. In some eyes, the outer regions of the cornea and lens have greater refractive power than the middle, while for others, the reverse holds. Further, the extent, and in many subjects even the direction, of this effect changes as the subject focuses on nearer objects (Ivanoff, 1956). The degradation of the retinal image caused by this property of the eye is called spherical aberration, even though none of the relevant surfaces is actually spherical.

Random Variation In addition to the systematic differences in refractive power across the pupil that are called spherical aberration, most eyes manifest a more or less random variation in power from place to place (Ivanoff, 1956; Van den Brink, 1962). Thus, rays from a point source that enter two adjoining parts of the pupil may come to focus in different planes. In many clinically normal eyes, this defect is a principle source of image degradation.

Light Scatter The media in the eye contain tiny particles that scatter light. In young, healthy eyes, a negligible proportion of the incident light is scattered in this way, but the density of scattering particles increases with age, and can seriously degrade the image in older people.

Another source of scattering that is much harder to evaluate, but which may well be of considerable significance, is the scattering of light by the structures within the retina itself. The reasons that this source is hard to measure will be explained later.

Diffraction All of the preceding discussion on image formation is part of the field called geometrical optics, in which images are located by straightforward principles of geometry. In order that the conclusions drawn from such geometrical diagrams be correct, two assumptions must be made, in addition to those already stated about refraction at surfaces. These assumptions are (1) that light travels in straight lines through any homogeneous medium, and (2) that when quanta in two paths intersect, they continue in their original directions.

The second of these assumptions is a good one except under very special conditions, such as when lights of extraordinarily high intensity meet in certain media, and those conditions are never met in studies of visual perception. However, the first assumption is incorrect, or at least misleading.

If a beam of light is directed toward a very small hole in an opaque sheet, quanta emerging from the hole spread out in all directions, so that a screen placed beyond the hole will be lighted all over, as illustrated in Fig. 3.20a. If the hole were infinitesimally small, quanta would diverge in a uniform distribution in all forward directions. As the hole is enlarged, the distribution becomes more and more directional, resulting in a pattern on the screen like the one plotted in Fig. 3.20b. When the hole is even larger, the distribution of light on the screen becomes flat on top, as in Fig. 3.20c. In the extreme case, when the hole has an infinite diameter, that is, when only a straight edge is present, the distribution is as shown in Fig. 3.20d. This divergence of the paths of quanta as they pass near an edge is called diffraction, and it has very important consequences in the visual process.[5]

The pupil of the eye is a hole in an opaque surface, and, particularly when the iris is strongly contracted, the hole is small enough to produce appreciable spreading of the quanta passing through it. For example, when the eye looks at a point source, as in Fig. 3.21a, the image, even if it is in perfect focus on the retina, is not really a point, but, instead, is a distribution of light with a shape like that indicated in the figure. The principles of geometrical optics are useful in that they determine the midpoint of this distribution, but they do not allow the detailed description of the light distribution that is necessary for the understanding of certain visual phenomena.

Figure 3.21b is a diagram of the formation of the image of an extended source or an object. Here each point on the object can be considered as a separate point source. The image of each point is a distribution like that in Fig. 3.21a, and all these distributions add up to give the distribution for the object as a whole. Again, the center of the

---

[5]The explanation of diffraction (and of refraction, too) is much easier when analyzed in terms of the wave nature of light. However, the discussion that must precede such an explanation is fairly long, and since the quantal concept of light is sufficient to understand most of the optical phenomena related to vision, wave mechanics will not be discussed here. The reader is referred, instead, to a superb elementary treatment by Weiskopf (1968).

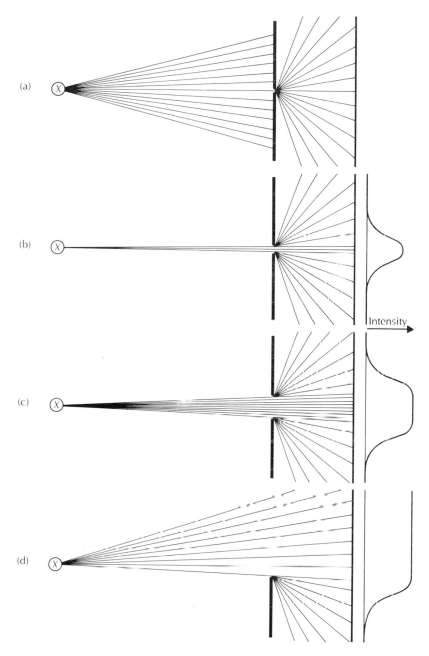

Fig. 3.20 **Diffraction of light by an aperture. This is not to scale. The light actually spreads over a much smaller angle.**

image can be located by geometrical optics, and its size, except for the spread due to diffraction, can also be determined, but the critical distribution of quanta at the edges must be determined from the principles of diffraction. The effects of diffraction upon vision will be discussed quantitatively in Chapters XI and XII.

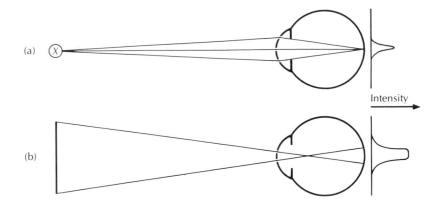

Fig. 3.21 **Diffraction of light by the pupil of the eye. The width of the retinal light distribution is exaggerated.**

MEASUREMENTS OF THE REAL RETINAL IMAGE

The effects of diffraction, aberrations, and scattering all combine to make the real retinal image different from the geometrical image. It is of great importance, when considering perceptual phenomena such as visual acuity and contrast, to know precisely what the distribution of light on the retina is for any object in space. Several workers have made measurements of such distributions and a particular set of them, made by Westheimer and Campbell (1962) will be discussed here.

One way to measure the light distribution in the retinal image would be to remove an eyeball, cut a tiny hole in the back of it, and measure the amount of light coming through the hole as the retinal image is moved slowly across the hole. This technique has been tried with steer eyes, fresh from a slaughter house, since steer eyes are more easily available than normal human ones and are reasonably similar to human eyes in structure. However, the technique is subject to serious difficulties (e.g., the cornea becomes cloudy soon after death, and the surfaces may change their shape).

A better way to measure the light distribution in the human eye would be to look into a subject's eye with some device that measures the distribution of the light, and this is essentially the technique used by Westheimer and Campbell.

The Ophthalmoscope

The white of the eye and the iris are opaque, so the only way to look into a subject's eye is to look through his pupil. However, the pupil ordinarily looks black, even when the subject is in a brightly lighted environment. This seems surprising, since the pupil is really a hole in front of a lighted retina.

The reason the pupil ordinarily looks black is illustrated in Fig. 3.22. Light from the screen enters the subject's eye through his pupil and falls on the retina, where some of it is absorbed by the visual pigments. Most of the remaining light passes through the layer containing the visual pigment and is absorbed by the black pigments that line the inside of the eye behind the receptors. A small proportion of the incident light is reflected from the back of the eye, and some of that light emerges from the pupil and returns toward the screen. (The amount of light coming back out of the eye is about 1/10,000 of the light that enters.)

Since light does emerge from the pupil, the pupil should look lighted, not black. However, most of the light reflected from the eye will travel back along roughly the same paths as it entered the eye. In Fig. 3.22, most of the reflected light will travel toward the screen. Therefore, if the experimenter places his eye off to the side, position 1 in Fig. 3.22, his eye will not intercept the reflected light and the pupil will

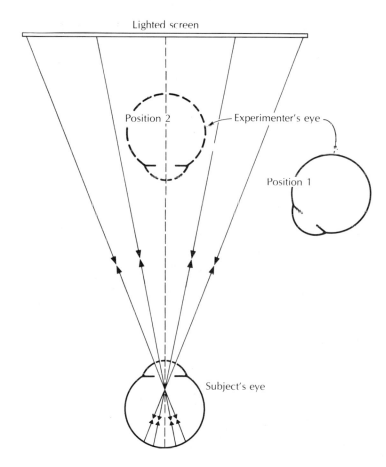

Fig. 3.22 **The reason a subject's pupils look black. If the observer's eye is off to the side (position 1), little light from the subject's retina enters the observer's eye. If he moves over to position 2, he cuts off the light from the screen, and the subject's pupil still looks dark.**

look dark. If the experimenter moves his eye over to position 2, the pupil will still look dark, because the experimenter's head has now blocked the light from the screen.

If he were to put a bright source between himself and the subject, close to the line between the subject's eye and his eye, the light reflected back from the subject's eye would enter his, but the light coming directly from the source to the experimenter's eye would be so much stronger that it would obscure his view of the retina.

The light reflected out of the pupil of the human eye can be seen by the use of the simple optical device shown in Fig. 3.23. This device optically places the experimenter's eye very close to the path of the incoming light without obscuring the light or the experimenter's view of the pupil. The light that is visible is that which is reflected from the retina along paths just very slightly different from the incoming light. The diagram in this figure is a diagram of the essential elements in the device called an opthalmoscope, which is used by physicians to ex-

Fig. 3.23 **Diagram of an opthalmoscope. The source of light is imaged in the subject's pupil, and a large area on the back of the eye is illuminated. Some of the light that is reflected from the retina emerges from the pupil, and half of that light gets past the mirror and into the examiner's eye. The correcting lens matches the optics of the subject's and the examiner's eyes. For example, if both the subject and the examiner are focused for infinity, light emerging from the subject's pupil will be collimated, and an image of the subject's retina will be formed on the examiner's retina if the power of the correcting lens is zero. If the subject is nearsighted (so that he cannot focus as far as infinity), and the examiner still focuses at infinity, then the correcting lens must have nonzero power.**

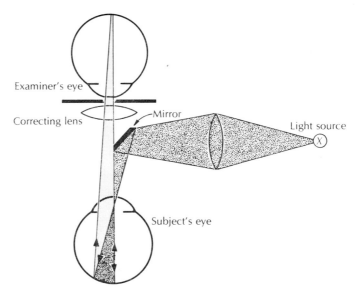

Examiner's eye

Correcting lens

Mirror

Light source

Subject's eye

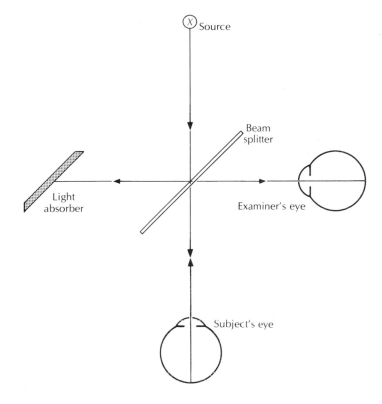

Fig. 3.24 **The rudiments of a different kind of ophthalmoscope. (To make this a useful device, the modifications described in Appendix III are required.)**

amine patients' retinas. If your doctor can spare the time when you next have a physical examination, ask him to let you use his opthalmoscope on him, or his nurse if you prefer her.

Figure 3.24 is a modification of the same principle. Light from the source strikes a device called a beam splitter, which may be simply a mirror on which the silver is coated so thinly that it reflects only about half the light and transmits the other half. The light reflected from the beam splitter falls on a highly absorbing surface, such as black velvet, while the transmitted light enters the subject's eye. Quanta reflected out of the eye along the same path again strike the beam splitter, half of it being transmitted back toward the source and the other half entering the experimenter's eye. Under these conditions, the light reflected from the subject's retina will cause his pupil to appear to the experimenter as if it were glowing with pink light.

The simple device diagramed in Fig. 3.24 would have a few defects if it were actually to be used for viewing a retina. Modifications to remedy these defects are illustrated in Appendix III. The modifications, however, do not involve any changes in the basic principle of the device. They are only changes in detail.

Westheimer and
Campbell's Apparatus

The device used by Westheimer and Campbell (1962) for measuring the light distribution in the retinal image of a fine bright line is basically the same as that shown in Fig. 3.24. Their apparatus is diagramed in Fig. 3.25. The source of light is an incandescent lamp whose filament is a straight, narrow, vertical wire. The diagram is a top view, and the filament is perpendicular to the surface of the page. The light from the filament passes through a colored filter to limit the wavelengths to a narrow band. Then, the light that is transmitted through the beam splitter, the lens, and the artificial pupil enters the eye. The lens is chosen to have just the right power that, in combination with the optics of the subject's eye, an image of the filament is formed on his retina. (The subject sees a bright vertical line.) Half of the light reflected from his retina and emerging from the pupil is reflected from the beam splitter toward a device for measuring light intensity. (The other half is lost.) From the law of reversibility, the optics of the eye (and the lens)

Fig. 3.25 **The optical system used by Westheimer and Campbell (1962) to measure the light distribution in a retinal image.**

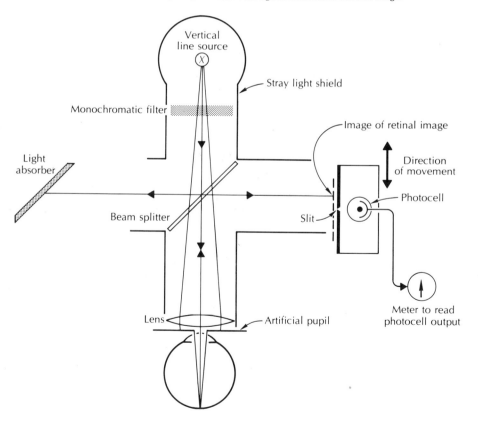

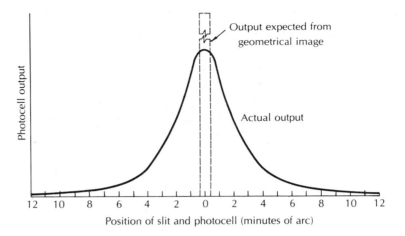

Fig. 3.26 **The photocell reading as a function of the position of the slit as it moves across the image of the retinal image. The solid curve is the obtained output pattern and the dashed lines are the output that would be expected if there were no aberrations or diffraction. The total area under the curve is a measure of the total light falling on the retina. If that same light were distributed in the geometrical image, the height of the geometrical image would be about ten times the height of the peak of the actual distribution.** [*After Westheimer and Campbell (1962), subject J.K., 3mm pupil.*]

will act on the light reflected from the retina, forming an image of the retinal image out in space at the same distance from the eye as is the source. Thus there will be an image of the retinal image superimposed exactly on top of the source (that image being formed by the light transmitted through the beam splitter), and another image of the retinal image will be formed in the plane so labeled in the diagram (formed by the light reflected from the beam splitter). A thin vertical slit is placed in this plane, allowing the light from a narrow region of the image to pass through to a photocell. The output of the photocell is proportional to the intensity of the light falling on it, and thus the reading of the meter indicates the intensity of the light wherever the slit is placed with respect to the image. The slit and photocell can be moved together across the image, and in this way the distribution of light in the image of the retinal image can be measured.

The solid line plotted in Fig. 3.26 shows the way in which the output of the photocell varies as the slit is moved across the image. The dashed line indicates how the plot would look if the retinal image were a true geometrical image.

The Results — Retinal Light Distributions

The distribution of light plotted in Fig. 3.26 is not quite the same as the distribution of light in the retinal image. It is the distribution in the *image* of the retinal image. That is, the aberrations and diffraction of the optics of the eye operate on the recorded distribution twice, while they operate only once on the actual retinal image. The light distribution in the retinal image may be determined by correcting the measured distribution to take the double passage into account, and the result is plotted in Fig. 3.27. The size of a receptor (cone) in the central retina is included for comparison.

Westheimer and Campbell also performed this kind of measurement for dark lines of varying widths and for gratings, that is fields containing dark and light stripes. Some of their results for dark lines are shown in Fig. 3.28a. As the line and its geometrical image are made narrower, the flat bottom on the light distribution disappears, and for all lines whose geometrical images are narrower than about 2', the distributions have essentially the same shape, but are reduced in amplitude.

Westheimer and Campbell's results for gratings are shown in Fig. 3.28b. As a grating becomes finer, the amplitude of the change in intensity on the retina becomes smaller. With gratings finer than about 1' of arc per cycle, the resulting light distribution is very close to a uniform one, and we know from independent psychophysical measurements that a subject cannot distinguish a grating finer than that from a uniformly illuminated field.

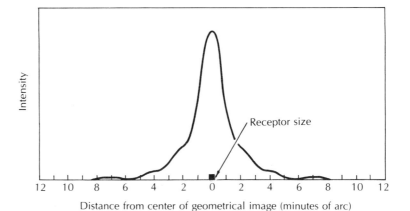

Fig. 3.27 **Light distribution on the retina for a fine bright line object, calculated from the curve in Fig. 3.26. The black rectangle represents the diameter of a retinal receptor in the central fovea.** [*After Westheimer and Campbell (1962), subject J.K. 3 mm pupil.*]

Distance from center of geometrical image (minutes of arc)

Fig. 3.28 **Light distributions in the images of retinal images. A series of dark lines on a bright field are shown in (a), and a series of black and white striped gratings are shown in (b). The curves are raw data from Westheimer and Campbell (1962), and contain irregularities caused by random electrical noise, eye blinks, etc.**

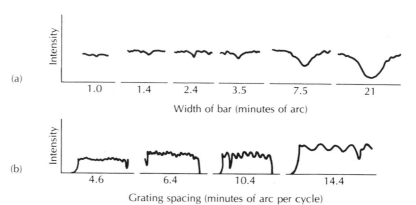

PROBLEMS

3.1   Explain, with a diagram, why the retinal image does not change size when the pupil of the eye changes size.

3.2   You are given a lens with a focal length of 100 mm, and an object 10 mm long, 500 mm from the lens. Where is the image, and how long is it?

Answer: 125 mm from the lens, 2.5 mm long.

3.3   Draw a lens and an object. Now dash in an image plane at any arbitrary distance from the lens. Then find the size of the image.

3.4   Find a lens. Any lens will do, as long as it is not concave (i.e., negative). It can be a camera lens, the lens from a slide projector, etc. Now find its focal length. (If you have a very thick lens or set of lenses, it is a complicated procedure to determine the focal length correctly, but for the purposes of this exercise, assume that the thick lens is the equivalent of a thin one located somewhere in the middle of the thick one.)

3.5   Assume that the focal length of the eye is 17 mm, that the diameter of the pupil is 5 mm, and that the eye is correctly focused on a point source 1.0 m away. If the source is then moved to 50 cm, and the eye does not change in any way, how big is the blur circle on the retina, in millimeters and in units of visual angle? (Neglect aberrations and diffraction.)

3.6   If 10 million quanta are incident on a set of filters, arranged in series, of densities 1, 2, and 3 log units, how many quanta will get all the way through (on the average).

3.7   (a) Given an eye with the properties that result in the curve in Fig. 3.27, graphically find and plot the light distribution on the retina when the object is two narrow bright lines, separated by 2′.
(b) Do the same when the entire visual field is filled with narrow bright stripes, infinitely long and spaced every 2′ across the field.

IV ◇◇◇ QUANTAL FLUCTUATIONS

HAVING covered the background material in the preceding chapter, we can begin to consider the perceptual phenomena involved in the experiments of Hecht *et al.* These phenomena are principally related to vision under conditions of low light intensity, but they also provide the necessary background for an understanding of phenomena at higher light levels, which will be discussed in subsequent chapters. The present chapter is an analysis of the effects of the quantal nature of light upon visual perception.

QUANTAL FLUC- Each quantum in a beam of electromagnetic radiation was generated
TUATIONS IN THE discretely when a particular electron shifted from one energy state to
STIMULUS another. The shifting of any electron is a random process, in the sense that the precise time of its occurrence cannot be predicted. All that can

be said of a given electron is that it has some particular probability of shifting energy levels per unit of time, and that the probability that a particular electron will radiate a quantum is independent of the states of the other electrons. Consider, for example, the light in the Hecht *et al.* apparatus. The filament was hot, and innumerable electrons were present that were capable of radiating quanta. Suppose that the temperature of the filament was such that any electron had a probability of 0.5 of radiating a quantum in 1 sec, and that there were 1,000,000 such electrons in the filament. Then, during a 1-sec period, the expected number of quanta radiated is 0.5 × 1,000,000, or 500,000 quanta. During a period of 1 msec, the expected number radiated is 500 quanta, and during 1 μsec, the expected number is 0.5 quanta. These are expected numbers, but for any single period of time, the actual number may well be larger or smaller than that amount. This is particularly evident for the 1-μsec period since, although the expected number is 0.5, that number is impossible, quanta being discrete events. Thus, during some particular 1-μsec period, zero quanta may be radiated, during another, 10 quanta, etc., the *average* of all these numbers equaling 0.5 quanta. In other words, if a perfect apparatus were constructed, one in which the filament were as constant as it could be and the shutter gave exposures of exactly 1 μsec every time, the number of quanta delivered by each successive flash would still vary, sometimes being zero, sometimes one, two, etc., the average number of quanta being 0.5 for a very large number of flashes. The fact that quanta are radiated discretely together with the fact that the occurrence of each is independent of the presence or absence of others, establish that the "frequency distribution" of quanta in a large number of flashes will necessarily be of a particular type called the Poisson distribution, as represented graphically in Fig. 4.1.[1]

If the exposure duration in the preceding example were increased to 1 msec, the expected number of quanta would be 500, and the frequency distribution of quanta for a large number of flashes would be a Poisson distribution with a mean of 500. This distribution is plotted in Fig. 4.2a. Note that it is almost perfectly symmetrical and, in fact, is virtually identical with a normal distribution. The other plots in Fig. 4.2 are Poisson distributions with other mean values. In general, as the means increase, the distributions approach normality.

---

[1]The term *frequency distribution* is commonly used in discussions of statistics, but it can be misleading, especially when the term *frequency* may be applied to some property of the events themselves. For example, the frequency distribution of quantal emission, as plotted in Fig. 4.1, has nothing to do with the frequencies of vibrations of the individual quanta. The distribution of frequencies of vibration of quanta emitted from a source is usually called the emission spectrum of the source (See Fig. 3.1, p. 30 for an example), and is really the frequency distribution of vibration frequencies emitted.

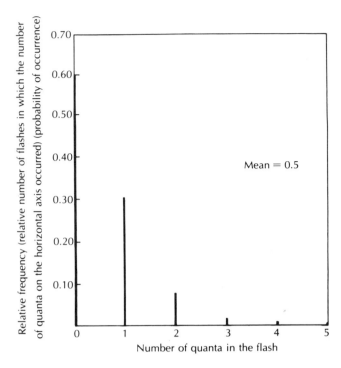

Fig. 4.1 **"Frequency distribution" of quanta in a large number of flashes when the average number per flash is 0.5. This is a Poisson distribution with a mean of 0.5.**

The filament in this example has some finite size, and let us assume that it is a ribbon similar to the one used by Hecht-*et al*. For a 1-msec opening of the shutter, the expected number of quanta delivered will be 500 and the distribution over a large number of flashes will be the one shown in Fig. 4.2a. Now suppose that the detector of quanta is very small and is placed in a position in the beam where it only catches quanta from one very small part of the filament, say 1/100 of the area of the filament. Then the expected number of quanta incident on the detector will be five, and the distribution will again be a Poisson one, as that in Fig. 4.2c. If the detector catches quanta from only 1/500 of the area of the filament, the expected number will be one quantum. On many of the exposures (37% of them), such a small detector will see no quanta at all, and the number it sees from flash to flash will vary according to the Poisson distribution in Fig. 4.2e.

The surface of a typical optical filter is coated with a large number of very small opaque particles with clear spaces between them. Suppose that a filter will transmit 10% of the light. That is, 10% of its area consists of clear spaces. Each of these spaces will, in a given 1-msec flash, have a very small expected number of quanta incident on it, and if there are, on the average, 50 quanta incident on the entire filter, all the

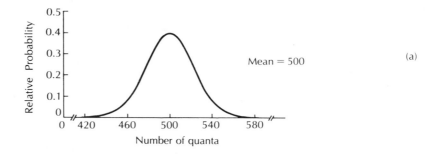

(a)

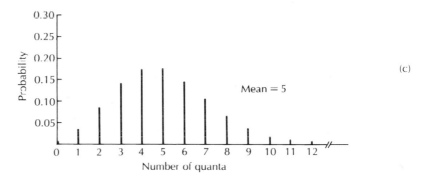

(b)

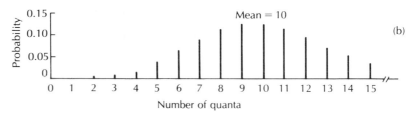

(c)

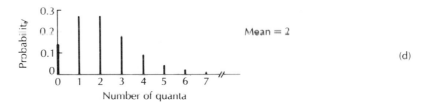

(d)

Fig. 4.2 **Poisson distributions for various average values. The breaks in the horizontal axes are meant to suggest that each plot should really extend to infinity. However, they have been cut short for convenience.**

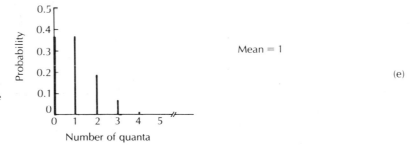

(e)

spaces combined will receive an average of five quanta. Therefore, quanta transmitted through the filter will be distributed in a Poisson distribution with a mean of five.

When Hecht *et al.* performed their experiment, they determined the setting of their apparatus for which the subject said he saw the flash on 60% of the exposures. The prism, the slits, and the filters in the apparatus all absorb some proportion of the incident quanta, and at the 60% threshold, the average number of quanta emerging from the apparatus was 90.[2] That is, the numbers of quanta in each of a large number of such flashes are distributed according to a Poisson distribution with a mean of 90. The reflections and absorptions in the eye and the absorptions by the visual pigment itself act in the same way as the filter described above, with the result that, at the threshold setting, the quanta actually absorbed by the visual pigment over a series of flashes are Poisson distributed with a mean of nine absorptions.

THE RELATIONSHIP BETWEEN QUANTAL FLUCTUATION AND THE SUBJECT'S VARIABILITY The fluctuation in the number of quanta present from flash to flash is of fundamental importance. When the apparatus is held at a fixed setting, some of the flashes deliver no quanta at all, more deliver just one quantum, some deliver 100 quanta, etc. When the apparatus is fixed at the 60% threshold intensity, the subject's responses also vary. Forty percent of the time he says he did not see the flash and 60% of the time he says he did see it. It is logically possible that all of the variability in his responses is a consequence of the actual variability inherent in the stimulus. It is certainly true that at least some of his variability results from these quantal fluctuations. Hecht *et al.* attempted to evaluate the relative contributions of the variability of the stimulus and of the subject himself, and to do so, they employed the following logic.

Suppose that there is no variability in the subject himself and further suppose that he says he sees the stimulus every single time that six or more quanta are absorbed and always says he does not see it when fewer than six quanta are absorbed. If the above is true, then it is easy to predict how often he should see the flash for each intensity setting of the apparatus, since the distributions of the quanta are known for each intensity setting. For example, suppose the apparatus is set so that an average of nine quanta are absorbed by his visual pigment. Figure 4.3 is a plot of the Poisson distribution, for a series of flashes at this intensi-

---

[2]This is the average of several measures on several subjects.

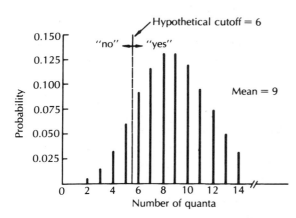

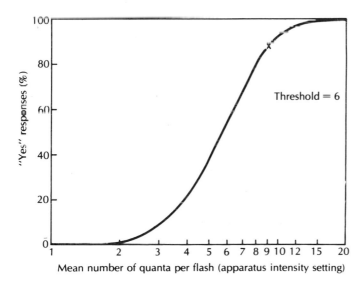

Fig. 4.3 **Poisson distribution with a mean of nine, the average number of quanta absorbed at threshold in the Hecht** *et al.* **experiment. The dashed line divides the distribution into those cases in which a subject with no variability would say "yes" and those in which he would say "no" if his threshold were six or more quanta.**

ty, that is, the mean is equal to nine. For every flash represented to the right of the dashed line in Fig. 4.3, the perfect subject will say "yes" and for every one on the left, he will say "no."

The sum of the heights of all the plotted lines is equal to 1.0. This is the sum of the probabilities of occurrence of every possible number of quanta. The sum of the probabilities to the left of the dashed line is 0.116, and to the right, 0.884. Therefore, a subject with absolutely no variability of his own and with a cutoff of six or more quanta, will say "yes" 88.4% of the times that he is shown a flash at this apparatus setting, and "no" 11.6% of the times. The same procedure can be followed to determine the expected percentages of "yes" responses for

Fig. 4.4 **The percentage of flashes on which a subject would say "yes" (he sees the flash) if the subject has no variability of his own, and always says yes when six or more quanta are absorbed by his visual pigment, as a function of the intensity setting of the apparatus (specifically, the mean number of quanta in each set of flashes). The point marked** *X* **is derived from Fig. 4.3. The horizontal axis is spaced as a logarithmic scale for reasons explained in the text.**

each of a number of apparatus intensity settings, ranging from a mean of one to a mean of 15 quanta absorbed by the visual pigment per flash. Such a curve is shown in Fig. 4.4. The point indicated by the X is the point derived from Fig. 4.3.

The curve in Fig. 4.4 is calculated for a subject whose cutoff was six absorbed quanta. Now the entire procedure can be repeated for a "perfect" (invariable) subject, assuming different values for his cutoff. Figure 4.5 contains a set of such curves, each curve based on the assumption of a different cutoff. The curve labeled "6 or more" is the one that was shown in Fig. 4.4.

The curves in Fig. 4.5 are theoretical curves to be expected from a perfect subject. Hecht *et al.* plotted the actual curves for their subjects to see how they compared with the theoretical ones. To do this, they delivered a long series of flashes to the subject at the different apparatus settings indicated on the horizontal axis of Fig. 4.5, and, for each setting, determined the percentage of times the subject said "yes." The obtained data for one of their subjects (S.S.) are shown in Fig. 4.6. For reasons that will be clear later, assume that the actual numbers of quanta absorbed by the visual pigments during these flashes are unknown, and that the data can only be plotted in the form shown in the figure, that is, with a *relative* intensity scale on the horizontal axis. Now suppose that the set of points in Fig. 4.6 is superimposed upon

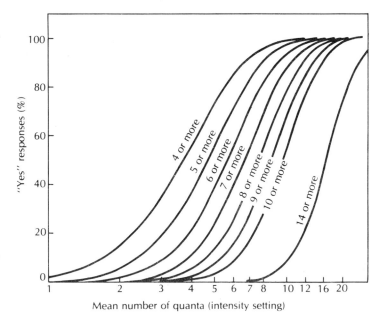

Fig. 4.5 **A set of curves like that in Fig. 4.4, for several different threshold values. The curve labeled "6 or more" is identical with that in Fig. 4.4. Note that the curves become steeper as the threshold number increases.**

Mean number of quanta (intensity setting)

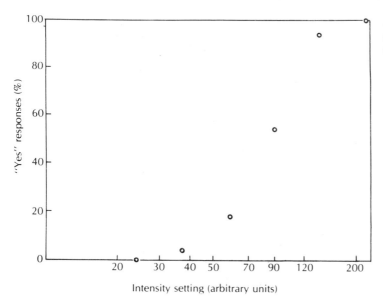

the theoretical curves in Fig. 4.5 and slid along horizontally to find the curve it most closely matches in shape.[3] This has been done in Fig. 4.7. The shape of the real frequency of seeing curve is most like that which would be obtained from a subject with absolutely no variability of his own, if he always said "yes" when his visual system absorbed seven or more quanta and always said "no" if fewer than seven quanta were absorbed. We may conclude then that, if subject S.S. really is perfect, in that he has no variability of his own, his threshold is seven absorbed quanta.

Now consider the situation if the subject were not perfectly consistent, but varied from time to time in sensitivity, so that, on some flashes his system required four absorptions, on other five, etc. Under these conditions, his frequency of seeing curve would be less steep. For example, if he varied from time to time, but required an *average* of seven absorptions, his expected frequency of seeing curve would be less steep than the curve predicted if he always required exactly seven or more quanta, as illustrated in Fig. 4.8. A new set of theoretical curves could be constructed assuming some particular amount of sub-

[3]Suppose you assume that the subject has no variability, i.e., that his "frequency of seeing" curve is entirely attributable to quantal fluctuations, but you do not know the actual mean number of quanta reaching his retina because you cannot estimate precisely the proportion of quanta absorbed by the filters in the apparatus, the media of the eye, etc. If you slide the points on his "frequency of seeing" curve horizontally along a logarithmic axis (as in Figs. 4.5, 4.6, and 4.7), that is equivalent to multiplying all the intensities by the same factor, which, in turn, is equivalent to trying out different proportions of quanta absorbed by the filters, etc.

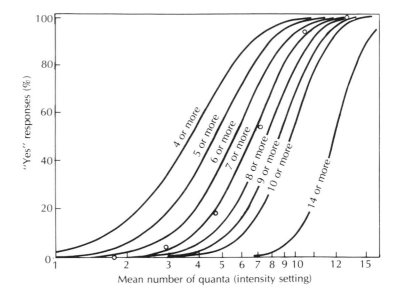

Fig. 4.7 **The set of data in Fig. 4.6 superimposed upon the curve that they most closely fit. The fit has been made by sliding the set of points horizontally over the set of theoretical curves.**

ject variability, corresponding to the set in Fig. 4.5. Such a set (for one particular amount of subject variability) is shown in Fig. 4.9. The actual data points (from Fig. 4.6) are also represented in this figure, and their slope matches the theoretical curve for a variable subject whose average threshold is 14. Comparing the data and curves in Fig. 4.7 with those in Fig. 4.9, it can be concluded that, if subject S.S. has no variability, his threshold is seven quanta, but if he does have variability of the kind assumed in Fig. 4.9, his average threshold is 14 quanta.

The curves in Fig. 4.9 were drawn under a particular set of assumptions about the way the subject varies. It is always true, however, that if the subject varies at all, the theoretical curves will be less steep than those for an unvarying subject, regardless of the nature of the subject's variance. It is also evident from Figs. 4.5 and 4.9 that, as the threshold number of quanta is greater, the slope of the frequency of seeing curve is greater. The conclusion follows, then, that if subject S.S. does, in fact, have no variability of his own, his threshold is seven quanta, but if he has any variability at all, his threshold must be greater than seven quanta (14 quanta for the particular kind of subject variability plotted in Fig. 4.9).

Taking these data alone, it is not possible to decide whether the subject is perfectly constant and always requires seven or more absorbed quanta for seeing, or whether he is variable and requires more. However, the first experiment of Hecht et al. was a direct determination of the average number of quanta that had to be absorbed in order for

Fig. 4.8 **The effect upon the frequency of seeing curve of variability within the subject. The solid curve is that expected when the subject's threshold is always exactly seven quanta, and the dashed curve would occur if his threshold varied randomly about an average of seven quanta.**

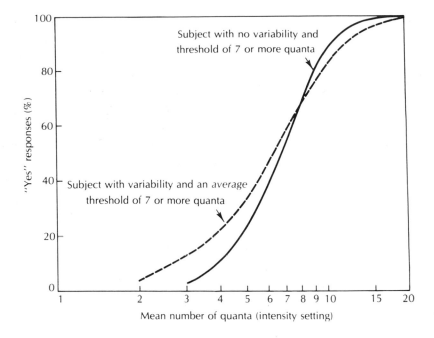

Fig. 4.9 **The Hecht** *et al.* **data for subject S.S. fitted to a frequency of seeing curve which assumes that the subject's threshold varies randomly about a mean value.**

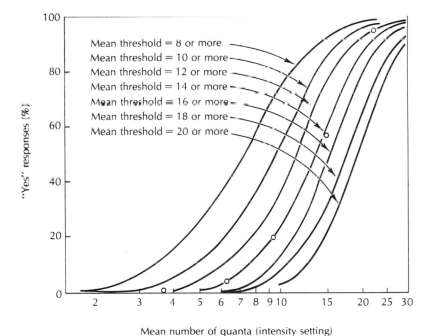

each subject to say "yes" 60% of the time, and, for subject S.S. that number was eight quanta.[4] Combining this finding with the previous one, it must be concluded that the major portion of the variability manifested in his responses results from quantal fluctuations in the stimulus itself. The discrepancy between seven and eight quanta cannot be taken as a precise measure of the subject's variability because the number eight is based upon estimates of the absorption by nonvisual parts of the eye that cannot be made with extreme precision. Nevertheless, those estimates are certainly sufficiently precise to permit the conclusion that a large portion of the variability in the subject's responses is a result of quantal fluctuations.

The Hecht *et al.* experiment is not the only one performed under such conditions. All of the experiments that were sufficiently well controlled to permit the drawing of firm conclusions agree in the finding that one quantum is sufficient to activate a rod. They differ somewhat in their conclusions concerning the number of rods that must be activated for threshold. However, even taking into consideration the most extreme findings, it must be concluded that very few rods need be stimulated, and that a large part of the variability of the judgments at threshold is a consequence of the quantal fluctuation in the stimulus.

SOURCES OF SUBJECT VARIABILITY While the results of the Hecht *et al.* experiments indicate that the subject displays little variability under their conditions, he still exhibits some. It is interesting to examine some of the possible sources of this variability.

Light is radiated in discrete quanta, and it is also absorbed discretely. That is, a pigment molecule cannot absorb half a quantum, and as a corollary, a single quantum cannot be absorbed by more than one molecule. Combining this property of light with the finding that the absorption of a single quantum is sufficient to activate a rod (as explained in Chapter II), it follows that the change of state of a single pigment molecule is sufficient to activate a rod.

In the area where the test flash is to be delivered, there are several hundred rods, and, each rod contains about 4,000,000 pigment molecules that are capable of activating the rod. No molecule, of any kind, is absolutely stable. There is always some finite probability that it will change its state spontaneously. We do not know the stability of rho-

---

[4]The mean number of quanta delivered to subject S.S.'s eye at his 60% threshold was 79 quanta, and correcting for losses in the media of the eye, between receptors, etc., it was estimated that eight quanta were actually absorbed by visual pigment.

dopsin at body temperature, but it is easy to calculate the amount of instability that would be required to produce variability in the subjects' responses during the Hecht et al. kind of threshold measurement.[5]

Since, once a molecule has changed its state, there is no way for the rest of the visual system to tell whether it did so spontaneously or because it absorbed a quantum, such spontaneous changes would look like flashes to the subject, and would thus be a source of subject variability. The critical duration, under the experimental conditions, is about 100 msec (see Fig. 2.9), and roughly ten quantal absorptions must occur during any 100-msec period and within some 10' disk on the retina, if the subject is to say he saw a flash. Considering that there are about 4,000,000 molecules per rod times about 300 rods per disk 10' in diameter equaling about 1,200,000,000 pigment molecules per test flash area, about ten molecules (per 100 msec per 10' disk) would spontaneously isomerize if the molecules were so stable that each molecule had a probability of 0.5 of spontaneously changing its state in any six-year period. In other words, the visual system is so sensitive that even an extremely low rate of spontaneous isomerization would produce, in the subject, the same events that are caused when he is actually presented with a flash of light at threshold intensity. Therefore, it is reasonable to expect that spontaneous isomerization of pigment molecules is a source of some of the variability within the subject.

When enough rods are activated, that information is somehow signaled to the rest of the visual system, as evidenced by the fact that the subject's reports correlate with the presence or absence of the stimulus. Many of the events that occur in the chain of connections in the visual system are unknown at present, but they certainly involve activity in neural elements, and this activity in turn depends upon the flow of molecules at synapses and across neural membranes. Such molecular flow also has some quantal characteristics. That is, the passage of each molecule through a membrane is a discrete event. Thus, it must be true that some fluctuations will occur in the neural events following the change of state of pigment molecules. These fluctuations will also contribute to the variability of the response. However, at the present time the extent of such fluctuations is not known.

---

[5]It is conceivable that only a few of the pigment molecules in each rod are actually capable of stimulating the rod. For example, it could be that only the molecules in the top layer of pigment are connected into the rod structure in a way that permits them to activate the rod. However, Hecht et al. assumed that all of the pigment present can absorb quanta, and on that basis, concluded that only about ten quanta need be absorbed at threshold. If most of the pigment could not activate the rod, one would have to conclude from their data that only a small fraction of a quantum need be absorbed at threshold. Since that is physically impossible, it must be concluded that all or at least most of the pigment molecules present in each rod, about 4,000,000, are capable of activating the rod.

The initiation of a nerve impulse probably involves very large numbers of molecules. Since the average of a very large sample of variable events is relatively stable (the variance of a set of averages is inversely proportional to the number of individual events contributing to each average), it is probably true that the variation involved in the generation of nerve impulses is very small. However, little is known about the way in which the change of state of a pigment molecule activates a rod. *That* event may result from the movement of a small number of molecules and, if so, the discrete nature of molecular events would impose variability upon the system. (Since the evidence indicates that the variability of the system is small under the conditions of Hecht *et al.* it is likely that the activation of a rod depends upon the movement of a large number of molecules.)

Still another source of variability is the fact that neurons from other parts of the subject's system are continually firing at times that are random with respect to the stimulus itself. Any of the systems that sense blood pressure, blood carbon dioxide content, pressure from clothing, sounds, etc., may interact with the signals from the visual system, resulting in variability. Changes in blood pressure within the eye may also stimulate neurons or change their sensitivity. Also, signals stored as memories of various kinds, including the memory of instructions to the subject, may, to some extent, bear random relations to the signals from the visual system. These events, which are often called psychological, may contribute to variability, and are worthy of analysis. The fact that, under the Hecht *et al.* conditions, all of these factors, combined, have a relatively small effect, suggests that such conditions might provide a sort of control or baseline against which variability under other "psychological" conditions can be compared.

Directly Observable Manifestations of Noise

The sources of variability described above are usually called noise. In common usage, the term "noise" refers to sounds that interfere with the sounds the listener wants to hear. These are generally sounds that are random with respect to the signal of interest. The term has now been generalized to include any signal, manifested in any form of energy, that occurs irregularly with respect to the signal of interest, and that tends to obscure that signal. (Some sources of disturbance are not irregular with respect to the signal. For example, the appreciative listener may stomp her foot in time with your serenade. Such events will not be included here under the label "noise," although what you do at home is your own business.)

Any subject, when confronted with the kind of conditions present in the Hecht *et al.* experiment, becomes very conscious of visual "noise." The dark field seems to be filled with little flickering specks and flashes. When the stimulus intensity is near the threshold level and the subject reports that he saw the stimulus, he is really saying that, during the click of the shutter and in the spatial region where he thinks the stimulus should appear, there seemed to be a little more flashing than there was before or after the click. It is only at intensities such that he reports seeing the stimulus close to 100% of the time that he is reasonably sure that what he saw was really the stimulus. Thus, the subject is not judging whether or not an event occurred, but rather, whether or not the events that did occur during the flash were very different from the events that occur at other times. It can be concluded on logical grounds that a subject is really judging the presence or absence of a signal imbedded in noise, and the subject himself is well aware that that is just what he is doing.

If you get up in the middle of a dark night and look at a blank wall, it will be very easy to observe the flickering and noisy appearance of the wall. Some of this noise is inherent in your system, arising from the sources described above. But if the room is not absolutely and completely light-free, much of the noise is actually a manifestation of quantal fluctuations. When the intensity of light on the wall is just about at the threshold for seeing in the totally dark-adapted state, each rod in the retina absorbs an average of about one quantum per hour. Since a flash is visible when about nine quanta are absorbed by nine rods within about 10' of each other and within about 0.1 sec, then a visual event should be expected about once every 3 sec in each square degree of the wall.

Some of the flashes seen in the dark are probably the result of small changes in the pressure exerted on the nerves in the eye, such changes resulting from pulse pressure, breathing, etc. In the dark, this effect can be easily seen in exaggerated form. Close your eyes and tap on your eyelid with your finger. The taps produce abrupt changes in pressure within the eyeball and result in easily visible flashes. (If you perform the same experiment in a lighted room, similar things can be seen, but these are, at least in part, changes in the sensitivity to light passing through the lids rather than direct stimulation of the nerves.)

QUANTAL FLUC-TUATIONS AT SUPRATHRESHOLD LIGHT LEVELS The stimuli discussed in the preceding sections were at intensities near the subject's threshold. Under those conditions, much of the variability in judgments is attributable to the quantal fluctuations in the stimulus. However, subjects' judgments also show variability at higher levels of illumination. For example, a large number of experiments have been performed where the subject is asked to discriminate between

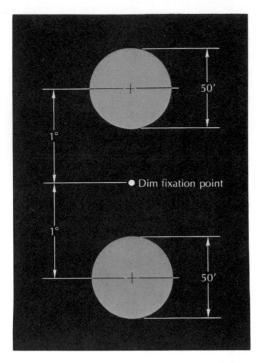

Fig. 4.10 **The stimulus pattern used by Cornsweet and Pinsker. The subject fixated the fixation point, and then the two disks were simultaneously flashed. One was more intensely illuminated than the other and the subject had to say which he thought was more intense.** [*From Cornsweet and Pinsker (1965).*]

two different levels of illumination, both of which are easily visible. It would be worthwhile to consider one such experiment here in order to evaluate the contribution of quantal fluctuations in the stimulus to the variability of the subject's responses.

This experiment, part of a set performed by Cornsweet and Pinsker (1965) was as follows. The subject was completely dark-adapted, and was then presented with the stimulus arrangement shown in Fig. 4.10. He fixated the dim fixation point in an otherwise dark field, and after a warning signal, the two disks were flashed simultaneously and briefly (4 msec). Each disk was evenly illuminated, one at an intensity I and the other at a somewhat higher intensity $I + \Delta I$. Sometimes the top one was the more intense and sometimes the bottom one, the location of the more intense one being chosen at random. The subject, after each flash, was to say either "top" or "bottom," indicating which one he thought had the greater intensity. (He was not permitted to say "I don't know." That is, he had to guess on every trial.) He was immediately told whether he was right or wrong. Then, after a period of readaptation to the dark, the disks were flashed again, and he responded again.

This procedure was carried out for a large number of flashes. On all of the flashes in any one experimental run, I was held constant, but between each pair of flashes the size of ΔI, that is the difference between the intensities, was changed, and the location of the more intense disk was or was not changed, according to a random schedule. If the size of ΔI were zero, that is, if the two disks were equal, the subject would of course be "correct" an average of 50% of the time. Using the procedure outlined above, a value for ΔI can be determined such that the subject is correct 75% of the time, and this value is called the *intensity difference threshold*.

For a single experimental run, the threshold value of ΔI was determined for some particular I. On different runs, different values of I were tested in the same way, so that, from the results of the entire experiment, it was possible to determine how great the difference in intensity had to be in order that the difference was detectable, as a function of the intensity itself.

The results of this experiment are plotted in Fig. 4.11. On the horizontal axis is the intensity of the dimmer disk. The line labeled "absolute threshold" indicates, on this scale, how intense the dimmer disk had to be in order that the subject could correctly distinguish it from a *dark* disk 75% of the time. (This corresponds roughly to the intensity at which the dimmer disk could be seen on 50% of its exposures.)

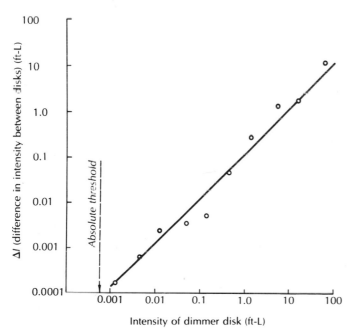

Fig. 4.11 **The amount by which the two disks had to differ in order for the subject to distinguish between them, as a function of the intensity of the dimmer disk. The data fall approximately on a straight line of 45° slope, indicating that the threshold intensity difference is directly proportional to the intensity. This is known as Weber's law. The arrow marks the intensity of the disk which could just be distinguished from zero intensity.** [*From Cornsweet and Pinsker (1965), Experiment I, subject D.O.*]

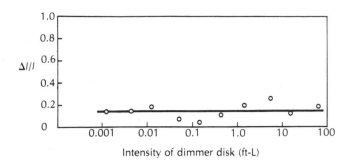

$\Delta I/I$

Intensity of dimmer disk (ft-L)

Fig. 4.12 **The results in Fig. 4.11 plotted a different way. When $\Delta I/I$ is plotted on the vertical axis, Weber's law is represented by a horizontal line. For these data, the best-fitting horizontal line falls at a $\Delta I/I$ ratio of 0.14.**

On the vertical axis is plotted the size of the difference in intensity necessary for the subject to be correct 75% of the time—the difference threshold. The data fall along a straight line of slope equal to one, indicating that the increment threshold increases in direct proportion to I. If one disk is twice as intense as it was before, the difference between it and the other disk will have to be twice as great. This relationship is known as Weber's law.

Exactly the same data have been replotted in Fig. 4.12.[6] However, the vertical axis in this figure is not the threshold, ΔI, but rather the ratio of ΔI to I. If I and ΔI are directly proportional to each other, then the points should fall on a horizontal line:

if

$$\Delta I = kI$$

then

$$\frac{\Delta I}{I} = k$$

where k is the constant of proportionally. Under the conditions in this experiment, the data are fitted by a horizontal line where $\Delta I/I = 0.14$.

The data from this experiment and comparable data from other experiments in vision and other sensory modalities are surprising. Why should the threshold intensity difference vary with the base intensity?

The visual pigment is essentially a device that registers each quantum that is absorbed. If there were no quantal fluctuations, and if the remainder of the visual system preserved all the information about incident light that is in the pigment, the difference threshold would be

[6]The data have been plotted on this figure only for intensities high enough that the dimmer disk is always seen. The curve must necessarily depart from a straight line at lower intensities for statistical reasons not relevant to the present discussion.

one absorbed quantum, regardless of the base intensity.[7] Thus, ΔI would not change as I changes. Suppose, instead, that the remainder of the system had a higher difference threshold than the difference in activity resulting from the capture of a single quantum. For example, suppose that the rest of the system required a difference of nine quanta absorbed by pigment. The difference threshold would then be nine absorbed quanta, i.e., still a constant. Thus the fact that the difference threshold is not constant means either that the visual system, after the pigment, behaves differently for different base intensities, or that quantal fluctuations in the stimuli account for the change in ΔI as I changes (or some combination of both these factors operates).

To decide among these alternatives, we can compute the consequences that quantal fluctuations would have upon the judgments of a perfect subject and compare the resulting predictions with the data actually obtained.

Suppose that the subject is perfect in the following sense: If, during a flash, the numbers of quanta absorbed from the two disks are not exactly equal, he will always identify the more intense disk as the one that produced the greater number of absorptions. If there were no quantal fluctuations, his difference threshold would be constant ($\Delta I = 1$ quantum) as I varied, and the resulting curve would be the dotted one in Fig. 4.13. However, quantal fluctuations do occur. If the intensities of the two disks are set so that, on the average, nine quanta are

---

[7]Based on the assumption that the quantum efficiency of pigment isomerization is 1.0, as discussed in Chapters V–VIII. If the quantum efficiency is E, then the expected difference threshold would be $1/E$ quanta.

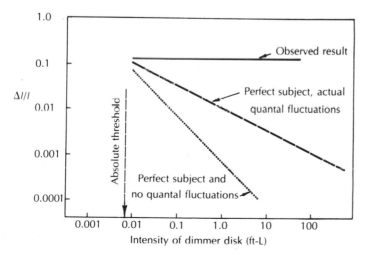

Fig. 4.13 **The result of the difference threshold experiment compared with the results expected on theoretical grounds. (The slopes of the three lines, on the log-log plot, are 0, -0.5, and -1.0.)** [From Cornsweet and Pinsker, (1965).]

Fig. 4.14 **The influence of quantal fluctuations on the intensity difference threshold. When the apparatus is set so that the bottom disk gives an average of ten quanta and the top disk nine, the actual numbers of quanta will be distributed as the plots in (a). When the pair of disks is flashed repeatedly, the intensity difference between them will vary according to the distribution in (b). The perfect subject will give a response that is called correct for every event contained in the shaded part of this plot, and he will also be "correct" on half of the trials on which the difference was zero (given that he is forced to say which of the disks was more intense).**

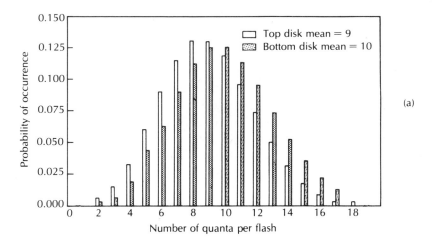

(a)

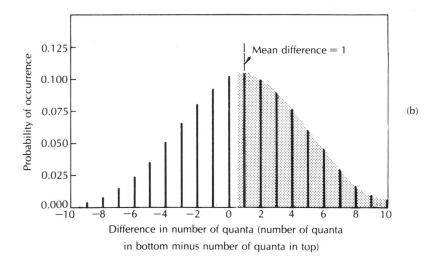

(b)

absorbed from the top one and ten from the bottom one, then, over a long series of exposures, the two disks will have intensities distributed as in the curves of Fig. 4.14a. On most of the exposures, the top disk will deliver fewer quanta than the bottom one, but on many exposures, the top disk will contain *more* quanta than the bottom one. If a long series of flashes is presented and the *difference* between the intensities of the two disks is measured on each flash, the resulting *differences* will have the distribution plotted in Fig. 4.14b.[8] For all the flashes in

[8]The distribution in Fig. 4.14b was calculated directly from the relationships in Fig. 4.14a by a statistical procedure that is beyond the scope of this book. Closely related procedures for normal distributions can be found in any statistics text.

the shaded area to the right of zero difference, the bottom disk contained more quanta than the top one, and the perfect subject will say that the bottom disk was brighter. Since, for all these flashes, the bottom disk was set to have the greater intensity, the experimenter will call all those responses correct. However, for each flash represented to the left of zero, the subject will say that the top disk was brighter and the experimenter will call those incorrect responses, since the apparatus was set to deliver more quanta in the bottom disk. For all flashes at zero, the subject must guess, and he will be correct half the time.

The area to the right of zero contains 53% of all the flashes. That is, on 53% of the flashes, the bottom disk will actually contain more quanta and the perfect subject's judgments will be called correct. The zero column contains 10%, and the subject will thus be correct on $0.50 \times 10\%$ of the trials, or another 5%. Thus the *perfect subject* will be correct on 58% of the trials altogether.

The preceding calculations are for $I = 9$ and $\Delta I = 1$. The comparable plots for $I = 100$ and $\Delta I = 1$ are shown in Fig. 4.15. Here the percentage of correct responses of the perfect subject will be 50.4%. In order for him to be correct 58% of the time, ΔI would have to be *increased* to 2.8 quanta. Thus, for a perfect subject, quantal fluctuations result in the requirement that ΔI must increase as I increases, if a constant percentage of correct responses is to be maintained. Even for the perfect

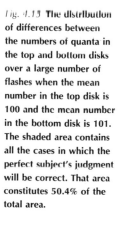

Fig. 4.15 The distribution of differences between the numbers of quanta in the top and bottom disks over a large number of flashes when the mean number in the top disk is 100 and the mean number in the bottom disk is 101. The shaded area contains all the cases in which the perfect subject's judgment will be correct. That area constitutes 50.4% of the total area.

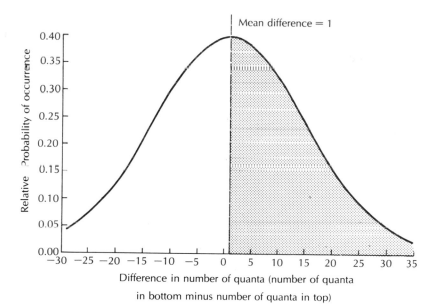

detector, then, we would expect ΔI must increase as I increases, and it therefore seems possible that quantal fluctuations might account for the results of the Cornsweet and Pinsker experiment.

When the calculation implied in the preceeding paragraphs is performed for the intensities tested in the Cornsweet and Pinsker experiment, the curve predicted for a perfect subject is as shown by the dashed line in Fig. 4.13.[9] This curve is closer to the data than that expected on the assumption of no quantal fluctuations, but it is still very clearly different from the obtained data. It can thus be concluded that, while quantal fluctuations must, in principle, set a lower limit on the subject's ability to discriminate the difference in intensity between two disks, that limit is far below the limits imposed by the properties of his visual system, except at levels of intensity very near the absolute threshold.

To summarize, then, while quantal fluctuations play a major role in visual phenomena at very low intensities, their importance diminishes rapidly as the illumination level increases, until, at moderate or high levels, their effects are negligible. Thus, the results of experiments like that of Cornsweet and Pinsker indicate that the sensitivity of the visual system itself is proportionately reduced as the illumination level is increased. The profound physiological and perceptual consequences of this conclusion will be discussed at length in subsequent chapters.

PROBLEMS   4.1   Suppose a subject has no variability and a cutoff of 3 quanta, i.e., he said he saw the flash every time his retina absorbed 3 or more quanta and said he did not see it every time fewer than 3 quanta were absorbed. Plot four points on this subject's frequency of seeing curve, using settings that yield 1, 2, 5, and 10 quanta absorbed by his retina, on the average.

(Sample Answer: For mean intensity equal to 1 quantum, the flash will be seen 8% of the time.)

4.2   Describe or plot a set of plausible threshold data that, if obtained from a given subject, would unequivocally prove he was not a perfect detector; that is, data that would prove that the subject's judgments manifested variability over and above quantal fluctuation.

4.3   If you can possibly arrange to obtain a "frequency of seeing" curve on *yourself*, for your completely dark-adapted eye, you will find it very instructive. Dark-adapt for about 30 min, in a completely dark room

[9]This (dashed) curve has a slope of $-\frac{1}{2}$, which, on a plot where both axes are logarithmic, represents the statistical fact that the uncertainty arising from quantal fluctuations is inversely proportional to the square root of the intensity of the dimmer flash.

(which, you will discover, is rare, and cracks will probably have to be patched up with opaque tape). Arrange some way of flashing a small spot of light with a flash duration no longer than about 1 sec. First, find the lowest intensity such that you can see the flash just about 100% of the time. Then choose seven or eight discrete intensity levels, ranging from the preliminary 100% level to a level almost never seen, spaced, if possible, by equal logarithmic steps (e.g., if you have a set of neutral filters, use 0.0, 0.2, 0.4, 0.6, 0.8, 1.0, and 1.2 densities as your steps). If you change the intensity some other way, try to get the steps to come out about like those (i.e., 1.0, 0.6, 0.4, 0.25, 0.16, 0.10, and 0.06 times the 100% intensity level).

Then have a friend present you with a total of 20 flashes at each of those levels, one flash every 10 sec or so, in a predetermined random order, and after each flash, you must say "yes" or "no" (no "not sure's" allowed). Then plot the data as in Fig. 4.6.

V ◇◇◇ THE ACTION OF LIGHT ON ROD PIGMENTS

THERE are two general classes of receptor in the human retina — rods and cones. These classes may be distinguished from each other on a number of different criteria that agree to varying extents. According to one criterion, rods are the class of receptors that mediate vision in an eye that has been dark-adapted for more than 10 min and that is stimulated by low levels of light. By this criterion (and all of the others), the results of the Hecht *et al.* experiment apply to the rods. By a different criterion, the rods are those receptors that contain a particular kind of visual pigment, called rhodopsin, or visual purple. The cones, as a class, contain several other pigments very similar to rhodopsin but differing in some important characteristics. The functioning of cones will be discussed in most of the chapters that follow the present one. In this chapter, our current knowledge about the interaction of light with rhodopsin will be discussed.

The absorption of quanta of light by rhodopsin molecules is the first of a long series of stages involved in visual perception, and the characteristics of this first stage impose crucial limits upon the entire perceptual process. If the rhodopsin cannot absorb some particular kind of quanta, those quanta can have no effect upon the rest of the visual system, and cannot be seen (unless they are absorbed by the cones). If the processes that occur within the pigment lose some aspect of the signal carried in the quanta, our perception must be correspondingly affected. For example, there is no mechanism within the rod system that can retain information about the wavelengths of the incident quanta, and, as a necessary consequence, rod vision, that is, vision under low illumination levels, is totally color-blind vision. It is also possible that the mechanism by which the absorption of a quantum excites the rod has factors inherent in it that result in Weber's law. That is, properties of very early states in the visual system may account for the results of the Cornsweet and Pinsker experiment described in the preceding chapter. Similar early processes probably play a vital role even in such "psychological" processes as contrast and brightness constancy, as will be discussed in Chapter XIII.

CHANGES IN RHO- The structural arrangement of the pigment within a single rod is too
DOPSIN MOLECULES fine to be examined in an ordinary microscope, but, through the use of
IN THE LIGHT the electron microscope, it has become evident that the pigment-bear-
AND IN DARKNESS ing part of the human rod is filled by a membrane arranged in the special way that is shown in Fig. 5.1. Adjacent layers of membrane are in contact with each other, and thus, the entire volume of that part of the rod is essentially filled with membrane. Membranes constitute an important part of every cell in every animal, and all cell membranes that can be examined appear to have extremely similar structures. They are composed primarily of protein and lipid molecules in orderly arrays. Probably, the membrane within the rod is similarly composed.

The molecules that constitute membranes absorb visible light only very slightly, but rods as a whole, absorb visible light strongly. Therefore, it is evident that rods contain pigment molecules as well as membranes, and this is verified by the fact that pigment molecules can be chemically extracted from rods. Since there is virtually no space between membrane surfaces in the rod, the pigment molecules contained in rods must be imbedded in the membranes themselves.

When pigment is extracted from dark-adapted mammalian rods, part of the extract consists of molecules with the structure shown in

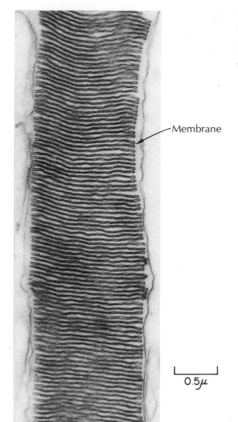

—Membrane

0.5μ

Fig. 5.1 **Cross section through the pigment-bearing part of a cone from the monkey retina. The rod structure is similar. Magnification: ×52,000. [One micron (μ) = one millionth of a meter]** [*From Dowling (1965) Copyright 1965 by the American Association for the Advancement of Science.*]

Fig. 5.2. This molecule is called retinal. When the retinal is in the rod itself, and when the retina has been dark adapted for a long time, virtually all of the molecules are in the state drawn in *a* of Fig. 5.3.[1] Each of several million retinal molecules per rod sits in a pocket in the surface of a protein molecule that constitutes part of the membrane. The retinal molecule is attached to the protein molecule at each end, and this combination of retinal and protein molecules is called rhodopsin. If a quantum strikes the retinal molecule and is absorbed by it, some of the energy from the quantum causes the bonds in the retinal molecule to be rearranged, and the molecule changes its shape, untwisting and straightening out. Such a change in state is called a cis–trans isomerization (the "cis" and "trans" referring to the two shapes of the molecule). The untwisting and straightening of the isomerizing molecule

[1]The drawing in Fig. 5.3 and the concepts of molecular structure and activity that it represents will be referred to throughout this chapter. Figure 5.3 is taken from an article by Wald *et al.* (1963), in which they amplified and modified a model first described by Kropf and Hubbard in 1958.

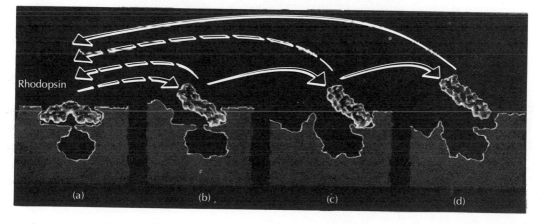

Fig. 5.2 **Molecular structure of the rod pigment extracted from a dark-adapted mammal. This molecule is called retinal.**

cause it to break loose from the protein at one end, as shown in stage *b* of Fig. 5.3.

The state in *b* is unstable at body temperature. If the incoming light were turned off so that no new quanta could be absorbed, the molecule would quickly undergo the series of changes indicated in *c* and *d* of Fig. 5.3.[2] The change from *b* to *c* is a schematic representation of a series of conformational changes in the *protein* molecule, and between *c* and *d*, the retinal molecule floats free of the protein. Molecules in state *d* will spontaneously regenerate, that is return to state *a*.[3]

---

[2]The dashed lines in Fig. 5.3 indicate reactions that usually require the absorption of light. (They may occasionally occur spontaneously, as discussed in Chapter IV.) The solid lines indicate reactions that do not require light. These reactions depend upon other factors, principally the thermal activity of the constituents. The reactions that occur regardless of the presence or absence of light will be called *spontaneous* reactions in this discussion, although it is important to remember that these reactions, too, require particular sets of conditions, e.g., body temperature.

[3]Under the appropriate conditions of temperature and chemical environment, the transitions schematized in Fig. 5.3 can be shown to occur in a series of substages. One or more of these substages may turn out to be critical to our understanding of visual excitation, but at the present time, our uncertainties about the excitation process are great enough that a more detailed description would be inappropriate.

Fig. 5.3 **The states of rod pigment. In a completely dark-adapted eye, virtually all of the pigment is in state *a*. The changes that can be produced by the absorption of quanta of light are indicated by the dashed arrows and the changes that occur independently of light are indicated by solid arrows.** [*After Wald et al. (1963).*]

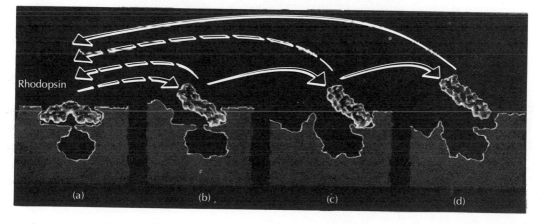

Once a molecule absorbs a quantum and isomerizes (from state a to state b in the figure), it will spontaneously undergo the series of changes described above and indicated by solid arrows in Fig. 5.3. However, if the molecule should absorb another quantum when it is in state b or c, it may be driven back to state a, as indicated by the dashed arrows. In order to evaluate the likelihood of occurrence of such photoreversals, one would need to know several properties of the reactions that have not yet been adequately measured. Specifically, the probability of quantal absorption per unit of time must be known for each stage in the process, and the time during which the molecules remain in each of those stages must also be determined.

Consider a simplified example. A regenerated pigment molecule (state a), upon absorbing a quantum of light, isomerizes (to state b). Suppose that, in this isomerized state, it is just as likely to capture a quantum as it was before it isomerized. Further, assume that the absorption of a single quantum in the isomerized state is sufficient to regenerate the molecule (to state a). Last, assume that the molecule will remain in the isomerized state for an average of 1 sec (if it does not absorb another quantum) before it spontaneously changes through state c to state d.

Now suppose that a flash of light 1 msec long is incident on a completely dark-adapted retina. If the flash is of extremely high intensity, so that a large number of quanta are incident on every pigment molecule in the stimulated region of the retina, then each molecule will flip back and forth between state a and state b a large number of times during the flash, and at the instant the flash is over, about half of them will be in state a and half in the state b. Then, several seconds later, half of the pigment will still be in state a and the other half will have continued on to state d. Now if the eye is allowed to dark-adapt and the experiment is repeated, except that the flash is made ten times more intense, the result will be exactly the same; several seconds after the flash, half of the pigment will be in state a and the other half in state d.[4]

Hagins (1955) reported evidence that corroborates these photochemical events for the rabbit eye. He subjected the dark-adapted rabbit retina to intense flashes of less than a millisecond duration and measured the subsequent proportion of bleached rhodopsin. The bleached proportion increased with increasing flash intensity up to a maximum of about one-half. That is, there is a critical intensity that bleaches about half of the pigment, and further increases in intensity do not increase the proportion of pigment bleached. However, if a

[4]A *long* flash of sufficient intensity will change nearly all the pigment molecules from a to d.

second flash is delivered several msec after the first, it will bleach half of the remaining pigment.

Brindley (1959) reported psychophysical results that seem to depend upon the same processes in the human. In essence, he found that there is a critical intensity for a 250-μsec flash such that its visual effects are indiscriminable from that of a flash of the same duration but of doubled intensity. However, if two such flashes are delivered in succession, separated by a few milliseconds, their effect is discriminable from that of a single flash.

Now consider the effects of a much weaker flash of light, weak enough that it is very unlikely that any one pigment molecule will absorb more than one quantum. In that case, virtually all of the molecules that are isomerized during the flash will go through the stages indicated by the solid arrows Fig. 5.3, and the dashed arrows pointing to the left can be ignored. In general, when the intensity of the stimulating light is low enough that the probability is low of a molecule capturing more than one quantum before it gets to state d, the photoreversals indicated by dashed arrows in Fig. 5.3 can be ignored. At the present time, the best estimates of the parameters of the photopigment system lead to the expectation that photoreversal can safely be ignored except at levels of intensity considerably higher than those normally experienced.

When a pigment molecule absorbs a quantum, the transition from state a to state b of Fig. 5.3 is virtually instantaneous. The transitions represented between states b and d probably require an average of about 1 sec, although at present that time is not firmly determined. The transition from d to a, the regeneration of the pigment, requires an average of 5 min. In other words, upon absorbing a quantum, a molecule will immediately isomerize to state b, change through c to d after about 1 sec, and finally return to state a after an average of 5 min.

These transition times — 1 sec and 5 min — require some explanation. Consider a molecule that just absorbed a quantum and entered into state b. It will change to state d after some particular time, which averages 1 sec. However, any individual molecule may stay in the intermediate states for a very short time or a very long time. This time can best be specified by saying that a given isomerized molecule has a probability of 0.5 of shifting to the d state in any 1-sec period. As a result, if a large number of molecules are in the isomerized state, about half of them will have changed to the d state within 1 sec, half of the remaining ones will shift in the next second, etc.

Similarly, if a molecule is in the d state, it has a probability of 0.5 of regenerating to the a state in any 5-min period. Thus, about half of the

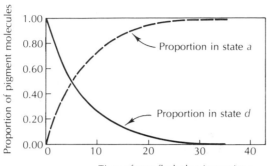

Fig. 5.4 **Proportion of pigment molecules in state** *a* **and state** *d* **as a function of the time after a flash of light so intense and so long in duration that is has isomerized every molecule. The solid curve falls half of the distance between where it is and zero during every 5-min period, and the dashed curve rises by the same amount.**

molecules will regenerate in the first 5 min (plus 1 sec) after absorbing a quantum, half of the remaining ones will regenerate in the next 5 min, etc.

The proportion still in the *d* state as a function of the time after a flash of light, is plotted as a solid line in Fig. 5.4. The proportion in state *a* is represented by the dashed line. These curves are based upon the assumption that each molecule in state *d*, considered alone, has a probability of 0.5 of regenerating in any 5-min period, and that that probability is unaffected by the states of the other pigment molecules in the system. There is good evidence that these assumptions are essentially correct (Rushton, 1962a).

We will now consider the perceptual correlates of each of these early stages in the visual process.

THE CHARACTERIS-TICS AND PERCEP-TUAL CORRELATES OF STATE *a*

The Absorption Spectrum of Rods

Visual pigment molecules that are in state *a* of Fig. 5.3 are capable of absorbing quanta of light, and if they do, the events that follow may produce a visual sensation. However, not all quanta are equally likely to be absorbed. The probability that any particular incident quantum will be absorbed by a pigment molecule depends upon the relationship between the structure of the molecule and the nature of the quantum. Quanta of different wavelengths are more or less likely to be absorbed. If the probability of absorption of some particular wavelength is great, it might be said that quanta of that wavelength fit well into the structure of the molecule, or resonate with the molecule. Regardless of the verbal "explanation" of such events, it is clear that the relationship between the wavelength of a quantum and its probability of being absorbed by visual pigment is of crucial importance, since quanta must be absorbed if we are to see.

Measurements of the relationship between the wavelength of a quantum and its probability of being absorbed by visual pigment are often carried out in the following way: Retinas from animals are dark-adapted and then subjected to procedures by which the rhodopsin is extracted from the retina and dissolved in a fluid. The solution is then placed in a device called a spectrophotometer, schematically represented in Fig. 5.5. Light from the source passes through a monochromator, and the monochromatic light emerging is divided into two paths by the beam splitter. Some of the light is reflected from the beam splitter to a photocell, which produces a voltage directly proportional to the intensity of the light falling on it. The remaining quanta are transmitted through the beam splitter and fall on a transparent container filled with the rhodopsin solution. As the quanta pass through this solution, some of them are absorbed, and the remaining ones fall on a second photocell. (Some of the quanta will also be reflected from the container. For this discussion, we will assume that this reflection has been taken into account.) Suppose the beam splitter transmits exactly 50% of the light and reflects the remaining 50%, and that the two photocells and meters are identical. Then, when the container is out of the path, the two readings will be equal, and when the container filled with the rhodopsin solution is placed in its path, the meter labeled "output" will read less than the "input" meter. If, for example, the output meter reading were 90% that of the input meter, then 90% of the quanta input to the container must have been transmitted and the

Fig. 5.5 Semischematic diagram of a spectrophotometer. If the beam splitter transmits and reflects equal proportions of the incident light, and if the photocells and meters are identical and their outputs are linear with light intensity, then the ratio of the reading of the output to the input meter equals the proportion of incident light transmitted by the rhodopsin solution.

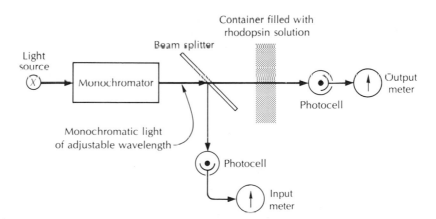

remaining 10% must have been absorbed by the container and its contents. In general:

$$\frac{\text{output reading}}{\text{input reading}} = \text{proportion of incident quanta}$$
transmitted by the container and its contents;

and

$$1 - \frac{\text{output}}{\text{input}} = \text{proportion absorbed by the container and its contents.}$$

This ratio is measured as the wavelengths of the quanta emerging from the monochromator are varied, and the resulting curve will be one like that shown in Fig. 5.6a. This curve is called the absorption spectrum of the rhodopsin solution and container. Next, the procedure is repeated when the container is in place and filled with the same fluid, but with no rhodopsin dissolved in it (as plotted in Fig. 5.6b). The curve for rhodopsin alone may then be found by the appropriate correction.[5] The resulting curve, shown in Fig. 5.6c, is the absorption spectrum for dark-adapted rod pigment.[6]

From the absorption spectrum of rhodopsin, it is evident that the rod pigment has a structure that forms the best fit with quanta of wavelength about 507 nm, and poorer fits with quanta of other wavelengths. That is, the probability that an incident quantum will be absorbed is greatest if the quantum has a wavelength of 507 nm, and quanta are very unlikely to be absorbed if their wavelengths are longer than about 800 nm.

This entire measurement could have been performed in a somewhat different way. Suppose that the monochromator in Fig. 5.5 is set to deliver flashes of quanta at, say 400 nm, and the measurement of the proportion of quanta absorbed by the rhodopsin is made. This will be

$$\frac{1}{10^{1.85}} = \frac{1}{70.8} = 0.014$$

according to Fig. 5.6c.

The reading of the input meter is a measure of the actual number of quanta incident on the rhodopsin. Suppose this meter and its photocell are properly calibrated, and indicate that 1,000,000 quanta were inci-

---

[5] The correction is simply to subtract the logarithm of the proportion absorbed by the cell and fluid from the logarithm of the proportion absorbed by the cell filled with rhodopsin solution, at each wavelength.

[6] If there is so much rhodopsin in the solution that it absorbs a substantial proportion of the incident light, the rhodopsin molecules will begin to screen each other from the light, and the absorption spectrum will change accordingly (in a predictable and relatively simple way). This effect is negligible at lower concentrations, and, to simplify this discussion, only low concentrations will be considered.

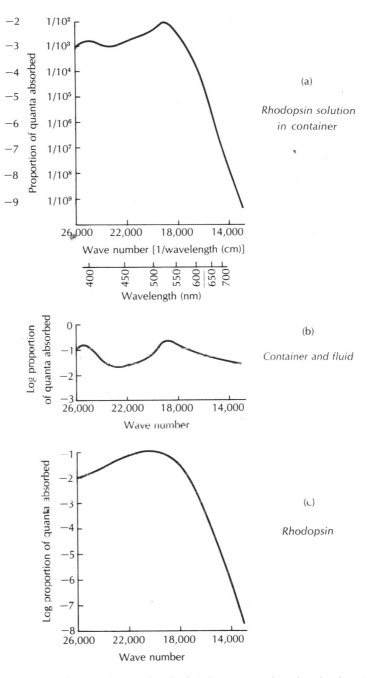

Fig. 5.6 **Absorption spectra for (a) a solution of rhodopsin in a container; (b) the container and the fluid without rhodopsin; and (c) the (calculated) spectrum for rhodopsin. There are several visual pigments that will be discussed later in addition to the mammalian rod pigment. The horizontal axes in these plots are linear with wave number (the reciprocal of wavelength) rather than with wavelength because the relations among the various pigments are more easily visualized when plotted this way.**

dent on the rhodopsin during the flash. This means that the rhodopsin will absorb 14,000 quanta during the flash. Now the wavelength is changed to, say, 410 nm, and the intensity of the beam leaving the monochromator is adjusted until the rhodopsin again absorbs 14,000 quanta in a flash. In order to do this, the intensity must be reduced to

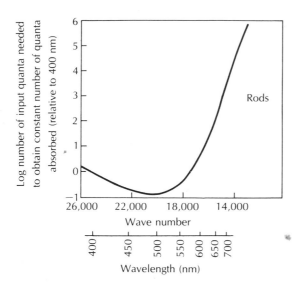

Fig. 5.7 **The absorption spectrum of rho-dopsin obtained by a procedure different from that in Fig. 5.6c.**

fewer than 1,000,000 quanta, since the proportion absorbed will be greater than at 400 nm. The reading for the intensity required to produce 14,000 absorptions may thus be measured for all wavelengths, and the resulting curve would be as plotted in Fig. 5.7. This curve bears a simple relation to the curve in Fig. 5.6c. The value of the vertical axis of either curve at any wavelength is inversely proportional to the value of the other curve at that wavelength. In other words, given either curve, the other may be easily deduced. Thus, the experimental determinations can be made in either of the two ways described above.

The Scotopic Spectral Sensitivity Curve

In order that a visual stimulus be seen, that is, in order that a subject be able to report correctly whether or not a flash of light occurred, the quanta must be absorbed by some elements in him that are capable of transmitting their signals to the rest of his nervous system. The quantum-catching molecules in the rods are not the only pigments in the eye. In fact, there is a layer of pigment lying behind the receptors which absorbs light even more strongly than the pigment in the rods. It is plausible that this pigment, called the choroidal pigment, is really the one that sends its signals to the rest of the visual system. The question of which pigment does, in fact, transmit the information about light in the world to the rest of the human system is a physiological question, but it is possible to decide it by psychophysical experiments,

experiments that involve only the delivering of stimuli to the subject and the recording of his verbal responses.

The isomerization of a visual pigment molecule is an event that is analogous to the firing of a pistol. The actual energy required to pull the trigger is much smaller than the energy released as a consequence of the pulling. The released energy is determined solely by the powder in the shell — it is the same whether the trigger was pulled hard or gently. Similarly, the isomerization of a visual pigment molecule is triggered by the absorption of a quantum, but the wavelength and energy of the quantum do not determine the nature of the isomerization. It is true that the wavelength of the incident quantum determines the probability that it will be absorbed by the molecule, but if it *is* absorbed, it produces the same isomerization regardless of its wavelength.

Hecht *et al.* determined that about nine quanta of wavelength 510 nm must be absorbed in order for a dark-adapted subject to see a flash. Since quanta of any wavelength, once absorbed, produce identical effects, it follows that nine quanta of *any* wavelength, if absorbed, will permit the subject to see the flash.

Suppose, then, that flashes of different wavelengths and intensities are presented to a dark-adapted subject, and that for each wavelength, the number of quanta is determined that must strike the eye in order for him to say he sees the flash. Since the same number of *absorptions* is required for a threshold flash regardless of the wavelengths of the quanta, this experiment is exactly analogous to the second procedure described above for determining the absorption spectrum of a rod solution. At each wavelength, a measurement is made of the number of quanta that must be incident in order that a fixed number of quanta are absorbed. The results of such an experiment are plotted in two ways in Fig. 5.8. This curve is usually called the scotopic spectral sensitivity curve. (The word "scotopic" refers to the fact that the eye is in its dark-adapted state during the measurements.)

The scotopic spectral sensitivity curve looks similar to the absorption spectrum of rods, and it must be related to the absorption spectrum of whatever pigment is the *visual* pigment. However, the spectral sensitivity curve is not quite identical with the absorption spectrum of any of the pigments in the eye. The media of the eye, and especially the lens, contain small amounts of pigment that absorb light. If those pigments are not visual pigments, that is, if they cannot transmit information about their absorption of quanta to the rest of the visual system, then they simply act as filters, absorbing some of the light on its way to the receptors themselves. These pigments play the same role in the eye

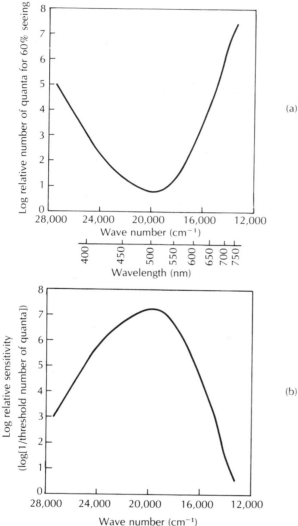

Fig. 5.8 **Two ways of plotting the scotopic spectral sensitivity curve.** [*From Wald (1945).*]

that the container and solvent played in the measurement of the absorption spectrum of rhodopsin.

Several workers have removed lenses and the other ocular media from human eyes, and have measured their absorption spectra. The results of these measurements are shown in Fig. 5.9. These media absorb relatively strongly in the short wavelength end of the spectrum and are almost completely transparent to long wavelengths. (The value of this curve at 510 nm, 50% absorption, is that used by Hecht *et al.* to correct for losses by absorption in the ocular media in their experiment.)

The pigment in the ocular media cannot be the visual pigment, because it is not in the image plane of the optics of the eye, and threshold determinations (and virtually all other visual determinations) depend upon the distribution of light in the retinal image plane. Therefore, this pigment merely acts as a filter in front of the receptors. To find the spectral sensitivity curve of the receptors themselves, the scotopic sensitivity curve must be corrected by the absorption curve of the ocular media.

The scotopic spectral sensitivity curve, corrected for absorption by the ocular media, is plotted as the set of x's in Fig. 5.10. If every absorbed quantum has the same effect upon the system, then this corrected curve must be the absorption spectrum of the *visual pigment*. The corrected curve is very close to the absorption spectrum of rhodopsin that is plotted as a dashed line in Fig. 5.10 (the fit is within the accuracy of the various measures), and is different from the absorption spectrum of any other pigment or combination of pigments that have been found in the retina. Therefore, it must be concluded, on the basis of *psychophysical* measurements, that rhodopsin, contained in rods, is the visual pigment.

(The scotopic spectral sensitivity curve, after correction for the losses in the ocular media, is properly called an action spectrum of the visual pigment, in that, what is measured is the relative number of quanta at each wavelength that are required to produce a constant "action," in this case, 60% seeing. This curve will be identical to the absorption spectrum of the visual pigment if it is true that the "action"

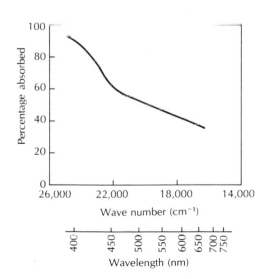

Fig. 5.9 **The absorption spectrum of the media of the human eye.** [*From Ludvigh and McCarthy (1938).*]

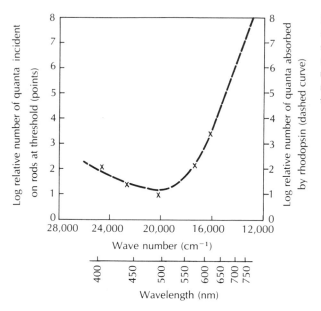

Fig. 5.10 **The dashed line is the absorption spectrum for rhodopsin. The points are the scotopic spectral sensitivity curve corrected for the absorption spectrum of the media in the eye. The points, therefore, represent the spectral sensitivity curve of the rods.**

resulting from the absorption of a quantum is the same regardless of the wavelength of the quantum.)

The reader may now wonder why Hecht *et al.* so carefully chose 510 nm as the wavelength of their stimulus. If they wanted to determine the smallest number of quanta required at the cornea for 60% seeing, then 510, or more probably 507 nm, was the appropriate wavelength. However, their really important finding, their determination of the number of quanta absorbed by the *visual pigment* at threshold, did not require the use of 510 nm. Any wavelength would have done equally well, since they included in their calculations an estimate of the proportion of the incident quanta that were absorbed by the pigment itself. That proportion simply would have been smaller for any other wavelength, according to the absorption spectrum of rhodopsin.

The preceding discussion indicates the way in which the threshold for seeing different wavelengths of light depends upon the absorption spectrum of the dark-adapted visual pigment molecules. Similarly, the brightnesses of dim but visible lights depend upon wavelength, other things being equal. A suprathreshold light at 507 nm looks appreciably brighter than one of the same physical intensity at 400 or 600 nm. Such an observation makes sense if it is assumed that, other things being equal, brightness increases when the number of pigment molecules isomerized per second increases, and that is a reasonable assumption. (A great many phenomena to be discussed subsequently demonstrate that the brightness at any point in the field does not depend *only* on the rate of isomerization of molecules at that point. However, there is such a dependence when all other factors are held constant.)

THE CHARACTERIS-TICS AND PERCEPTUAL COR-RELATES OF STATES *b*, *c*, AND *d*   When a pigment molecule in a rod absorbs a quantum, the molecule undergoes an isomerization and for a period averaging about 1 sec, it remains attached at one end to the protein in the membrane, as in *b* and *c* of Fig. 5.3. Some event that accompanies either the transition to this state, or the transition from state *c* to state *d*, results in the activation of subsequent stages in the retina. Very little is known at the present time about the perceptual correlates of states *b* and *c*.

A solution of rhodopsin extracted from a dark-adapted eye (state *a*) looks purple when viewed in white light (hence its alternative name, visual purple). It looks purple for the following reason: Rhodopsin absorbs light most strongly in the middle region of the spectrum (see Fig. 5.6c). The light that is not absorbed by the rhodopsin solution reaches the viewer's eye. It contains relatively more quanta of short and long wavelengths than does white light, and a mixture of lights of short and long wavelengths is purple to an observer with normal color vision.

If a solution of rhodopsin is exposed to an intense light for a long time, it will bleach. That is, it will become relatively transparent, turning from purple to a pale yellow. The fact that it bleaches means that the absorption spectrum of the solution has changed, the amount of absorption being reduced for all or most visible wavelengths. It looks somewhat yellowish because the peak of the new absorption spectrum has shifted from the middle to the short wavelength region of the spectrum. This same bleaching can be observed in the intact human retina when it is subjected to high light intensities, and the technique for measuring this will be discussed later in the present chapter. In terms of the model shown in Fig. 5.3, this means that the visual pigment, when it is in state *d*, has a low probability of capturing quanta of any visible wavelength.

The states represented by *b* and *c* in Fig. 5.3 probably consist of a series of changes in the structure of the protein molecule, accompanied by corresponding changes in the absorption spectrum of the system. However, the actual sequence, as it occurs in a living eye, has not yet been fully determined.

When a molecule is in state d, it is very unlikely to absorb incident quanta (that is, it is bleached), and if it does, it probably does not signal that fact to the rest of the visual system. Therefore, if a subject's eye could be stimulated with a light so intense and long that all of the pigment molecules absorbed quanta and subsequently changed to state d, his visual threshold would become infinite. That is, he would be unable to see. Then, if he remained in darkness, more and more of his visual pigment molecules would spontaneously regenerate to state a, and his threshold should thus fall. Finally, after a very long time in darkness, virtually all of the molecules would be regenerated, and his threshold would approach a low asymptote such as that in the Hecht *et al.* experiment. Thus, for many years, the fact that the threshold falls during dark adaptation was attributed to the increase in the number of regenerated pigment molecules available for capturing quanta. It is now clear, however, that such an explanation is grossly insufficient to account, quantitatively, for the dark-adaptation curve. The concentration of unbleached pigment must set a limit below which the threshold cannot fall, but the actual threshold level is evidently limited by features of the visual system beyond the pigment itself.

The data that lead to this conclusion came from many sources, but the most directly relevant observations are measurements of the amount of rhodopsin actually bleached in the living human retina by flashes of light of various intensities. The measurements by Rushton (1962) were made by a rather elaborate procedure, but the procedure has yielded such important data in many fields of human vision that it will be discussed in detail here.

Retinal Densitometry If one could look into a dark-adapted subject's eye, the retina might be expected to appear purple, since it contains a layer of rhodopsin. It might further be expected that, just after the subject looked at a bright light for a minute or two, the retina would look transparent, or slightly yellowish, and then, as time in the dark increased, the retina would gradually return to its purple state. Measures of this change in color would reflect the relative amount of bleached pigment as a function of time in the dark. Therefore, comparisons of these changes in color with perceptual data, such as the changes in threshold during dark adaptation, would provide a means of testing theories about the relationship between visual phenomena and the state of the visual pigment.

However, for several reasons, it is very difficult to measure the changes in the color of the retina. First, the amount of light reflected back out of the eye is a very small proportion of that entering the eye. Therefore, in order for the experimenter to see the color of the subject's retina, he would have to put a very intense light into the subject's eye. This light would produce a large amount of bleaching, and the color of the dark-adapted retina could never be seen. Second, there are many pigments in the eye that are not visual pigments, such as the pigments in the blood and in the choroid layer, and some of these pigments absorb light more strongly than the visual pigment itself. Therefore, the color of the subject's retina is primarily determined by these other, nonvisual, pigments (see Fig. 6.2).

In 1955, Campbell and Rushton described a technique that overcomes these difficulties and measures changes in the light reflected from the living human retina. Their apparatus is schematized in Fig. 5.11. (This diagram is somewhat different from that described by Campbell and Rushton. Their actual apparatus contains many elements that are not essential to the discussion here, and they have therefore been omitted. Furthermore, in the course of their research over several years, they modified the apparatus in a number of ways, and the diagram in Fig. 5.11 includes the essential modifications.) Monochromatic light emerging from a monochromator is incident upon a sectored disk, which is redrawn in an inset to Fig. 5.11. This disk is made of glass and mounted so that it can be spun by a motor. Two of the sectors of the disk are transparent, and the other two are coated with silver to form a mirror. Thus, when the disk is spinning, the light from the monochromator is alternately transmitted to the eye and reflected away from it. During the times that a mirrored sector is in the path, light from another source, the adapting field source, is reflected to the eye. In other words, when the disk is spinning, the eye is alternately stimulated with monochromatic light and with light from the adapting field source.

Consider first, what would happen if the disk is stopped with a transparent sector in the path, so that light from the monochromator can enter the eye. This light is incident on a beam splitter that transmits some of the light to the eye and reflects some of it to a photocell labeled "input." The signal from this photocell indicates the intensity of the light input to the eye. The light transmitted by the beam splitter falls on the subject's retina and a small fraction of it is reflected back out of the eye along the incoming path. Some of this light is transmitted by the beam splitter and effectively lost, but the remainder of the light from the retina is reflected to a second photocell, labeled "output,"

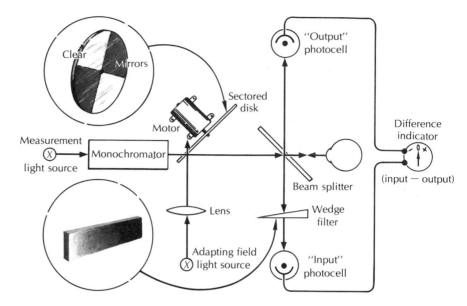

Fig. 5.11 **Schematic diagram of apparatus to measure the change in light absorption by retinal pigments in the living human eye.** [*This is a modified version of that described by Campbell and Rushton (1955).*]

since its signal is a measure of the amount of light reflected from the retina.

In the path between the beam splitter and the input photocell is a device called a wedge filter, and this device is drawn in the other inset to Fig. 5.11. It is a neutral filter like those described in Chapter III, except that its density varies smoothly from one end to the other. Thus, as it is moved back and forth perpendicular to the path between the beam splitter and the input photocell, the intensity of light falling on the photocell will change smoothly. Such a filter is conventionally represented by a wedge-shaped symbol, as in this diagram. (Unfortunately, this symbol is essentially the same as the symbol for a prism. It should be noted that the wedge shape of the filter symbol refers, schematically, to the *density* of the filter and not to its actual shape.)

The signals from the two photocells are fed into a device that processes them so that the output reading of the device is an extremely sensitive measure of the difference between the two photocell signals.

A subject is completely dark-adapted and positioned in the apparatus (with the sectored mirror set to transmit light from the monochromator to the eye). Since the intensity of the light falling on the input photocell will be much greater than that reflected from the retina and falling on the output photocell, there will be a strong signal on the difference indicator. Now the wedge is moved into the path, reducing the intensity on the input photocell until the difference indicator signals zero difference. (If the other elements of the apparatus were properly calibrated, the position of the wedge for this "null" between the photocells would then indicate the proportion of incident light reflected by the retina. However, that is not the measurement of interest, since that measure is determined by many pigments in addition to the visual pigment itself.)

Now suppose that the sectored disk is rotated until the monochromatic light is cut off and the light from the adapting source enters the eye. (The photocells are automatically switched off whenever the sectored disk is in this position.) An image of the lens in front of the adapting light will be formed on the subject's retina, and he will see a very bright disk of light. This light will isomerize some of the visual pigment, which will then bleach (as in Fig. 5.3). Next, the sectored disk is returned to its other position, and the monochromatic measuring light again enters the eye. Since some of the pigment in the eye is now in the bleached state (that is, it is less likely to absorb quanta from the measuring light), the light falling on the output photocell will be more intense than it was before the eye was light-adapted, and the difference indicator will signal this difference. The wedge must thus be moved part of the way out of the path in order to restore the null. The change in the density of the wedge that is required to establish the new null is equal to the change in the density of the pigment in the path of the light falling on the output photocell. Since most of the light falling on the output photocell passed through the retina twice, once on its way in and once again after reflection from the back of the eye, the change in wedge density actually equals approximately twice the change in density of the pigment. In this way, the amount of bleaching that results from the adapting light may be measured.

However, this measurement must be carefully evaluated. If the change in wedge setting is to be interpreted as a measure of the amount of pigment bleached by the adapting light, one assumption that must be made is that the bleached pigment is completely transparent to the measuring wavelength. That is, it must be assumed that the probability of a bleached molecule absorbing a quantum of the measuring light is very small compared with the absorption by unbleached pigment. In these experiments, Rushton used a measuring wavelength for which it is known that bleached rhodopsin in solution has a very small absorption coefficient so that, unless unsuspected nontransparent products result from the bleaching of rhodopsin in the living eye, the measurements are not subject to this problem.

A second observation about this technique is also very critical. What is being measured here is the change in the amount of light absorbed by pigments in the eye as a result of exposure to the adapting light, but these pigments are not necessarily the *visual* ones. For example, it is plausible that the choroidal pigment, when in the living eye, actually bleaches when light falls on it. It is even possible, although unlikely in the human eye, that the position of the visual pigment changes during adaptation. There is excellent evidence that this actually occurs in the eye of the frog, where, during dark adaptation, the pigment migrates to a position where it is more likely to catch light. Any such change in retinal absorption would be registered by Campbell and Rushton's technique.

It is very likely that the results of this procedure do represent the bleaching of *visual* pigments, so long as the bleaching light is not too intense, because the only pigment ever extracted from the mammalian eye that does bleach is rhodopsin, and there is no indication that pigment migration occurs in humans. Further, the relationship between the amount of bleaching and the wavelength of the bleaching light as measured by this technique, agrees with the absorption spectrum of rhodopsin. However, Weale (1964) who has performed measurements similar to those of Campbell and Rushton (1955), pointed out that the heat produced at the retina by very strong adapting lights may actually cause the retina to swell locally. The consequent redistribution of the blood could seriously affect the measurements.

One more limitation of the technique should be noted. It cannot work unless some of the measuring light is actually absorbed by the visual pigment, and the process of measuring itself will, therefore, change the result. Campbell and Rushton designed their apparatus to be as sensitive as possible in order to reduce this difficulty, and Weale reduced the artifact even further.

Visual Pigments during Dark Adaptation   With the preceding qualifications in mind, it is possible, using retinal densitometry, to measure the amount of pigment bleached for different intensities, durations, and wavelengths of the adapting light. The course of bleaching and regeneration may also be traced. The points in Fig. 5.12 are readings taken as a function of the time after an adapting light was turned off. This particular adapting light resulted in the bleaching of virtually 100% of the pigment. Then, over the course of about 40 min, the bleached pigment regenerated (that is, went from state d to state a, Fig. 5.3).

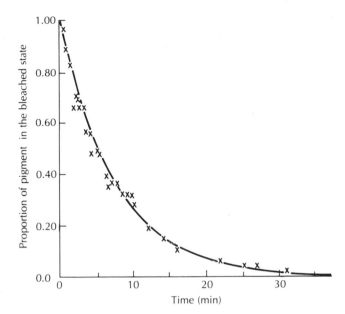

Fig. 5.12 **The time course of regeneration of rhodopsin in the living eye. At zero time, an adapting light strong enough to cause virtually all of the pigment to bleach was extinguished. The x's are Rushton's measurements and the smooth curve is an exponential with a time constant of 7.5 min (a half-life of 5 min).** [*From Rushton (1965).*]

The smooth curve plotted here is an exponential curve. Remember that each molecule, if in state *d* (i.e., bleached), will have some fixed probability of returning to state *a*, that probability being independent of the states of the other pigment molecules in the receptor. For rhodopsin, that probability can be stated as follows: Any molecule in state *d* will have a probability of 0.5 of having returned to state *a* in any 5-min period. Whenever a very large number of molecules behaving in this way are observed, the characteristics of the group will be described by an exponential curve. Half of the molecules will have regenerated during the first 5 min, half of the remainder during the next 5 min, etc.[7]

It would be expected from this curve that the intensity of a threshold flash would decrease correspondingly with time in the dark. That is, suppose that the visual system always required the activation of nine rods, each absorbing a single quantum, in order that the subject see the flash. After total dark adaptation, this would require about 100 quanta incident on the cornea. However, immediately after adapting with the light in Fig. 5.12, virtually all of the pigment molecules will be in state *d*, and therefore unreceptive to quanta incident on them. As a consequence, the threshold would be infinite. After 5 min in the dark,

[7]Another, probably more common, way of describing this curve is to say that it is an exponential with a time constant, that is, the time required to fall to $1/e$ of the final level, of 7.5 min. (The symbol e represents the base of Natural, or Naperian logarithms, 2.718.)

half of the pigment molecules have regenerated, and the intensity of the flash must be 200 quanta at the cornea in order that nine quanta will still be absorbed by "receptive" pigment molecules. In general, if it is true that the absorption of nine quanta is always required for seeing, the threshold at any instant should simply be inversely proportional to the fraction of pigment molecules in the regenerated state (assuming that the pigment is not so dense that an appreciable proportion of the molecules are shielded from the light by other bleachable molecules).

A direct comparison of the threshold during dark adaptation and the proportion of regenerated pigment shows very clearly that this relationship does not hold. For example, Rushton found that a light which results in the bleaching of 25% of the pigment molecules will cause the threshold to rise not by 25%, but 100,000 times as high. (These figures are based on data taken from a patient whose eyes contained only rods.) According to Rushton's data, the threshold is not simply inversely proportional to the proportion of pigment in state a. Rather, the *logarithm* of the threshold is proportional to the fraction of pigment in the bleached state. Specifically, for his conditions:

$$\log_{10} \frac{\Delta I}{\Delta I_0} = aB,$$

where ΔI is the threshold intensity, ΔI_0 is the threshold after complete dark adaptation, a is a constant of value about 20, and B is the fraction of rod pigment in the bleached state. The relationship is plotted in Fig. 5.13. It must be concluded from these data that the threshold during dark adaptation is not limited by the quantal-catching capacity of the pigment. More specifically, it must be true that the number of quanta that must be captured in order for the subject to see the flash increases as the proportion of bleached pigment increases, as plotted on the right-hand vertical axis in Fig. 5.13. The reasons for this decrease in the sensitivity of the visual system are not yet fully understood, but will be discussed in some detail in Chapter XIV.[8]

Visual Pigments during Light Adaptation Using the procedure outlined above, Rushton also studied the course of events during light adaptation. To measure the propor-

[8]The slope of the relation in Fig. 5.13 varies somewhat under different experimental condition (e.g., for different test flash sizes). Thus, a light that bleaches 25% of the pigment might raise the threshold 75,000-fold instead of the 100,000-fold found by Rushton. However, this variation is trivial with respect to the point that the changes in threshold during dark adaptation cannot be attributed to the depletion of quantum-catching visual pigment.

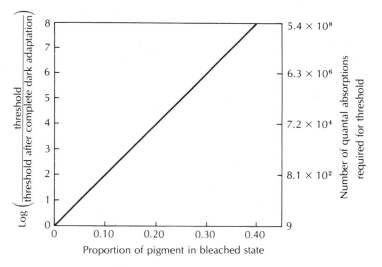

Fig. 5.13 **Relationship between the threshold and the proportion of rod pigment in the bleached state. These data were obtained by Rushton (1965) from a subject whose eyes contained only rods. The correspondence is mostly obscured in the normal eye by the activity of a different set of receptors, the cones. The vertical axis on the left is the quantity represented by Rushton's equation in the text. The axis on the right is the number of quanta that must be absorbed by visual pigment in order for the subject to see the flash**

tion of bleached pigment while the eye is actually being light-adapted, the sectored disk (Fig. 5.11) is continuously spun by the motor. Then on half of the disk's cycle, the eye is being light-adapted (and the measuring device is disconnected), while on the other half the measuring light enters the eye, and the wedge is continuously adjusted to maintain a null. Since light adaptation is much faster than dark adaptation, the amount of dark adaptation that occurs during each measuring period is very small relative to the amount of light adaptation that occurs during the remainder of the cycle.

The results of such a procedure are shown in Fig. 5.14.[9] Let us consider, step by step, the factors that produce these curves. The eye is first completely dark-adapted. Then the apparatus is turned on and the measurements are made while the sectored mirror is spinning. During the first short time that the adapting light is on, unbleached pigment molecules are isomerized at a rate directly proportional to the intensity of the adapting light. That is, twice as many quanta per second will isomerize twice as many pigment molecules. The isomerized

[9]The procedure that Rushton actually followed was slightly different from the one illustrated here. This version is presented because it more clearly illustrates the relevant points.

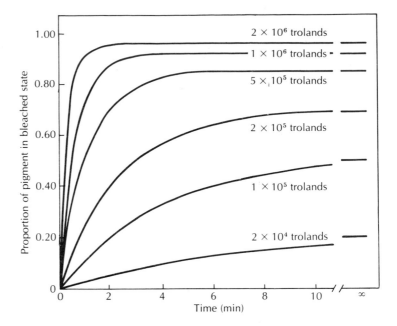

molecules (in state *b*) will then spontaneously change through state *c* to state *d*, bleaching in the process. Thus, at the end of the first short time in the light, some proportion of the pigment will no longer be capable of capturing quanta, and, as a consequence, during the second light adapting period, the number of molecules that bleach will be smaller than the number during the first period. If there were no regeneration of pigment (from state *d* to *a*), this process would continue, each succeeding short light-adapting period bleaching a fixed proportion of the remaining pigment, and the curve would be a simple exponential with its asymptote at 100% bleached. After a given period of time, half of the pigment would be bleached; after another equal period, half of the remaining pigment would be bleached, etc.

However, during all of this time, any molecules in state *d* have a finite probability of returning to state *a*, and some of them will. That means that the proportion of pigment in the bleached state is at all times smaller than would be expected if there were no regeneration, and 100% bleaching can never be reached.

Some of Rushton's data confirm the assumption mentioned earlier in this chapter that the probability of *regeneration* of a bleached molecule is independent of the state of the other molecules. He showed that the rate at which the pigment changes from the bleached to the regenerated state depends directly, and only, upon the number of bleached molecules. (If each molecule has a fixed probability of regenerating in a given time period, then the more there are, the more will regenerate in that time period, and, therefore, the greater will be the rate of regeneration of the pigment as a whole.) For any given amount of bleached pigment present, the rate of regeneration is the same whether the eye is in the light or in the dark. Therefore, while the eye is light-adapting and an increasing proportion of the pigment is driven into the bleached state, the rate of *regeneration* will also increase. Since regeneration has an effect opposite to that of bleaching (it is unbleaching), the two processes will eventually come into equilibrium. That is, after a long time in the light, the curves in Fig. 5.14 will approach levels at which the rate of regeneration and the rate of bleaching are equal.

This can be explained in another way. After a long period of light adaptation, if the pigment were bleaching faster than it was regenerating, the proportion of bleached pigment would increase, but this would result in an increase in the rate of regeneration. If the regeneration rate were greater, more pigment would be in the ready-to-bleach state, and bleaching would go on at a greater rate. Thus, the system must come to a stable equilibrium such that the rates of bleaching and regeneration are equal.

The various curves in Fig. 5.14 represent equilibration at different adapting light intensity levels. As the intensity is increased, the slope of the curve increases and the asymptotic level is also higher. Note, however, that the asymptotic levels get closer and closer together as the intensity is increased; the level approaches but cannot exceed 100%.

The relationship between the asymptotic level and the intensity of the light is shown in Fig. 5.15. This is a very useful curve, because if a subject has been looking for a long time at a field of any intensity represented on the horizontal axis, the proportion of his rhodopsin that is bleached may be read directly from the vertical axis.

By the same reasoning as that presented above during the discussion of dark adaptation, it must be expected that the sensitivity of the visual system will decrease during light adaptation, and there is ample evidence to support that expectation. It seems much darker in a matinee movie when you first go in than after you have dark-adapted there for a few minutes. Similarly, it seems much brighter when you first walk back out into the sunlight than it does after a short period of light adaptation. Just as with dark adaptation, however, the change in sensitivity during light adaptation does not depend simply upon the number of unbleached pigment molecules present. It is limited by other aspects of the visual system, which will be discussed further in later chapters.

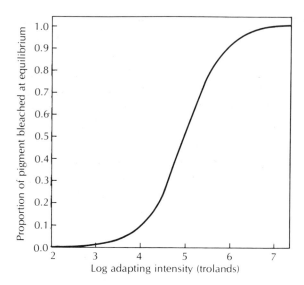

Fig. 5.15 The proportion of rod pigment that will be in the bleached state after an infinitely long period of adaptation to the intensities on the horizontal axis. [*Calculated from the data of Campbell and Rushton (1955).*]

PROBLEM 5.1 An eye is first completely dark-adapted. Then, a 1-μsec-long, extremely intense flash is delivered, intense enough that the site of every visual pigment molecule is likely to have received a large number of quanta. The eye is then dark-adapted for 5 min, and then another identical flash is delivered. What is the proportion of rod pigment in state a, that is, regenerated, immediately after the second flash?

Answer: 37.5%

VI ◇◇◇ THE EXCITATION OF RODS

THE discussion of visual pigments in the preceding chapter is relevant to visual perception because the action of light on these pigments is the very first stage in the long series of processes that culminate in visual perception. If the presence of an object does not alter the absorption of light quanta by visual pigment molecules, the object cannot be seen, and if the object is seen, the way in which the light from it interacts with the visual pigments has a profound influence on our perception of the object.

When pigment molecules are isomerized, processes are set in motion that activate some of the neural units in the retina, and this activation, after processing by subsequent stages, is transmitted to other parts of the brain where further processing takes place. There still are serious gaps in our knowledge of the ways in which the isomeriza-

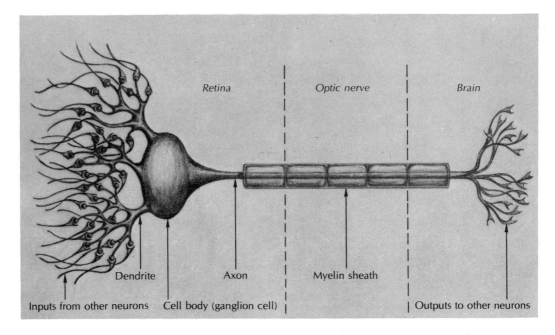

Fig. 6.1   **Semischematic diagram of one of the neurons in the optic nerve.**

tion of pigment molecules activate rods. Both the knowns and un-knowns, and their implications for perception, will be discussed in detail in this chapter.

THE FUNDAMEN-TALS OF NEURAL ACTIVITY   Most of the stages that process and transmit visual information are built of neurons. In order to understand the process of visual excitation, some fundamental properties of neuronal activity must be briefly reviewed.[1]

The optic nerve, running from the retina out of the back of the eyeball and into the brain, is a bundle containing about a million individual neurons that are typical of neurons found throughout the body. (The term "nerve" refers to a group of individual nerve fibers, or neurons, usually held together mechanically by a sheath that surrounds the nerve.) A neuron of the optic nerve may be represented schematically by the drawing in Fig. 6.1. The cell bodies of the neurons that make up the optic nerve are called retinal ganglion cells. The ganglion cells are spread over the surface of the retina, where each of

[1]For a more extensive, but elementary and clear discussion of neural activity, the reader should examine "Neurophysiology," by Charles F. Stevens, Wiley, New York, 1966.

them receives inputs from the endings of other neurons (to be discussed below) which comprise earlier stages in the visual process. When the input to a retinal ganglion cell is strong enough, the cell is activated to generate an impulse that is propagated down its axon. These impulses in turn act upon other neurons in the brain.

The axons of ganglion cells from all over the retina converge on the region of the eye called the optic disk, where they emerge from the back of the eye to form the optic nerve (see Fig. 3.11). During most of their course across the retinal surface the axons are transparent, but from the point where they enter the optic disk to their termination in the brain, they are covered with the myelin sheath, which is white and translucent. When the retina is viewed through an ophthalmoscope as in Fig. 6.2 (see the color insert), the myelin usually causes the optic disk to look whitish.

Neural Excitation The membrane that forms the walls of any neuron is semipermeable. This means, in effect, that it has holes through it that permit the passages of some molecules and ions into and out of the cell, but hinder or prevent the passage of others. This membrane also manifests a phenomenon called the "sodium pump." While the mechanics of the sodium pump are not yet understood, it seems to be true that the membrane actively pumps sodium ions from the inside to the outside. As a result of the sodium pump and the differences in permeability of the membrane to different ions, the concentration of positive ions is greater on the outside of the cell than on the inside. This concentration difference appears as a voltage across the membrane, called the resting potential; the outside of any living, resting neuron is between about 0.06 and 0.09 volts positive with respect to the inside.

Most of the mammalian neurons that have been studied are normally stimulated into action in the same way. If the endings of one neuron are in close proximity to second neuron and those endings are stimulated, they release a chemical, called a neural transmitter, that changes the permeability of the receiving cell membrane. Since there is an excess of positive ions on the outside of the membrane (i.e., the resting potential), the rate of flow of positive ions into the cell will become greater if the permeability increases. The difference in ionic concentration across the membrane is called a polarization (since it is manifested in positive and negative poles across the membrane), and the action of the excitatory chemical transmitter substance thus results in the depolarization of the membrane. In other words, the chemical transmitter increases the permeability of the membrane so that ions can flow through it, reducing the difference in charge.

What we have just described is the first step in the excitation of the neuron. If a region of a neuron undergoes enough depolarization, a further series of events are triggered in the membrane that result in a wave of strong depolarization that self-propagates, sweeping over the entire neural membrane. Even a single molecule of chemical transmitter probably causes some increase in the permeability of the membrane, but the membrane will not propagate the resulting depolarization unless that depolarization reaches some threshold level. That is, a single molecule of transmitter substance will not excite the neuron as a whole, but some minimum number of such molecules will produce enough depolarization to trigger the processes of propagation. Thus, there is machinery in the neuron that may be adequate to account for the presence of sensory thresholds.

When the number of molecules of transmitter substance acting on the membrane becomes large enough, a single wave of depolarization will sweep down the neuron. However, the propagation process is self-limiting. Once a given region of the axon has become depolarized, it will quickly restore itself to its initial, polarized state. As a consequence, only a short region of the neuron is depolarized at any given instant, and this region will sweep progressively over the surface. The wave of depolarization is called a spike, or nerve impulse.

The magnitude and duration of this propagated change depend entirely upon the characteristics of the membrane and the surrounding media, and not at all upon the nature of the input signal that initiated it. However, the strength of the input signal does effect the spacing between successive impulses as shown in Fig. 6.3.[2] Note, in this figure, that as the strength of the input stimulus increases from zero, it must exceed a threshold before any impulses are generated. Above that threshold, the frequency of firing of the neuron first increases almost linearly with input strength, and finally, at high input strengths, the frequency asymptotically approaches its maximum level.

Neural Inhibition The neurons in the body are normally stimulated (depolarized) by inputs from either receptors or other neurons or both. The places in which the receptors and neurons come into contact—where chemical

[2]The size of each impulse, in turn, depends slightly upon how rapidly it follows the preceding impulse because the state of the membrane just before it fires depends somewhat upon how much time has passed since the previous impulse. A stronger input will result in impulses that are closer together and slightly *smaller*.

mediator substances are released by the input neurons or receptors and act upon the receiving cell membrane — are called synapses. The action at the synapse that has been discussed previously is called excitation.

Some of the input endings that synapse with the retinal ganglion cells produce excitatory effects, but some of the endings on the same cell body may have the opposite effect, that is, an inhibitory effect. The mechanism by which inhibitory effects are produced at synapses is not as well understood as the mechanism for excitation. It is clear that inhibitory synapses produce hyperpolarization of the membrane of the receiving cell (that is, increases in the resting potential). However, the neuron only propagates *depolarizations* of the membrane, and therefore, the presence of the inhibitory input will not result in a signal being sent down the axon. On the other hand, if inhibitory and excitatory synapses both operate at the same time and in the same region of a receiving neuron, the net depolarization will be smaller than if the excitatory synapse acted alone. Therefore, the presence of the inhibitory input will, under these conditions, be signaled by a reduction in the number of propagated nerve impulses.

Figure 6.4 shows a set of recordings of nerve impulses from one of the neurons that form the optic nerve of the arthropod, *Limulus* (the horseshoe crab). The *Limulus* eye and the records shown here will be discussed extensively in Chapter XI, where such recordings will be re-

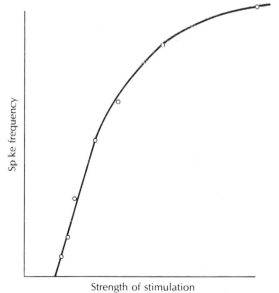

Fig. 6.3 **The relationship between the strength of the input to a neuron and resulting frequency of its firing impulses. The data plotted here are from Hodgkin (1948).**

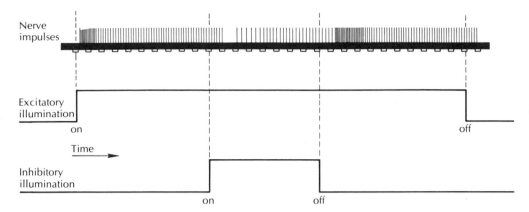

Fig. 6.4   **A record of the nerve impulses occurring in a single optic nerve fiber from the lateral eye of** *Limulus* **when a receptor is illuminated that excites the fiber and others are illuminated that inhibit the fiber. The deflections of the baseline are 0.2-sec intervals.** [*From Hartline et al.* (1952); *and Hartline et al.* (1956).]

lated to brightness and color contrast phenomena. For the present purposes, however, it is sufficient to understand that the neuron in Fig. 6.4 receives inputs from two receptors, one of which excites it and the other of which inhibits it. First, the excitatory receptor is illuminated, and the neuron fires a train of impulses beginning at a high frequency and leveling off at a lower steady rate. When the inhibitory receptor is illuminated, the rate of firing is abruptly reduced to zero, and then gradually returns to a low level. When the illumination on the inhibitory receptor is turned off, the firing rate again increases to its uninhibited level.

It may be seen from Fig. 6.4 that the excitatory and inhibitory effects do not occur at exactly the instants that the lights are turned on or off. The onsets and offsets of excitation and inhibition are delayed, and these delays are called latencies. Such latencies can have important perceptual consequences, and some of them will be described in subsequent chapters.

Neural Summation   If the input endings at an excitatory synapse are more strongly stimulated, they will cause an increase in the rate of firing of the neuron. However, the rate of firing of the neuron depends not directly upon the intensity of any local depolarization, but rather upon the total rate at which ions flow across the cell membrane. Because of this fact, the neuron will also fire more rapidly if *more* excitatory endings are activated, producing a greater *area* of depolarization.

The fibers leading to the endings that synapse with retinal ganglion cells come from many different neurons. As a consequence, the activity levels in these input neurons are added together by the receiving ganglion cell, and its output frequency signals the sum of the activities in all of the input neurons. This process is called summation.

One example of the perceptual consequences of summation has already been discussed in Chapter II. Most human retinal ganglion cells indirectly receive excitatory inputs from a large number of rods. One result is the relationship between threshold and test spot area that was shown in Fig. 2.5, p. 13, which was useful in interpreting the results of Hecht *et al*. The effects of inhibitory inputs also summate. In general, the effects of all inputs, excitatory and inhibitory, may be thought of as undergoing an algebraic summation at the synapse, the excitatory inputs having a positive sign, and the inhibitory ones a negative sign. The resulting signal, the frequency of firing of impulses in the neuron, depends upon the sum of all of the excitation inputs minus the sum of all the inhibitory inputs, so long as the net quantity is equal to or greater than zero. (Whenever the sum of the inhibitory inputs is greater than the excitatory ones, the frequency of firing will be zero.[3])

The Excitation and Inhibition of Neurons by Ion Flow   When the excitatory chemical transmitter substance increases the permeability of a cell membrane, an ionic current flows across the membrane. This current, in turn, induces depolarization in adjacent areas of the neuron, resulting in the propagation of what is called the nerve impulse. While the chemical transmitter causes a change in permeability, it is the resulting ion flow that actually initiates the nerve impulse. If, by any means at all, a current is driven across the membrane in a direction so as to reduce the membrane potential, that depolarization will also be propagated down the axon. For example, a neuron can be made to fire a train of impulses if electrodes are placed one inside and the other outside the cell membrane, and an electric current is passed between the two electrodes. If the current is in the direction that reduces the polarization of the membrane, impulses will be propagated, and if the current is driven in the opposite direction, the effect will be similar to inhibition in that the neuron will not propa-

---

[3]There is another kind of inhibition that acts to change the *sensitivity* of the input endings. There are important differences between the consequences of this kind of inhibition and the additive one described above, but they are beyond the scope of the present treatment.

gate impulses unless a *stronger-than-normal* current is driven across the membrane in the depolarizing direction at the same time.

Ions may be driven across neural membranes in normal, living tissue by the action of other neural elements. In other words, it is possible that excitation and inhibition in neurons under normal conditions may sometimes, or in some places, be produced by direct ion flow instead of by the ion flow resulting indirectly from the action of chemical transmitter substances. As yet, there is no evidence of such electrical excitation in normal mammalian neurons. However, there is evidence of electrical transmission in the nervous systems of some fishes, and it is quite possible that electrical transmission may naturally occur in some of the neural tissue of the human retina.

The Neurons in the Human Retina   There are several types of neurons in the retina, the types being distinguished by their shapes and locations. The ganglion cells are the last in the chain of neurons running from the receptors to the optic nerve itself. At the time of this writing, it is probably premature to try to describe the specific connections among all of the neural elements in the human retina, but recent superb electron microscopy work in Dowling's laboratory at Johns Hopkins suggests that a real explosion of knowledge about the interactions among these units is about to occur. In the (probably short) interim before that work is completed, it would be consistent with what is presently known to accept, as a working assumption, the idea that every type of cell *may* be connected with every other type, and that each of these connections may be either excitatory or inhibitory. Figure 6.5 is a semischematic drawing of the kinds of cells and connections that were known to be present in the primate retina when this book was written.

THE EXCITATION OF RETINAL STRUCTURES AS A CONSEQUENCE OF THE ABSORPTION OF QUANTA   In some way, the isomerization of visual pigment molecules produces changes in the activity of retinal neurons. While there is no unequivocal evidence concerning the nature of the process by which this is accomplished, it is probably true that isomerization excites neurons by one of two general processes, which will be described below.

Somehow, the occurrence of the isomerization, or the subsequent changes of the rhodopsin molecule, must cause a change in the excitation of neural tissue. Figure 6.6 shows, again, the model of rhodopsin that was discussed in Chapter V. A pocket has been drawn in this fig-

Fig. 6.5 Semischematic
diagram of the connec-
tions among neural ele-
ments in the primate
retina that were identi-
fied as of 1966. R, rod;
C, cone; MB, midget bi-
polar nerve cell; RB,
rod bipolar; FB, flat bi-
polar; H, horizontal
cell; A, amacrine cell;
MG, midget ganglion;
and DG, diffuse gang-
lion. The regions where
the cells are contiguous
are synapses. [From
Dowling and Boycott
(1966). Copyright, 1966,
by the American Asso-
ciation for the Advance-
ment of Science.]

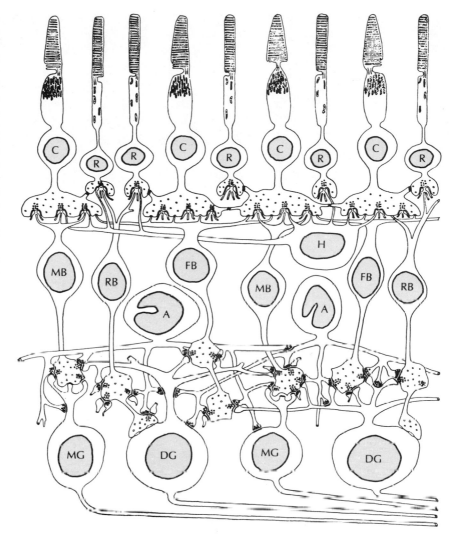

Fig. 6.5 **Semischematic diagram of the connections among neural elements in the primate retina that were identified as of 1966. R, rod; C, cone; MB, midget bipolar nerve cell; RB, rod bipolar; FB, flat bipolar; H, horizontal cell; A, amacrine cell; MG, midget ganglion; and DG, diffuse ganglion. The regions where the cells are contiguous are synapses.** [*From Dowling and Boycott (1966). Copyright, 1966, by the American Association for the Advancement of Science.*]

ure beneath the socket into which the retinal molecule fits. When the system is in state *a* this pocket is buttoned, but when it isomerizes to *b*, the pocket is unbuttoned and begins to open up. According to this model, then, the isomerization of the pigment molecule opens a path between the inside of the pocket and the surrounding media.

There are two ways in which such an occurrence might result in the activation of any nearby neural tissue. This site and the millions like it in each rod are imbedded in a folded membrane, and the membrane is almost certainly semipermeable. It might, in fact, be similar or identical to the membranes surrounding neuronal cell bodies. If this is true, the pocket could act as a hole in the membrane, permitting ion flow as

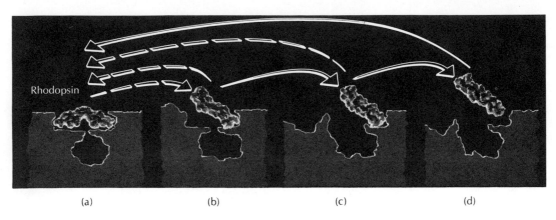

Rhodopsin

(a)   (b)   (c)   (d)

Fig. 6.6 **Semischematic diagram of the states of a rod pigment molecule.**
[*From Wald et al. (1963).*]

long as it is open. The ions that would flow through the hole might
well pass across neighboring sensitive neural membranes on their migration, depolarizing these neighboring neurons. If the neurons or the
membrane of the rod itself were capable of propagating the depolarization, the information that a quantum had been absorbed would thus
be transmitted away from the rod, and begin its way through a chain of
neurons to the brain.

There is another way in which the opening of the pocket could activate subsequent neurons. Suppose that the pocket encloses an active
site on the protein molecule, and that the active site generates an excitatory neural transmitter substance. The substance might be generated
in the pocket and then be released when the pocket is unbuttoned, or
it might be formed by the interaction of the site with the surrounding
media, and thus generated only while the site is exposed. If either of
these processes were to occur, the excitatory substance could find its
way to any neighboring excitable neural tissue, causing its depolarization and the eventual transmission of an impulse or impulses along the
optic nerve. (Of course, there is no reason to believe, *a priori*, that the
absorption of a quantum produces *excitation* of neurons. It is possible
that an opened pocket releases inhibitory substance, reducing the
level of some steady activity, and that the reduction in activity signals
the presence of the light.)

Within each of the models mentioned above, there are several possible modifications in detail, and many models or theories basically
different from the ones already described might also be proposed.
Since, at the present time, there is so little evidence upon which to
base a choice among the models and their modifications, it would not

be fruitful to discuss them in detail here. However, it is instructive to examine how some of these models might be related to two perceptual phenomena, dark adaptation and the perception of brightness.

DARK ADAPTATION AND ROD EXCITATION In the preceding chapter, the relationship between the amount of unbleached visual pigment and the visual threshold was discussed, and evidence was presented that the number of quanta that must be absorbed by visual pigment molecules in order to see increases as the proportion of pigment in the bleached state increases. For example, when the eye is completely dark adapted, so that the proportion of pigment in state d is virtually zero, about nine quanta must be absorbed for a flash to be seen. When 25% of the pigment is in state d, however, approximately half a million quanta must be absorbed by the molecules that are in state a, in order for a flash to be seen. It is known that, if a molecule in state a absorbs a quantum, it isomerizes, regardless of the state of the other pigment molecules. If we accept the reasonable assumption that an isomerization will have roughly the same local effect (for example, release the same amount of excitatory substance) regardless of the state of the other molecules, then the half a million quanta will have a much greater effect than the nine quanta. It follows that the rest of the visual system requires a stronger stimulation (e.g., more excitatory substance) to exceed its threshold if more molecules are in state d. The visual system seems, in some way, to sense the fact that molecules are in state d, since it behaves differently if they are in that state.

The following discussion will illustrate the way in which one theory accounts for these facts about dark adaptation. This theory is chosen somewhat arbitrarily from among a large number of possible theories, and it incorporates a great many specific subtheories or assumptions, each of which is debatable. There is too little evidence at the present time to permit a sensible choice among many theories; the one discussed here is chosen merely to illustrate the kind of theorizing that guides the thinking of workers doing research in this area, as well as the way in which theory dictates the kinds of psychophysical and physiological experiments that such workers perform. At each stage in this presentation, alternative assumptions or theories may occur to the reader, but alternatives will not be discussed here.

We may begin by stating what is known about dark adaptation. A totally dark-adapted subject will say he sees a flash when it results in the isomerization of about nine or more visual pigment molecules, and will say he does not if fewer isomerizations occur. There will be one isomerization in each of about nine rods, and the flash will be seen if the rods are relatively close to each other spatially and the isomerizations are close to each other temporally. If some of the pigment is in the bleached state, a greater number of isomerizations are required for the same response.

The basic element in the theory under consideration is the following: We will hypothesize that the site at the bottom of the pocket in Fig. 6.6 is one that generates chemical mediator substance whether or not the pocket is open. Assume that this generation is a simple chemical reaction, in that the rate at which the substance is generated is reduced when the concentration of the substance in the neighborhood of the site of generation is increased. Also assume that when the molecule is in state a, the pocket is securely buttoned, so that none of the mediator can leak out. Given those assumptions, it follows that while a pocket is in state a, it fills up with mediator substance, and, after it has been buttoned for a long time, the concentration of the substance becomes so great that the generation of new substance effectively ceases. Then when the molecule is isomerized, the pocket opens, releasing its contents in a burst. Furthermore, as the pocket remains open, the site will again begin to generate mediator substance (since the concentration immediately adjacent to the site has been greatly reduced), and the mediator will continue to leak out at a low rate until the molecule finally regenerates again. We will assume, further, that released mediator substance is diffused away or deactivated by some other agent.

For convenience in this discussion, the variability inherent in the subject can be neglected and his dark-adapted threshold will be taken as nine quantal absorptions. That is, when he is dark-adapted, he will always say "yes" if nine or more isomerizations occur, and always say "no" if fewer than that occur.

The theory is summarized by the schematic diagram in Fig. 6.7. Some of the quanta incident on the receptors isomerize pigment molecules, and mediator substance flows out of the pockets (Stage 1). Now a crucial assumption will be made, namely that the excitation resulting from this chemical mediator is a negatively accelerated function of the amount of mediator, as shown in Stage 2 of the figure. In other words, the output of the excited part of each rod is not directly proportional to the amount of mediator substance present, but follows the general type of relation shown in the plot in Fig. 6.7. (Without some nonlinear relationship somewhere in the visual system, no theory could possibly be consistent with the data of dark adaptation.)

Stage 3 in the diagram in Fig. 6.7 is simply a spatial summation stage, that is, one that adds the outputs from a number of different rods.

Fig. 6.7 **Diagram of a model of the visual system to account for the change in threshold during dark-adaptation. It is explained in the text.**

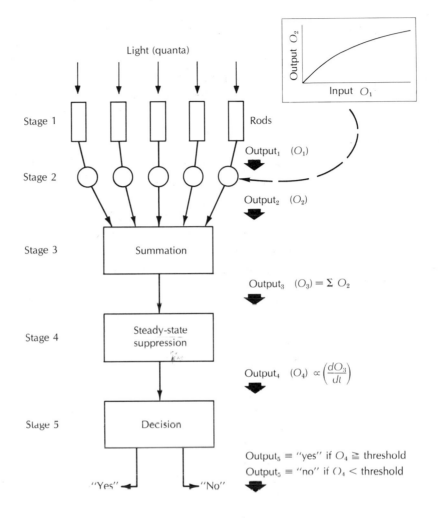

Light (quanta)

Stage 1   Rods

$Output_1$ (O_1)

Stage 2

$Output_2$ (O_2)

Stage 3   Summation

$Output_3$ $(O_3) = \Sigma\ O_2$

Stage 4   Steady-state suppression

$Output_4$ $(O_4) \propto \left(\dfrac{dO_3}{dt}\right)$

Stage 5   Decision

$Output_5 \equiv$ "yes" if $O_4 \geqq$ threshold
$Output_5 \equiv$ "no" if $O_4 <$ threshold

"Yes"   "No"

(Graph in figure: Output O_2 vs Input O_1)

Stage 4 has another special property that is required by this theory and that is also a critical part of theories of many other perceptual phenomena. Stage 4 gives an output only when the input to it *changes*. That is, if the input is steady, or changing only very slowly, it will give no output, or only a very small one. The faster the input is changing, the greater will be its output. (There is excellent evidence that stages with this property occur in various places in the nervous system, and their structure as well as their profound perceptual consequences will be discussed in a number of other places in this book.)

The last stage in this model is called a decision stage. It simply says "yes" if the input to it is greater than some fixed amount and "no" if the input is smaller than that. This stage corresponds to the fact that, in the typical dark-adaptation experiment, the subject is only permitted two response categories, "yes" and "no."

Now let us examine the properties of this theory as a whole. If the eye is completely dark-adapted, and then a flash is delivered of sufficient intensity that nine quanta are absorbed by the visual pigment contained in the rods feeding Stage 3, each rod will contribute a certain output to the summation stage. Since this is a change (from the zero output before the flash), it will be transmitted through Stage 4 to the decision stage, and from the Hecht *et al.* experiment and the assumptions set forth above, we know that the input to the decision stage will be great enough that its output will be "yes." Let us arbitrarily call that input level to Stage 5 (that is, the threshold level for Stage 5), nine units of excitation.

Now the eye is light-adapted until 1000 of the pigment molecules are in the bleached state, and then the adapting light is turned off. A few seconds later, almost all of the 1000 molecules will still be in the bleached state (since regeneration is relatively slow), but all of those bleached sites will have been unbuttoned for a long enough time that their initial bursts of chemical mediator will have subsided. Now assume, merely for the sake of discussion, that the amount of mediator per unit of time leaking out of any pocket that has been unbuttoned for awhile is, say, one twentieth of that which pours out when it is first unbuttoned. Then the total amount of chemical mediator present in the neighborhood of the visual pigment will be 1000/20, or 50 units, as compared with the nine units that were present when the threshold flash was presented to the dark-adapted eye. We might expect that such a large amount of excitatory substance would result in strong stimulation of the rest of the system, and the decision stage would say "yes" continuously (until most of the molecules regenerate to state *a*). However, the signal resulting from the leakage of chemical mediator from open pockets *changes* only very slowly (as the pigment regenerates). As a consequence, there will be virtually no output from Stage 4, and the decision stage will say "no."

Now suppose that under these conditions, with 1000 molecules in the bleached state, a test flash is delivered that is intense enough to result in the absorption of nine quanta by regenerated pigment molecules. (This will require a flash slightly more intense than the equivalent flash for the dark-adapted eye, since there are slightly fewer molecules in state *a*.) Each of the nine resulting isomerizations will release a burst of transmitter substance. However, the resulting input to the decision stage will be smaller than nine units, for the following reason.

The curve in Fig. 6.7 has been redrawn in Fig. 6.8. When nine isomerizations occurred in the *dark-adapted* eye, the result was the change in output shown on the figure (nine units). However, after

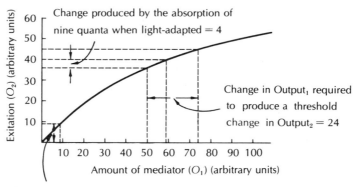

Fig. 6.8 **Hypothetical curve of the relationship between the input and the output of Stage 2 in Fig. 6.7. The curve represents any negatively accelerated relationship.**

light-adaptation, the flash produced a change in mediator substance from 50 to 59, and because the curve is negatively accelerated, this results in an output change of only four units. A change of four units, when transmitted through the system to the decision stage, results in the response "no." It can be seen from Fig. 6.8 that when 1000 molecules are in the bleached state, 24 new ones must be isomerized in order that the resulting change be large enough to yield the response "yes." Thus this theory provides a possible explanation for the fact that the number of quanta that must be absorbed for a flash to be seen increases as the amount of bleached pigment increases. (This "explanation" is obviously incomplete. Each of the stages in this model must consist of substages, which must themselves be explained. For example, what causes the nonlinear relationship in Stage 2?)

THE EARLY STAGE OF DARK ADAPTATION In the preceding chapter, it was explained that when a subject steadily views a lighted field for a long time, an equilibrium is established in his retina, such that the rates of isomerization and regeneration of visual pigment are constant and equal. Suppose that a subject has been looking at such an adapting field, then it is turned off, and his threshold for a flash of light is measured very shortly after the offset of the adapting light.

According to the theory outlined in the preceding section, the following events should occur: While the adapting light is still on, each newly isomerized molecule contributes its supply of mediator substance, and since the rate of isomerization is constant, the rate of release of mediator substance will be constant. The theory also assumes

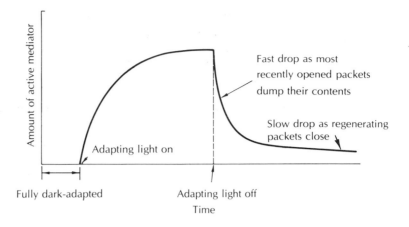

Fig. 6.9 **Hypothetical amount of active chemical mediator substance during light and dark adaptation.**

that a substance that inactivates the chemical mediator is present, or that the mediator diffuses away. This will result in a second equilibrium such that the rate at which mediator substance is released will equal the rate at which it is inactivated (or diffused away). Therefore, after the adapting light has been on for a long time, a constant amount of active mediator substance will be present. (According to the theory, Stage 4 in Fig. 6.7 should block the resulting output, and the subject should not see the adapting field. The fact that he *does* see the field under these circumstances should not be taken as a refutation of the theory, as will be explained in detail in Chapter XI.)

The amount of mediator substance present when the adapting light has been on for a long time will be the sum of the amount contributed by newly isomerized molecules and the amount slowly leaking out of pockets that have previously opened and not yet regenerated. Now, if the adapting light is suddenly turned off, the contribution by newly isomerized molecules will cease, and the amount of mediator present will drop rapidly (with a speed that reflects the rate at which any newly opened pocket dumps its contents, and the rate of deactivation of mediator) to a lower level, and then continue to fall slowly at a rate determined by the regeneration of pigment. This progression is plotted in Fig. 6.9.

One of the essential consequences of the excitation theory under discussion is that the light intensity required for a flash to be seen depends upon the amount of chemical mediator substance present during the flash. This results from the nonlinearity of Stage 2 in Fig. 6.7. It follows from the theory, then, that the threshold should drop sharply when an adapting light is first turned off, and then should undergo the gradual reduction usually called dark adaptation.

What actually happens during dark adaptation is shown in Fig. 6.10. These plots all show an early rapid drop followed by a slow phase, as predicted. However, at the higher adapting intensities, the curves are different from the theoretical prediction in that there is a rise in the threshold just when the adapting light goes off. To account for this rise, a new feature must be added to the model under discussion.[4] For example, the output of stage 4 may be made proportional to the *absolute value* of the rate of change of its input, and a stage added

[4]The rises in threshold begin slightly *before* the adapting light is extinguished. Although this appears to demonstrate the action of extrasensory perception on the subject's part, there are several alternative explanations. The simplest is as follows: The test flash is considerably less intense than the adapting light, and there is ample physiological evidence that the activity of the neural stages in the retina begins more slowly when the stimulus is less intense. Thus, although the test flash may actually be delivered before the adapting light is extinguished, the neural change resulting from the test flash may nevertheless occur after the neural effect of the extinction of the adapting light.

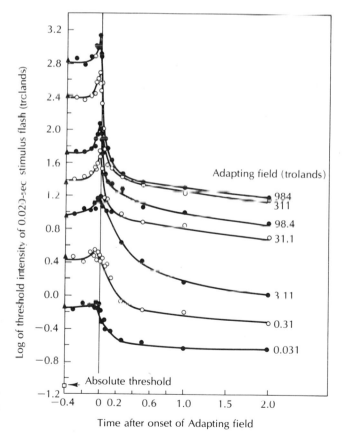

Fig. 6.10 **Threshold intensity of a short flash during the early stages of dark adaptation, for several intensities of light adaptation. (Trolands are units of retinal illumination.) The value of the absolute threshold, that is, the threshold that all curves finally reach after forty minutes in the dark, is shown near the bottom of the figure.** [*From Baker (1953).*]

Log of threshold intensity of 0.020-sec stimulus flash (trolands)

Adapting field (trolands)

984
311
98.4
31.1
3 11
0.31
0.031

Absolute threshold

Time after onset of Adapting field

between Stages 4 and 5 that has the simple property that its output is a negatively accelerated function of the input, just like the nonlinearity in Stage 2. These additions would account for the rise in threshold when the adapting light is extinguished, for the following reasons: After the adapting light has been on for a long time, the output of the early stages becomes steady, and the output from Stage 4 is thus zero. A test flash that occurs well before the adapting light is extinguished would produce a certain increase in the input to Stage 4, and this change would be signaled through Stage 4. However, if a flash were presented very close to the time when the adapting light is extinguished, the input that it would contribute to the new nonlinear stage would be superimposed upon the very large input produced by the offset of the adapting light. The effect of the flash would, therefore, be smaller than it would have been had the flash not occurred near the time of offset of the adapting light, and the threshold would consequently be increased.

VII ◇◇◇ CONES AND CONE PIGMENT

THE preceding discussion in this book has dealt exclusively with rod vision. In this chapter, the relationships between rods and cones will be described, and the remainder of the book will treat the properties of cones and cone vision.

HISTOLOGICAL PROPERTIES OF RODS AND CONES Figure 7.1 is a drawing of a typical rod and two typical cones. All the rods are shaped more or less like rods, and the peripheral cones (that is, ones found away from the fovea) are cone-shaped. However, the cones in the fovea look as rodlike as rods do. Thus, rods and cones cannot always be distinguished on the basis of their general shapes.

Fig. 7.1 **Receptors in the human retina.**
[*After Greeff (1900).*]

Direction of incident light

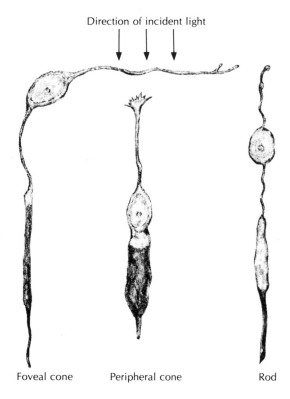

Foveal cone   Peripheral cone   Rod

Nevertheless, there are reliable differences in the structural details of rods and cones; on this basis, a receptor may be classified as a rod or cone under the microscope, and the distribution of rods and cones over the whole of the retina may thus be measured. Figure 7.2 is a plot of these distributions, along with a drawing of the eye for reference. (The rod distribution has already been discussed in relation to choice of location made by Hecht *et al.* for their test flash.) In the center of the retina, there is a region that contains only cones, and the cones there are very densely packed. The density of cones rapidly declines as the distance from the center increases. The rods begin to appear about 1° from the center, and their density increases to a maximum at about 20°, thereafter falling to a low level.

The plot in Fig. 7.2 represents a horizontal section through the eyeball, and such a section cuts through the optic disk. The optic disk is the region where the axons from all of the ganglion cells converge and exit from the eyeball, and through which the retinal arteries and veins pass. It contains no receptors, and objects imaged on it cannot be distinguished. The region is therefore called the blind spot.

Except for presence of the optic disk, the distribution of receptors is radially symmetric about the fovea.

Figure 7.3 is an enlargement of a section through the fovea itself. The receptors are at the back of the retina. The other neural elements of the retina are interposed between the front of the eye and the receptors, and since they are not completely transparent, they interfere

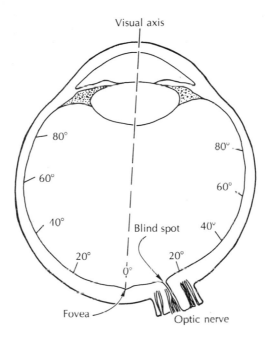

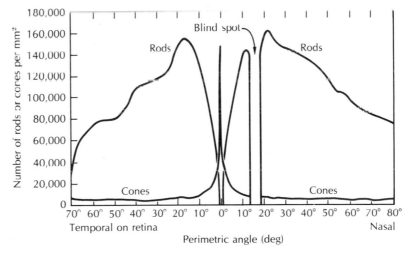

Fig. 7.2 **Top view of the left eye, and the corresponding densities of rods and cones across the retina.** [*From Pirenne (1967) "Vision and the Eye," 2nd ed. Associated Book Publishers, London.*]

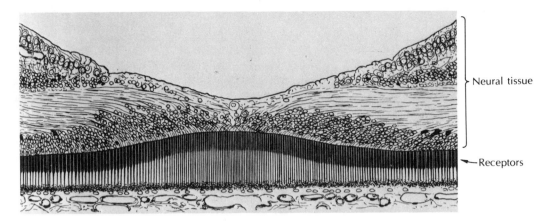

Neural tissue

Receptors

Fig. 7.3 **Sketch of a cross section through the region of the fovea in the human eye. The front of the eye would be above the top of the page.** [*From Polyak (1957) Copyright © 1957 by the University of Chicago Press.*]

slightly with the passage of light to the receptors themselves. However, in the very center of the fovea where the cones are most densely packed, some of the neural tissue is displaced to the sides, giving the light more direct access to the cones. A slight depression thus appears in the surface of the retina in this region, and that depression gives rise to the name of the region, the fovea. (*Fovea* means a small pit in Latin.)

Figure 6.5 (p. 125) is a semischematic representation of the kinds of neural elements present near rods and cones. As this drawing shows, the kinds of elements connecting with rods seem to be different from those connecting with cones. However, the actual connections of rods and cones have not yet been established with certainty, and all that can be said at present is that the neural elements in regions where the rods predominate are different from those that contain mostly cones.

One statement that is often made about the neural connections of the rods and cones is very misleading. The total number of ganglion cells (and their axons, the optic nerve fibers) that are present in the periphery of the retina is far smaller than the total number of rods themselves. If it is assumed that most rods are capable of stimulating ganglion cells, then it must be true that each ganglion cell receives input from a large number of rods. This conclusion is supported by many kinds of physiological and psychophysical studies (for example, spatial summation of threshold flashes, as discussed in connection with the choice of size of the test flash in the Hecht *et al.* experiment).

However, if the numbers of receptors and ganglion cells are counted in the region of the retina that contains predominantly cones, it is found that there are almost the same number of ganglion cells (and optic nerve fibers) as there are cones. This observation has lead to the statement that each cone is connected to a single ganglion cell, and that while the rods have "party lines" to the brain, the cones have "private lines." That statement is incorrect. There is ample evidence, much of which will be discussed later, that ganglion cells in cone-dominated regions of the retina receive inputs from many cones. While it is true that there are almost as many ganglion cells as cones in the cone region of the retina, the activity in each ganglion cell is affected by the actions of a large number of different cones, and further, each cone influences the activity of a large number of ganglion cells. These interactions are of crucial importance to brightness and color perception, and will be extensively discussed later.

PSYCHOPHYSICAL DISTINCTIONS BETWEEN RODS AND CONES

The psychophysical characteristics and perceptual correlates of cone activity differ in many respects from their rod counterparts. Three principal differences will be described here.

Dark Adaptation

The discussions of dark adaptation in the previous chapters of this book have been restricted to conditions under which only the rod system is operating. For example, the curves shown earlier, representing the way the threshold changes during dark adaptation, were taken under conditions in which the test flash was presented far out in the periphery of the retina, where very few cones are present. If such an experiment is repeated when the test flash is delivered only to the small rod-free region in the central fovea, the results look quite different. The solid curves in Fig. 7.4 are plots of the threshold changes during dark adaptation for one test spot that stimulates the rods only and another that stimulates the cones only, the same adapting light having been used for both. Note that the dark adaptation of the cones is virtually complete in about 5 min, while rod adaptation takes about 30 min. Also note that, while the rods are less sensitive than the cones at first, they are more sensitive after about 7 or 8 min.

Now suppose that the test flash is delivered to a region that contains both rods and cones. For the first 7 min after the adapting light is turned off, the cones are more sensitive. Therefore, if the intensity of the flash is adjusted until the subject just barely sees the flash, the resulting dark adaptation curve will follow the curve of the cones alone,

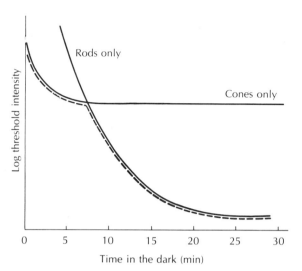

Fig. 7.4 **Change in the visual threshold during dark adaptation. The solid curves are for a test flash that affects the rods only and another that affects the cones only. The dashed curve is that obtained when the test flash affects both systems.**

leveling off after about 5 min. Then, 7 or 8 min after the adapting light was turned off, the rods will have become more sensitive than the cones, and the threshold will begin to drop again, finally leveling out after about 30 min. The dashed curve in Fig. 7.4, then, represents the plot of threshold against time of dark adaptation when the test flash stimulates both rods and cones as it would, for example, when the test flash is large.

The Stiles—Crawford Effect   Figure 7.5a is an optical diagram of an eye looking at a point source of light. All of the quanta traveling in paths within the cone formed by the source at the apex and the edges of the pupil at the base enter the eye and contribute to the retinal image of the source. If a small hole is placed in front of the pupil, as in Fig. 7.5b and 7.5c, the hole will restrict the quanta striking the retina. In Fig. 7.5b, only those quanta traveling very close to the visual axis will contribute to the retinal image, while in Fig. 7.5c, all of the quanta forming the image will pass through the outer edge of the natural pupil. Note, however, that as the hole is moved across the pupil, say from its position in (b) to that in (c), the location of the retinal image does not change at all, nor will its physical intensity.[1] All that happens when the hole is moved is that the quanta forming the image will have traveled along different paths. As the hole is moved across the pupil, the subject will report seeing a sta-

[1]Ignoring the effects of spherical abberation, which are easily compensated.

tionary bright point of light, but, despite the fact that its physical intensity is not changing, he will report that its brightness changes appreciably, being brightest when the hole is centered over the pupil, and dimmest when it is near the margin of the pupil. Similarly, if the intensity of the source is varied, and his threshold for seeing it is measured as a function of the position of the hole with respect to his pupil, the result will be as shown in Fig. 7.6. His visual system is most sensitive to quanta entering the eye near the center of the pupil, and progressively less sensitive as the quanta enter farther from the center of the pupil. This is called the *Stiles–Crawford* effect, after its discoverers W. S. Stiles and B. H. Crawford.

The Stiles–Crawford effect only appears when the stimulus is acting on the cone system. Consider the following experiment: The subject fixates a fixation point and the test spot is presented, say 1° away from the fixation point, so that its image falls on a region containing both rods and cones. If the subject is light adapted and the threshold for the test spot is measured immediately after the adapting light is turned off, the cone system will have a lower threshold than the rod system, and the threshold for the test spot will thus be determined by the cones. The Stiles–Crawford effect will appear under these conditions. However, if exactly the same measurements are made after 10 min of dark adaptation, when the rod threshold is lower than the cone threshold,

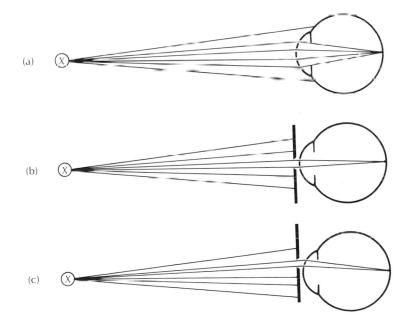

Fig. 7.5 **An eye forming a retinal image of a source through different pupils. In (a), the natural pupil is the effective one. In (b), a small artificial pupil is placed in front of the natural pupil and centered on it. In (c), the artificial pupil is displaced to the side so that the light enters the eye near the edge of the natural pupil. Note that as the artificial pupil is shifted from its position in (b) to that in (c), the retinal image does not move with respect to the retina (so long as the eye is correctly focused for the distance of the source.)**

(a)

(b)

(c)

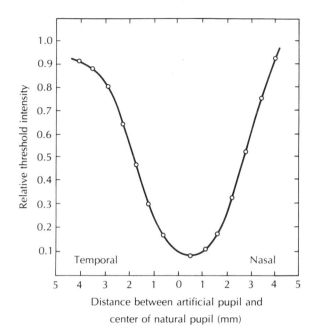

Fig. 7.6 **Variation in threshold as a
function of the point of entry of the
quanta with respect to the center of
the natural pupil.** [*From Stiles and
Crawford (1933), subject BHC, right
eye.*]

there will be no Stiles–Crawford effect. That is, when only rods are stimulated, the threshold will be essentially the same regardless of the position of the hole with respect to the natural pupil.

The Stiles–Crawford effect might be thought to be due to some difference in the transmission of light through the eye. That is, it is possible that light traveling near the edges of the pupil is more strongly absorbed or reflected by the cornea, the lens, or the media of the eye. However, careful measurements of these factors show that they are far too small to account for the effect (except possibly for blue test lights, which are strongly absorbed by the lens, especially in older eyes). Therefore, the effect must be attributable to the properties of some part of the retina. Also, since once a quantum is absorbed, information about its direction of incidence is lost, it is very likely that the Stiles–Crawford effect is a function of the properties of the receptors or the pigment itself. Evidently the cone pigments are more likely to capture quanta when those quanta are traveling close to the visual axis of the eye than if the quanta are off-axis.

O'Brien (1951) described an interesting theory to account for the Stiles–Crawford effect. In essence, this theory states that the inner segment of the cone (the shaded part of the peripheral cone in Fig.

7.1) acts like a funnel, gathering all the quanta incident on the end that faces the cornea, and concentrating those quanta into the outer segment, where the pigment is located. These funnels, according to O'Brien, are not perfect, in that, if a quantum enters the inner segment at an angle to the axis of the cone, it is less likely to be reflected into the region containing the pigment, and thus, less likely to be absorbed by the cone pigment. According to this theory, the axes of the cones are pointed toward the center of the pupil, and therefore quanta entering through the edges of the pupil will strike the cones at angles that render them less likely to be captured. As a consequence, the threshold will be higher for light entering the edges of the pupil.

O'Brien estimated the speed of light in the material making up the walls of the inner segments of the cones and in the media inside and outside of the inner segments. (Reflection of light at a boundary between two media is governed by the angle of incidence of the light and the relative speeds of light in the two media.) He then made a model of a set of cones, scaled in the following way: The model cones were plastic foam with dimensions about 80,000 times that of the cones in the eye. Instead of light as a stimulus, he used microwaves (such as those used in radar), which are electromagnetic radiations whose wavelength is about 80,000 times that of visible light. The plastic foam was chosen so that the ratio of the speed of microwaves in the foam to their speed in air was equal to the ratio of the speed of light in cones to its speed in the surrounding ocular media. Therefore, he had a model of a set of cones that matched, in its relevant dimensions, the characteristics of the cones when they are in the retina. The model is shown "looking" out of a window, in Fig. 7.7a.

To test his theory of the Stiles–Crawford effect, O'Brien pointed the outer segments of his set of model cones toward a small source of microwaves and measured the intensity of the waves transmitted through to the other ends as a function of the angle between the axis of the model and the direction of the incident microwaves. He found that the sensitivity of the model fell off as the angle of incidence increased, and that the shape of the relationship was very similar to the shape of the curve in Fig. 7.6. Later, Enoch and Fry carefully repeated O'Brien's measurements under a variety of conditions, and obtained results such as those in Fig. 7.7b. In general, the sensitivity curves for the model have a shape similar to the Stiles–Crawford effect, but the curves for the model are narrower. Thus, if the theory is correct, it is evident that the individual cones have "tuning" curves narrower than that of the eye as a whole, and the overall shape of the Stiles–Crawford effect is

Fig. 7.7 **A photograph of O'Brien's model is shown in (a). The results of Enoch and Fry's measurements are compared with the psychophysical data in (b). The solid lines connecting the circles represent measurements from the model at two different wavelengths, while the dashed curve is a plot of psychophysical measurements made by Stiles and Crawford.** [*(a) is from O'Brien (1951), and (b) from Enoch and Fry (1958).*]

(a)

(b)

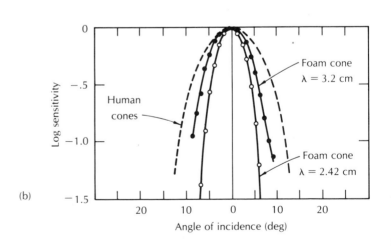

the result of the combined actions of many cones whose axes are distributed over a small range of angles.[2,3]

The Purkinje Shift The scotopic spectral sensitivity curve (the sensitivity of the dark-adapted eye as a function of the wavelength of the stimulus) has already been described. That curve is a consequence of the absorption spectrum of rhodopsin in rods, modified somewhat by the filtering action of the media of the eyeball. Whenever the spectral sensitivity of the eye is measured after the eye has been in the dark for more than ten minutes and the test flash falls at least partly on regions of the retina containing rods, a curve of this particular shape will result, since under these conditions, it is the rods that are most sensitive and thus determine the threshold. However, if the same kind of measurement is made during the *early* stages of dark adaptation, when the *cones* are more sensitive, the resulting curve is somewhat different. This curve is called the photopic spectral sensitivity curve, or sometimes, the photopic luminosity curve.

Figure 7.8 shows both the scotopic (rod) and photopic (cone) curves on the same plot. The scotopic curve in this figure represents the sensitivity after complete dark adaptation. The photopic curve would be obtained after about 5 min of dark adaptation. The heights of the two curves at any wavelength obviously depend upon the extent of dark adaptation. For example, if the scotopic curve were taken just 10 min after dark adaptation had begun, it would have the same shape, but it would be lower everywhere, since the sensitivity would not yet have reached its maximum. Similarly, if the photopic curve were measured after fewer than 5 min in the dark, that curve would also be lower at every point.

---

[2]This conclusion has been given further support by a recent set of measurements of the Stiles-Crawford effect (Safir and Hyams, 1969). These authors conclude that the shape of the Stiles–Crawford effect curve is not exactly that predicted for each single cone, according to the O'Brien model, but is probably the result of a normal distribution of axes of such cones.

[3]If the O'Brien theory is correct, then the cones in the very center of the fovea should exhibit a reduced Stiles–Crawford effect, since they are less funnel-shaped. Recent data collected by Westheimer (1967) verify this prediction.

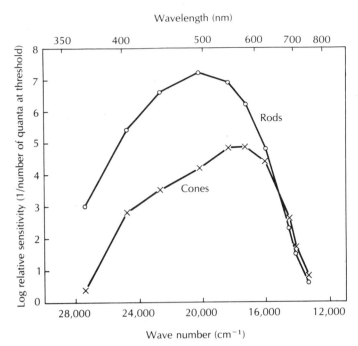

Wavelength (nm)

Fig. 7.8 **Photopic (cone) and scotopic (rod) spectral sensitivity curves.** [*After Wald (1945).*]

The photopic curve in Fig. 7.8 represents the spectral sensitivity of the eye when the cones are fully dark-adapted but are still more sensitive than the rods, and the scotopic curve represents the condition when the rods are fully dark-adapted. Several features of the comparison between these curves are important. First, the rods are more sensitive than the cones at all wavelengths except for the very long ones, where the two sensitivities are about the same. Second, while the shapes of the two curves are roughly the same, the cone curve is shifted about 50 nm to the right with respect to the rod curve, the rods being maximally sensitive to light of about 505 nm and the cones to a light of about 555 nm. Third, the rod curve is smooth but the cone curve has a dent in it (and when the cone curve is measured in more detail, it can be seen to contain several bumps.) Each of these features will be discussed in turn.

Earlier in this chapter, it was stated that when dark adaptation is measured under most conditions, the curve of threshold versus time consists of two segments, the rod and the cone segments (e.g., the dashed curve in Fig. 7.4). From Fig. 7.8, it is clear that such a compound curve will be found only when the test flash contains enough light of wavelengths shorter than about 650 nm (and the flash falls on a region of the retina containing both rods and cones). If the test flash contains only wavelengths longer than about 650 nm, the fully dark-adapted rods will exhibit no more sensitivity than the dark-adapted cones, and the resulting overall dark-adaptation curve will look the same as the one labeled "cones only" in Fig. 7.4.

In many textbooks, the comparison between the rod and cone spectral sensitivity curves is plotted in a different and misleading way. That kind of plot is shown in Fig. 7.9. The highest points in the two curves have arbitrarily been given the same value on the vertical axis, and the rest of each curve is scaled accordingly. The vertical axis in this figure should really be labeled something like "relative sensitivities of the rods and of the cones but not the relation between the sensitivities of the two of them." That is, each curve by itself is correctly proportioned, but the relationship between rod and cone sensitivities cannot be determined from this kind of plot. The reason that the data are often plotted in this way is to emphasize the shift of one curve with respect to the other along the wavelength dimension. However, plotting them this way loses important information, and gives the false impression that the cones are actually much more sensitive than the rods in the long wavelength end of the spectrum.

The peak of the spectral sensitivity curve of the cones is shifted about 50 nm toward the red end of the spectrum with respect to the

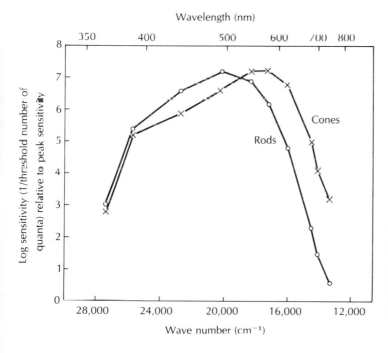

Fig. 7.9 **A common and misleading way to plot the photopic and scotopic sensitivity curves on the same graph. The highest points on each curve have arbitrarily been assigned the same value, and the remainder of the points have been correspondingly scaled.** [After the data of Wald (1945).]

rods. This is a reflection of the fact that the absorption spectrum of the visual pigment in the cones is correspondingly different from that of rhodopsin. This difference will be discussed in detail in Chapter IX. The shift from one curve to the other that occurs during dark adaptation is called the *Purkinje shift*, after J. E. Purkinje (1825).

Purkinje passed white light through a prism and looked at the resulting spectrum during the early and the late stages of dark adaptation, and noticed that the brightest region shifted toward the shorter wavelength end of the spectrum after about 10 min in the dark. The fact that the brightest part of the spectrum shifts during dark adaptation would lead to the expectation that the wavelength at which the threshold will be lowest will also shift during dark adaptation, and the plot in Fig. 7.8 shows that this is true.

The scotopic sensitivity curve is smooth. That is because the fit between a quantum and a rhodopsin molecule need not be exact in order for the quantum to be captured, and the goodness of the fit is continuously graded. Thus the absorption curve and scotopic sensitivity curve are correspondingly smooth.

This smooth absorption curve is characteristic of each of the pigments found in receptors. However, the absorption spectra of different kinds of pigment molecules are usually shifted along the wavelength dimension with respect to each other, and therefore a mixture of several different pigments may well have an overall absorption curve that is bumpy. There is ample evidence that the cones of the human eye do, in fact, contain three different pigments, each with a different absorption spectrum (these will be discussed fully in Chapter VIII), and the bumpy appearance of the photopic spectral sensitivity curve is in part a consequence of this fact.

The photopic curve may also be bumpy for a different reason. In the typical human eye, there is region lying on the surface of the retina, and covering an area approximately 5° in diameter centered on the fovea, that contains a yellowish pigment called the macular pigment. Macular pigment molecules do capture quanta, but the capture does not generate any neural signals. The pigment merely absorbs some of the light before it arrives at the receptor layer. This pigment contains a variety of kinds of molecules, and, as a result, has a bumpy absorption spectrum. Since the light must pass through the macular pigment before it arrives at the receptors, the macular pigment can affect the spectral sensitivity curve of the eye, introducing some small bumps of its own. This pigment is only present near the fovea, and therefore does not appreciably affect the scoptic curve so long as the test stimulus extends more than about 2 or 3° from the fovea.

INDIVIDUAL DIFFERENCES There is remarkably little variation between different subjects for most of the kinds of measures discussed thus far. The visual pigments, if they are present at all, may well be identical in all humans. (Color blindness will be discussed in Chapter VIII.) The time course of dark adaptation is also very similar in all humans (unless they are suffering from nutritional deficiencies or circulatory defects). The principle differences between the sensitivity curves of different individuals seem to arise from differences in the amounts of visual and nonvisual pigments in the eye.

Some individuals (about 1% of men and 0.1% of women) are missing one or more of the several visual pigments in the normal eye, and this absence can change the shape of their spectral sensitivity curves. Such individuals are also color blind, and an extensive discussion of this condition will be presented in succeeding chapters. Among individuals who possess all of the normal visual pigments, there may be considerable variation in amounts. While there is not yet enough evidence on this point to provide quantitative statements about the variation in pigments in the population, there is excellent evidence that the amount of at least one of the cone pigments can vary over a three-fold range from one subject to another (Wald, 1964). Such variations in the amount of pigment result in changes in the heights and the shapes of the spectral sensitivity curves.

Differences in nonvisual pigments also affect the spectral sensitivity curve. The density of the macular pigment is highly variable among individuals, and this produces some differences among photopic spectral sensitivity curves. Similarly, the lens becomes less transparent, and absorbs relatively more strongly in the short wavelength region of the spectrum in older people, resulting in elevated thresholds there. Racial differences in pigmentation have similar effects.

THE NATURE OF CONE PIGMENTS To study rhodopsin, the retinas of, say, cattle are subjected to processes that extract the pigment, and the characteristics of the extract are studied. When this is done, it always turns out that the extracted pigment is rhodopsin. There is no evidence in these extracts of any other pigment or pigments that might be present in the cones, even though it is known that cattle retinas contain many cones. Evidently the total amount of cone pigment in the eye is extremely small compared with the rhodopsin, and the characteristics of the rhodopsin swamp any cone pigment that might be present. This is partly a consequence of the fact that there are many more rods than cones, but it also appears that there is actually less pigment in each cone than in each rod.

The retinas of chickens and many other birds contain only cones, and Wald successfully extracted a pigment from chicken retinas that has an absorption spectrum more like the photopic than the scotopic human spectral sensitivity curve (Wald *et al.,* 1955). However, it is not likely that this pigment is actually the same as any of the cone pigments present in the human eye.

Two techniques have been recently developed that can directly measure the absorption characteristics of cone pigments in human eyes, and these will be discussed in Chapter VIII. In general, the cone pigments are probably very much like rhodopsin in their behavior and structure, differing only in their absorption spectra. In fact, Wald and his co-workers have concluded that the only differences among the different visual pigments in humans are in the underlying protein molecule, the retinal molecule being identical in all of them. They have drawn this conclusion primarily on the basis of studies of the many different visual pigments found in different animals. For example, the rod pigment in the porpoise has a different absorption spectrum than that in the cow, but both contain identical retinal.

The dynamics of the cone pigments are clearly different from the dynamics of rhodopsin — regeneration proceeds much more rapidly in cones than in rods — and this may well be a function of the difference in the protein molecules. Furthermore, while the absorption of a single quantum is sufficient to trigger a rod, probably more than one but fewer than five are required to trigger a cone (Zegers, 1959; Brindley, 1960, pp. 187–188). This difference, too, may be a consequence of the protein structure underlying the retinal.

THE KINETICS OF CONE PIGMENTS Rushton, using a modification of the technique discussed in Chapter V, has made extensive studies of the bleaching and regeneration of cone pigments. When he and Campbell used the technique to measure rod pigments, their test lights were made to fall on the peripheral retina. To measure cone pigments, Rushton projected the test light on to the very small rod-free region in the central fovea, and because there is little cone pigment in such a region, he had to increase greatly the sensitivity of the measuring device. The present discussion will be confined to his measures of the cone pigments as a whole, considering them as one single batch of pigment. (His studies of the individual cone pigments will be discussed in Chapter VIII.)

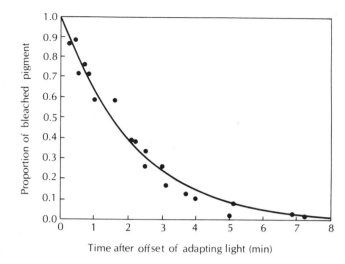

Fig. 7.10 **The regeneration of a cone pigment during dark adaptation.** [*After Rushton* (1963).]

Time after offset of adapting light (min)

Figure 7.10 shows Rushton's measures of the proportion of bleached cone pigment as a function of the time after an adapting light has been turned off. This curve has the same shape as the corresponding curve for the rods, but it falls much more rapidly, leveling off in 6 or 7 min, just as does the psychophysical curve of cone dark adaptation.

The implications of this curve are very important. Before Rushton made these measurements, there was no evidence that the cone pigments actually bleached as a consequence of the absorption of quanta. A pigment molecule need not change its absorption spectrum appreciably (that is, bleach) in order to signal the absorption of a quantum, nor is bleaching required to account for the changes in threshold that occur during dark adaptation. (Bleaching is not a sufficient explanation of dark adaptation, and it may not be necessary either.) But Rushton's measurements show that the cone pigment does in fact bleach, just as the rod pigment does. This lends support to the notion that the basic dynamics of quantal absorption by cone pigments are similar to that of rhodopsin, although the bleached cone pigment molecule returns to its regenerated state in an average of about 1.5 min, as compared to about 5 min for the rod pigment.

When a quantitative comparison is made between the proportion of pigment in the bleached state and the threshold for a flash of light, it is found that the relationship is similar to that for the rods. That is, more quanta must be absorbed by cones in order for the subject to see a flash when some of the cone pigment is in the bleached state. The equation that Rushton uses to describe the relationship between the cone threshold and the fraction of pigment in the bleached state is:

$$\log_{10}\left(\frac{\Delta I}{\Delta I_0}\right) = aB,$$

where ΔI is the threshold intensity, ΔI_0 is the completely dark-adapted cone threshold, B is the fraction of pigment in the unbleached state, and a is a constant of value about 3. This is identical with the corresponding rod relationship except that, for the rods ΔI_0 is the *rod* dark-adapted threshold, and $a = 20$.[4] These two relationships are plotted in Fig. 7.11.

Figure 7.12 is a plot of the time course of light adaptation for a cone pigment. When the adapting light is first turned on, the proportion of bleached pigment begins to rise from zero, and approaches an asymptote as the adapting light continues. This asymptote is the level at which the rate of bleaching and the rate of regeneration of pigment are equal. The level at asymptote obviously depends upon the intensity of the bleaching light.

The middle curve (adapting intensity is equal to 12,000 trolands) represents an intensity such that after a very long adaptation period, half of the pigment is bleached. The other curves, calculated from Rushton's data, represent the results that would be obtained for other intensities of the adapting light.

[4]The values in these expressions may vary somewhat with the testing conditions (e.g., the size of the test flash). The values presented here were reported by Rushton in 1963.

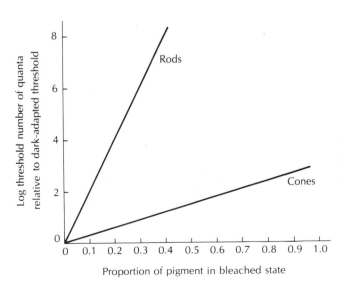

Fig. 7.11 **The relationship between the proportion of bleached pigment and the threshold stimulus intensity, relative to the fully dark-adapted threshold. (The values on the rod curve are relative to the rod dark-adapted threshold and the cone curve to the cone dark-adapted threshold.)** [*Plots of Rushton's equations in the text.*]

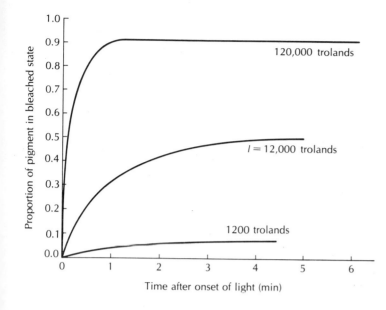

Fig. 7.12 **Proportion of bleached cone pigment as a function of the time an adapting light has been on. Before the light was turned on, the eye was fully dark-adapted. The curves are calculated from the equation:**

$$1 - x = \frac{K}{K + CI} + \frac{CI}{K + CI} \cdot e^{-t(K + CI)},$$

where I **is the adapting intensity, in trolands;** x **is the proportion of unbleached pigment; and** $C = 64 \times 10^{-8}$ **and** $k = 0.0077$, **on the basis of Rushton's data.** [*The derivation of this equation can be found in Cornsweet (1962) and the data are from Rushton (1958).*]

The asymptotic levels of these curves may be plotted as in Fig. 7.13. From this plot, the amount of bleached pigment can be determined for any intensity of an adapting light that has been viewed for a long time.

The absorption of quanta by receptor pigments is the first stage in the perceptual process, and it is clear, as a consequence of the events discussed above, that the relationship between the intensity and timing of the incident light and the strength of the resulting neural signal is a

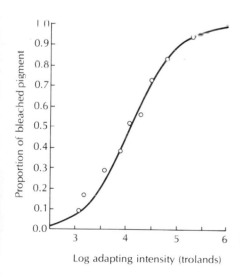

Fig. 7.13 **Proportion of pigment in the bleached state as a function of the adapting intensity at equilibrium (i.e., when the subject has been exposed to the adapting light for a long time.)** [*From Rushton (1963).*]

complicated one. Our perceptions of the incident light are necessarily distorted in accordance with these processes. The particular ways in which cone pigment kinetics may influence our perceptions will be discussed in many of the remaining chapters.

PROBLEM 7.1 It is common practice for people who are about to perform some visual task under very low illumination (e.g., pilots flying at night) to wear deep red goggles during the period just before going into the dark. These goggles transmit only light of very long visible wavelengths. Why are they worn?

VIII ◇◇◇ COLOR VISION I—DISCRIMINATIONS AMONG WAVELENGTH MIXTURES

COLOR NAMES WHEN the light from an ordinary lamp is passed through a prism and falls on a screen, a spectrum will appear. Each region of this spectrum reflects to the eye quanta of different wavelengths, and if the intensity of the light is not too low, the spectrum will look colored, as illustrated in Fig. 8.1 (see the color insert). For the normal human observer, each color corresponds to a different wavelength. If, for example, a spot of light containing a moderate number of quanta per second of wavelength 578 nm is shown on a dark background, the spot will look yellow, and if the wavelength is, say, 650 nm, it will look red.

The color of any such spot depends strongly upon the wavelength of the light coming from it. Let us briefly analyze what this means. When light of wavelength 578 nm strikes the retina, activity must result that is different in some respect from the activity resulting from light of other wavelengths, and we have learned, if we speak English, to use the word "yellow" to apply to that aspect of the activity. We have learned a variety of names to apply to the activities resulting from a variety of wavelengths and combinations of wavelengths.

The fact that we reliably use different names for certain sets of different wavelengths necessarily means that we can discriminate between those sets of wavelengths. However, the converse is not true. That is, there are many sets of wavelengths that are easily discriminable to the normal human observer, but which are given the same color name. For example, lights of 530 and 550 nm are both called green, but they are easy to tell apart if they are shown side by side. A subject with normal vision can learn to give them different names even when they are seen one at a time, although that may require some practice. In other words, we do not have a distinct color name for each discriminable set of wavelengths.

Of all the sets of wavelengths that are discriminable, the choice of those that are given unique color names is strongly culture-dependent. Natives of the jungle have lots of names for wavelengths in what we call the green region of the spectrum, although it is unlikely that they would be better able to discriminate among those wavelengths than we would be, if the wavelengths were presented side by side in a properly controlled measurement. Painters, weavers, chemists, etc., all use different color names to refer to and remember different combinations of wavelengths that are important to them.

A primary question of interest to workers in the area of visual perception relates to the underlying discriminations among wavelengths, and how those discriminations are made. Without such discriminations, different color names could not be reliably used to refer to different wavelengths and mixtures of wavelengths. (The fact that there are groups of discriminable lights that look *similar* is also of great relevance to the area of visual perception. We will return to that point later.)

MONOCHROMACY

As a consequence of disease or genetic factors, some peoples' retinas contain only rods. Let us consider such an individual's capacity for wavelength discrimination.

The absorption spectrum of the rods is redrawn in Fig. 8.2a. Suppose that a subject whose retinas contain only rods is presented with two flashed patches of monochromatic light, side by side, one of which

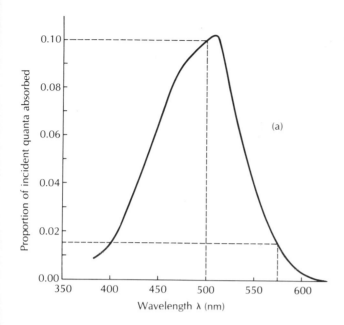

Fig. 8.2 **(a) The absorption spectrum of rhodopsin. This curve has an unfamiliar shape because the scale on the vertical axis is linear, instead of the usual logarithmic one. The linear scale is used here to simplify the numerical illustrations in the text. (The data plotted here are identical with those plotted the more usual way in Fig. 5.6.) (b) When two patches of light are flashed, one of wavelength 500 and the other 575 nm, the table indicates the numbers of quanta absorbed by rhodopsin from each patch.**

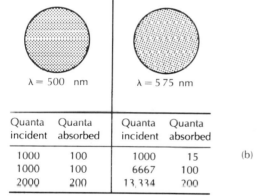

λ = 500 nm		λ = 575 nm		
Quanta incident	Quanta absorbed	Quanta incident	Quanta absorbed	
1000	100	1000	15	(b)
1000	100	6667	100	
2000	200	13,334	200	

delivers 1000 quanta at 500 nm to his retina and the other 1000 quanta at 575 nm. From Fig. 8.2a it is evident that 100 quanta from the 500-nm patch will be absorbed and 15 quanta will be absorbed from the other patch. This condition is represented in the top row of the table in Fig. 8.2b. Since the two patches have different effects on the retina, it is possible, in principle, for the subject to tell the two patches apart.[1]

[1]A real subject might not actually be able to tell these two patches apart. He would not even see the patches unless all the viewing conditions were optimal, since the intensities that happen to have been chosen are very low. For this example, however, it is only important that he *could*, in principle, tell them apart.

Now suppose that the intensity of the 575-nm flash were increased to 6667 quanta, while the 500-nm flash remained at 1000 quanta. The 500-nm patch would still produce 100 absorptions but now the 575-nm patch will also produce $6667 \times 0.015 = 100$ absorptions (line 2 of the table in Fig. 8.2b). If the intensity of the 500-nm patch were increased to 2000 quanta, a new intensity for the 575-nm patch could be found such that the numbers of quanta absorbed from the two patches are again equal (13,334 quanta, line 3, Fig. 8.2b). In general, given any intensity of one of the patches, an intensity can be found for the other patch such that the numbers of quanta absorbed are equal.

Now let us combine this with a crucial assumption. The wavelength of an incident quantum determines the likelihood that it will be absorbed by a visual pigment molecule, but if a quantum *is* absorbed, we will assume that it produces exactly the same effect on the pigment molecule regardless of its wavelength. Each absorbed quantum isomerizes a pigment molecule, and the isomerization and its consequent effects on the visual system are identical, regardless of what kind of quantum happened to produce the isomerization. It will be shown in Chapter IX that this assumption is almost certainly correct. (The differences in energy among absorbed quanta of different wavelengths are manifested in negligible differences in the temperature of the receptors.) Therefore, in the example under discussion, when the intensities of the two disks are in the proper ratio, the disks will have effects on the visual system that are identical in every respect except their locations, and there is no way for the subject to tell them apart on the basis of his visual information. The two patches really are different, both in the numbers of quanta radiating from them and in the wavelengths of the quanta, but the subject's visual system loses the information that they are different, and he cannot discriminate between them.

Two particular wavelengths, 500 and 575 nm were arbitrarily chosen in the preceding example, but exactly the same analysis could be applied to any pair of wavelengths at all. In general, then, a subject whose retinas contain only rods can discriminate between two patches of different wavelengths unless their intensities happen to be in a particular ratio, the inverse of the ratio of the heights of the rod absorption spectrum at each wavelength. If the intensities are in that ratio, he cannot make the discrimination.

In order to say that a subject has *wavelength discrimination* and in order to use that term sensibly, we must be able to show that he can discriminate between two patches strictly on the basis of wavelength. That is, he must be able to discriminate two patches of different wavelengths, *regardless* of any other dimensions, such as intensity. Using the term in that way, we must conclude that a subject whose retinas contain only rods cannot have wavelength discrimination.

A subject's visual system can be tested for this property simply by presenting him with two patches of light of differing wavelength, one of which is adjustable in intensity. If it is possible to find an intensity of the adjustable one such that he cannot discriminate between the two patches, it may be said that he cannot discriminate between those two wavelengths; and if such an adjustment can be made for all possible pairs of wavelengths, then it follows that he has no wavelength discrimination. Such a subject is called a *monochromat,* and his state is called *monochromacy*. (If it is further known that his defect stems from the fact that the only working receptors he has are rods, he is called a rod monochromat.)

The term "monochromat" is a somewhat confusing one. The roots of the word mean "single color," and it might be expected, then, that a monochromat sees everything as the same color. To use the term this way is very misleading, however, because a subject with monochromatic vision may very well tell you that one of the patches is yellow and other is green. If he has no way of knowing what the relative physical intensities of the patches are, his color names will bear no consistant relation to the wavelengths of the patches, but he still may use the color names. If you want to, you can say that he isn't *really seeing* any colors, but if he argues with you, you have no grounds to stand on other than to say what has already been said, namely that his color names are not reliably related to the wavelengths. It is probably safest to say of a monochromat that he may see colors, but that he has no *wavelength* vision, his system having lost all information that might be present in the stimulus concerning its wavelength.

(If the subject does have information about the relative intensities of the stimuli, he may well give color names that are reliably related to the wavelengths, so long as the intensities do not happen to be in the one critical ratio. For example, he may be able to label correctly the colors of flowers, because there is a consistent relationship between the intensities and the wavelengths of lights reflected from most ordinary garden flowers and he has learned, for example, to call the brightest flower yellow. However, if he were shown a garden in which the yellow tulips were coated with a paint that reduced their reflectance but did not change the wavelength composition of the reflected light, he would probably call them red or blue.)

Given the assumption that all absorbed quanta have identical effects on the visual pigment, it follows that if all of the receptors in an individual's visual system have identical absorption spectra, that individual must necessarily be a monochromat.[2] His visual system loses all the information that is carried exclusively by the wavelengths of the quanta striking his retina, and it is therefore impossible for him to make discriminations or to 'use color names that are reliably related to the wavelengths of the stimuli. It is not necessary that all his receptors be rods. For example, he might have the normal complement of rods and cones in his retinas, but if all of those receptors contained the same pigment, be it rhodopsin or one of the pigments normally found in cones (and if the physical shapes of the different receptors did not influence their absorption spectra), he would be a monochromat.

DICHROMACY Suppose that a subject's retinas contained two kinds of visual pigment whose absorption spectra were different, and these pigments were isolated in different receptors, so that one class of receptors contained only one of the pigments and the other class contained only the other pigment. Figure 8.3 is a plot of the absorption spectra of two such classes of receptors, A and B. These spectra have been drawn so that there is no overlap between them. If this subject were presented with patches of light, one at λ_1 and the other at λ_2 and if their intensities were adjusted properly, he would not be able to discriminate between them, for exactly the same reasons that applied to the monochromat. In general, he would not be able to discriminate between two patches on the basis of their wavelength whenever the two wavelengths both fell under the same absorption curve. However, if one patch delivered a wavelength lying under the curve labeled A, say λ_1, and the other one lying under B, say λ_3, it would, in principle, be possible for him to discriminate the patches no matter what the relative intensities were, provided that the rest of his system is capable of maintaining the separation between the outputs of systems A and B. (This proviso will be discussed later.) This subject would therefore have a rudimentary form of wavelength discrimination.

The curves in Fig. 8.3 do not overlap, but there are, in fact, no known instances where this condition actually obtains.[3] A more general case, and one that is actually found in the retinas of some humans and lower animals, is represented in Fig. 8.4a. Here, the absorption spectra of the two classes of receptors are different, but they overlap to

[2]Unless his macular pigment is unusually dense or he is wearing trick glasses, as discussed later.

[3]The probability that a quantum will be captured by a pigment molecule never falls to zero. There is some finite percentage of quanta absorbed at any wavelength. Therefore, any two or more real absorption spectra actually overlap at all wavelengths.

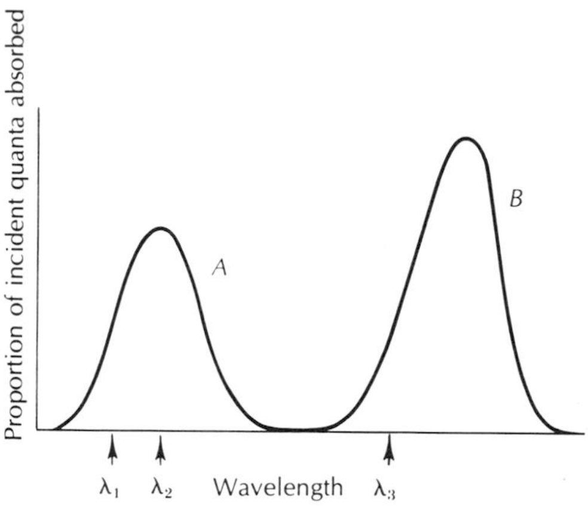

Fig. 8.3 **Absorption spectra for two hypothetical visual pigments.**

a large degree. We will consider this case intensively, since it provides the basis for understanding all forms of color vision.

Suppose that a subject whose retinas contained only receptors with absorption spectra A and B in Fig. 8.4a were presented with two flashed patches of light, side by side, one patch containing 1000 quanta at wavelength λ_1 and the other 1000 quanta at λ_2.[4] This condition is represented in Fig. 8.4b, Condition 1. Of the 1000 quanta of wavelength λ_1, 460 would be absorbed by the A receptors and 150 by the B system. Of the 1000 quanta at wavelength λ_2, 260 would be absorbed by the A system and 410 by the B system. The subject would then be able to tell the two patches apart, because they produce different effects on his visual system. Now suppose we adjust the intensity of one of the patches, say λ_2, in an attempt to make the two patches have the same effect on his visual system, as we did for the monochromat. When the intensity of λ_2 is increased to 1770 [(460/260)×1000] as in Condition 2, Fig. 8.4b, the two patches will result in identical effects on the A system. However, they will still have different effects on the B system, and the subject has thus not lost the information that the two patches are different. If the intensities are adjusted to make the effects of the two patches the same for system B, as in Condition 3, then the patches have different effects on system A, and again the subject may be able to discriminate the patches. There is no setting of the relative intensities of the two patches such that each of them will have the same effect on both the A and the B systems at the same time, and therefore the subject's system as a whole does not lose the information that the two

[4]For this discussion, absorption by nonvisual pigments in the eye will be ignored. Such absorption can change the effective shapes of the absorption spectra of the pigments, but the argument presented here is unaffected. The consequences of nonvisual pigments will be discussed later.

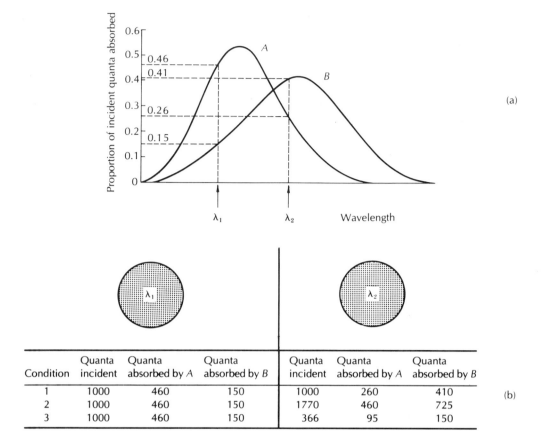

(a)

(b)

Fig. 8.4 (a) Absorption spectra for two hypothetical visual pigments that are like the ones actually found in the eye. (b) The effects of two patches of light of different wavelengths upon a visual system with those pigments. The intensities of the two patches can be adjusted so that the effects are identical on either the A or the B system, but there is no intensity setting such that *both* the A and the B systems are equally stimulated at the same time.

patches are at different wavelengths. In other words, such a system is capable of wavelength discrimination, and is not monochromatic.

Exactly the same argument can be applied to any pair of wavelengths, with one class of exceptions. Suppose that two wavelengths can be found such that the ratio of the heights of the two absorption spectra is the same for both. For example, in Fig. 8.5, A is twice as high as B at λ_1 and also twice as high as B at λ_2. If the wavelengths of two test patches happen to be λ_1 and λ_2, then it is easy to show that there is a setting of the relative intensities of the two patches such that the effects of the two patches will be identical on both the *A* and the *B* systems.

There is considerable evidence that the absorption spectra of the various visual pigments all have similar shapes (when absorption is plotted against wave number, the reciprocal of wavelength), and differ simply by being shifted with respect to each other along the horizontal axis. Further, their shape is such that pairs of wavelengths do exist for which the heights of the two curves are in approximately the same ratio, but these pairs occur at wavelengths where the absorption is very small. That is, the exception cited in the preceding paragraph occurs only in the extreme regions of the spectrum.

However, there is a situation where the exception being discussed becomes very important. Suppose that a subject's visual system contained only one kind of pigment, but there were two classes of receptors in his retina that differed in their overall ability to capture quanta. For example, suppose that one class of receptor had a wider aperature through which quanta were funneled into it, or that there were twice as many of one class of receptor as another, both classes containing the same kind of pigment. Then the absorption spectra of the two classes would be different, but in the special way shown in Fig. 8.6. These curves are such that the ratio of *A* to *B* is the same for *every* wavelength. Thus, a subject whose retinas contained only these two classes of receptors would be a monochromat.

Now let us go back to a consideration of the retina that contains two classes of receptors with different but overlapping absorption spectra. This case is redrawn in Fig. 8.7a. It has already been pointed out that if any one wavelength is presented in one patch and another in the other

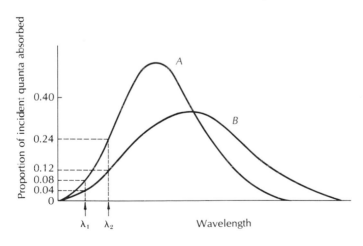

Fig. 8.5 **Absorption spectra for two hypothetical pigments so shaped that the ratio of** *A* **to** *B* **is the same for the two wavelengths** λ_1 **and** λ_2.

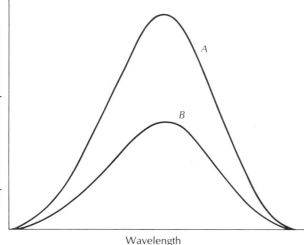

Fig. 8.6 **Absorption spectra for two hypothetical sets of receptors that contain the same kind of pigment, but set** A **catches twice as many quanta as** B **at every wavelength (because, for example there are twice as many** A **receptors).**

patch, the subject can discriminate them regardless of their relative intensities. That is, if he is allowed to adjust the intensity of one of the patches, there is no setting he can find for which the two patches produce identical effects.[5] However, we will now prove that, if one wavelength is presented in one patch and a *mixture* of *two* other wavelengths is presented in the other patch, there are a set of intensities for which the two patches, which are very different physically, will look exactly alike.

Suppose that one patch is lighted by a flash at the wavelength labeled λ_1 in Fig. 8.7, and other by a mixture of λ_2 and λ_3, all of the wavelengths being at the same intensity, 1000 quanta, incident at the retina. "Condition 1" on the chart in Fig. 8.7b indicates the effects on the two systems, A and B, of each of these two patches. The patch containing λ_1 produces 530 absorptions by the A system and 260 by the B system, exactly as they have been determined in the preceding examples. In the other patch, λ_2 results in 360 absorptions by the A system and 110 by B, and, at the same time, λ_3 produces 270 absorptions by A and 410 by B. Now, since we are assuming that each quantum that is absorbed produces the same effect on a pigment molecule regardless of its wavelength, the total effect from the right hand patch on the A system is completely described by the sum of the numbers of absorptions from λ_2 and λ_3. The right hand patch will therefore produce 630

[5]Again assuming a perfect subject for the purposes of this explanation. For example, if both intensities were almost zero, a real subject might not be able to discriminate between the two patches (they would both look dark), but our perfect subject could.

quantal absorptions in the *A* system, and similarly, 520 absorptions in the *B* system. An examination of the "total effect" row in Fig. 8.7b, Condition 1, shows that the effects of the two patches on the visual system will be different.

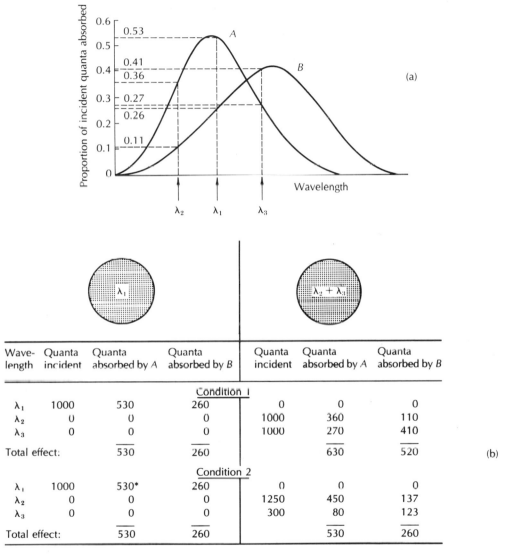

(a)

(b)

Wave-length	Quanta incident	Quanta absorbed by *A*	Quanta absorbed by *B*	Quanta incident	Quanta absorbed by *A*	Quanta absorbed by *B*
			Condition 1			
λ_1	1000	530	260	0	0	0
λ_2	0	0	0	1000	360	110
λ_3	0	0	0	1000	270	410
Total effect:		530	260		630	520
			Condition 2			
λ_1	1000	530*	260	0	0	0
λ_2	0	0	0	1250	450	137
λ_3	0	0	0	300	80	123
Total effect:		530	260		530	260

Fig. 8.7 **(a) Absorption spectra for two hypothetical visual pigments, and (b) the corresponding effects of lights upon a visual system containing only those two pigments. It is always possible to find intensities for λ_2 and λ_3 such that the effects of their mixture (the right-hand patch) will be identical to the effects of λ_1 (left-hand patch).**

However, it is possible to adjust the intensities of *both* λ_2 and λ_3 until the effects of the two patches are identical. The values labeled "Condition 2" represent the results of such an adjustment. The intensities of λ_2 and λ_3 have each been changed. As a result, each of those wavelengths, by itself, still has effects upon the visual system that are different from λ_1, but the total effect of the light in the right-hand patch is identical with the total effect in the left-hand patch, and the two patches must therefore look exactly alike to the subject, even though their wavelength compositions are different and the subject is *not a monochromat.*

The particular intensities for λ_2 and λ_3, Condition 2, were found in the following way: Consider first how each number of absorptions in the table was determined. The number identified by an asterisk in the table is the number of quanta of wavelength λ_1 absorbed by the *A* system when there are 1000 quanta incident on that system. This number is simply the proportion of incident quanta absorbed by the *A* system at that wavelength, multiplied by the number incident.[6] The number absorbed is equal to the proportion absorbed times the number incident, or

$$530 = 0.53 \times 1000.$$

In general,

$$N = P \times Q,$$

where N is the number of quanta absorbed, P is the proportion of incident quanta absorbed (i.e., the absorption coefficient), and Q is the number of incident quanta in the flash.

Now we will assign some subscripts to these quantities in order to label which wavelength and absorbing system they apply to. For example, N_{1A} is the number of quanta of wavelength λ_1 that are absorbed by the *A* system. (In the example in Condition 2, Fig. 8.7b, $N_{1A} = 530$.) N_{1B} is the number of quanta of wavelength λ_1 that are absorbed by the *B* system ($N_{1B} = 260$).

This subscript system will be used for all the quantities. For example, Q_2 is the number of incident quanta of wavelength λ_2.

Now if the effects of the two patches are to be identical, then:

[6]This calculation actually yields the *expected* or average number of absorptions, the particular number of absorptions on any given flash varying about this value, as a consequence of the stochastic nature of light and its interactions with matter. (See Chapter IV.) For the purposes of the present discussion, statistical fluctuations will be ignored.

$$N_A \quad \text{for the left patch} = N_A \quad \text{for the right patch}$$

and

$$N_B \quad \text{for the left patch} = N_B \quad \text{for the right patch}$$

That is, the number of quanta absorbed by the A system in the left patch must equal the number absorbed by the A system in the right patch, *and*, the numbers of quanta absorbed by the B system must also be the same for the two patches.
Since:

$$N_A = N_{1A} \quad \text{for the left patch,}$$

and

$$N_A = N_{2A} + N_{3A} \quad \text{for the right patch,}$$

then

$$N_{1A} = N_{2A} + N_{3A}, \tag{1}$$

and similarly,

$$N_{1B} = N_{2B} + N_{3B}, \tag{2}$$

if the two patches are to have exactly the same effect on the system.
   We have already seen that $N = P \times Q$. Substituting $P \times Q$ for N in Eqs. (1) and (2):

$$P_{1A} \times Q_1 = P_{2A} \times Q_2 + P_{3A} \times Q_3, \tag{3}$$

and

$$P_{1B} \times Q_1 = P_{2B} \times Q_2 + P_{3B} \times Q_3, \tag{4}$$

   We are given that the intensity of λ_1 is 1000 quanta, that is $Q_1 = 1000$, and we are also given all of the values of P, from the curves in Fig. 8.7a. If values of the intensities of λ_2 and λ_3 can be found such that Eqs. (3) and (4) are both fulfilled, then it must be that the two patches will match exactly for that set of intensities.
   The only unknowns in the two equations are Q_2 and Q_3. Given two equations in two unknowns, the equations can be solved for the two unknowns by simple algebra. The resulting expressions are:

$$Q_2 = \frac{Q_1(P_{3B} \times P_{1A} - P_{1B} \times P_{3A})}{P_{3B} \times P_{2A} - P_{2B} \times P_{3A}} \tag{5}$$

and

$$Q_3 = \frac{Q_1(P_{1B} \times P_{2A} - P_{2B} \times P_{1A})}{P_{3B} \times P_{2A} - P_{2B} \times P_{3A}} , \tag{6}$$

Substituting the appropriate values from Fig. 8.7b.

$$Q_2 = 1250,$$

and

$$Q_3 = 300.$$

The important point of this discussion is that a perfect match between these two patches is described by two equations in two unknowns, and, since such equations *can* be solved, the match can be made. In general, then, if a subject's retina contains two different sets of receptors with different but overlapping absorption spectra, he can always make a perfect match between two disks if one of them contains any one wavelength and the other contains any two other wavelengths, and he is allowed to adjust the intensities of two of the wavelengths.

In the preceding example, the two wavelengths that were mixed (λ_2 and λ_3), fell on either side of the single wavelength (λ_1). That is, the wavelength λ_2 was shorter than λ_1, and λ_3 was longer than λ_1. Suppose, instead, that the wavelengths indicated in Fig. 8.8a were presented to a subject whose retina contained only receptors with the two absorption spectra plotted in Fig. 8.8a. The intensity of λ_1 is set at 1000 quanta per second and the subject is to adjust the intensities of the other two wavelengths until the two patches match.[7] These necessary intensities may again be found by Eqs. (5) and (6) as in the previous example, and the result is shown in the chart in Fig. 8.8b.

This result is peculiar, because it requires that a negative number of quanta at λ_3 be added to the right-hand patch, and while that conclusion is correct mathematically, it is impossible physically. However, if, instead of adding a negative 710 quanta of λ_3 to the right-hand patch, 710 quanta are positively added to the left-hand patch, the resulting equations will also yield the proper solution, as shown in the chart in Fig. 8.8c. That is, the effects of the mixture of 1000 quanta at λ_1 and 710 quanta at λ_3 will be identical with the effects of 1280 quanta at λ_2.

The following general statement can, therefore, be made about the wavelength mixture matches of any subject whose visual system contains only two receptor systems with different, but overlapping, ab-

---

[7] In the examples given so far, the stimuli have always been presented in flashes and the "intensity" at each wavelength can then be considered as the total number of quanta in each flash. However, identical arguments apply when the stimuli are presented steadily and the intensity is in quanta per unit of time. In that case the symbol N stands for the number of absorptions per unit of time.

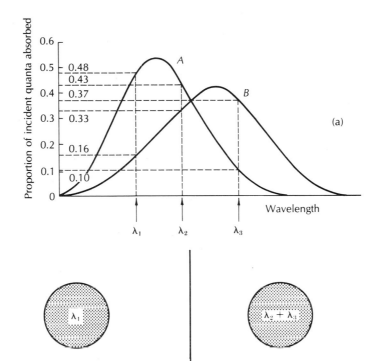

(a)

Wave-length	Quanta incident	Quanta absorbed by A	Quanta absorbed by B	Quanta incident	Quanta absorbed by A	Quanta absorbed by B	
λ_1	1000	480	160	0	0	0	
λ_2	0	0	0	1280	551	423	(b)
λ_3	0	0	0	−710	−71	−263	
Total effect:		480	160		480	160	

Wave-length	Quanta incident	Quanta absorbed by A	Quanta absorbed by B	Quanta incident	Quanta absorbed by A	Quanta absorbed by B	
λ_1	1000	480	160	0	0	0	
λ_2	0	0	0	1280	551	423	(c)
λ_3	710	71	263	0	0	0	
Total effect:		551	423		551	423	

Fig. 8.8 (a) The absorption spectra for two hypothetical visual pigments; and
(b) the corresponding effects of lights upon a visual system containing only
those two pigments.

sorption spectra. If he is given any three wavelengths and permitted to adjust the intensities of two of them, he will be able to find a mixture of two that exactly matches the third one.[8] This condition is called dichromacy, and such a subject is called a dichromat.

TRICHROMACY   Suppose that you are studying the visual system of a particular subject in the laboratory. You present him with two patches of light, one at one wavelength and the other at a different wavelength. If it is possible to adjust the intensity of one of them until he cannot tell the two patches apart, and if this can be done for all pairs of wavelengths that are visible to him, then he is, by definition, a monochromat. It is necessarily true, then, that only one color system is functioning in his visual system under your conditions of testing. That system might contain many different pigments, but it is only one "system" or "channel." (This point will be discussed later.)

If he can discriminate wavelengths regardless of their relative intensities under those conditions, he is *not* a monochromat. Then, if he cannot discriminate between two patches when three wavelengths are mixed in them in the right proportions, he is a dichromat, and his visual system contains two and only two "color" systems that have different absorption spectra.

The typical human subject *is* able to discriminate two patches of light when one of them contains one wavelength and the other a mixture of two wavelengths, regardless of their intensities (so long as the intensities are great enough to stimulate cones). That is, most human beings are neither monochromats nor dichromats. However, if you give the typical subject *four* wavelengths, and he is permitted to mix them in two patches (e.g., λ_1 in one patch and λ_2, λ_3, and λ_4 in the other; or λ_2 and λ_1 in one patch and λ_3 and λ_4 in the other, etc.) and is allowed to adjust the intensities of *three* of them, he will be able to make a perfect match between the two patches. This condition is called trichromacy, and it follows, by extension of the same logic that was applied to dichromacy, that such a subject's visual system contains three color systems.

Figure 8.9 is a plot of a good estimate of the absorption spectra for the three color systems present in a normal human eye, corrected for absorption by nonvisual pigments. (The ways in which these curves have been determined will be discussed below.)

[8]Provided that no pair of the wavelengths are at places on the absorption spectra where their ratios are equal (as in Fig. 8.5).

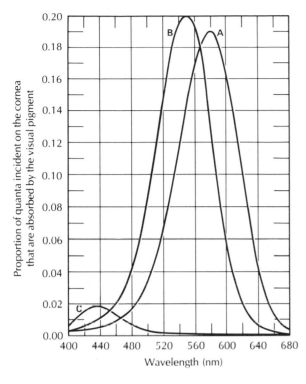

Fig. 8.9 **Estimates of the absorption spectra of the three color-systems in a human subject with normal color vision. These curves are actually derived from psychophysical measurements that agree well with direct physical measurement, such as will be described in the text. They are estimates of the absorption spectra of the visual pigments as seen from the cornea, that is, after having been affected by the absorption of the nonvisual pigments of the eye, and by the relative numerosities of cones containing the different pigments. According to Wald, who published these curves, the C curve is about three times higher in this subject than that in the average subject.** [*From Wald (1964) assuming 80% losses. Copyright, 1964, by the American Association for the Advancement of Science.*]

If a light of wavelength λ_1 is presented at intensity Q_1 in one patch and three other wavelengths, each of adjustable intensity, are mixed together in another patch, the two patches will have identical effects on the subject's system if the strengths with which λ_1 stimulates each of his three color systems are exactly the same as the strengths with which the mixture of the other wavelengths stimulate the three systems.

That is, a perfect match will obtain if:

$$N_{1A} = N_{2A} + N_{3A} + N_{4A} , \qquad (7)$$

and

$$N_{1B} = N_{2B} + N_{3B} + N_{4B} , \qquad (8)$$

and

$$N_{1C} = N_{2C} + N_{3C} + N_{4C} .^{9} \qquad (9)$$

---

[9]Compare these equations with the corresponding ones for the dichromat [Eqs. (1) and (2), p. 167].

The values of these N's (that is, the numbers of quanta absorbed by each of the systems) can be found in the same way as in the dichromatic case described above. When the appropriate $(P \times Q)$'s are substituted for the N's, the result is three equations in three unknowns, the three unknowns being the intensities of the three adjustable wavelengths. A group of three equations in three unknowns is solvable for the three unknowns, and therefore the match is possible for a subject whose retinas contain three different absorption spectra. Conversely, if such a match is possible for a given subject, he must have no more than three color systems (and if matches involving only one or two variables are impossible, that is, he is neither a monochromat nor a dichromat, he must have *at least* three color systems).

If a subject is a trichromat, he can make a match among four wavelengths when he is allowed to adjust the intensities of three of them. This can be restated by saying that, if he is given a mixture of any three wavelengths, each of variable intensity, he can adjust the proportions of the mixture to reproduce the effect of any other wavelength.[10] (In order to avoid elaborate phrasing, it will be assumed in this discussion that the intensity can be adjusted to any positive *or negative* level. The physical implementation of any negative intensity is always simply that the desired intensity is added, with a positive sign, to the other patch, as shown in Fig. 8.8b,c. Later, the implications of this physical limitation, i.e., no negative light, will be examined.)

It follows that if a trichromat is provided with a mixture of any three wavelengths, each of adjustable intensity, he can make a perfect match not only to any other wavelength, but also to any *mixture* of wavelengths at all. Any single wavelength in a patch will produce a particular number of quantal absorptions by each of the three color-systems, and these numbers can be exactly duplicated by the proper mixture of any other three wavelengths. In general, the effects on a trichromatic visual system of any patch of light can be completely described by stating the effects of the patch on the three color systems, and those effects can also be produced by the mixture of any three wavelengths, when their intensities are properly adjusted.

COLOR BLINDNESS If a person's body contains no device that can convert quanta of light into biological activity, he is blind. The word "blind" means that he is

---

[10]This generalization is correct except for the special case in which one of the three mixed wavelengths can be perfectly matched by a mixture of the other two. For that case, three equations in three unknowns reduce to two equations in three unknowns, and are therefore no longer solvable for all values of the unknowns.

unable to use the information about the world that is contained in quanta of light. If the subject's visual system contains only one class of receptors, he is not blind, but he *is* said to be totally *color*-blind, and this means that he is unable to use information contained in the *wavelengths* of quanta, although he does assimilate information conveyed by differences in the rates at which quanta are radiated or reflected from objects. Specifically, for a totally color-blind subject, it is possible to find two patches of light that are physically different, in that they radiate different wavelengths to his eyes, but that he is unable to tell apart. His visual system has therefore lost the information that the two patches are really different.

A subject whose retinas contain two different color systems, as defined above in the discussion of dichromacy, is also color-blind. He cannot distinguish between two patches that are physically different when one contains one wavelength and the other contains the correct mixture of two other wavelengths. His system does not lose wavelength information so completely as does a monochromatic system, but a very large amount of wavelength information is lost.

Similarly, the trichromatic system loses an enormous amount of wavelength information. Two patches that are utterly different in wavelength composition can be made to be completely indistinguishable to the normal subject. Thus, normal human beings are really very color-blind.

Examine Fig. 8.10 (see the color insert). The two areas in this figure are each composed of inks that reflect different sets of wavelengths to the eye. Assume, for the sake of this discussion, that each kind of ink reflects only a single wavelength, the red ink reflecting 640 nm, the green 550 nm, and the orange 610 nm. (That is a good enough approximation for the present discussion. The consequences of the fact that each kind of ink really reflects a set of wavelengths will be discussed later.) Prop the book open to Fig. 8.10, light it with an ordinary light bulb (not fluorescent nor sunlight) and look at it from across the room. The two disks will then approximately match. When the figure is far enough from your eyes, the aberration, diffraction, and scatter of light within the eyes blur each small square so much that quanta from neighboring squares are superimposed at the retina, and the result is a mixture of 640 and 550 nm in the top disk. Obviously, if the proportion of one class of squares is increased, for example, if a greater percentage of the squares in the upper disk were red, the effect would be the same (to a distant eye) as increasing the intensity of the 640-nm component relative to the 550-nm component. The proportion of each kind of ink in Fig. 8.10 has been adjusted so that for the normal eye, the mixture of wavelengths in the top patch matches the single one in the lower patch.

The two disks in this figure are very different from each other physically. They reflect completely different sets of wavelengths. However, even to a normal eye, they are indistinguishable (or almost so, depending upon how well this particular figure has been reproduced and upon the particular lamp by which it is being illuminated). Thus your eyes have lost the information that the two disks are different. Your visual system loses much wavelength information; you are only a little less color-blind than those people whom we usually call color-blind.

This fact, that the normal human visual system is extremely color-blind is of enormous practical significance. Virtually every object in the world reflects a complicated combination of wavelengths to the eye. For example, ordinary grass in sunlight reflects a mixture of wavelengths with the relative intensities represented in Fig. 8.11. The numbers of quanta absorbed by each of the three color-systems in a normal eye can be calculated for a subject looking at this mixture of wavelengths (i.e., grass) in the following way: At every wavelength, the value of the reflectance curve is multiplied by the height of the spectral sensitivity curve of the A system, and all of these values are added up to give the total effect of grass in sunlight upon the A system (just as in

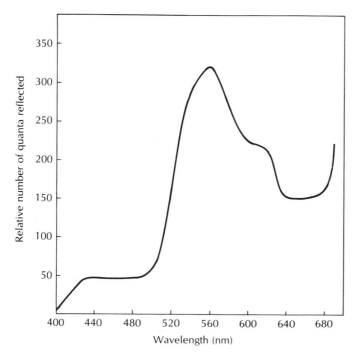

Fig. 8.11 **The spectral reflectance of grass in sunlight. This curve is the product of the reflectance of green grass** [from Krinov (1947)], **and the irradiance of direct sunlight at sea level** [from Moon (1940)] **corrected from energy units to quanta.**

the preceding examples where mixtures of wavelengths stimulate the eye). Then the same procedure is repeated for the B and C systems. These three numbers (the numbers of quanta absorbed by each color system), then, completely describe the wavelength information introduced into the visual system by a patch of grass. Suppose, now, that a printer wished to reproduce a picture of grass. He might select three wavelengths to be used as primaries. When they are mixed in the proper proportions, say by printing small dots of each wavelength, they will produce effects on the three color-systems that are the same as those produced by grass, and their mixture will therefore look just like grass.

In this example, we must consider negative intensities with some care. If the mixture that matches grass requires that one of the primaries have a negative intensity, the reproduction obviously can not be produced. However, it is possible to find a set of primaries such that no negative values will be needed to match most of the colors of objects, such as grass (see below for an explanation). Therefore, the printer need only use those few kinds of inks in order to reproduce the colors of most objects.

WAVELENGTH MIXTURE SPACE It may help in understanding what is involved in color reproduction if the information about human color systems that has already been presented in this chapter is examined in a different form. Plots of the absorption spectra of the retinal color systems, such as the ones in Fig. 8.12a, clearly represent the effects of various wavelengths of light *on the pigments*. However, such plots are not an efficient way of presenting the effects of mixtures of wavelengths on the visual system as a whole. The effects of lights on the visual system of a dichromat can be much more efficiently described by a two-dimensional plot, one dimension being the effect on one of the color systems and the other dimension the effect on the other system. The effects of any patch of light on the normal (trichromatic) visual system can similarly be described by a three-dimensional plot.

Absorption spectra and the corresponding two-dimensional plot for a dichromat are shown in Fig. 8.12a. The following procedure was used to derive the plot in Fig. 8.12b from that in Fig. 8.12a. We must again assume that all quanta absorbed by a pigment have identical effects on that pigment. Now suppose, for example, that 1000 quanta of wavelength 560 nm are incident on the retina. From Fig. 8.12a, 165 of them will be absorbed by the A system and 193 by the B system. Those

Fig. 8.12 (a) (top) Absorption spectra of the color
systems of a dichromat;
and (b) (bottom) the cor-
responding wavelength
mixture space. The two
absorption spectra are two
of the three curves found
in the normal eye, A and
B in Fig. 8.9.

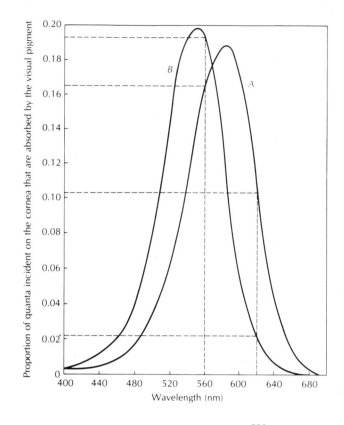

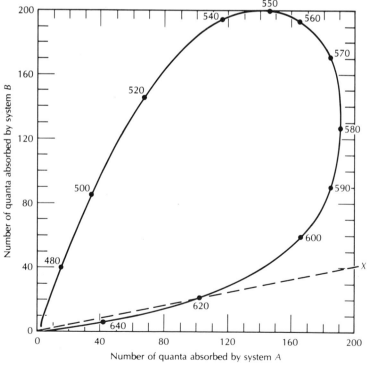

two effects, on the A and on the B systems, are represented by the point labeled "560" in Fig. 8.12b. This point represents the effects on the A and the B systems of 1000 quanta at 560 nm. A thousand quanta at 620 nm result in the absorptions of 102 and 21 quanta by the A and B systems, respectively, and this point is labeled "620" in the figure. When such points are plotted for all wavelengths, the intensity at each wavelength being held constant at 1000 quanta, the oblong shape in Fig. 8.12b results. We will call this curved shape a *spectral locus*.

Now suppose that a flash of 2000 quanta (or a steady light at 2000 quanta per second) at 620 nm is presented. This will produce twice as strong an effect on each system, an effect represented by the point labeled X. Point X lies along the line connecting "620" with the origin, and is twice as far from the origin as "620." (If the lights were so intense that they bleached an appreciable proportion of the pigment, then twice as many quanta would not result in twice as many absorptions, and X would not be twice as far from the origin as "620." However, since lights so intense that they bleach an appreciable proportion of the pigment are rarely encountered, the present linear simplification is acceptable for most viewing conditions.) In general, the effect of any intensity at a given wavelength is represented by a point somewhere on the straight line from the origin through the point on the spectral locus that represents that wavelength, and the distance of the point along the line is proportional to the intensity of the light.

Suppose, now, that two wavelengths, λ_1 and λ_2, each at an intensity of 1000 quanta, are mixed together in a patch. The point labeled "1" in Fig. 8.13a represents the effects of λ_1 by itself on the A and the B systems. Similarly, point "2" represents the effects of λ_2. When the two lights are mixed, the total effect on the two color systems may be found as follows: The effect of the two wavelengths on the A system is the sum of each of the individual effects. That is, the total effect on A is $N_1 + N_2$, $140 + 34 = 174$. Similarly, for the B system the total effect is $37 + 80 = 117$. Therefore, the total effect of the mixture of λ_1 and λ_2 is represented by the point ($A = 174$, $B = 117$), which is labeled "(1 + 2)" in Fig. 8.13a.

There is a simple graphical technique for determining the effects of any particular mixture of wavelengths, such as the point "(1 + 2)." To understand it, we will back up a little. Figure 8.13b is a graphical representation of the way in which the point "1" in Fig. 8.13a was found. The arrow along the horizontal axis is the effect on the A system of 1000 quanta at wavelength λ_1. The length of this arrow is determined by the height of the absorption spectrum of the A system at wavelength λ_1 multiplied by the intensity of the light. Similarly, the vertical arrow

Fig. 8.13 **Finding the effects of a mixture of two wavelengths on the eye of a dichromat. See the text for explanation.**

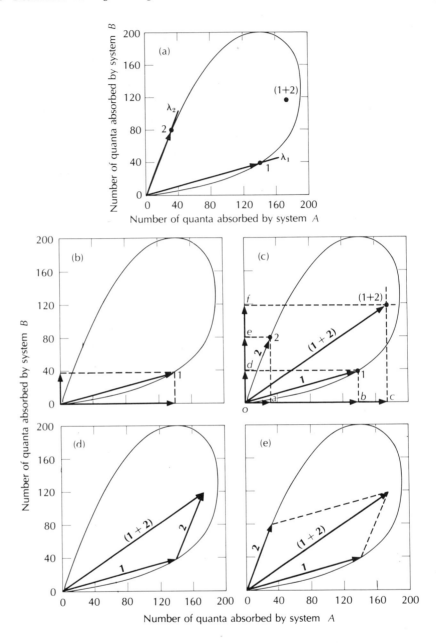

in Fig. 8.13b is the effect of the same light on the B system. The effect of this light on *both* systems can be found by drawing the vertical and horizontal dashed lines to find the point labeled "1." The effect on both systems may also be represented by an arrow from the origin to the point labeled "1." For the rest of this discussion, the effects of lights on retinal systems will be represented by arrows such as this one.

Arrows, when used symbolically in this way, are called *vectors*.[11]

The point "(1 + 2)" in Fig. 8.13a was found by adding together the effects of each of the lights on each of the systems. This operation is represented graphically in Fig. 8.13c. The effects of λ_1 plus λ_2 on the A system are found by adding the effect of λ_2 on the A system (vector **oa**) to the effect of λ_1 on the A system (vector **ob**). This addition is done simply by adding the length **oa** to the end of **ob**, and the result is the effect **oc**. Likewise, the effect of the mixture on the b system is **of**, which is **od** added to the end of **oe**. The single vector that represents the effect of this mixture upon both systems is then found by drawing a vertical line from c and a horizontal line from f; the point where those lines meet is point "(1 + 2)," and the arrow from the origin to that point is the vector (**1 + 2**).

Exactly the same result may be achieved by simply adding the vectors **1** and **2** end to end, maintaining their directions, as shown in Fig. 8.13d, or by completing the parallelogram as in Fig. 8.13e. All of these techniques are equivalent, and are called vector addition.

The point "(1 + 2)" from Fig. 8.13 is redrawn in Fig. 8.14. It lies on the line connecting the origin with some other wavelength, λ_3. There-

[11]In the text, vectors will be represented by boldface type.

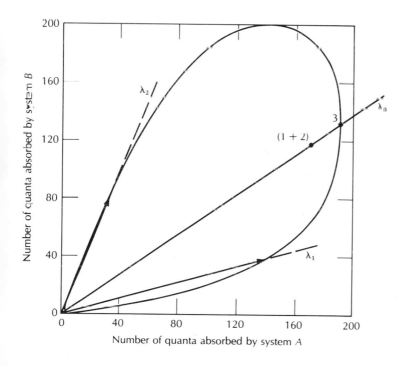

Fig. 8.14 **The point "(1 + 2)," from Fig. 8.13, lies on the line labeled λ_3, and is 312/350 of the way from the origin to the spectral locus. Therefore, the mixture "(1 + 2)" is perfectly matched by $1000 \times 312/350 = 892$ quanta at λ_3.**

Number of quanta absorbed by system B

Number of quanta absorbed by system A

fore, if a second patch of light is introduced that contains slightly fewer than 1000 quanta at λ_3, this second patch would produce effects on systems A and B that are identical to the effects of the mixture of λ_1 and λ_2, and the two patches would match exactly.

The number of quanta of wavelength λ_3 at point $(1 + 2)$ is simply:

$$Q_3 = 1000 \times \frac{[0 - (1 + 2)]}{(0 - 3)},$$

where $(0 - 3)$ is the length of the line from the origin to the point labeled 3, and $[0 - (1 + 2)]$ is the length of the vector $(\mathbf{1} + \mathbf{2})$.

$$Q_3 = \frac{1000 \times (3.12 \text{ inches})}{(3.50 \text{ inches})}$$

$$Q_3 = 892$$

Thus, if a dichromatic subject whose absorption spectra are those plotted in Fig. 8.12a were presented with two patches of light, one delivering 1000 quanta at λ_1 plus 1000 quanta at λ_2 and the other patch delivering 892 quanta at λ_3, he would be unable to discriminate between the two patches.[12] This result is simply a graphical restatement of the algebraic expressions discussed on pages 166 through 168.

Now consider the converse. Suppose that 1000 quanta at wavelength λ_1 (Fig. 8.15a) are presented in one patch, and two other wavelengths of adjustable intensity, λ_2 and λ_3, are mixed in a second patch. From the diagram in Fig. 8.15a, it can be seen that, when the intensity of λ_2 is set at 1700 quanta and the intensity of λ_3 at 133, the effects of the mixture will be plotted on the same point as was the effect of λ_1, and the two patches will match exactly. (The vector sum of 1700 at λ_2 and 133 at λ_3 equals the vector for 1000 at λ_1.)

Given a patch of, say, 1000 quanta at λ_1, *any* two primaries might have been chosen to match it. That is, the actual wavelengths of λ_2 and λ_3 might have been chosen from anywhere in the spectrum, and the same procedure could be applied, yielding a match. In other words, the system represented in the diagram is dichromatic. For example, suppose that the two wavelengths chosen as primaries were those labeled λ_3 and λ_4 in Fig. 8.15b. Since the point representing 1000 quanta at λ_1 lies above both of the lines representing those primaries, a negative amount of one of them must be used in order to achieve a match. That simply means either that the effects of one of the primaries

---

[12]If the two patches produce identical effects on each kind of receptor, the information that the two patches are really different is lost, and no matter how the rest of the subject's nervous system is organized, there is no way that it can recover that information.

Fig. 8.15 **A given light (wavelength λ_1, intensity 1000 quanta) can be matched for a dichromat by finding the correct intensities of two other wavelengths. In (a), the two wavelengths to be mixed, λ_2 and λ_3, lie on opposite sides of λ_1, and positive amounts of each are required. In (b), the two wavelengths to be mixed, λ_3 and λ_4, lie on the same side of λ_1, and a negative amount of one (λ_3) is required.**

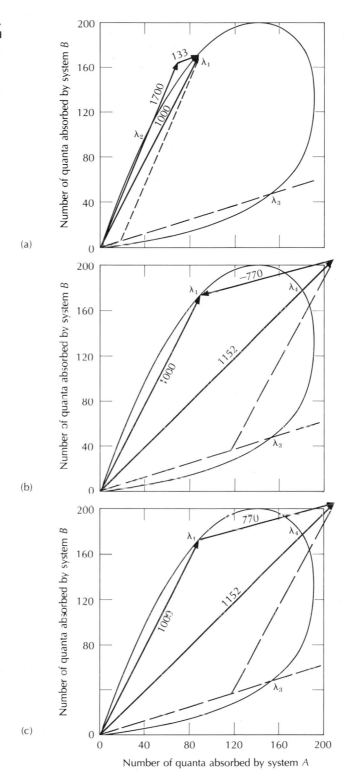

must be subtracted from the effects of the other (as shown in Fig. 8.15b by the fact that the λ_3 vector points in the negative direction), or that it must be added to the patch containing λ_1 (as in Fig. 8.15c).

If the lines representing the two primaries fall on either side of the point to be matched, then it is always true (for the dichromat) that the necessary intensities of the primaries will both be positive. For example, if the two primaries to be mixed together are λ_1 and λ_3 in Fig. 8.15c, then any patch that is represented by a point within the area between their two lines can be matched by positive mixtures of the two primaries.

COLOR REPRO-DUCTION FOR THE DICHROMAT

The two-dimensional space in Fig. 8.15 contains the effects of any mixture of wavelengths on a dichromat's visual system. Obviously, any mixture of wavelengths whatsoever will produce some particular magnitude of effect on the A system and some other magnitude of effect on the B system, and a point representing any such pair of effects can be found somewhere in the two-dimensional space of the diagram. If one wished to make a good color reproduction of any object by the proper mixture of just a few "primary" wavelengths, he could locate the point in the wavelength mixture space that represents the effects of the object on the two color systems, and then determine the intensities of the primaries required so that the vector sum of their effects on the two systems is plotted at the same point in the mixture space.[13]

The first problem, then, is to locate the point in the mixture space that corresponds to the object. To illustrate this process, we will locate a point corresponding to the hypothetical object represented in Fig. 8.16a. This is a plot of the spectral composition of the light reflected from an imaginary substance when it is illuminated with white light of some particular intensity. It reflects only three wavelengths and absorbs the rest.

The spectral locus in Fig. 8.16b is again that for the dichromat whose absorption spectra were shown in Fig. 8.12a. To determine the effects of the stimulus of Fig. 8.16a on this subject's system, the following procedure is followed: The stimulus delivers 1000 quanta per second at 540 nm, and the effects of that component of the stimulus are

---

[13]In the preceding discussion, wavelength-mixture space has been used to map perfect matches. That is, if two mixtures of lights produce effects that plot at the same point in the wavelength-mixture space, those two mixtures are indiscriminable, and two patches each containing one of the mixtures are said to match each other perfectly. Obviously, if the printer wishes to make a perfect reproduction of some *object*, he must reproduce its shape, smell, etc. So the words "matching" and "reproducing" as used in that context have a less rigorous meaning than the "perfect match" that is referred to in other sections of this book.

Fig. 8.16 (a) The reflection spectrum of a hypothetical object. (b) The object's effect on a dichromatic visual system is the vector sum (1 + 2 + 3). (c) The visual effect of this object can be matched by the proper mixture of λ_a and λ_b.

(a)

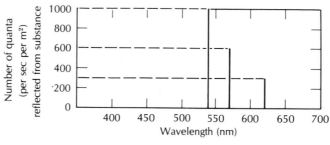

(b)

(c)

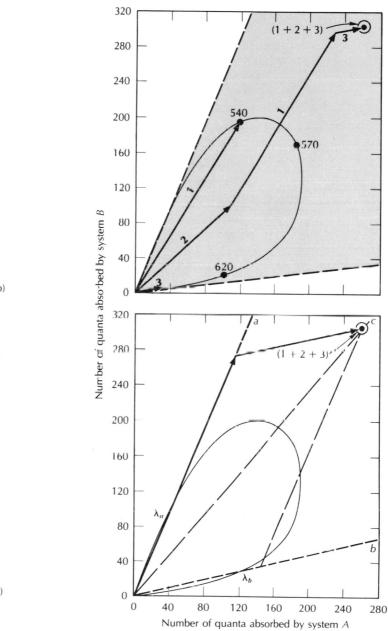

thus represented by vector **1**. The effects, on his system, of the stimulus component at 570 nm are represented by vector **2**, which lies on the straight line plotting the effects of various intensities at 570 nm, and which is 600/1000 of the way from the origin to the (1000 quanta) spectral locus. The effects of the 620 nm component are represented by vector **3**. The effect of the mixture of all three components is then simply the sum of the three vectors.

It is obvious from this example that the effects on the dichromat's visual system of any mixture of wavelengths whatsoever can be found by simply adding up the vectors corresponding to each of its spectral components, and that procedure will result in a point somewhere in the mixture space.[14] Furthermore, the point representing *any* mixture (of nonnegative intensities) must lie somewhere in the space that is shaded in Fig. 8.16b. The borders of the shaded space are the lines tangent to the spectral locus and running through the origin. They are the lines representing wavelengths whose relative effects on the *A* and the *B* systems are in the greatest and the smallest ratios. The effects of every wavelength on the visual system lie somewhere in the shaded space, and therefore, the effects of all mixtures of wavelengths must also lie somewhere in that same shaded space.

The lines *oa* and *ob* in Fig. 8.16c represent the effects of two wavelengths near the two ends of the visible spectrum. While there are some wavelengths that lie outside these lines, the visible light reflected from any object is likely to consist mainly of wavelengths lying between the limits set by the lines. Therefore, the effect on this visual system of almost any object is representable as a point somewhere in the space between those two lines. Certainly, if the light is monochromatic and its wavelength lies between λ_a and λ_b, its effects on systems *A* and *B* will be represented somewhere in that space, and the vector sum of *any* set of wavelengths between λ_a and λ_b (of positive intensity) must also fall within that region. Therefore, if a printer were manufacturing a set of color reproductions that were to be seen only by the kind of dichromats whose color systems are as diagrammed in Fig. 8.12, and if he could find just two kinds of ink, one reflecting λ_a and the other λ_b, he could, by mixing them in the right proportions, produce an effect lying along a line from the origin through the desired point (e.g., line *oc* in Fig. 8.16c). If this picture is viewed under an illumination with varying intensity, its effect will move along the line *oc*, and when the intensity

---

[14]The reflection spectrum in Fig. 8.16a is discontinuous. That is, only a few discrete wavelengths are reflected. Most real objects actually reflect continuous spectra, and the vector sum must either be found by integration, or else the spectrum must be approximated by a set of discrete wavelengths, whose vectors are then added.

is correct, the effect will fall on top of the effect of the hypothetical object. That is, the reproduction will match the object. (This is true only for the dichromat. The reproductions would not be perfect for any person whose visual system contained two color systems with different absorption spectra from those plotted here, or that contained more than two color systems.)

Thus, in principle, if a printer can find two inks that reflect wavelengths near the two extremes of the visible spectrum, he can reproduce almost any color to the eye of a dichromat.[15] However, in practice, color reproduction is seriously limited. To understand this limitation, consider how a printer might actually attempt to manufacture a reproduction.

To simplify the conditions somewhat, assume that the picture to be produced is printed on paper that is perfectly black, that is, which absorbs all of the light incident on it, and that the printer has two inks available, each of which reflects 100% of the incident light at one wavelength and 0% at all other wavelengths. The inks are laid down in tiny dots that never overlap. If an area is entirely covered by dots reflecting λ_1 (Fig. 8.17), 100% of the incident illumination at that wavelength will be reflected; if it is half covered by λ_1 dots, 50% will be reflected, etc. If the area is covered, for example, in the following way: 20% covered by λ_1, 40% covered by λ_2, and therefore 40% black, and if the incident light has an intensity of 1000 quanta per second per unit area *per nanometer* (i.e., the same amount of quanta at every wavelength), then the reflected light will contain 200 quanta per second at λ_1 and 400 at λ_2, and its effect on the visual system may be plotted as the open circle in Fig. 8.17.

By varying the proportions of the area covered by the two kinds of inks, the printer can, in this way, produce any effect within the shaded area of Fig. 8.17, and, thus, can perfectly reproduce the color of any object whose effect is also plotted in the shaded area.

In this example, it has been assumed that the inks reflect monochromatic light, but all real inks reflect a broad mixture of wavelengths. Thus it may appear that the physical structure of real inks invalidates the foregoing analysis. However, in that analysis, the monochromaticity of the inks was assumed merely for convenience of phrasing. In fact, it makes no difference at all whether the inks reflect a narrow or a broad band of wavelengths, for the following reason: It has already

---

[15] If the printer were allowed to use negative intensities, he could of course reproduce *any* color (for the dichromat). Since he can neither subtract light from his product nor add light to the object he is trying to reproduce, he is restricted to positive intensities, and thus to the area between the lines in the wavelength mixture space that represent the primaries he has chosen.

Fig. 8.17 **Representations, in a dichromat's wavelength mixture space, of color reproduction using λ_1 and λ_2 as primaries. When the light illuminating the page delivers no more than 1000 quanta per second per unit of area at λ_1 and λ_2 (and the inks are perfect, as explained in the text), the resulting mixtures all fall within the shaded triangle.**

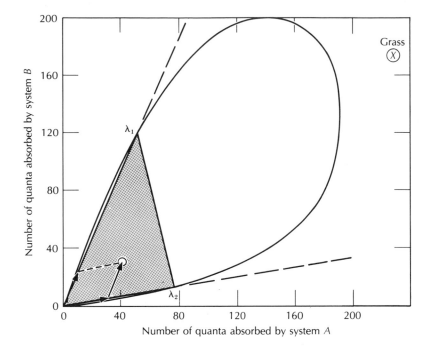

been shown that a single wavelength can always be found that perfectly reproduces the effect on the visual system of any mixture of wavelengths (for the dichromat). Therefore, the effect of an ink that reflects any broad band of wavelengths will be exactly the same as the effect of an ink that reflects some particular monochromatic light. In the example under discussion, it does not matter whether the printer uses two inks that reflect monochromatic lights of λ_1 and λ_2, or two inks that reflect broad bands whose effects on the visual system are the same as monochromatic lights at λ_1 and λ_2. Thus, the broadness of the spectral reflectance of available inks does not limit the printer's ability to make perfect reproductions for the dichromat.

Examination of Fig. 8.17 suggests the nature of the printer's real limitation. On the one hand, it is desirable to choose two primaries that are as close as possible to the ends of the visible spectrum, so that they will enclose, between them, as large a part of the mixture space as possible. (Any objects whose effects are represented outside the area enclosed by the primaries cannot be matched by any mixture of positive amounts of the primaries.) On the other hand, the more extreme the wavelength, the weaker is its effect on the visual system (as represented by the fact the distance from the origin to the spectral locus becomes shorter near the ends of the visible spectrum). Therefore, mixtures of wavelengths from extremes of the spectrum will only be able to match objects whose effects are near the origin. The significance of this point is explained as follows.

The intensity of the light reflected from any part of a printed page equals the intensity of the light incident upon the page multiplied by the reflectivity of that part of the page. Therefore, it is obvious that the light reflected from a reproduction can be made arbitrarily intense if the intensity of the source that illuminates the picture can be made arbitrarily great. If a reproduction can be viewed under an arbitrarily intense light, the appearance of any object whose effect lies between the lines representing the primaries can be perfectly reproduced. However, if the picture is to be viewed under ordinary lighting conditions, a serious problem arises.

Suppose that one wished to reproduce grass in sunlight for a dichromat. Let us assume that the reflectance curve in Fig. 8.11 was used to determine the effects on his two systems, resulting in the point labeled "grass" in Fig. 8.17. Obviously, if the printer used an ink that reflected about the same proportions of the incident light at all wavelengths as grass does, and if the picture were viewed in sunlight, the reproduction would be faithful. However, if the printer tried to reproduce grass by the use of the two primaries λ_1 and λ_2 and the pictures were viewed in sunlight, the effects on the two color systems would always fall short of the point labeled "grass." In general, the more extreme the primaries, the worse this effect becomes, and the printer must compromise. Extreme primaries permit him to reproduce objects reflecting a broad range of wavelengths but the reproduction is faithful only if the illumination on the picture is appreciably greater than the illumination on the object to be reproduced.

The printer (or painter, color film maker, etc.) can overcome this problem either by compromising on his choice of primaries and using wavelengths farther from the extremes of the visible spectrum, or he can use more than two primaries, adding, say, a third one from the middle of the spectrum. The problems of reproducing colors for trichromatic vision are essentially the same (as will be explained soon), and in practice the printer both compromises on the wavelengths of his primaries and uses more of them.

THE COLOR MIXTURE SPACE OF THE TRICHROMAT The dichromat's color vision is two-dimensional; two intensity adjustments are required to match the effects on his system of any wavelength or mixture of wavelengths. For this reason, the space containing all possible dichromatic matches may be represented graphically in two dimensions. All possible matches lie in a plane. The monochromat's color vision may be similarly represented in one dimension; that is, all possible matches lie on a line. Normal color vision is three-dimensional, and must be represented by a three-dimensional diagram, in which all possible matches are represented by a volume. The procedure for making such a plot is a simple extension of the dichromatic, two-dimensional diagram, but it is much harder to present on a flat page. Therefore, many of the features of trichromatic vision will be discussed here by making analogical extensions from the discussion of dichromacy.

Figure 8.18 is a representation of the three-dimensional effects on the normal human visual system of lights of all the wavelengths in the visible spectrum (all at an intensity of 1000 quanta per second). It is derived from the three curves in Fig. 8.9 in just the same way as Fig. 8.12b was obtained from Fig. 8.12a. For example, consider 1000 incident quanta at wavelength 460 nm. From the absorption spectra of the three color-systems (Fig. 8.9), the following effects can be determined: The stimulus results in the absorption of nine quanta by the system labeled A, 21 by B, and 13 by C. The dot on the line labeled 460 represents that point in the three-dimensional space. If the intensity at that wavelength were changed, the new effect on the three systems would fall somewhere on the straight line from the origin through the point, the dashed line in the figure. The effects of all other wavelengths are similarly represented by lines running from the origin through the corresponding wavelength points on the spectral locus. To locate the effects of any mixture of wavelengths, the effect of each wavelength alone may be plotted as a vector whose direction is determined by the wavelength and whose length is determined by the intensity at that wavelength. The various vectors are then added, end to end, preserving their angles, just as in the dichromatic case. The point at the end of the combination of all these lines represents the effects on the visual system of that mixture. Any other mixture whose effects when similarly plotted, are coincident with that point, must necessarily be indistinguishable from the first mixture.[16]

Suppose, now, that the three wavelengths 450, 550, and 620 nm are mixed together, in adjustable intensities, in one patch. The effects of all possible mixtures of those three primaries are included within the triangular pyramid determined by those wavelengths, as indicated in

[16] The spectral locus plotted in Fig. 8.18 represents the vision of one particular subject. Subjects differ, especially in the relative heights of the C system, and thus, this particular plot does not accurately represent every person with normal vision.

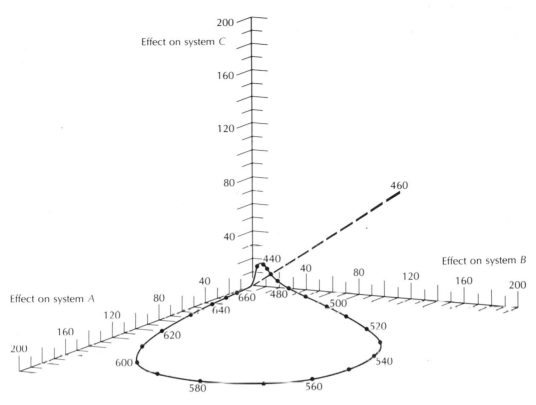

Fig. 8.18 The (three-dimensional) wavelength mixture space of a normal human. The solid curve is the 1000 quanta spectral locus, and the effects of any wavelength upon the three color-systems are represented by a straight line from the origin through the corresponding point on the spectral locus. Note that the *C* system makes a relatively small contribution, even though the subject whose vision is represented by this plot is reported to have an unusually *sensitive C* system. This figure is the three-dimensional representation of the curves in Fig. 8.9 [*from* Wald (1964)]. The scales on the axes are the numbers of quanta incident on the cornea that are absorbed by each system, assuming 80% losses in the media of the eye and interstices between receptors.

Fig. 8.19. Any other wavelength or mixture of wavelengths that falls within this volume may be matched exactly by the proper mixture of these three primaries. Note, however, that there are a number of wavelengths that lie outside of the pyramid. Those wavelengths, and some mixtures that contain those wavelengths, cannot be matched by any mixture of positive amounts of the primaries in Fig. 8.19. Thus, if primaries are chosen that enclose as much as possible of the volume included within the tangents to the spectral locus, the colors of most objects can be reproduced.

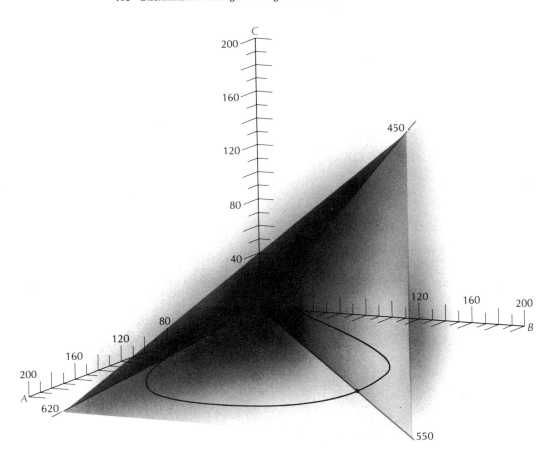

Fig. 8.19 **The shaded pyramid contains the effects of every possible combination of lights at wavelengths 450, 550, and 620 nm, and, conversely, any mixture of wavelengths whose effects lie within the pyramid may be exactly matched by the appropriate combination of 450, 550, and 620 nm.**

For example, the effects of grass illuminated at various intensities are represented by the dashed line labeled "grass" in Fig. 8.20. (This line is the one through the origin that contains the point found by adding the effects of all the wavelengths plotted in Fig. 8.11.) If the grass to be reproduced is lighted at some particular intensity, its location will be at some point, say the point labeled X in Fig. 8.20. In Fig. 8.21 (see the color insert), three classes of dots are present (plus black to permit the adjustment of their intensities), and the vectors representing the effects of those three sets of dots are represented in Fig. 8.20. When they are combined at the retina, by lighting the page well and then looking at it from across the room, their effect is the same as that of grass, as indicated by the vector addition in Fig. 8.20.

Using just these three classes of dots in various proportions, a match can be made to any color whose location lies within the pyramid they determine, providing that the intensity of light incident on the set of dots is sufficient. (Under dim illumination, only grass-under-dim-illumination can be perfectly replicated.)

The volume enclosed by these three classes of dots does not include all possible colors. By choosing the three inks carefully, the volume they enclose can be increased, but as the wavelengths reflected by the inks approach those needed to enclose the volume of all possible colors, their effects upon the visual system become very weak, and, as a consequence, the only objects whose appearances they can faithfully reproduce are those that are illuminated much more dimly than the reproduction itself is illuminated. By using more than three inks, the volume enclosed by the primaries may be increased, and therefore, the printer often uses more than three colors of ink. Each additional

Fig. 8.20 **The vector addition of the effects of the three classes of dots in Fig. 8.21, resulting in an effect upon the visual system that is identical with that of grass.**

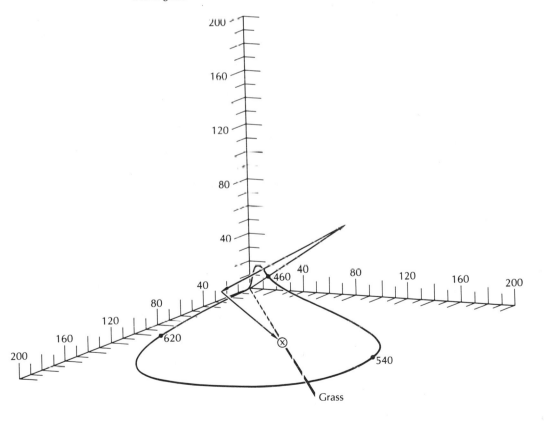

color, however, adds greatly to the printing expense. For this reason, the funnies are cheap but not very colorful (they usually use only three primaries, and the primaries are not very close to tangents of the spectral locus), while very high quality color reproductions use many primaries, some of which are fairly close to the tangents of the spectral locus, and are, correspondingly, very expensive.

The extent of the color-blindness of the normal human visual system is represented clearly in Fig. 8.20. There are an infinite number of physically different combinations of wavelengths and intensities all of which are represented by the same location in this diagram, and thus all will have identical effects on the normal subject's system. Certainly, grass in sunlight delivers to the eye a very different array of quanta than does the corresponding combination of the three primaries in Fig. 8.20 and yet the normal visual system is blind to this extreme difference. If the normal retina were not at all color-blind, the only ways that a printer could produce a patch of color that looked like grass would be either to extract the pigments from grass and paste them on the paper or to make a new pigment that had exactly the same spectral reflectivity as grass (that is, the plot in Fig. 8.11), and if he wanted to reproduce the sky, the first alternative would be very difficult.[17]

The human auditory system contains an enormous number of sound receptors. These receptors are imbedded in a structure within the ear that is driven into vibration by sound, and it is likely that the extent to which an auditory receptor is excited depends upon its amplitude of vibration. If the amplitude of vibration of any single auditory receptor is measured as a function of the wavelength or frequency of the stimulating sound, the results will be as plotted in Fig. 8.22. The structure of the receptor and its surroundings are such that each has a "spectral" sensitivity curve roughly like that of a light receptor in the retina. However, in the ear, each receptor, or each small group of receptors, has a different "spectral" sensitivity, and the entire array of auditory receptors contains an enormous number of different classes of receptors, each class having its sensitivity curve peaking at a different wavelength. Figure 8.23 shows the sensitivity curves for a small sample of auditory receptors, and there are many other receptors with curves in between the ones that are plotted.

---

[17]Note, in Fig. 8.18, that the scales on the three axes are all equally spaced. There is no *a priori* reason, other than simplicity, for scaling them equally. (It might even be easier to visualize the shape of the spectral locus if the vertical scale were magnified.) In fact, it would be interesting to determine whether or not it is possible to change the relative magnifications of the three scales in such a way that all pairs of points whose effects are just distinguishable from each other are equally far apart in the wavelength mixture space. [A related operation is discussed in a series of articles by MacAdam, e.g., MacAdam (1965).]

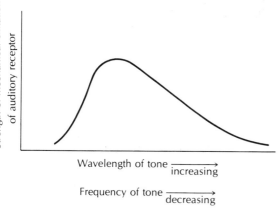

Fig. 8.22 **The "spectral sensitivity" curve of a typical auditory receptor in the ear.**

In other words, the auditory system is equivalent to a visual system with an almost infinite number of color systems. The auditory system is essentially "infinite-chromatic." It is impossible to find, say, three different tones which, when combined, sound indistinguishable from some other single tone. In fact, any chord always sounds different from any single note (except perhaps at extreme frequencies or amplitudes). A trained subject can, in fact, identify the individual tones that make up a chord, but no subject, no matter how much training he has, can ever identify the particular wavelengths that are mixed together in grass. Wavelength information is present as the light passes through the media of the eye, but the media contain no machinery for detecting it, and, at the very first stage where quanta are detected, that is,

Fig. 8.23 **"Spectral sensitivity" curves of auditory receptors at six different locations in the ear.** [*From von Bekesy (1949).*]

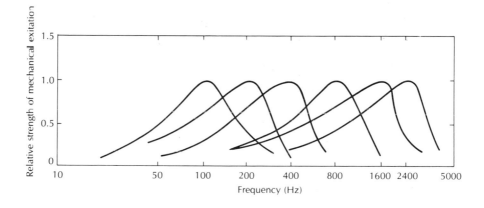

where the quanta isomerize pigment molecules, a large part of the wavelength information is lost. It can never be recovered by the remainder of the subject's system.

A CURE FOR COLOR-BLINDNESS   Until the present, virtually no mention has been made in this discussion of the experience of color — what colors look like, and what names we give to them. That topic will be discussed extensively in the following chapters. In fact, the most meaningful definition of color-blindness must be given without reference to the experience of colors. Color-blindness has been discussed in some detail here in terms of the subject's ability or lack of ability to distinguish between physically different mixtures of lights.

If we agree that even the normal person is quite color-blind, it is very hard to develop a sensible definition of color blindness that involves color experience. We would have to imagine some color experiences that none of us has ever had and then say that, since we have not had them, we are color-blind. That kind of exercise might be entertaining, but a discussion in terms of discriminations between physically differing stimuli leads to a number of very useful conclusions. For example, in the following discussion, we will see how a monochromat can be changed into a dichromat or trichromat, and how, in fact, normal human vision can be made much less color-blind. The procedures for producing such changes are derived from considerations of wavelength discrimination. It is unlikely that they would ever have been developed from consideration of the *experiences* of colors.

Making a Monochro-mat Dichromatic   A subject is defined as a monochromat if, when he is presented with two patches, each containing one of two arbitrarily chosen wavelengths, it is possible to adjust the intensity of one of them so that he cannot tell the two patches apart. However, that statement, as it is phrased, is internally inconsistent, since, if there are *two different* patches, they must, by definition, be distinguishable on *some* basis. For example, if the two patches are side by side, the subject will see one to the right of the other, and hence they are discriminable. What is really meant by the statement is that he cannot tell the two patches apart *solely* on the basis of wavelength.[18] This can be tested by decid-

[18]The definition of a monochromat can also be rectified by saying that he cannot discriminate one patch from another if he cannot tell that anything has changed when one patch is substituted for the other. The arguments presented here are consistent with either wording.

ing, randomly, which wavelength will appear in which patch on each of a set of trials, and then by seeing if the subject's responses are correlated with the locations of the wavelengths. For example, we can ask him to say which patch is green, or which patch is x. On each trial, if he says that the patch containing the shorter wavelength is, say, x, he is told that he is correct; if he says the other patch was x, he is told he is wrong. Then, over a long series of trials, he can be said to be able to discriminate the two patches on the basis of wavelength alone if, for all possible values of the intensities for the two patches, his responses are correlated with the locations of the two wavelengths. If the subject is a monochromat, there will be a set of pairs of intensities such that his responses are random with respect to the locations of the two wavelengths. That is really what is meant by saying that he cannot tell the two patches apart.

Now suppose we perform the experiment just described, and find that our subject cannot distinguish the two patches when one of them contains 1000 quanta per second at 500 nm and the other contains 1375 quanta at 525 nm (this would be the case if the subject's retina contained only rods). (We would also find pairs of intensities at all other wavelengths that were indistinguishable, but we will only consider these two in this example.) Now we give this subject a pair of glasses in which the left lens is perfectly transparent but the right lens absorbs quanta of different wavelengths differentially. Such a pair of glasses and their absorption spectra are shown in Fig. 8.24. The solid curve in Fig. 8.25 is the absorption spectrum of the rods in each of the subject's eyes (corrected for absorption by the media of the eye) and is, therefore, the absorption spectrum of the rods in the left eye when the glasses are being worn. The absorption spectrum of the right eye when the glasses are in place is shown by the dashed curve. That is, if monochromatic lights of various wavelengths were delivered to this eye through the glasses, the percentages of quanta, at each wavelength, that are actually absorbed by the visual pigment must be corrected for the absorption of the glasses. At very short wavelengths, the glasses absorb little, and the net absorption by the receptors of the right eye will be almost the same as if the glasses were not present. At a wavelength of 500 nm, the glasses absorb 40% of the quanta and therefore the absorption by the receptors will be only 60% of what it would have been without the glasses. In general, to obtain the dashed curve, the solid curve is multiplied, at each wavelength, by the proportion of light transmitted by the right lens.

The absorption curve for the left eye wearing glasses has a different shape from the corresponding curve for the right eye wearing glasses.

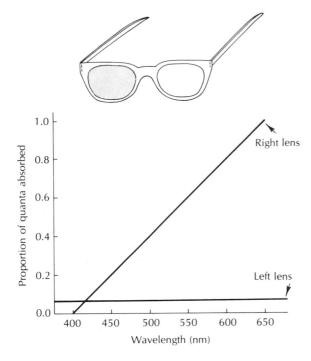

Fig. 8.24 **A pair of glasses in which the left lens is perfectly transparent and the right lens has the absorption spectrum plotted below.**

Therefore, the subject's visual system (including the glasses now) contains two systems with different but overlapping spectral sensitivity curves, one system in the right eye and the other in the left. Now, if we perform wavelength discrimination measurements, we will find that the subject will no longer be a monochromat. (He will be a dichromat.) For example, suppose that we put 1000 quanta at 500 nm in one patch and 1375 quanta at 525 nm in the other. These two patches will have identical effects on his left eye (110 quanta absorbed from each patch), but if he closes that eye and looks with the right one (while he is wearing the glasses), the two patches will have different effects (66 quanta absorbed at 500 nm and 55 at 525 nm). In general, there is no pair of intensities that will make the two patches match in both eyes, and thus the subject will always be able to discriminate between the patches. Whenever the patches are set to look the same to his left eye, he can close that eye and look with his right. He will then learn to call the wavelength that stimulates his right eye more strongly the shorter wavelength. If the intensities are adjusted to stimulate his *right* eye equally, then he can look with his left eye, and will learn to call the one that stimulates the left eye more weakly the shorter wavelength. It is impossible to find any setting of the two intensities such that he is unable to tell them apart, and he is, therefore, not a monochromat.

On the other hand, if this subject, wearing his glasses, is shown two patches one of which may contain any wavelength and the other a mixture of any two wavelengths, it is possible to adjust the intensities of two of the wavelengths so that the patches are indiscriminable to both eyes. This fact follows from exactly the same analysis as was presented in the preceding section on dichromacy. In other words, the subject, wearing the glasses, is a dichromat.

It is true that the information that allows this artificial dichromat to distinguish wavelengths is manifested in a different way in his nervous system than is the information available to a natural dichromat, but that is irrelevant to the present discussion. The point to be emphasized here is that a subject with only one kind of visual pigment, but who wears the glasses described above, exactly fits the definition of a dichromat.

A monochromat can be made into a dichromat in several different ways, differing in the manner by which the information about wavelength differences is manifested in the nervous system. For example, the top half of each spectacle lens might be clear, while the bottom half is tinted in the same way as the right lens was tinted in the previous example. Then the subject would need to tilt his head, causing the light that enters his pupils to pass alternately through the top and the bottom halves of the glasses, in order to distinguish the patches. If the glasses were made in three areas instead of two, each area having a different spectral absorption curve, then the monochromat who wears them would become a trichromat.

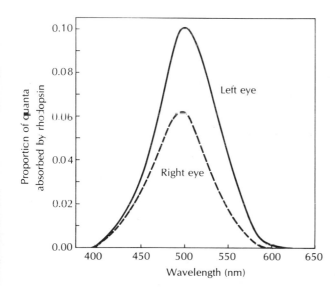

Fig. 8.25 Absorption spectra of the two eyes-plus-glasses, when wearing the glasses shown in Fig. 8.24.

Improvements over Normal Color Vision   If a subject with normal (trichromatic) color vision wears the glasses in Fig. 8.24, his vision will be tetrachromatic (four-color). He will be able to distinguish between mixtures of wavelengths that look identical to the normal subject. For example, he could easily distinguish between the two colored areas in Fig. 8.10. A distillery painted to match the green of the hills (for normal observers), would not be a safe camouflage to use against revenuers wearing these special glasses. If the still matched the woods when seen through the clear parts of the glasses, it would probably not match when seen through the tinted parts. If the federal agent could be equipped with glasses whose absorption spectra were unknown to the still operators, the only safe camouflage would be either to paint the rig with pigments extracted from the local vegetation or to cover it with living leaves.

PROBLEMS   8.1 Prove that a monochromat wearing a *neutral* filter over one eye will still be a monochromat. (A neutral filter transmits the same proportion of incident quanta at all wavelengths.)

8.2 Prove that a natural dichromat will manifest *tri*chromatic vision (not tetrachromatic) if he wears a tinted glass over one eye.

8.3 If you give a monochromat the right kind of glasses, he will fit the definition of a trichromat. "Yes", you say, "but, of course, he is still really color blind. Just putting on the glasses doesn't let him see colors." Can you prove that a monochromat who is experienced at wearing these glasses really doesn't *see* colors?

8.4 Plot the spectral locus in wavelength mixture space for a protanope, that is, a subject from whose retinas the long-wavelength sensitive pigment (A in Fig. 8.11) is absent.

8.5 In Fig. 8.17, prove, either by algebra or by plotting representative points, that the line between λ_1 and λ_2 should truly be a straight line.

8.6 It would obviously be useful in certain industries (e.g., textiles) to have a device that, when shown two colored-patches, would indicate whether or not they would match for a normal observer. How would you make such a device?

IX ◇◇◇ COLOR VISION II – RETINAL COLOR SYSTEMS

THE wavelength mixture matches obtained from 99% of the population are characteristic of trichromacy. Given a patch containing a mixture of any three wavelengths, the typical subject can make the patch exactly match any other wavelength or mixture of wavelengths if he is allowed to adjust the intensities of the three wavelengths to any values, including negative ones. It was explained in Chapter VIII that this behavior, trichromacy, would be evident if the subject's visual system contained three color-systems whose absorption spectra overlapped but were shifted with respect to each other along the wavelength dimension. A three-dimensional space was derived that represented the effects of any mixture of wavelengths on the entire system. For the particular examples in Chapter VIII, this derivation depended upon the absorption spectra of the three color systems, and upon two assumptions: that every quantum absorbed has an equal probability of isomerizing a pigment molecule, and that all isomerizations within any given color system have identical effects on that system. These assumptions will be evaluated later in this chapter.

POSSIBLE TRICHROMATIC MECHANISMS

The state of trichromacy, as defined by its characteristic psychophysical data (from wavelength mixture matches), implies that the trichromat's visual system contains three different "color" systems. The following is a brief discussion of some physiologically reasonable ways in which such color systems might be constructed.

A very simple trichromatic system would be one in which there are three classes of cones, each class containing a different pigment, the pigments having different but overlapping absorption spectra. If the neural structures in the visual system were able to preserve the information contained in the signals from each of the three classes of receptors, then the individual would be a trichromat. This simple system was the one used in the preceding chapter to illustrate trichromacy. If the visual system were really organized in this way, the spectral sensitivity curves of the three color-systems would depend simply upon the absorption spectra of the three types of pigment. (The spectral sensitivity curves would be the absorption spectra corrected for any absorption by the media of the eye.)

This simple arrangement, in which each of three kinds of pigment is isolated in a separate class of receptors, is only one of several structures that would yield trichromacy. As an example of a different kind of trichromatic structure, consider the following retina: The visual pigment in all receptors is identical; each receptor also contains, interposed between the front of the eye and the visual pigment, a droplet of a nonvisual pigment, that is, one that absorbs light but does not send signals to the nervous system. Now if there were three kinds of these nonvisual pigments, each with a different absorption spectrum, and if each cone contained only one of these three kinds of nonvisual pigments, the system would be trichromatic. Here, while the visual pigments all have identical absorption spectra, the absorption spectrum of each receptor as a whole would be the product of the absorption spectra of the visual and the nonvisual pigments, and there would thus be three classes of receptors, having different absorption spectra. (This system is closely related to the system that was discussed in the preceding chapter for making a monochromat into a dichromat.)

There is no evidence to suggest that the human receptors contain nonvisual pigments of the kinds required by this model, and it is very unlikely that the human visual system operates in this way. However, there is a real possibility that such a system is present in birds, amphibians, and reptiles. The retinas of some of these animals contain droplets of colored oil that lie immediately in front of the receptors. For example, Fig. 9.1a is a photomicrograph of the retina of the chicken. This retina contains three classes of oil droplets with the absorption spectra shown in Fig. 9.1b. There is quite good evidence that birds are not monochromatic. (Whether or not they are trichromatic or tetrachromatic is not known.) Certainly, the presence of three classes of oil droplets is sufficient to account for trichromacy if the bird's neural structures are capable of retaining the wavelength information available at the receptors. (It appears from Fig. 9.1 that many receptors contain no oil droplets. Therefore, the bird should be capable of tetrachromacy.[1])

Another mechanism that would permit trichromacy is the following: In Chapter VII, a theory was presented that may explain the Stiles-Crawford effect. This theory proposes that there is a funneling of light within the cones as a consequence of their shape and of the refractive indices of the media forming the cones and their environment. The extent of the funneling must depend upon the relationship between the shape of a cone and the wavelength of the incident light, both because the index of refraction of a medium depends upon the wavelength of the incident light, and because the dimensions of cones are of the same order as the wavelength of light, producing wavelength dependent resonances (which are beyond the scope of this book). Therefore, if all of the receptors in the retina contained the same kind of pigment, but if the *shapes* of the cones fell into three different classes, then the retina would contain cones with three different absorption spectra.

Brindley and Rushton (1959) performed a very simple experiment that conclusively disproves this hypothesis for human vision. They stimulated subjects' retinas with two sources of monochromatic light. Light from one source entered the eye normally, that is, through the pupil, while the other source was focused on the white of the eye, the sclera. The intensity of the light passing through the sclera and thus passing into the retina backwards was made comparable to that of the light falling on the retina from the other, normally viewed, source. Since the light entering the pupil was incident on the cones in the normal direction but the trans-scleral light passed through the cones in the reverse direction, any differential funneling would be expected to

[1]Some writers have concluded "that the oil droplets have no part in the mechanism of color vision" (Duke-Elder, 1958, p 632). However, the logic upon which this conclusion is based (that animals without colored droplets have color vision) is not convincing.

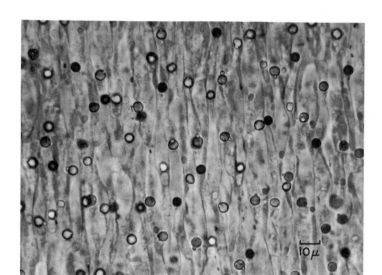

(a)

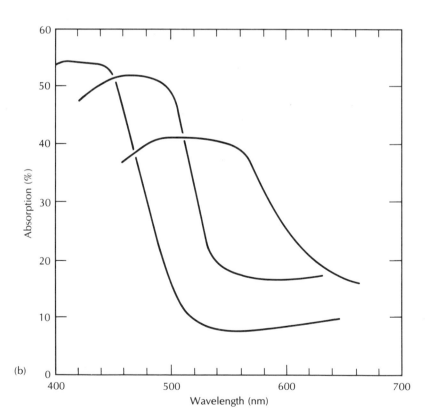

(b)

produce different effects on the absorptions of the two lights. However, Brindley and Rushton found that the light of normal incidence was essentially the same color as the trans-scleral light when the two were at the same wavelength. Therefore, differential funneling can only explain human trichromacy if the funnel happens to be constructed in such a way that it is equally effective regardless of the direction of the incident light, and there is no evidence to support the idea that the cones are symmetrical funnels.

From Brindley and Rushton's experiment, it is also clear that the kind of filtering that occurs in the retinas of chickens cannot be responsible for trichromacy in humans, since light entering the cones from the back of the eye would not be filtered by the oil droplets. However, their experiment does not eliminate the possibility that each class of cones contains visual and nonvisual pigments mixed up together, the different classes differing only in the spectral absorption characteristics of the nonvisual pigments.

The facts of trichromacy are psychophysical, and therefore involve a lot more of the elements in the subject than just his retina. The facts do require that the normal retina contains *at least* three different sensing systems as described above, since with fewer than three, the discriminations that normal subjects do make would not be possible. However, the normal human retina might contain any number of different kinds of pigments greater than three, each isolated in a different class of cones, and still the entire system could be trichromatic. For example, suppose there were six different kinds of visual pigments, each in a separate class of cones, which we will call classes *a, b, c, d, e,* and *f.* If all of these classes of cones fed their outputs to the ganglion cells indiscriminately, that is, if each ganglion cell were equally strongly coupled with cones from all these classes, then the system as a whole would be monochromatic. The complete system could be described by saying that there is only one color-system, its absorption spectrum being the composite of the absorption spectra of all six pigments.

On the other hand, if cone types *a* and *b* fed to one set of ganglion cells, *c* and *d,* to another, and *e* and *f* to a third set, and if the outputs from these three sets of ganglion cells were independently represented throughout the rest of the visual system, then the subject would be tri-

Fig. 9.1 (a) A photomicrograph of the retina of the chicken. Each gray globule is a droplet of oil that is interposed between the front of the eye and the visual pigment in a cone, the different colors of globules appearing in this photograph as different shades of gray. (b) The absorption spectra of the classes of globules. [*From Wolkin (1966) "Vision," Thomas, Springfield, Illinois. Reproduced by permission of the publisher.*]

chromatic. His visual system would contain three sets of color-systems, the absorption spectrum of each being a combination of the absorption spectra of two pigments. (If all of the outputs of all three classes of ganglion cells fed indiscriminately to a single kind of neuron later in the system, then the subject would obviously be a monochromat.)

In general, then, the facts of trichromacy do not necessarily indicate the number of visual pigments present in the retina. They only indicate that there are three systems whose outputs are at least partly separated throughout the visual system, the systems having different but overlapping spectral characteristics.

One more point should be clarified here. The spectral characteristics of the three color-systems that were analyzed in Chapter VIII were taken as the absorption spectra of three pigments (corrected for absorption by the media of the eye). The explanation of the resulting wavelength mixture space was then based upon the assumption that each quantum isomerizes one pigment molecule. That assumption, however, is not a necessary one. What is really of interest is not the exact numbers of absorbed quanta, but rather the *effect* or *action* on each system of quanta incident at each wavelength. If, for example, *two* quanta must be absorbed at all wavelengths in order to produce one isomerization, then all of the arguments given so far apply equally well.

Suppose, however, that the number of quanta that must be absorbed in order to produce a single isomerization varied with the wavelength. Then the curves showing the *actions* of quanta as a function of wavelength (called *action* spectra) would have different shapes from the absorption spectra. In that case, the absorption spectra are no longer the appropriate curves to use in plotting the wavelength mixture space. Instead, the action spectra must be used. In general, an action spectrum is a curve that relates the wavelengths of the incident quanta to the magnitude of their effects on the system under study, and the action spectra are really the ones that determine the kinds of matches that a subject will make.

In Chapter VIII, for ease in explanation, the assumption was made that the number of quanta that must be absorbed per isomerization (the quantum efficiency of isomerization) was the same at all wavelengths, and therefore the absorption spectrum and the action spectrum were taken as identical. Although that assumption is not essential to the arguments presented (the axes of the wavelength mixture space could have been labeled as numbers of isomerizations), there is good evidence, to be presented later, that the assumption is probably correct.

MEASUREMENTS OF THE MECHANISMS OF HUMAN COLOR SYSTEMS The general psychophysical data of trichromacy have been known for a long time [since the 1850's and 1860's, when James Clerk Maxwell (1861) described them]. Because these data are consistent with a number of different possible physiological mechanisms, the different possibilities described above, and many more, have been discussed at great length in the literature. Few if any areas of scientific endeavor include more miscellaneous facts and more confused theoretical discussions than the area of color vision. However, very recently (beginning in about 1957), direct measurements of the spectra of human cone pigments have been published, and these measurements have enormously clarified the confusion of the preceding century. It is now relatively clear that the human retina contains four different visual pigments, a rod pigment (rhodopsin) and three cone pigments. The measurements that have produced this clarification will now be discussed.

Cone Pigments in the Living Human Eye In Chapter V, Campbell and Rushton's device for measuring the bleaching of rhodopsin in the living human eye was described. (See Fig. 5.11, p. 108.) Rushton has used this device, with a few modifications, to make measurements from which the action spectra for bleaching the visual pigments may be inferred. The measurements of the action spectrum of rhodopsin will be described first, since they provide a good introduction to the measurement of the cone pigments.

Action Spectrum for Bleaching Rhodopsin To measure the action spectrum for bleaching rhodopsin, Rushton, in effect, measured the amount of light necessary to bleach 30% of the rhodopsin at a series of different wavelengths (Rushton, 1962, p. 13). The result of this set of measurements is an *action* spectrum for *bleaching,* since it is a measure of the bleaching action of light of various wavelengths upon rhodopsin. Over the visible region, the action spectrum for bleaching is essentially identical with the absorption spectrum of rhodopsin. Therefore, the number of quanta that must be absorbed in order to bleach a pigment molecule is the same regardless of the wavelength of the quanta. Whether each absorbed quantum isomerizes one pigment molecule (which then bleaches, following the sequence described on p. 93), or whether more than one absorption is required for each bleached molecule cannot be determined from these data, but it *is* evident that the quantum efficiency for bleaching rhodopsin is the same at all wavelengths.

A Cone Pigment in a Dichromat

To measure the spectral characteristics of cone pigments, Rushton restricted the measuring lights to the central area of the retina, in a disk 2° in diameter. In that region, cones are plentiful and rods are few.

In his first measurements of the cone pigments, Rushton (1963a) used, as his subject, a protanope, that is, a person whose color vision is a particular form of dichromacy. This form of dichromacy was presumed to be a consequence of the lack of one of the cone pigments, and Rushton's measurements verified that presumption.

Measurements were made first on the dark-adapted fovea as follows: The wavelength of the measuring light was set at some value, the amount of that light that was reflected from the back of the eye was determined, and such determinations were made for various wavelengths of the measuring light that sampled the visible spectrum.[2] Rushton does not present the resulting measurements, since, as will be clear, they are unimportant by themselves. However, to facilitate the present explanation, assume that they came out as shown by the "x's" in Fig. 9.2a. The retinal reflectance as it is plotted here depends upon the way in which light is absorbed by all the pigments that happen to be in the path of the measuring lights, including, for example, blood. The "x's" then really depend upon the absorption spectrum for the central 2° region of the eye as a whole.

After these measurements had been made on the dark-adapted fovea, the eye was bleached by a strong adapting light whose predominant wavelength was about 600 nm. After the adaptation to this light was essentially complete, the measuring procedure described above was repeated, this time on a retina that had been strongly light-adapted. The resulting readings might have been those represented by the small circles in Fig. 9.2a.

The only difference between the conditions under which these two sets of measurements were made was that in one case the eye was dark-adapted while in the other it was light-adapted. Therefore, the differences between the two sets of data constitute a measurement, across the spectrum, of the effects of the *adapting* light, and are very likely a manifestation of the bleaching of visual pigment. Consider, first, the results at 700 nm. There is no difference between the measurements under the two conditions. Therefore, whatever pigment was bleached by the adapting light must have been absorbing negligible quanta at 700 nm. If it were absorbing appreciable quanta at 700 nm

---

[2]While this description of Rushton's procedure is correct in its relevant aspects, his actual procedure was somewhat more elaborate, permitting him to overcome certain difficulties in instrumentation. If the reader is interested in the details of this procedure, he should examine Rushton (1963a).

and then some of it were bleached (i.e., rendered transparent), the amount of the measuring light that would have been absorbed by the eye would have been smaller after light-adaptation, the amount of measuring light reflected would thus have been greater, and the corresponding circle would have been higher than the "x." It can be concluded, then, that the pigment that is bleached by the adapting light absorbs little if any light at 700 nm.

At 605 nm, the amount of light reflected from the fovea changed upon bleaching, and therefore, the pigment that was bleached must have been absorbing quanta at 605 nm before it was bleached. In general, the difference between the "x" and the "o" at each wavelength is

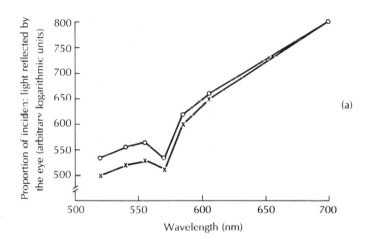

(a)

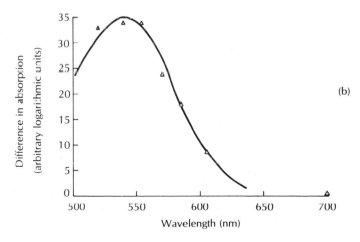

(b)

Fig. 9.2 (a) Hypothetical absorption spectra for the back of the eye before (x's) and after (o's) bleaching. (b) The difference between the two sets of measurements in (a). This is the difference spectrum for bleaching a cone pigment in the eye of a protanope. There are no data at wavelengths shorter than 510 nm because such data were too difficult to obtain, for reasons that are explained in the text. The smooth curve in (b) is the spectral sensitivity curve of a protanope, measured psychophysically by Pitt (1944). [From Rushton (1963a).]

a measure of the extent to which the pigment that was bleached by the adapting light actually absorbed quanta at that wavelength before it was bleached. The curve in Fig. 9.2b is a plot of these differences as a function of wavelength, and is called a *difference* spectrum.

Table 9.1. *A Brief Review of the Kinds of Spectra Discussed*

Absorption spectrum	*The proportion of incident light that is absorbed as a function of wavelength*
Reflection spectrum	*The proportion of incident light that is reflected as a function of wavelength*
Action spectrum	*Any measure of the action of light as a function of wavelength*
Action spectrum for isomerization	*The efficiency with which light isomerizes pigment as a function of wavelength*
Action spectrum for bleaching	*The efficiency with which light results in the bleaching of pigment as a function of wavelength*
Difference spectrum	*The difference between any two of the same kind of spectra (e.g., between two action spectra)*

The difference spectrum in Fig. 9.2b must be identical with the absorption spectrum for the pigment that is bleached by the adapting light if two conditions are met: (1) that the quantum efficiency of bleaching is independent of wavelength, and (2) that the likelihood that a bleached molecule will absorb quanta is constant over the spectrum. Condition (1) has already been explained (p. 205). An example should clarify condition (2). If all the bleached molecules were completely transparent, then the difference spectrum for bleaching would be the same as the absorption spectrum of the bleachable pigment. Suppose, instead, that each bleached molecule absorbed no quanta at wavelengths greater than, say, 550 nm, but at wavelengths shorter than 550 nm, the bleached molecules absorbed just as strongly as the unbleached ones. Under those conditions, the *difference* spectrum below 550 nm would fall to zero (since bleaching would produce no *change* in the amount of light at those wavelengths that is reflected from the retina), but the *absorption* spectrum of the pigment would be nonzero at those wavelengths. In general, any absorption of light by bleached molecules that is not uniform across the spectrum will cause the difference spectrum for bleaching and the absorption spectrum to be different.

There are, as yet, no unequivocal ways to measure the absorption spectrum of the *bleached* pigment in the living eye and thus to overcome this possible error. However, most bleached visual pigments that have been studied in solution are relatively transparent over most of the visible spectrum, absorbing appreciably only in the very short wavelength region. Therefore, it will be assumed for the remainder of this discussion that the difference spectrum is the same as the absorption spectrum for wavelengths greater than about 450 nm, recognizing that this assumption may be in error.

The difference spectrum in Fig. 9.2b was the result of bleaching the eye of a dichromat with strong light at a wavelength of about 600 nm. Rushton then repeated the entire set of measurements, but substituting an adapting wavelength of 500 nm instead of the original 600 nm, and the results were identical. In fact, the results for this dichromat were the same regardless of the wavelength of the adapting light. That result is a very important one, since it indicates that this subject's retina contains only *one* bleachable pigment that absorbs light over the range of wavelengths plotted in Fig. 9.2b. The logic underlying this conclusion is as follows.

First, remember that once a quantum has isomerized a visual pigment molecule, information about the wavelength of the quantum is lost. That is, the molecular condition that occurs after isomerization is the same regardless of the wavelength of the quantum that triggered the isomerization. Then, if there is only one kind of pigment being bleached, the difference spectrum must be the same regardless of the wavelength of the adapting light.

However, if there were two different pigments with different absorption spectra in the bleached region of the eye, the difference spectrum for bleaching *would* depend upon the wavelength of the adapting light. For example, suppose that there were two pigments, the first absorbing quanta maximally at 500 nm and only slightly at 600 nm, while the second absorbed strongly at 600 nm and weakly at 500 nm. The difference spectrum that would result from the bleaching of the pigments by any adapting light would depend upon a combination of the absorption spectra of the two pigments. When the adapting light was at 500 nm, the first pigment would be more strongly bleached than the second, while with a 600 nm adapting light, the second pigment would be more strongly bleached. Therefore, the difference spectrum after bleaching with 500 nm would primarily reflect the absorption spectrum of the first pigment, while the difference spectrum after 600-nm bleaching would be more influenced by the second pigment. Thus, because the absorption spectra of the two pigments are different, the resulting difference spectra must be different.[3]

In general, if the difference spectrum for bleaching is independent of the wavelength of the bleaching light, then all of the pigment that was bleached must have had the same absorption spectrum. Since the difference spectrum of the protanope as measured by Rushton is independent of the adapting wavelength, the protanope's fovea must contain only one bleachable pigment that absorbs quanta in the region of the spectrum studied, and the difference spectrum in Fig. 9.2b is the absorption spectrum of that pigment.

The measurements just described are based upon the bleaching of pigments, but what are really of interest are the *visual* effects produced by lights of various wavelengths, and the relationship between bleaching and visual excitation is not necessarily simple. For example, molecules might be bleached without having any effect on the rest of the visual system, and quantal absorptions might excite the visual neurons without causing the bleaching of pigment (although, if the theory of excitation described in Chapter VI is valid, bleaching *is* a good measure of visual excitation).

To verify the relationship between his measures of bleaching and the visual excitation itself, Rushton performed a series of experiments in which the measures of bleaching could be directly compared with the subject's responses. In essence, he chose a pair of wavelengths and adjusted their relative intensities until they produced identical amounts of bleaching of the foveal pigment, as measured by his instrument. Then he presented these same pairs of wavelengths to the subject, the two wavelengths alternating rapidly, and asked the subject to adjust their relative intensities until the apparent flickering was minimized. Presumably, the two wavelengths then appeared equally bright. He repeated these kinds of measurements over a range of wavelengths, and found that the relative intensities that produced the same amount of bleaching also were those that were equally bright. The data also agree with the sensitivity curve of the protanope measured a different way by a different investigator, plotted as the smooth curve in Fig. 9.2b. This experiment provides a very important confirmation of the hypothesis that the difference spectrum in Fig. 9.2b is really the *action* spectrum (for brightness) for that subject. That is, Fig. 9.2b is a plot of the relative action on the visual system of lights of different wavelengths.

---

[3]Of course, this argument does not hold for sets of adapting lights so intense that they bleach away virtually *all* of each kind of pigment.

The subject on whom these measurements were made was a dichromat, and it is therefore to be expected that his foveas contain *two* visual pigments, rather than just one. Note, however, that Rushton's measurements do not cover the short wavelength end of the visual spectrum. His measurements are made upon the light reflected from the retina and back out of the eye, and only between about 0.1 and 0.01% of the light entering the eye actually emerges from the pupil. This fact, combined with the losses in the measuring apparatus itself, means that in order to get enough light to measure, the light sent into the retina must be intense. If the measuring light is very intense, however, it will, itself, bleach an appreciable part of the visual pigment, and will therefore disrupt the measurements. In other words, these measurements are extremely difficult to perform.

In the short wavelength region of the spectrum, the measurements are especially difficult for a number of reasons. One of the most important ones is that the nonvisual pigments in the eye absorb short wavelengths much more strongly than long ones, and the light available to the measuring instrument is thus very weak. A related difficulty is that short wavelengths scatter more strongly in the media of the eye than do longer wavelengths, and thus fewer of the quanta that are reflected from the retina find their way straight back out of the pupil and into the measuring system. Still another problem is that, while the products of bleaching of visual pigments are transparent in the middle and long wavelengths, "bleached" visual pigment molecules generally absorb light of short wavelengths, obscuring the measurements and making them hard to interpret.

At the present time, these technical difficulties have not been overcome, and reliable measurements have not been made at short wavelengths. Therefore, it is possible that the foveas of the protanope contain a second pigment that absorbs strongly in the short wavelength region of the spectrum and negligibly in the spectral region tested by Rushton. (It will be shown below that this is almost certainly the case.) Thus the fact that Rushton's subject was dichromatic can be reconciled with his measurements showing only one bleachable pigment absorbing light in the region of the spectrum he tested.

The Cone Pigments in the Normal Retina   The filled circles in Fig. 9.3 are Rushton's measurements of the difference spectrum (before and after bleaching) for the fovea of a subject with normal color vision. For these measurements, the wavelength of the adapting light was about 620 nm. (Thus, the curve described by the filled circles represents the difference between the absorption spectrum of the completely dark-adapted retina and the absorption spec-

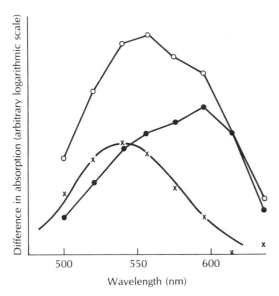

Difference in absorption (arbitrary logarithmic scale)

500   550   600

Wavelength (nm)

Fig. 9.3 **Difference spectra for bleaching the fovea of a normal subject, first with a light of long wavelength (filled circles) and then further with a white light (open circles). The fact that one of the spectra is shifted with respect to the other is evidence that the normal fovea contains more than one bleachable pigment that absorbs light over the range of wavelengths plotted. The differences between the filled and open circles are plotted as x's, and they fit the absorption spectrum of the pigment found in the fovea of the protanope, the solid curve.** [*From Rushton (1958).*]

trum after bleaching with light of long wavelength.) The open circles in Fig. 9.3 represent the corresponding spectrum after subsequent bleaching with a *white* light (that is, a light containing all wavelengths in the visible spectrum).

If the normal fovea contained only a single pigment, then these two spectra would not be shifted with respect to each other along the wavelength dimension. The white adapting light would bleach more of the pigment and therefore yield a higher curve, but not a shifted one. The fact that one curve *is* shifted with respect to the other means that there is more than one bleachable pigment in the normal fovea. The long-wavelength bleaching light evidently bleaches one of the pigments more strongly than the other(s), and the difference spectrum with a long wavelength bleach primarily represents the absorption spectrum of the long-wavelength-sensitive pigment. However, when the bleaching light is white, all of the pigments are bleached, and the resulting difference spectrum (the open circles) is the difference spectrum for the combination of all of the bleachable pigments that are present.

Suppose that the normal human fovea contained two pigments, one of which was the same as the pigment found in the protanope (as plotted in Fig. 9.2b), and the other with an absorption spectrum peaking at longer wavelengths. It is clear from Fig. 9.2b that the protanope's pigment absorbs very little light at wavelengths as long as 620 nm. Therefore, if the normal fovea is flooded with light at 620 nm, any bleachable pigment that absorbs the longer wavelengths may be strongly bleached while the protanopic type of pigment will remain largely intact. This is the state of the retina represented by the filled circles in Fig. 9.3. If, now, after the eye has been adapted to strong light at 620 nm and the measurements taken, it is further bleached with a strong white light, the pigment that had remained after the 620 nm bleach (that is, the protanopic type of pigment) will bleach away as well, producing the new curve represented by the open circles in Fig. 9.3. Therefore, the difference between the solid circles and the open circles should be the difference spectrum of bleaching of the protanopic type of pigment in the normal fovea.[4]

The difference between the two curves is plotted by the "x's" in Fig. 9.3, and the smooth curve in Fig. 9.3 is the absorption spectrum of the protanope's pigment, redrawn from Fig. 9.2b and appropriately scaled. The fact that the 620 nm and the white-bleach curves are shifted with respect to each other is firm evidence that the normal human fovea contains more than one bleachable pigment, and the fact that the x's fall on the curve of the protanopic pigment is good evidence that one of the pigments in the normal eye is the same as the protanope's pigment.

The difference spectrum represented by the filled circles in Fig. 9.3 is the composite spectrum for whatever pigments absorb light at a wavelength of about 620 nm. If there were more than one such pigment present, then changing the wavelength of the bleaching light over the range between 620 and about 750 nm (the longest wavelength that produces measurable bleaching), would produce difference spectra that were shifted with respect to each other along the wavelength dimension, for the reasons already discussed. However, Rushton found that changing the adapting wavelength over this range produced no measurable change in the resulting difference spectrum. It can therefore be concluded that there is only one bleachable pigment present in the normal fovea that absorbs appreciable quanta at wavelengths longer than 620 nm. In general, no matter what wavelengths are used to adapt the human fovea, the resulting difference spectrum is always either the one shown by the filled circles, or that shown by the x's, or some predictable combination of those two. Therefore, Rushton concludes that there are only two bleachable pigments in the normal human fovea that absorb appreciable light over

---

[4]This is strictly true only if the 620 nm light bleached *all* of one kind of pigment and none of the other, and the white light bleached all of the remaining pigment.

the range of wavelengths he can measure. Their absorption spectra are represented by the filled circles and the x's in Fig. 9.3. (There is almost certainly a third pigment as well, which absorbs more strongly in the short wavelength end of the spectrum, but, as explained above, Rushton's technique was not sensitive enough to detect the bleaching of that pigment if it indeed bleaches at all.)

Two further limitations of Rushton's technique should be mentioned: First, as already explained, the difference spectra he measures would not accurately represent the absorption spectra of the pigments themselves if the *bleached* pigment molecules absorbed different wavelengths differentially. Second, it cannot be concluded unequivocally from Rushton's results that there really are two different *pigments* in the fovea. The same result might be obtained if there were only one kind of pigment but it was contained in two classes of cones of different shapes, the two shapes causing differential absorption across the spectrum. If so, what Rushton actually measured was the absorption spectra of two different classes of cones, rather than two types of pigment. However, as explained earlier in this chapter, that is an unlikely possibility.

MICROSPECTROPHO-TOMETRY OF THE HUMAN RETINA

Recently, a technique has been perfected by which the absorption spectra of individual receptors in the human retina may be measured (Marks et al., 1964; Brown and Wald, 1964). At the time of this writing, only a small amount of data have been collected using this technique, but these preliminary data are surely representative of the more refined data that will, no doubt, be published soon. Therefore, the technique and the preliminary data are worth describing here.

No adequate technique has yet been developed that can be applied to the living human retina. However, there are many surgical procedures that require the removal of an eye. When such an operation is to be performed, preparations are made to obtain the retina, relatively dark-adapted and in as fresh a state as possible. This retina, or a small part of it, is separated from the rest of the tissues that form the back of the eye and flattened against a glass plate that is placed under a modified microscope. In the retinal regions a few degrees away from the center of the fovea, the rods and cones are distributed roughly as shown in Fig. 9.4. A very small spot of light is projected backwards through the optics of the microscope and focused in the plane of the retina, and the retina is moved under the spot until the light passes through a single cone (a large circle in the figure). On the other side of

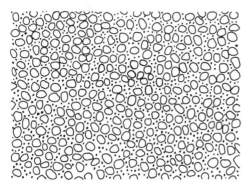

Fig. 9.4 **Outline drawing of a section through the receptor layer of a human retina, parallel with the surface of the retina, about 2° away from the center of the fovea. The larger circles are cones and the small ones are rods.** [Redrawn from Osterberg (1935).]

the cone, a sensitive light detector records the intensity of the light transmitted through it. The measurements are essentially made by passing light of different wavelengths through a cone and determining the proportion of the incident light that passes through it and falls on the photodetector.

The absorption spectrum of the cone and all the other tissue in front of and behind the cone may thus be measured. Since it is virtually impossible to prepare the specimen in such a way that the only light-absorbing material between the source and the photocell is the *visual* pigment, two different procedures have been used to correct for the absorption in nonvisual pigments. One procedure is very similar to the one Rushton used on the living eye. The difference spectrum before and after bleaching is measured, and this is taken to be the absorption spectrum of the visual pigment in the cone.

A second procedure is based upon the assumption that the nonvisual pigments are evenly distributed over the area of the retina. Two beams of light are passed through the retina at the same time, one being directed through a cone and the other passing through a region nearby that contains no receptor. The absorption spectrum of each of these spots is measured (by finding, at each wavelength, the proportion of incident quanta that do not arrive at the photocell), and the difference between these two absorption spectra is taken as the absorption spectrum of the pigment in the cone itself. If it is further assumed that the only pigment in a cone that is different from the surrounding pigments is the *visual* pigment, then such difference spectrum is the absorption spectrum of the visual pigment contained in that cone.

These two measures, described in the preceding paragraphs, should agree if the quantum efficiency for bleaching is independent of the wavelength of the quanta, an assumption that has been discussed on

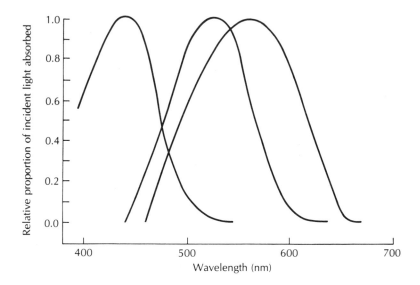

Fig. 9.5 **Absorption spectra for three classes of cones found in the human retina. The heights have been adjusted arbitrarily to have maxima at 1.0.** [*These curves are from Wald and Brown (1965) and they are very similar to the curves found by the other group of workers (Marks et al., 1964).*]

page 205. The results of the two procedures are, in fact, in good agreement.

When such microspectrophotometry is performed on various cones in the human retina, different cones yield different absorption spectra, and as might be expected, there are three sets of cones, each with a different absorption spectrum.[5] The absorption spectra of these sets are plotted in Fig. 9.5.[6]

CLASSES OF CONES IN THE RETINA All of these findings, taken together, seem to establish firmly that there are three different classes of cones in the normal human retina, each with a different absorption spectrum, each spectrum being shifted with respect to the others along the wavelength dimension.

As yet, there has been no wide agreement about names for these three classes of cones. For the purposes of this discussion, however, they will be called the red-absorbing, green-absorbing, and blue-absorbing pigments, each name referring to the color of the wavelength at the maximum absorption. These names may be abbreviated to R, G, and B, respectively.[7]

[5]One cone was found whose absorption spectrum has a shape suggesting that the cone may contain a mixture of two of the normal pigments (Wald and Brown, 1965) but at the time of this writing, no replication of that observation has been published.

[6]The agreement between these spectra and those published by Rushton is poor, and, at present, the data from both kinds of procedures seem somewhat unreliable. However, descriptions of the present procedures are valuable pedagogically, and presumably their reliability will be improved upon in the future.

[7]Rushton has proposed the names erythrolabe and chlorolabe (red-catching and green-catching, respectively, from Greek roots) for the two pigments he measured.

It is important, in this regard, to point out that the red-absorbing pigment, if extracted from the retina, would not look red. If it were illuminated with white light, it would absorb the long wavelengths most strongly, and therefore reflect to the eye predominantly the middle and short wavelengths. When a mixture of middle and short wavelengths strike the normal eye, the observer calls this mixture bluish-green. Thus the red-absorbing pigment has a bluish-green color, and likewise, the green-absorbing pigment has a purplish color and the blue-absorbing pigment a reddish color. Similarly, "visual purple" (another name for rhodopsin) is a blue-green absorbing pigment (that is, it absorbs maximally at a wavelength of 507 nm; this wavelength, when exposed at intensities great enough to stimulate the cones, is called bluish-green). The pigment is called visual purple because that is the color of the pigment when seen under white light.

TETRACHROMACY

According to the evidence from microspectrophotometry, the normal retina contains cones with three different spectral sensitivity curves, and each of those curves is different from the spectral sensitivity curve of rhodopsin, the rod pigment. Therefore, the normal retina contains *four* classes of receptors with different absorption spectra. Such a retina should then be expected to be tetrachromatic, rather than trichromatic.

Much of the data on matches between mixtures of wavelengths has been collected when the patches to be matched are small, and under these circumstances (when the patches are no larger than about 2° in diameter), normal vision is exactly trichromatic. This is to be expected if the subjects fixate the two patches in turn, and make their matches on the basis of the activity resulting from each while it is being fixated, since there are very few rods in the central 2° of the retina. However, when the patches are larger than 2°, tetrachromacy should be expected. The fact that trichromacy has generally been reported even for large fields has been taken as evidence that the rod system simply does not operate when the intensity of the field is great enough to stimulate the cones. It has been hypothesized, for example, that the rods are inhibited when the cones are active. However, when the measurements are made under special conditions, normal human vision is, in fact, tetrachromatic for large fields.

To distinguish between trichromacy and tetrachromacy, measurements must be made with great care. Very few of the published measurements have used sufficiently sensitive procedures. The technique that is usually followed in collecting data on wavelength matches is simply to present the subject with two patches illuminated by different combinations of wavelengths of light and ask him to adjust the intensities of some of the components until the two patches match, that is, look the same. The subject is almost never tested to determine whether or not he can *discriminate* between the two patches. It is quite possible that a subject will say that two patches look alike even when the effects of the two patches on his visual system are different enough to permit him to discriminate between them if he is asked to do so. This is an extremely important point. The logic (explained in Chapter VIII) by which the color mechanisms of the visual system can be deduced from wavelength mixture data depends critically upon the assumption that, when two patches are "matched," their effects on the visual system as a whole are *identical*, and that when two patches have identical effects on the visual system, they cannot be discriminated.[8] The number of color systems in the retina *cannot* be deduced from wavelength matching data taken simply by finding mixtures of wavelengths that "look alike." It must either be demonstrated or assumed that the stimuli are indiscriminable, and it is a very poor (almost always incorrect) assumption that, when a subject sets two patches to look the same, he will be unable to discriminate between them. If he is given some training, he can usually distinguish between wavelength mixtures that he had previously adjusted to look alike, no matter how careful he was in his original adjustments.

To reach firm conclusions about retinal color systems from wavelength mixture data, the experimenter should always make the final adjustments himself, adjusting the intensities until the subject *cannot learn to discriminate* between the patches. However, this procedure is so time consuming, and the logical arguments that show why it is required are so widely ignored, that experimenters have rarely collected wavelength mixture data in that way.

When large stimulus patches are used, and only three intensity adjustments are permitted, the subject will often report that the patches match well in the regions where he is looking but do not really match very well in the parts that fall on the periphery of the visual field. Mea-

---

[8]In essence, the logic is as follows: You wish to test the physiological theory that there are only three sets of receptors (with different action spectra), all operating at the same time. If that theory is correct, and a subject is presented with two patches of light containing mixtures of four wavelengths, it must be possible to find intensities for three of the wavelengths such that the two patches will have *identical* effects upon his system as a whole. If the two patches have identical effects, the subject cannot discriminate between them. Therefore, the theory is disproved if the subject can discriminate between the patches at all intensity settings. (There is no set of operations by which this theory, or any theory, can be proved.)

surements by Bongard et al. (1957), using a careful procedure in which differences far from the fovea were made more easily noticeable, indicate that the normal subject really is tetrachromatic for large fields. Those measurements did not employ discrimination testing procedures, but at least the stimuli were arranged in such a way that peripheral differences between the patches were more noticeable, and the subjects were instructed not to ignore them. The experimenters found that the normal subject is trichromatic for patches smaller than 2° in diameter, but that he requires four intensity adjustments to equate two larger patches. Thus it is evident that the rods are not inhibited and do contribute to wavelength discrimination, at least under their conditions of measurement. They did find, however, that, even for large patches, three intensity adjustments were sufficient to provide reasonably good matches. In other words, for practical purposes, such as designing color television sets, the trichromatic data in the literature are only slightly in error, and may be taken as a useful description of normal color vision.

EVALUATION OF THE ASSUMPTION THAT ALL ABSORBED QUANTA PRODUCE IDENTICAL EFFECTS While the probability that a quantum will be absorbed certainly depends upon the relationship between the nature of the pigment molecule and the wavelength of the quantum, most of the preceding discussion of color vision depends heavily upon the assumption that, once a quantum is absorbed, it will have an effect on the molecule that is the same regardless of the wavelength of the quantum. That assumption will be evaluated in this section.

It is firmly established that all lights at near-threshold intensities look the same when presented to the periphery of the dark-adapted eye, regardless of their wavelengths. That is, the dark-adapted eye exhibits monochromacy. (If the lights are presented to the fovea, long-wavelength stimuli look colored because, at long wavelengths, the cone threshold is somewhat lower than the rod threshold. When the stimuli are restricted to the rods, however, there is no wavelength discrimination.) Specifically, if any two lights of different wavelengths are adjusted in intensity so that they produce equal numbers of quantal absorptions, the two lights will be indiscriminable (other factors, e.g., size of test patch, being equal). Therefore, the information contained in the wavelengths of the quanta is certainly lost somewhere in the visual system.

Similarly, the trichromacy of normal vision can only be reconciled with the presence of three kinds of cone pigments if it is true that wavelength information is lost within each of the systems characterized by one of the pigments. (If, for example, one of the systems did not lose wavelength information, normal vision would be better than trichromatic.)

The question, then, is whether wavelength information is lost in the interaction between light and the visual pigments or later in the system. That question cannot be answered unequivocally at the present time, but there is a large body of evidence that is consistent with the hypothesis that wavelength information is lost during the photoisomerization of visual pigment.

When a visual pigment molecule is in the regenerated state, it could have one of several twisted shapes (probably, only one of these physically possible forms actually occurs in the eye). However, there is strong evidence that the effect of a quantum of light on regenerated visual pigment is always to isomerize it to the same straight form (called the all-trans form). That is, if a quantum of light does isomerize the molecule, the result is a molecule of one particular shape. There is no evidence that quanta of any wavelengths ever change a regenerated molecule into one with any shape other than the all-trans isomer. Thus, the molecular result of the absorption of a quantum is almost certainly the same regardless of the wavelength of the quantum.

It is possible that the events that initiate neural activity in the retina do not depend upon the isomerization of pigment molecules. If that were so, then the fact that all quanta produce identical isomerizations would be irrelevant. For example, it is possible that the energy in the quantum being absorbed drives some electronic structure into oscillation, the amplitude of which determines the nature of the neural response. Since quanta of different wavelengths contain different amounts of energy, that mechanism could result in a neural response that maintained wavelength information. Since the sequence of events that actually excites the retinal neurons is still largely unknown, such a theory cannot be rejected with certainty. However, at the present time, the evidence strongly favors the hypothesis that it is the isomerization itself that is the first crucial event the process of visual excitation.

A large body of psychophysiological data are reconcilable if it is assumed that, within any given kind of pigment, all absorbed quanta have identical effects. The fact that the absorption spectra for visual pigments, the action spectra for bleaching, and the spectral sensitivity curves are all identical (when the appropriate corrections are made) is easily explained if the equal-effect assumption is made, but if it is assumed that different quanta have different effects, then the explanation of this identity must become very involved.

In summary, it is firmly established that wavelength information is lost somewhere in the visual system, and there is a large amount of evidence consistent with, and none contradictory to, the hypothesis that this information is lost during the very early stage of visual processing when quanta of light isomerize molecules of visual pigment.

THE STABILITY OF WAVELENGTH MIXTURE MATCHES Suppose that a subject is looking at two patches each of which is a mixture of different wavelengths, the intensities having been adjusted so that the two patches are completely indiscriminable. This means that the red-absorbing system captures equal numbers of quanta from the right and from the left patches, the green-absorbing system catches equal numbers from each patch, etc. Now suppose that the entire retina is light-adapted in such a way that half of each kind of pigment is bleached, and then the same two patches are viewed again. In each patch, half as many quanta will be absorbed, and the brightnesses of the two patches will certainly be lower than before light adaptation. Nevertheless, if the general theory of visual process presented here is correct, it should still be true that the left patch will excite each of the retinal systems to the same degree as the right patch. Therefore, the two patches should still be indiscriminable, even though both of them look different from the way they originally looked.

Now suppose that the entire retina is adapted to a light containing only very long wavelengths, so that it bleached most of the red-absorbing pigment, but less of the green-absorbing and little of the blue-absorbing pigment. After such an adaptation, the colors of both of the patches will be very different from their original colors (for reasons to be discussed in Chapter X), but they should still match each other exactly. They must still match, since, while fewer isomerizations will occur in each color system after bleaching than before, the *same* reduction in this number of isomerizations will result from both patches (so long as the adapting light covered the entire retinal area being tested), and the excitations produced by two patches will thus still be equal *within each* color system. In general, when any two patches are matched under any state of retinal adaptation, they should still match under any other state of adaptation (unless, of course, the regions of the retina where the two patches are falling are not adapted to the same light).

This prediction, which follows from the assumptions about quantal absorption and visual processes discussed in Chapter VIII, has been extensively tested, and found to be correct under almost all conditions.

However, there is evidence that matches break down when the adaptation is extremely strong, bleaching a large proportion of the pigment. Such a breakdown would be expected if the absorption spectrum of at least one of the retinal systems actually changed during adaptation. For example, suppose that the "bleached" molecules of the red-absorbing pigment were not completely transparent to visible light, but actually absorbed appreciable quanta of short wavelengths. Then, after adaptation to a very strong light, the bleached red-catching pigment would act as a wavelength-selective filter, filtering the light falling on the remaining, unbleached pigment. The action spectrum for these cones, as a whole, would thus be changed. The particular intensities of the various wavelengths in a pair of matched patches depend upon the action spectra of the retinal systems involved, and therefore, if, after bleaching, one or more of these spectra were different, the match would no longer hold.

When the background surrounding a stimulus patch is changed in color or intensity, the color and brightness of the patch itself will change strongly. This effect, called simultaneous contrast, will be discussed extensively in Chapters X–XII. If contrast effects are a consequence of interactions among neurons in the visual system (as will be demonstrated in Chapters X–XII), then they should be expected not to disturb wavelength mixture matches. For example, suppose that two patches match exactly when each is on a dark background. When they are both placed on a background that is bright and colored, both patches will look dimmer and may change in hue, but they will still match each other.

The reason for this is as follows: We have argued that the two patches matched in the first place (when they were presented on a dark background) because the quanta incident on the retina from the two patches had identical effects on the three sets of receptors. These effects are identical at the very first stage in the visual process, when the quanta are absorbed by pigment molecules. Once the quanta have been absorbed, the activities in the retinal regions corresponding to the two patches are identical in every respect. Therefore, any factor that effects this activity, a background light for example, must effect the activity in precisely the same way in both patches. Put another way, before the quanta are absorbed by visual pigments, the visual system has no information about the patches at all. As soon as the quanta *are* absorbed, the system has no information that the two patches are different, even if they really are physically different. Since the information that the two patches are different is lost at the first stage in the visual process, no subsequent processing can recover that information, and the two patches will thus remain indiscriminable. Any factor that affects the excitation from one of the patches must effect the other in exactly the same way. The match can only be disturbed by factors that actually change the shape of the action spectrum of one or more of the classes of receptors.

For normal human subjects, wavelength mixture matches do exhibit this expected stability — they are not disturbed by changes in the background illumination. However, it is possible that matches might be disturbed in certain forms of color-blind subjects. The logic in the preceding paragraph depends upon the assumption that the wavelength information is lost at the instant that quanta are absorbed by pigment molecules, but suppose that this information were lost at a later stage in the system, as in the following example. Once in a great while, a subject is found who manifests the wavelength matches of a monochromat, but who otherwise seems to possess a functional cone system. Such a person is called a cone monochromat. All of the cones possessed by a cone monochromat might contain the same kind of pigment (which might be any one of the normal pigments), or every cone might contain all three of the normal pigments, all mixed in the same proportions. In either of these cases, he would show monochromatic wavelength matching data.

However, it is also possible that the retinas of such a subject contain the normal three classes of cones, each class with a different absorption spectrum, but that all of these classes feed their outputs equally to a single set of ganglion cells. If that were true, then his visual system, as a whole, would contain only one action spectrum, a composite of the curves from the three classes of receptors. In such a retina, the wavelength information is not completely lost until the level of the ganglion cells. Now if whatever processes produce contrast effects operated among the neurons lying between the receptors and the ganglion cells in the retina, then wavelength matches *could* be disturbed by contrast effects.

PROBLEM 9.1 Prove or show by a quantitative example that if a pair of physically different patches match for an eye adapted to white light, they will still match after chromatic adaptation (e.g., light adaptation to a monochromatic light).

X ◇◇◇ COLOR VISION III — THE PERCEPTION OF COLOR

IN the preceding chapters, almost nothing has been said about the experience of color. The data and principles previously discussed could have been obtained without ever asking the subject to describe the stimuli. All that was required was to determine sets of wavelengths and intensities such that the subject could not discriminate between patches; that is, he could not reliably attach any response to one patch and any different response to the other. The relationship between data from such pure discrimination studies and ones in which a subject is asked to describe the appearance of a stimulus is of considerable importance, and will be discussed at length in this chapter. The principles involved in this analysis are applicable to all aspects of the study of perception.

224

To begin this discussion, it is necessary to distinguish among several terms that will be used to designate different aspects of the perception of patches of light. These terms will be defined very roughly here, and then somewhat more precisely later in the chapter.

We will use the word *hue* to refer to that aspect of perception commonly called "color"; for example "redness" or "greenish-yellowishness." Hue is the aspect that changes most strongly when the wavelength of the stimulus is changed. *Brightness* will be used in its common meaning. That is, brightness is that aspect of the perception of a patch of light that varies most strongly when its intensity is changed. Saturation refers to the purity of a hue. For example, scarlet is more saturated than pink. Saturation is the aspect that changes most strongly when white light is added to a monochromatic patch. (When the wavelength of a patch of light is changed while its intensity, say in quanta per second per square millimeter, is held constant, its hue changes, but its saturation and brightness will generally change too. Similarly, when the intensity is changed, all three attributes generally change. Thus, the kind of definitions given above cannot be made precise. Nevertheless, they are adequate for the present purposes.)

The term *color* will hereafter be used to refer to the overall effect of the stimulus, that is, its hue, saturation, and brightness. Thus, two patches may be said to differ in color even if their hues are the same.[1]

THE RELATIONSHIP BETWEEN PERCEIVED COLOR AND THE PHYSICAL STIMULUS

Color and Wavelength

Figure 10.1 (see the color insert) is the excitation space that was discussed in Chapter VIII. This is the space that represents, for the normal eye, the effects on the three color-systems of any combination of wavelengths. Each point in this space represents a different particular combination of the activities of the three components of the visual system. When we see any given patch of light, its effects can be found somewhere in this space, and if a different patch gives us a different experience, it must have produced a different set of excitations in our visual system, and therefore must be represented at some different point in the space.[2] This means that our sensations of color and our color names may be plotted in excitation space, as indicated in

[1] These usages follow the definitions of the terms that have been officially adopted by scientists and engineers working in the area of visual perception.

[2] In the present discussion, we will consider only stimuli that are patches of light on dark backgrounds, to which the eye is adapted. Contrast effects and the results of chromatic adaptation, both of which can change the color of a patch, will be considered later.

Fig. 10.1. The colored lines are loci of points that appear to have the same hue and saturation. For example, the yellow line is the locus of all points that are called pure yellow by a normal observer. This line is essentially the same as the line representing the effects upon the visual system of a single wavelength, 578 nm, at varying intensities. Thus, the wavelength 578 nm always looks yellow regardless of its intensity, and no combination of excitations that is not plotted along that line looks pure yellow.[3] The yellowish-green line next to it is the locus of points that have a particular shade of yellowish-green. This line curves a little. At low intensities, a wavelength of 565 nm looks yellowish-green, but as the intensity of a 565-nm light is increased, it tends to look more yellow. Therefore, in order to maintain the hue of the light at a particular yellowish-green, its wavelength must be shortened somewhat as its intensity is increased. (The Bezold-Brucke effect is the name given to the fact that the hues of most wavelengths change with intensity.) In general, there are three lines, representing about 475, 505, and 578 nm, that are straight (Purdy, 1937). These are the three wavelengths whose hues do not change as their intensities are increased. All the other lines curve a little, and if the diagram were extended to very high intensities, all of the lines would curve strongly, as will be discussed below.

The purple line in Fig. 10.1 does not intersect the spectral locus; there is no single wavelength that produces the sensation we call purple. Purple is produced by mixing short and long wavelengths.

There is a dashed line in Fig. 10.1 that represents a white line. (If the line were actually white in the figure, unfortunately, it would not show up well.) Any mixture of wavelengths whose effects on the three color-systems yield a point on this line will appear white. For example, a mixture of all the wavelengths in the spectrum at equal intensities (i.e., an equal number of quanta per second at each wavelength) would appear white. In fact, the term "white light" usually refers to light that contains all the wavelengths of the spectrum in roughly equal amounts. (People use the word "white" to refer to many discriminably different colors, e.g., slightly yellowish, slightly bluish, etc., which result from different wavelength mixtures. The particular

---

[3]At extremely high intensities, the colors of monochromatic stimuli change strongly as a function of their duration, an effect which will be discussed later. For ease of exposition, the plot in Fig. 10.1 does not extend to such high intensities, but covers the range experienced under all ordinary conditions.

"white" represented by the white line in Fig. 10.1 is that produced by equal numbers of quanta at all wavelengths.)

The axes in Fig. 10.1 represent the excitations of the three retinal color systems, and the colored lines represent loci of perceptual events, that is, color sensations. Therefore, Fig. 10.1 is essentially a map, in three dimensions, showing the locations of the various colors in excitation space. To determine the excitations that are occurring when a given color is being seen, find the color and then locate the corresponding values on the axes; conversely, to find the color that will result from any given set of excitations, locate the corresponding point in the space and see what color it is.

Obviously, Fig. 10.1 is not a complete map, since most of the points in excitation space have not been labeled with any color. The complete map would be a solid volume of color, and could not be drawn. However, a complete color map can be constructed for any surface within the three-dimensional excitation space. For example, in Fig. 10.2, a plane is indicated that is the section through the wavelength-mixture space perpendicular to the line from the origin that makes equal angles with all three axes. Lines representing the effects of various wavelengths have been drawn to their intersections with this plane.

Figure 10.3 (see the color insert) is a view of this plane that has been made in such a way that the hue of each point in the figure is approximately the hue that would result from the corresponding combination of excitations. Figure 10.3 is, thus, a complete map of this one surface. If all the colored lines in Fig. 10.1 were perfectly straight, then a set of maps like that in Fig. 10.3, taken in parallel planes at different distances from the origin, would all be identical (except for being more or less magnified). However, since most of the colored lines in Fig. 10.1 curve slightly, such a set of maps (representing different intensities) are all slightly different from each other.

Any plane section through excitation space, for example, the one in Fig. 10.3, has the following useful property: If light of any hue is mixed with light of any other hue, it is approximately true that the hue and saturation of the mixture will lie on the straight line between the two components. For example, if a red light of 640 nm is mixed with a green light of 512 nm and the intensities are such that the two lights produce approximately equal total numbers of quantal absorptions, the mixture will look yellow, the color of the point in Fig. 10.3 that is halfway along a straight line between 640 and 512 nm. If the propor-

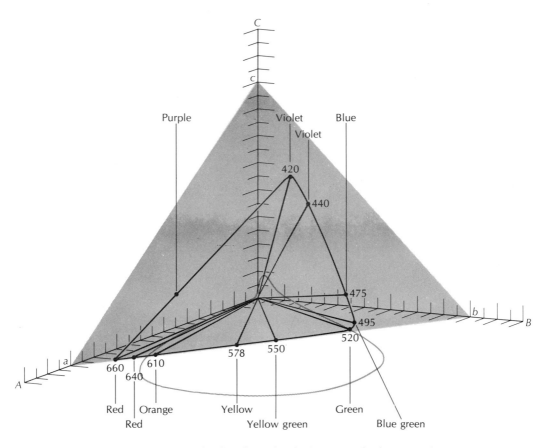

Fig. 10.2 **A section through wavelength mixture space that forms an equi-lateral triangle with the axes. The (1000 quanta) spectral locus is plotted in mixture space, and the intersections between the plane and the lines representing the effects of various wavelengths are shown. (The set of intersections is a different kind of spectral locus from the ones discussed so far, one in which the numbers of quanta incident are *not* constant at all wavelengths.)**

tion of green is increased, the mixture will look yellowish-green, etc. Similarly, if a yellow light at 578 nm is mixed with a blue one at 477 nm, the hue and saturation of the mixture will change from blue through white to yellow as the proportion at 578 nm increases from zero.

This property of such surfaces would follow exactly from geometry if it were true that all the color lines like those in Fig. 10.1 were straight. Figure 10.4 may aid in understanding this point. When lights of any two wavelengths (λ_1 and λ_2) are mixed, the effect of their mixture may be found by adding the two vectors representing the two lights. Since all vectors representing wavelengths can be drawn with one end at the origin of the space, any two such vectors will define a plane through the origin, as shown in Fig. 10.4. Further, the vector representing the effects of the mixture of the two components ($\lambda_1 + \lambda_2$) must also lie in this same plane, somewhere between the vectors of the two components. The intersection of this vector plane with a hue-map plane (the

Fig. 10.4 **The vector representing the mixture of any two wavelengths ($\lambda_1 + \lambda_2$) lies in the plane formed by the two components (λ_1 and λ_2). The plane intersects the hue map plane in a line. If the proportions of λ_1 and λ_2 are varied, the mixture vector, ($\lambda_1 + \lambda_2$), will move in the vector plane, and therefore, will always intersect the hue-map plane in the straight line that joins the component wavelengths. Then, if the hue is the same everywhere on the vector ($\lambda_1 + \lambda_2$), the hue of any mixture of λ_1 and λ_2 will be one that is found along the straight line connecting λ_1 and λ_2 in the hue map.**

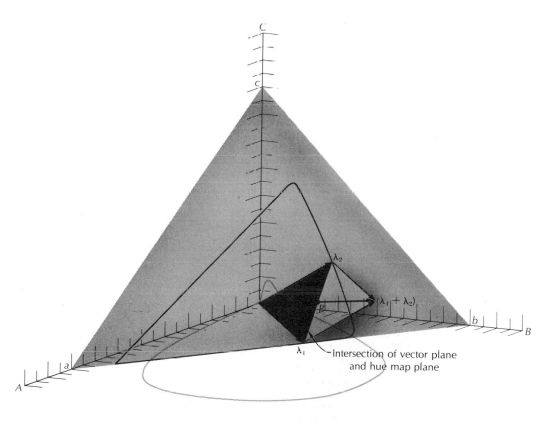

plane in Fig. 10.2) will be a straight line with one of the two component wavelengths at each end. This line is the intersection of the hue-
map plane with the vectors representing all possible mixtures of the
two components.

Now if all the color lines are straight, then the vector representing
any mixture of wavelengths will have the same hue and saturation all
along its length. For example, in Fig. 10.4, the hue and saturation produced by any of the points that lie along the vector $\lambda_1 + \lambda_2$ would always be the same. Therefore, the hue of the mixture of the two wavelengths would be the same as the hue of the point labeled p. In general
if the color lines were straight, the hue and saturation of any mixture of
λ_1 and λ_2 would be the same as the hue and saturation of some corresponding point on the straight line that connects λ_1 and λ_2 in the color
map.

If the color lines are not straight, then the hue of the point p may be
different from the hue of the point $(\lambda_1 + \lambda_2)$, and the hues of mixtures
would not necessarily lie on the straight line connecting the components. However, it has been established empirically that the color lines
actually are not very curved over the normal range of intensities, and
therefore the property under discussion is a reasonably good approximation.[4]

[4]People working and teaching in the area of color are most familiar with one particular form of
map like that in Fig. 10.3, called the "CIE (Commission International de l'Eclairage) chromaticity diagram for the XYZ system." Those interested in the specific relationship between that diagram and the
ones in Figs. 10.1 and 10.3 should examine any of the general references on color listed at the back
of this book. With a lot of brain work, and luck, the logic of the CIE system may reveal itself. The following brief discussion might serve as an aid in relating the color system used in this book with the
CIE system.

While the discussion of color in this book was developed as an aid to understanding the basic processes and properties of color vision, the CIE system was developed primarily to serve an applied
function, namely to enable manufacturers of paints, fabrics, etc., to specify and to communicate the
colors of their products. Thus, the CIE system was designed to be convenient to use, rather than to be
consistent with any particular physiological data (although, of course, in order for it to work, it must
be consistent with the *psychophysical* data of color mixture).

The mixture space in Fig. 10.1 was originally derived from a set of three curves that are the current
best estimates of the action spectra of the three retinal color systems. The known data of color mixture, that is, the various mixtures of wavelengths that are known to match each other, fit into this
space. (To the extent that the action spectra are correct, they must fit correctly in this space, as explained in Chapter IX.) Conversely, if a large set of color mixture data are known, it is possible to find
a set of hypothesized action spectra that would account for the matches. In fact, there are an infinite
number of sets of hypothetical action spectra that correctly fit the data of color matching (although
there can be only one set of color matches that fit the correct action spectra).

The CIE chromaticity diagram was derived from a set of hypothetical action spectra in the following way: First, a complete set of color mixture data were collected under carefully controlled conditions. Specifically, three "primary" bands of wavelength were arbitrarily chosen, and the relative
amounts (energies) of each of them were determined that must be mixed in order to match each
wavelength in the spectrum. (As explained in Chapter IX, an energy was called negative when that
amount had to be added to the patch containing the nonprimary wavelength.) A set of three action
spectra for the three retinal color systems was then calculated that fit the obtained color mixture data.

An infinite number of spectra would all fit the observed color mixture data, and a choice among

Complementaries Any mixture containing all wavelengths at equal intensities looks white, and is represented somewhere on the dashed line in Fig. 10.1. However, there are many other mixtures of wavelengths that are indistinguishable from that "equal-intensity" mixture. For example, if the wavelengths 477 and 578 nm are mixed in the proper proportions, their effects on the three color-systems lie on the dashed line in Fig. 10.1. The effect of that mixture is identical with the effect of the proper mixture of all wavelengths, and therefore the mixture of 477 and 578 nm must produce the same appearance as "white" light. Any two wavelengths which, when mixed in the proper proportions evoke the sensation of white, or appear without hue, are called complementary wavelengths.

---

them was made on the following basis. It was convenient to assume that the brightness of a light (under photopic conditions) is determined solely by the color system whose action spectrum peaks in the middle wavelengths (analogous to the B system in Fig. 8.9, p. 171), and therefore the action spectrum of one of the systems was set equal to the photopic spectral sensitivity curve. (The spectral sensitivity curve actually used by the CIE was much smoother than the spectral sensitivity curve as we now know it, e.g., Fig. 7.8, p. 146.) Given this one action spectrum, the spectra of the two remaining systems were fixed.

The resulting curves are similar to the spectra on which the space in Fig. 10.1 was based, but they differ in three ways. First, Fig. 10.1 is based upon equal quanta spectra, while the CIE curves were based upon equal energy spectra. That is, for the CIE system, the effects were plotted on the basis that every wavelength band of equal width contained the same amount of energy, rather than the same number of quanta, yielding a systematically different result because the energy per quantum is inversely proportional to the wavelength. (Equal energy spectra were used because it was much easier to measure energy than number of quanta.) Second, there are minor discrepancies resulting from differences in the ways the basic data were obtained. Third, the setting of the middle curve to equal the photopic spectral sensitivity curve was arbitrary, and the resulting action spectra would thus only agree with directly measured ones if that arbitrary setting happened to coincide with the true action spectrum of the B system. (It does not.)

The first and third factors result in major differences between the CIE diagram and the color map in Fig. 10.3, but they have no bearing on the accuracy of either map. Obviously, the use of equal energy versus equal quanta spectra is purely a matter of the units one wishes to use. While it is not so obvious, it is also true that, so long as the three action spectra are consistent with the color-matching data, any set of three spectra will give equally correct color maps (although their shapes will differ). The reason for this is that the system is linear [e.g., Eqs. (7)-(9) p. 171, are linear], and different sets of action spectra, so long as they are all consistent with the color-matching data, are all linear transformations of each other.

Suppose that these hypothetical CIE action spectra were used to construct a spectral locus in three-dimensional space, just as was done for Fig. 8.18, p. 189. This would result in a figure similar to Fig. 8.18 (and Fig. 10.1), but with a differently shaped spectral locus. If a section were then taken through that space, and the spectral locus projected on to it, just as in Fig. 10.2, the resulting diagram would be very close to the CIE chromaticity diagram. The only difference between that figure and the CIE diagram is that the standard CIE chromaticity diagram is a right triangle instead of an equilateral triangle.

In geometrical terms, the right triangle is achieved by projecting the equilateral triangle and its contents on to a plane at an angle to the plane of the equilateral triangle. For example, examine the triangle in Fig. 10.3. If this triangle were tilted backwards, pivoting about its base, the angle at the top, as projected onto the plane of the paper, would increase from its present 60° until, if the triangle were tilted all the way perpendicular to the paper, the top angle would become 180°. At some particular intermediate angle, it would be just 90°, as projected on to the plane of the paper. That is essentially the way in which the equilateral triangle in the CIE system is converted into a right triangle.

Fig. 10.5 **Complementary pairs of wavelengths.** [*From Sinden (1923).*]

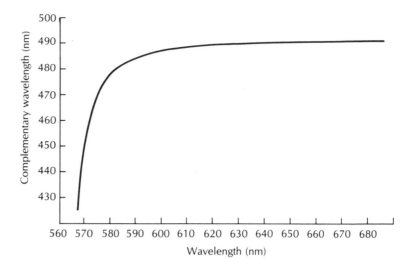

Fig. 10.5 **Complementary pairs of wavelengths.** [*From Sinden (1923).*]

There is an infinite number of such complementary pairs, but a set of wavelengths centered around 550 nm have no complements. Figure 10.5 is a plot of all the pairs of complementary wavelengths. The points on this curve were determined experimentally, but since they merely represent a special case of wavelength mixture matching (i.e., they are matches between one mixture containing all wavelengths and another containing just two), they could also be determined directly from the wavelength mixture space.

Saturation, Hue, and Brightness   Any mixture of wavelengths may be plotted in excitation space and the resulting hue and saturation found from a map like that in Fig. 10.3. For example, when 477 and 578 nm are mixed in the proper proportions, the mixture will appear white, as described above. Also, if the same two wavelengths are mixed in *any* proportions, the hue and saturation of the mixture will lie somewhere along the line connecting the two wavelengths on the hue map. If the mixture contains a lot more light at 477 than 578 nm, it will appear blue, and as the relative amount of 578 is slowly increased, the mixture will look first a whiter and whiter blue, then white, then a yellowish-white, and finally yellow. The perceptual dimension of "whitishness" is called the saturation or desaturation of the color. For example, a yellowish-white is called desaturated yellow, and the more whitish the color appears, the more desaturated it is said to be.

The various hues and saturations of mixtures of 495 and 650 nm are represented in Fig. 10.6. (What are actually represented in this two-dimensional map are the intersections of the vectors representing various mixtures with the plane of the map.) When those two wavelengths are mixed in one particular proportion, the resulting color (x in Fig. 10.6) lies on the line connecting 578 nm (yellow) and white. Therefore, when the wavelengths are mixed in that proportion, the mixture will look like a desaturated yellow, and will be indistinguishable from, say, a particular mixture of 477 and 578 nm, a mixture of 578 nm and a white light, etc.

The projection of the spectral locus onto any color mapping plane forms a convex curve from the blue end of the spectrum to wavelengths of about 520 nm. Therefore, a mixture of any pair of wavelengths in that region will produce a color that is the same hue as an intermediate wavelength but is somewhat desaturated. However,

Fig. 10.6 **The proper mixture of lights at 495 and 650 nm (point x) produces a color that is the same as the color of a mixture of 578 nm and white. It is called a desaturated yellow.**

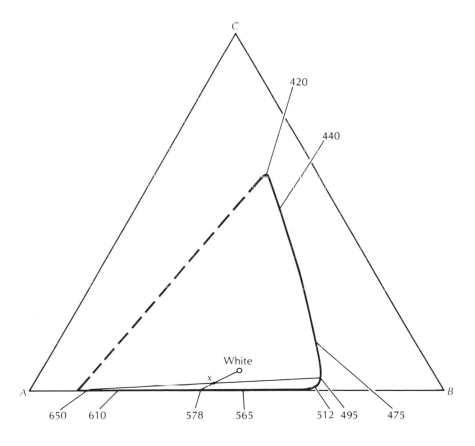

because the curve is almost straight from about 520 nm to the red extreme of the spectrum, a mixture of any pair of wavelengths in that region will yield a color that is almost identical with the color of a monochromatic light at the appropriate intermediate wavelength.

The term "hue" refers to "redness," "greenness," etc. For example, it is correct usage to say that the proper mixture of red and green monochromatic lights will produce a *hue* that is the *same* as the hue of a monochromatic light at 578 nm (the hue is yellow), but the saturation of the mixture is less than the saturation of the monochromatic light.

A perceptual dimension not represented in Fig. 10.1 is the fact that as the intensity of a stimulus is increased, its brightness increases. Thus, for example, as the intensity of a monochromatic light at 578 nm increases, it continues to appear yellow, but becomes brighter. To represent this dimension in Fig. 10.1, each colored line should be dark at the origin and increase in brightness as the distance from the origin increases.

(All of the perceptual dimensions under discussion, the brightness, saturation, and hue of a patch, depend strongly upon the nature of the background, and it is important to remember that the diagram in Fig. 10.1 applies only to the case in which the background is dark.)

DIFFERENCES BE-TWEEN HUE, SATU-RATION, AND BRIGHTNESS

The meanings of the terms hue, saturation, and brightness can roughly be distinguished from one another by reference to certain perceptual continua. We can define "brightness" as that aspect of the perception of a patch of light that varies as the intensity (quanta per second per unit of retinal area) varies. Similarly, "saturation" is that aspect of the perception that varies as more and more white light is added to a monochromatic light, and "hue" as the variation when the wavelength is changed. None of these "definitions" is sharply delimiting, since, when the wavelength, the intensity, or the amount of white light in a patch is changed, hue, saturation, and brightness *all* change. Nevertheless we can say, roughly, that the aspect of the perception that is changing most strongly when the intensity is changed is what we wish to call brightness, etc. Such definitions are not completely satisfactory, but they do, nevertheless, have a lot of meaning.

The fact that these three different aspects of the perception of lights are so frequently distinguished from each other implies that the distinctions among them are useful. On the other hand, since they all co-vary during most physical manipulations of the stimulus, and since we always experience all three simultaneously when we see a patch of light, it seems very difficult to clarify the distinctions among them, and thus to establish a firm base upon which they may be related to the physiology of the visual system. However, there is a set of psychophysical observations that greatly aid in making the distinction between hue and brightness more rigorous, and comparable observations could easily be made to clarify the differentiations between these terms and saturation. These observations are as follows.

First, consider brightness matches. A subject is presented with two patches, one of which contains a monochromatic light at fixed intensity, and the other a light adjustable in both wavelength and intensity. If the two wavelengths are made equal and the subject is instructed to adjust the intensity of one until the two patches "have the same brightness," he will do so easily, and his successive settings will differ very little from each other; that is, the variance of his settings will be small. (Under this condition, the patches will look identical when he has made his intensity setting.)

Now suppose that the wavelength of the second patch is set at a fixed value that is different from the wavelength of the first, and the subject is again asked to adjust the intensity of the second until the two patches "have the same brightness." For example, one of the patches might be red and the other blue, and he is asked to set them to look equally bright. This is called heterochromatic brightness matching. The subject will report that it is a much harder task than when the two patches have the same spectral composition, and the variance of his settings will be very much greater than for a homochromatic match.

Now consider hue matches. The subject is again presented with the two patches. If the two intensities are held equal (e.g., the two patches always deliver equal numbers of quanta per second to the eye) and he is asked to adjust the wavelength of the second patch until the two patches "have the same hue," the variance of his settings will be very small. (Again, under this condition, the two patches will look identical when he has made his setting.) Now, if the intensity of the second patch is set at a fixed level that is *different* from the intensity of the first patch, and the subject is asked to adjust its wavelength until the two patches "have the same hue," the variance of his settings will be only slightly greater than when the two patches were at the same intensity.

In summary, when two patches are different in wavelength, equal brightness settings are very unreliable, whereas when they are different in intensity, equal hue settings are highly reliable. To put it very generally, it is extremely hard to judge the relative brightnesses of different hues, but it is easy to judge hue, regardless of brightness. This result suggests that the aspect of the activity in the visual system that is the physiological correlate of "hue" is almost independent of the intensity of the stimulus, while the aspect that is the correlate of "brightness" is strongly linked with wavelength. Any theory attempting to relate the physiology of the visual system to our perceptions of hue and brightness, such as those described later in this chapter, must take this fact into account.

FACTORS OTHER THAN WAVELENGTH THAT INFLUENCE HUE

The preceding discussion was restricted to the case in which the subject is presented with a patch of light of moderate intensity on a dark background, and the composition of the light radiating from the patch is varied. However, the subject's perception can also be strongly influenced by illuminating the background and by adapting his retinas to lights of different wavelengths. The perceptions of hue, brightness, and saturation are also markedly affected when the intensity of the stimulus is extremely high or extremely low.

The Hues of Stimuli of Very Low Intensity

Figure 7.8 (p. 146) is a plot of the spectral sensitivity curves of a dark-adapted and a light-adapted eye. The rods are more sensitive than the cones at all wavelengths except very long ones. Therefore, if the eye is dark-adapted (for more than 10 min) and a monochromatic light at, say 500 nm is flashed on the peripheral retina at an intensity near the threshold for seeing the flash, only the rods will be excited.[5] Under these conditions, the flash will be white or grey, without hue.[6] As the intensity is raised, the flash will finally take on hue when it is intense enough to excite cones. (The intensity range between rod and cone thresholds is called the photochromatic interval.) If the wavelength of the flash is greater than about 650 nm, it will appear red when it is first seen, since the cone threshold is a little lower than the rod threshold beyond that wavelength.

[5]There is some evidence that the scotopic and photopic curves shift with respect to each other in a direction that reduces their differences when the test flash is quite small (Walters and Wright, 1943). That would be the expected result if the greater sensitivity of the rods was due partly or wholly to a greater degree of spatial summation. Nevertheless, when the test field is not very small, stimuli presented to the peripheral retina at near threshold intensities appear colorless, except for the very long wavelengths.

[6]Some subjects report that lights that excite only rods appear as very desaturated blues or violets. You can decide for yourself what color you wish to call such lights by contemplating any nonred object under starlight or dim moonlight.

The Hues of Stimuli of Very High Intensity The hue map in Fig. 10.1 represents the range of intensities ordinarily encountered in the world. However, in the laboratory, the hues of extremely intense stimuli have been studied, and it is clear that such stimuli are not well represented in Fig. 10.1. While a thorough mapping of the hues of high intensity stimuli has not yet been accomplished, a few stimulus conditions have been carefully studied (Cornsweet, 1962). They will be described here.

When a very intense monochromatic light of any wavelength shorter than about 560 nm is steadily viewed, it will appear colored when it is first turned on (its hue and saturation are roughly that to be expected from Fig. 10.1), but it will rapidly desaturate, and if it is intense enough, will soon appear to be essentially white. All very intense stimuli of wavelengths *longer* than about 560 nm undergo a series of striking changes in hue as they are steadily viewed, and if they are intense enough, all finally appear orange.

Perhaps the most striking sequence of changes in hue occurs when an extremely intense stimulus in the long-wavelength end of the spectrum, for example 620 nm, is continuously viewed. When it is first turned on, this wavelength looks orange, but it rapidly changes through yellow to a deep, saturated green during the first 10 to 50 sec of viewing, and then it slowly returns through yellow to a yellowish-

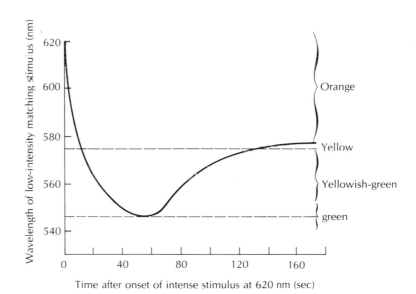

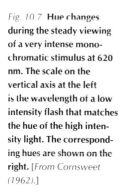

Fig. 10.7 **Hue changes during the steady viewing of a very intense monochromatic stimulus at 620 nm. The scale on the vertical axis at the left is the wavelength of a low intensity flash that matches the hue of the high intensity light. The corresponding hues are shown on the right.** [*From Cornsweet (1962).*]

Time after onset of intense stimulus at 620 nm (sec)

orange. Figure 10.7 illustrates this sequence for one particular intensity. The color changes progress more rapidly at greater intensities.[7]

While no explanation for these color changes has been unequivocally established, the data are consistent with the theory of excitation of receptors that was discussed in Chapter VI. In essence, if it is assumed that the output of a receptor is proportional to the rate at which quanta isomerize its pigment molecules, and if the resulting equations to describe the outputs as a function of time are solved, the result is as follows: When a very intense long wavelength light is first turned on, the output of the A system (long wavelength absorbing) will be greater than that of the B or C systems, but as time passes, the A output will fall faster than the B and C outputs, and if the intensity is great enough, there will be a period during which the output of the B system actually exceeds that of the A system. Therefore, the stimulus, during that time,

[7]It is relatively easy to observe this phenomenon. Set up the apparatus diagrammed in Fig. 10.8. Dark-adapt for about 5 min, then turn on the lamp and stare at the fixation point as steadily as you can with one eye while covering the other eye with your hand. (If you squint it closed instead of covering it, you will tend to close your viewing eye too, and the effect will be weakened.) You will probably see at least some of the changes described above. However, since the face of the lamp is not of uniform intensity, different regions will change color at different rates, reducing the effectiveness of the demonstration. Under good laboratory conditions, the phenomenon is always strong.

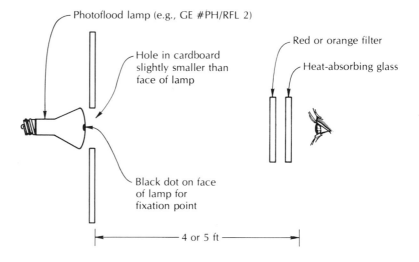

Fig. 10.8 **Diagram of apparatus to demonstrate hue changes. Heat-absorbing glass can be purchased from many camera stores, or pirated from almost any slide projector, where it is used to protect the slide from the heat of the lamp. The colored filter can be any object that is transparent and red or orange, as long as it is not too dense or dark. Red cellophane is perfectly adequate.**

Photoflood lamp (e.g., GE #PH/RFL 2)

Hole in cardboard slightly smaller than face of lamp

Red or orange filter

Heat-absorbing glass

Black dot on face of lamp for fixation point

4 or 5 ft

Important Note: Do not stare at a photoflood lamp *without* a heat-absorbing filter between you and it. Otherwise, it is possible to burn your retina.

If the color does not change to a deep green in this demonstration setup, try the following. Dark-adapt again, turn on the light and stare with one eye covered until it turns to as close to green as it seems to be able to do, and then back away to about 10 ft from the lamp and look at it through the heat glass and red filter with each eye in turn. It should look red to the dark-adapted eye and green to the light-adapted one.

would be expected to have the same hue as a less intense stimulus from the middle of the spectrum (that is, green).[8]

Chromatic Adaptation   The hue of a stimulus depends strongly upon the state of the retina being illuminated. The color map in Fig. 10.1 is correct for a retina that is either dark-adapted, adapted to the stimulus itself, or adapted to a white field. However, if a stimulus is presented to a part of the retina that has previously been adapted to a colored light, the hue of the stimulus will be changed. In general, the hue will tend to move toward the hue of the wavelength that is the complement of the adapting light. For example, if a patch that is white under ordinary conditions is viewed after strong adaptation to a red light, the patch will appear to be a bluish-green; yellow adaptation will make it appear blue, etc. The color thus induced by chromatic adaptation is called a negative afterimage, and demonstrations of such afterimages can be found in almost any introductory book of psychology. (Negative afterimages are usually demonstrated by viewing a neutral patch after chromatic adaptation, but the hues of *colored* patches are similarly affected. A patch that normally looks yellow will appear as orange after adapting to a blue-green light, etc.)

A qualitative explanation of negative afterimages is fairly easy to generate, within the framework of the discussion of receptor excitation contained in Chapter VI. For example, suppose that a dark-adapted subject looks at a patch of light that contains all wavelengths in equal amounts. That stimulus will excite his three retinal systems to various degrees, and he will call the stimulus white. Now let his retina be flooded with light for a few minutes at 650 nm. This will cause more isomerizations in the A system than in the others, and the A system will become more strongly bleached and less sensitive than the B or C systems. As a result, when the original "white" stimulus is presented again, the A system will be relatively less strongly excited. Hence, a "white" stimulus presented to a retina adapted to 650 nm will produce a combination of excitations that is the same as that produced by a stimulus containing a preponderance of wavelengths around 500 nm presented to a dark-adapted retina, and the name given to that combination of excitations is "blue-green."

Clearly, the changes in hue resulting from steady stimulation at very

[8]For a more complete explanation, see Cornsweet (1962).

high intensities, discussed in the preceding section, are special cases of chromatic adaptation, in which the adapting wavelength and the test wavelength are identical. Thus any quantitative theory of one phenomenon should also explain the other.

Simultaneous Contrast   Negative afterimages are sometimes said to be examples of successive contrast; the hue induced into a stimulus by previous chromatic adaptation is a hue that contrasts with the adapting hue. The hue of a patch of light will also be strongly affected by the wavelength composition of light that forms the *background* of the patch, and this phenomenon is called simultaneous contrast. For example, if a patch that appears achromatic against a dark surrounding is placed on a red background, it will tend to look blue-green. In general, the hue of any patch of light will tend to move in the direction of the hue of the complement to the wavelength of the surroundings.

Although simultaneous contrast appears to be quite similar to successive contrast, the mechanisms that account for the two effects are probably not the same. Successive contrast depends upon the photochemical state of the retina, while simultaneous contrast is probably mediated by a particular, highly significant, set of interactions among neurons in the retina. A discussion of these interactions will be reserved for Chapters XI and XII, where they will be treated extensively.

STIMULUS GENERALIZATION   Two patches containing different sets of wavelengths can be made to be completely indistinguishable if the intensities of the components are properly adjusted. These two patches then produce identical effects on each of the three retinal color systems, and therefore are plotted at the same point in excitation space. Now consider two patches that match in hue and saturation, but are different in brightness. For example, suppose that one patch delivers some particular number of quanta per second at 578 nm and the other delivers quanta of the same wavelength but at twice the rate. Under these circumstances, the subject will report that both patches are yellow, but that the second one is brighter than the first.

Let us approach that situation in a slightly different way, now. Suppose that the subject is given one patch at 578 nm and a particular intensity, and another patch whose wavelength is adjustable, but which always delivers twice as many quanta per second as the first. If a subject is told to adjust the wavelength of the second patch until the two patches match, he will adjust until the second patch is also at 578 nm, and he will say, now, that the two patches match in hue but *not* in brightness. Here, he is clearly making an adjustment that is related to the one he makes when he can achieve a *perfect* match, but the nature of the relationship between the two kinds of matches is difficult to clarify.

Let us analyze this relationship by describing still a different way in which the match might be made.

As explained in Chapter IX, the experimental procedure by which a perfect match may be defined is as follows: The subject is presented with the two patches, side by side, and he is asked to make some specific response to one of them. For example, he might be asked which patch contains the mixture of wavelengths, or which patch is *x*, or which patch is ugly. The particular response is irrelevant. On each presentation, he must apply the response to only one of the patches, and is told whether he is right or wrong, the experimenter having decided in advance which is *x*. On successive trials, the positions of the two patches are rearranged randomly. If the subject can learn to apply the correct name to one of the patches, he is, by definition, able to discriminate between the two patches. A perfect match is one for which the subject cannot learn to assign the name to the correct one reliably, and is thus correct 50% of the time.

Now suppose that the subject is given two patches that are clearly discriminable—say, one is red and the other green—and again he is trained, say, to call the green patch "green," or *x*, or any name. He will learn to label the green patch correctly. If the wavelengths in the green patch are then replaced by others such that the new green patch is a *perfect* match for the old one, he obviously will continue to respond in the same way, since he will not even know that one of the patches has been changed.

If the green patch is replaced by another patch that contains the wavelengths of the original patch, but at doubled intensities, he will almost certainly continue to call that patch green, or *x*, even though it does not look identical with the patch on which he was trained. That is, if he has learned to respond in some particular way to a given stimulus, he will be likely to give the same response to a new stimulus if it has the same wavelength composition as the old one, even if its intensity has been changed a little. Here, the response that the subject gives is *identical* for green patches at two different intensities,[9] but the two

[9] It is possible that the subject might say "green" a little louder when shown the more intense stimulus. (If he is responding by pressing a lever, he might press it differently for different intensities.) However, we will assume that the responses are identical (within statistical variations) in the absence of

patches could be shown to be discriminable if a different procedure were used. Similarly, if the subject learns to make a particular response to a given patch, and then the wavelength composition of the patch is changed *slightly*, he will also be likely to give the original response even if he is capable of discriminating between the two patches. Under these conditions, the subject is said to be *generalizing*.

The phenomenon of stimulus generalization is usually discussed at length in books on learning, but is rarely discussed, at least under that label, in modern books on perception. However, stimulus generalization is an extremely fundamental aspect of perception, and must be clearly understood in order to make sensible analyses of perceptual phenomena. The usual definition of stimulus generalization states that stimulus generalization has occurred when a subject makes the same response to two stimuli that are physically different. Following that definition, all perfect wavelength mixture matches are examples of generalization. However, the term stimulus generalization is almost always used to refer, instead, to the situation in which the subject is *capable* of discriminating between the two stimuli, but, under the particular conditions of the experiment, he makes identical (or apparently identical) responses to all of them.

Consider, again, the subject who has been trained to call a patch of a given intensity at 550 nm x. He is now presented with a new patch at twice the intensity of the old one, and the wavelength of the new patch is varied from trial to trial. It will be found that the probability of his calling the new patch x will be greatest at some particular wavelength, close to 550 nm. This wavelength is recorded and then the procedure is repeated for a new intensity. Following this procedure over a large range of intensities, one can plot the wavelength that is most likely to be called x as a function of intensity, and that is essentially what the colored lines in Fig. 10.1 represent. In that figure, the subject has been trained, probably by his parents, to call certain of his experiences "green," and the green line in Fig. 10.1 represents the combinations of excitations on his three color-systems that produce that experience. It may be that he has actually learned by trial and error to give the name "green" to each of those locations in the mixture space; or he may have learned the name for just a small number of intensities and then, as a consequence of his genetically determined anatomy, he applies

---

evidence to the contrary. Alternatively, we could define the response to be what the experimenter actually observes about the subject's behavior, and then, under many conditions (e.g., when the subject responds by throwing a switch one way or the other), it is clear that the responses can be identical even if the stimuli are of differing intensities.

the same name to all the other points along the green line. The question of whether the generalization he manifests is learned or inborn is not relevant to this discussion (although it will be discussed in detail later). The only important point to be made here is that, at the time a normal human adult appears as a subject in the laboratory, he has in him machinery such that he will give the same name to this wide variety of physical stimuli. (Of course the complement is also important; namely that he gives different names to different sets of stimuli. For example, he calls 578 nm, at almost all intensities, "not green," and specifically, "yellow.")

If identical responses are given to sets of discriminably different stimuli, it must be true that these different stimuli produce identical effects at *some* stage or stages in the subject's nervous system. If the two stimuli constitute a perfect match, it has already been explained that their effects are identical at all stages in his system that follow the visual pigments themselves. Similarly, if he says "yellow" in exactly the same way to each of two lights of discriminably different intensities, he is making exactly the same movements of his vocal cords, tongue, etc., as a final consequence of the excitations resulting from the lights; therefore, at least at that final stage, the lights produce identical effects.[10] However, since he is capable of discriminating between the lights, their effects cannot be identical at *every* stage in his system. Somewhere between the retinal surface and the muscles controlling speech, the effects of the two stimuli converge and become identical. By analyzing the relationships among the physical stimuli that are generalized, we can attempt to understand the nature of this convergence. We can ask what mechanisms might be found in a nervous system that would, in fact, lose information about the differences in the excitations resulting from those stimuli that *are* generalized, but would not lose the corresponding information about stimuli that are *not* given the same name.

THE PHYSIOLOGI-CAL CORRELATES OF PERCEIVED COLORS

If a subject is shown two flashes, both at 510 nm, one flash delivering 1,000,000 quanta to his eye and the other 2,000,000 quanta, he will call them both green. The effects of these two flashes on his visual sys-

---

[10]You may wish to *insist* that his responses are really always different, but in some way that is not observed by the experimenter. Then the identity resides in the experimenter's data sheets. What is of interest in this discussion is to generate plausible hypotheses about where the responses change from different to identical, and about the mechanisms of the change. That is, where and by what machinery is the difference information lost. The hypothesis that this information loss is entirely attributable to the experimenter is tenable but the hypotheses to be presented later in this chapter seem more plausible to me.

tem are not identical, since he could be shown to be capable of discriminating between them; but there must be *some* aspect of these two effects that is the same if, under the experimental conditions, he makes the same response to both; that is, if he generalizes between the two flashes.

Obviously, one aspect that is the same for both flashes is the fact that both excite cones. If some part of the subject's visual system responded in one way (resulting in the verbal response "green") whenever any cones were excited, and did not so respond when they were not, then he would call both flashes "green," even though he might be able to discriminate between them by using some other part of his visual system. If that were true, he would call all flashes green, regardless of wavelength, and, since he does not, this aspect is obviously not the one that is uniquely correlated with the fact that he generalizes the two flashes. Nevertheless, it is worth discussing the example a little further. We can perform an experiment, similar to the one described above, in which the two flashes are of very different wavelengths. If the subject is asked to name the hues of the two flashes, and if he has normal color vision, he will certainly respond differently to the two flashes. Therefore, for the normal subject, the mere fact that cones are excited is not what determines the perception of hue. (It may do so for the cone monochromat.) However, even a subject with normal color vision will generalize flashes of all wavelengths when the instructions are different. For example, he always will say that he *saw* a *flash* regardless of wavelength (in the visible spectrum). The mechanism that mediates *this* response may well depend upon the excitation of *any* visual receptor.

We know that the normal subject, when asked to report about hue, generalizes among flashes of the same wavelength but differing intensities, and does not generalize among flashes of widely different wavelengths. We also know that when a flash of 1,000,000 quanta at, say, 510 nm is presented, about 0.2% of the quanta, that is 2000 quanta, are absorbed by the C system (from Fig. 8.9, p. 171), and assuming that each absorption isomerizes a pigment molecule and each isomerization adds an equal increment of excitation, the flash will result in 2000 "excitation units" in the C system. Similarly, the flash will result in 113,000 excitations in the B system and 50,000 in the A system. When a field at the same wavelength but twice the intensity is flashed, the resulting absorptions are doubled in each system. These absorptions are summarized in Table 10.1. (In this discussion, the fourth pigment, rhodopsin, will be neglected.) Some aspect of the effects of these two different stimuli yield identical responses, that is "green."

Put another way, some aspect of the effect of the flashes is the physiological correlate of "green." Let us examine some possible physiological correlates.

Table 10.1

Stimulus	Incident quanta	Number absorbed		
		System C	System B	System A
1	1,000,000	2000	113,000	50,000
2	2,000,000	4000	226,000	100,000

One very common form of neural interaction is the process of subtraction. If two neurons are simultaneously active, one producing excitation and the other inhibition at a synapse, the output of the postsynaptic neuron will be proportional to the difference between the two inputs, as diagramed in Fig. 10.9. Suppose that this simple mechanism operates among neurons connected to the three types of cones in the retina, as in Fig. 10.10. If so, the retinal outputs resulting from the first flash in Table 10.1 would be proportional to the differences between A, B, and C excitations as in Table 10.2, and these new outputs might be the correlates of the response "green." However, it is clear from Table 10.2 that this possibility must be rejected, since stimulus 2 is also called green but the retinal outputs are not the same for both flashes. Clearly, the same response could not be given to both stimuli if the physiological correlate of the response were the output of a neural system that simply subtracted some cone outputs from others.

Table 10.2

Stimulus	$A-C$	$B-A$	$B-C$
1	48,000	63,000	111,000
2	96,000	126,000	222,000

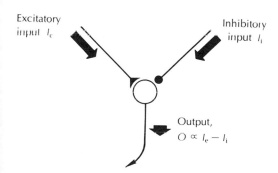

Excitatory input I_e

Inhibitory input I_i

Output, $O \propto I_e - I_i$

Fig. 10.9 **Schematic representation of a synapse that, in effect, computes the difference between the two inputs.**

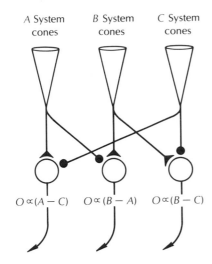

A System cones   B System cones   C System cones

$O \propto (A - C)$ $O \propto (B - A)$ $O \propto (B - C)$

Fig. 10.10 **Hypothetical set of neural interactions among different color systems. The outputs of the complete system are proportional to the differences among the input excitations. This mechanism would give a different set of outputs for two monochromatic stimuli that differ only in intensity, and is, therefore, inconsistent with the hue lines in Fig. 10.1. (If the output of this mechanism were really the physiological correlate of hue, the lines of constant hue in excitation space would all be straight but they would be parallel instead of converging at the origin.)**

Returning to Table 10.1, it is obvious that the *ratios* of the excitations of the various color systems are the same for both flashes. If the visual system contained some machinery that measured the ratios among the excitations of the three systems, and the output of that machinery was the physiological correlate of hue, then it would necessarily be true that the two stimuli in Table 10.1 would have identical hues. In general, that kind of neural machinery would yield the same hue for any set of patches that differed only in their intensities, that is, stimuli whose effects could be plotted along a straight line through the origin in excitation space. Thus such a neural mechanism would come very close to accounting for the loci of constant hue that are plotted as colored lines in Fig. 10.1.

How could the visual system measure these ratios? There is no convincing evidence that neural circuits exist which directly calculate ratios (although, in principle, presynaptic inhibition provides that capability). However, a circuit that includes only elements found extensively in the body, and which indirectly takes ratios, is relatively easy to imagine.

Examine the diagram in Fig. 10.11. Light falls on an *A* and a *B* receptor, resulting in E_A absorptions and isomerizations in the *A* receptor and E_B isomerizations in the *B* receptor. Now we will assume that the excitation in the neurons themselves is proportional to the *logarithm* of the number of isomerizations in the receptor. In other words, the relationship between the input to the receptor and its output is a logarithmic one, as indicated in the figure. (Later, evidence related to this assumption will be presented, but before discussing the logarithmic, or approximately logarithmic, process itself, let us simply assume it in order to see its consequences.) According to the model in Fig. 10.11, one of these outputs excites a synapse while the other inhibits it. If the interaction at the synapse is a simple subtraction, the output from the synapse will be proportional to the difference between the inputs, which is the difference between the logarithms of the quantal absorptions, and the difference between the logarithms of two numbers equals the logarithm of the *ratio* of the numbers. Therefore, in the system in Fig. 10.11, the output will be constant when the ratio of the quantal absorptions is constant.

Suppose that the three types of cones are interconnected in the way schematized in Fig. 10.12. The two outputs, O_1 and O_2, will be identical for the two flashes in Table 10.1, or for any two flashes that differ in intensity but not in wavelength composition. Therefore, if these two outputs are the physiological correlates of hue, the two flashes in Table 10.1 would have the same hue. Furthermore, if the ratios of the isomerizations in the various cones were changed by changing the wavelength composition of the flash, the outputs would be different, and the hue would then be different. In fact, this model approximately fits all of the data thus far presented on hue, since stimuli that have different hues (e.g., in Fig. 10.1) would yield different sets of outputs, and to the extent that the hue lines are straight, every set of wavelength mixtures that have the same hue have identical outputs. However, the hue lines are *not* all straight, and this theory is therefore in error. Probably, the

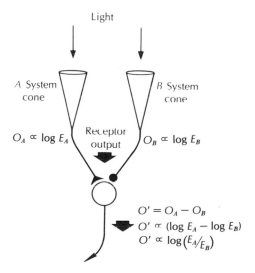

$$O' = O_A - O_B$$
$$O' \propto (\log E_A - \log E_B)$$
$$O' \propto \log(E_A/E_B)$$

Fig. 10.11 **Hypothetical neural interaction between two receptors. Light falling on the receptors isomerizes pigment molecules in proportion to the intensity of the light and the absorption coefficients of the pigments. The outputs of the receptors are assumed to be proportional to the logarithms of the numbers (or rates) of isomerization. One receptor excites and the other inhibits the synapse. Therefore, the final output depends upon the ratio of the receptor isomerizations.**

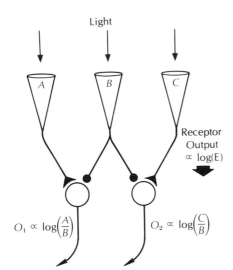

Light

A

B

C

Receptor
Output
∝ log(E)

$O_1 \propto \log\!\left(\dfrac{A}{B}\right)$

$O_2 \propto \log\!\left(\dfrac{C}{B}\right)$

Fig. 10.12 **A system of interactions among the three color-systems that agrees reasonably well with the hue lines in Fig. 10.1. The particular interactions are arbitrary, but the subtraction of logarithmic functions and the fact that there are (at least) two output channels are essential.**

receptor transformation is not perfectly logarithmic, but only approximately so. This will be discussed below.

The particular connections in Fig. 10.12 were arbitrarily chosen. The model would work equally well if, for example, an A/C synapse were substituted for either of the two represented, or was simply added as a third output channel. Furthermore, the signs of any pair of synaptic inputs could be reversed (e.g., a B/A synapse could be added or substituted for the A/B one). Later, physiological evidence will be discussed indicating that, in the *Macaca irus* monkey, the units actually present are A/C, C/A, and B/C, but as yet, there is no evidence from which to choose among these different possibilities in the human visual system.

Note that this model is only intended as a possible explanation of human *hue* perception. It accounts for matches between patches of like hue even if their intensities are discriminably different. If the neural paths in Fig. 10.12 were the *only* paths present between the cones and the rest of the nervous system, then the subject would not be able to discriminate between patches of different intensities if their wavelength compositions were the same, and that is clearly not true of humans. The fact that only two channels are required here, while three are required to account for trichromacy, means that the subject is demonstrating that he has retained more information when he is making trichromatic matches than when he is making hue matches. The information that is missing from hue matches is that which codes the intensities of the stimuli. Thus, the model in Fig. 10.12 represents a hypothesis about the neural circuits that control hue perception, while intensity discrimination (and trichromacy) require other pathways *as well*, pathways presumably in parallel with the ones in Fig. 10.12.

LOGARITHMIC TRANSFORMATIONS AND APPROXIMATIONS TO THEM The color naming measurements described here are only one group of a fairly large set of psychophysical observations that suggest the presence of a logarithmic-like transformation early in the visual system. Other observations will be discussed in the remaining chapters. However, there is ample direct physiological evidence to support the supposition that the relationship between the light intensity input to the visual receptors and the neural output level is approximately logarithmic. A critical evaluation of these physiological studies is not appropriate here, but a few of the results will be described briefly.

Physiological Evidence A set of very elegant measurements of the electrical properties of nerve cells in the eye of the horseshoe crab have been performed by Fuortes (1959). His results fit the hypothesis that light falling on the receptor cell causes it to release a chemical mediator that decreases the resistance of the membrane of a cell lying next to the receptor. This decrease in resistance in turn causes a change in the generator potential, that is, the voltage that is recorded between the inside and the outside of the cell, and the change in generator potential is related to the frequency with which the cell fires nerve impulses. Furthermore, as Rushton (1961) has pointed out, the membrane resistance is proportional to the logarithm of the light intensity (plus a constant that Rushton suggests represents "noise" or spontaneous breakdown of pigment molecules), and the frequency of firing of impulses is linearly related to the membrane resistance. Thus, in the relatively primitive eye of the horseshoe crab, there is a relationship between the light intensity and the resulting impulse frequency that is approximately logarithmic.

Data of Fuortes are plotted as points in Fig. 10.13. The points fall very close to a straight line when the change in membrane resistance or the impulse frequency is plotted against the logarithm of the light intensity. Thus, it appears that there is some set of processes in the *Limulus* eye, interposed between the absorption of light quanta and the generation of nerve impulses, that result in a logarithmic relationship between the two events.

If a microelectrode is inserted into the retina of a mammal, a multi-

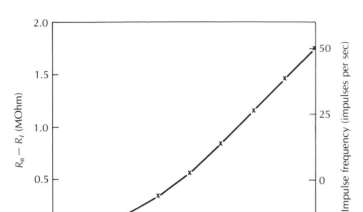

Fig. 10.13 **The effects of different light intensities upon a neuron in the eye of the horseshoe crab. The vertical axis on the left is the change in the resistance of the cell membrane (R_0 is the resistance in the dark and R_1 the resistance under illumination), the horizontal axis is the logarithm of the intensity of the stimulating light, and the vertical axis on the right is the frequency of firing of impulses by the cell.** [After Rushton (1961), from the data of Fuortes (1959).]

tude of electrical changes can be recorded when the eye is illuminated. Under a special set of conditions, electrical activity originating in the receptor cells themselves can be recorded (Brown et al., 1965). When an intense flash is delivered to the retina, two receptor responses can be observed. One is a voltage change that begins virtually simultaneously with the onset of the light and the other is a further change that begins about 1 msec after the onset of the flash. The evidence suggests that the first response, called the early receptor potential, is a reflection, at the recording electrode, of the fact that the absorption of quanta has shifted the positions of a large number of electrical charges, as might be expected if a large number of molecules changed shape upon absorbing quanta. The second response, called the late receptor potential, probably reflects some subsequent stage of activity, since it occurs later in time, but its origin is still unknown.

Cone (1965) has shown a very interesting relationship between the amplitudes of these responses and the intensities of the lights evoking them. The amplitude of the early receptor potential is directly proportional to the number of visual pigment molecules isomerized by the flash. Thus, the amplitude of this potential is essentially linear with intensity for all normally encountered levels, and begins to depart from linearity only with flashes so intense that they isomerize an appreciable fraction of the pigment. This is precisely what would be expected if the early receptor potential is a measure of the motion of oriented and electrically charged pigment molecules as they isomerize.

On the other hand, Cone shows that the late receptor potential is more closely proportional to the *logarithm* of the stimulus intensity over a moderate range of intensities. Thus a logarithmic transformation occurs somewhere between these two very early stages in the visual process. Cone's data are plotted in Fig. 10.14. They do not fit a true logarithmic relationship very well nor over a very large range. This will be elaborated below.

There are many other studies in the literature that show similar relationships between the intensity of a stimulating light and the strength of the resulting neural activity. Most of these studies indicate that the relationship is roughly logarithmic over a moderate range of intensities.

A Plausible Approximation to a Logarithmic Process Very little is presently known about the processes that intervene between the absorption of quanta and the generation of nerve impulses, that is, the processes that produce the transformations in Figs. 10.13 and 10.14. The accurate measurement of the nature of this transformation and the analysis of the reasons for its occurrence are certainly among the most important problems currently being studied by visual physiologists and psychophysicists. There are a large number of preliminary theories about the transformation processes, and while it is not appropriate to examine any of them here, one result is common to many superficially different theories, and seems consistent with both

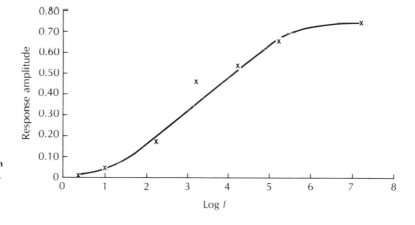

Fig. 10.14 **The relationship between the amplitude of the late receptor potential and the logarithm of the intensity of the stimulus.** [*From Cone (1965), a wave.*]

the physiological and the psychophysical data. Theories involving hypotheses about chemical processes, about electrical properties of the receptor, and about the effects of various kinds of neural feedback all lead to the prediction that the relationship between the intensity of illumination and the resulting neural activity will have the general form:

$$A = \frac{K_1 I}{K_2 + I}, \tag{1}$$

where A is some measure of neural activity, I is proportional to the intensity of the incident illumination, and K_1 and K_2 are constants.[11]

[11]For example, suppose that each isomerized molecule uncovers a hole in the membrane of the receptor, through which ionic currents, driven by the membrane potential, can flow. To simplify the case, assume that each covered hole has an infinite resistance to ion flow and each uncovered hole has a resistance R_h. Then the equivalent circuit is:

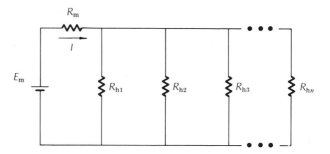

where E_m is the membrane potential, R_m is the membrane resistance, and R_h is the resistance of each uncovered hole. Thus,

$$\text{Current, } I = \frac{E_m}{\dfrac{R_h}{N} + R_m} = \frac{E_m N}{R_h + N R_m}$$

where N is the total number of uncovered holes.

If the further plausible assumption is made that the excitable tissue of the next stage in the visual system is stimulated by the total current flow, and it is recognized that for all but extremely great intensities, N is proportional to the intensity of the incident light I, ($N = CI$), then the "output" O is

$$O = \frac{ECI}{R_h + R_m CI}$$

Because E, C, R_h, and R_m are all constants, this expression has the form of Eq. (1).

An equation of identical form describes the concentration of a substance (e.g., chemical transmitter) at equilibrium, when the substance is constantly being generated at a rate depending upon I and the limited availability of its precursors, and being destroyed or diffused away at a rate proportional to its own concentration. The same equation results again from certain forms of neural feedback, which essentially constitute neural analogs of these chemical reactions.

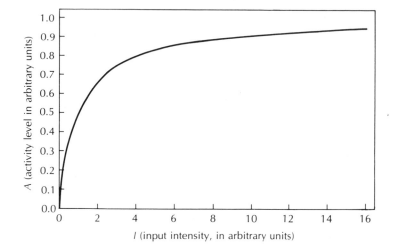

Fig. 10.15 **A plot of the expression** $A = (K_1 \times I)/(K_2 + I)$, **for** $K_1 = K_2 = 1$.

Equation (1) is plotted in Fig. 10.15, for the case where $K_1 = K_2 = 1$. In Fig. 10.16, A is replotted against the *log* of *I*. From Fig. 10.16, it is evident that the relationship in Eq. (1) is approximately logarithmic[12] over a moderate range of intensities, and resembles the curve in Fig. 10.14. Over this region, the curve also resembles Fig. 10.13, and it is possible that, had Fuortes been able to make measurements at higher and lower intensities, his curve might have begun to decelerate, as the curve in Fig. 10.16 does.

Since so many different theories all yield this form of relationship, and since Eq. (1) seems approximately consistent with the physiological data, we will use it as an example to illustrate how such a transformation can be related to the perception of hue. The use of this relationship is not intended to imply that it is the correct one nor even that its consistency with the data lends much support to its validity. It is used here merely because it is a plausible and simple relationship with which to illustrate the point that such nonlinear transformations are crucial to the perception of hue.

APPLICATION OF A NONLINEAR TRANSFORMATION TO THE PERCEPTION OF HUE Consider the condition in which a subject is looking at a monochromatic light whose intensity can be varied, and he is asked to indicate its hue by adjusting the wavelength of another patch until the two hues are the same. We will call the first patch the variable and the other the matching patch. Suppose that the subject has normal color vision, that the absorption spectra of his three retinal systems are those that were plotted in Fig. 8.9, p. 171, and that the wavelength of the variable in-

---

[12]If the relationship were exactly logarithmic, the plot in Fig. 10.16 would be a straight line.

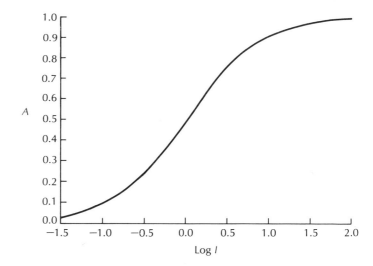

Fig. 10.16 **A plot of the**
same relationship as in Fig.
10.15 [$A=(K \times I)/(K + I)$],
but showing the relation-
ship between the *logarithm*
of *I* **and the resulting** *A*.

tensity patch is 620 nm. At that wavelength, the C system has a negligible sensitivity, and the ratio of the heights of the A to the B systems is
4.9:1. Therefore, the effective intensity on the A system is 4.9 times the
effective intensity on the B system. (The "effective intensity" is, of
course, the rate of incident quanta multiplied by the probability that
the quanta will be absorbed.)

Let us examine the hypothesis that the hue of the stimulus is exclusively dependent upon the algebraic difference between the outputs of
the A and the B systems, and that those outputs are related to the "inputs" by the relationship in Eq. (1).

The difference in outputs,

$$\Delta_{A-B} = \frac{K_{A1}I_A}{K_{A2} + I_A} - \frac{K_{B1}I_B}{K_{B2} + I_B} . \tag{2}$$

For convenience, we will make the simplifying assumption that
all the K's are equal. Then letting R be the ratio of the heights of the
two absorption spectra (I_A/I_B),

$$\Delta_{A-B} = \frac{KRI_B}{K + RI_B} - \frac{KI_B}{K + I_B} . \tag{3}$$

Figure 10.17 is a plot of Eq. (3) for a wavelength of 620 nm (i.e., $R =$
4.9). (For convenience, K is set equal to 1.0.) As the intensity of the
stimulus increases from a low level, the resulting difference between

the outputs of the *A* and *B* systems increases, but then at still higher intensities, the difference begins to fall, approaching an asymptote of zero as the intensity approaches infinity. Therefore, if the physiological correlate of the hue of a stimulus is really the difference between the outputs of the color systems, then the hue of a light at 620 nm should first move in one direction and then reverse as its intensity is raised.

Now we know that yellow is the color name given to wavelengths near where the absorption spectra of the two systems are equal (around 575 nm). Thus, if the hypothesis is correct, "yellow" is the hue corresponding to a very small difference in outputs. Further, for long wavelengths, the excitation of the *A* system is greater than that of the *B* system, and such wavelengths are called "red." Thus the hue of a light of 620 nm should first move from yellowish red to redder and then back toward yellow as its intensity is raised.

Now examine the set of curves in Fig. 10.18. Each curve is a plot of Eq. (3) for an *R* corresponding to a different wavelength. (The curve for 620 nm is the same as that in the preceding figure.) If the theory is correct, wavelengths greater than about 575 nm should become redder and then yellower as their intensities are increased, wavelengths shorter than about 575 nm should become greener and then yellower as their intensities are increased, and 575 nm itself should not change in hue as its intensity is changed.

There have been very few careful measurements of the hues of monochromatic lights at different intensities. The plot in Fig. 10.19 is based upon data taken by Purdy in 1931.[13] The lines in the figure

[13]Purdy also collected data for the short-wavelength end of the spectrum, but they have been omitted from this figure and will be neglected in the present discussion, since their interpretation requires several additional assumptions that are even more tenuous than those already discussed. For an example, see Walraven (1961).

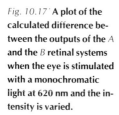

Fig. 10.17 **A plot of the calculated difference between the outputs of the** *A* **and the** *B* **retinal systems when the eye is stimulated with a monochromatic light at 620 nm and the intensity is varied.**

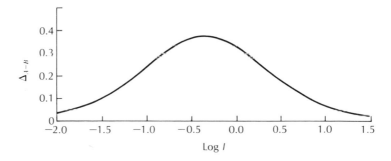

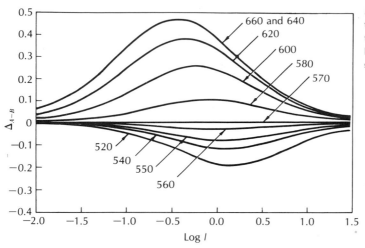

Fig. 10.18 **Calculated differences between excitations of the** A **and** B **systems for a number of different wavelengths (based upon the absorption
spectra in Fig. 8.9, p. 171.)**

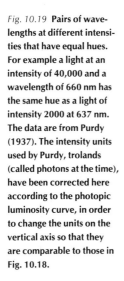

Fig. 10.19 **Pairs of wavelengths at different intensities that have equal hues.
For example a light at an
intensity of 40,000 and a
wavelength of 660 nm has
the same hue as a light of
intensity 2000 at 637 nm.
The data are from Purdy
(1937). The intensity units
used by Purdy, trolands
(called photons at the time),
have been corrected here
according to the photopic
luminosity curve, in order
to change the units on the
vertical axis so that they
are comparable to those in
Fig. 10.18.**

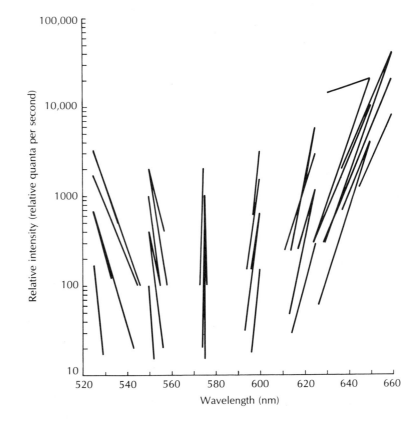

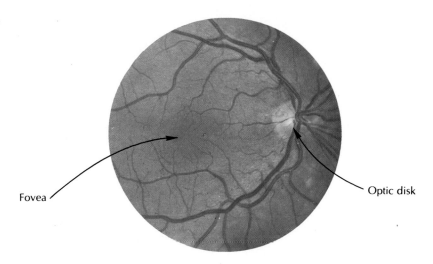

Fig. 6.2 **The appearance of the back of the normal human eye, as seen through an opthalmoscope. The optic disk is the region through which the nerve fibers and blood vessels enter the eyeball.**

Fovea

Optic disk

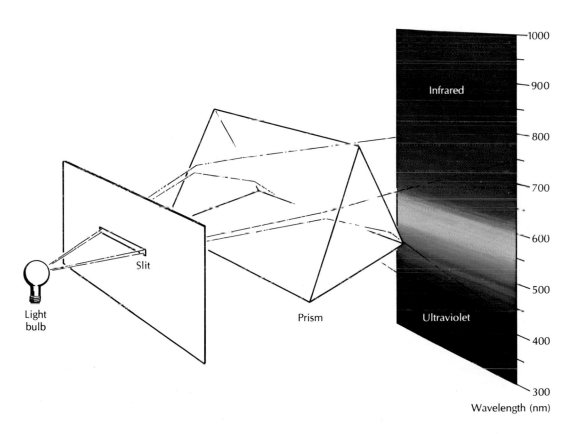

Fig. 8.1 **A prism spreading the various wavelengths of light emitted from an ordinary light bulb into a spectrum.**

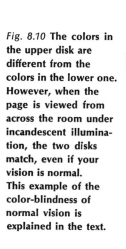

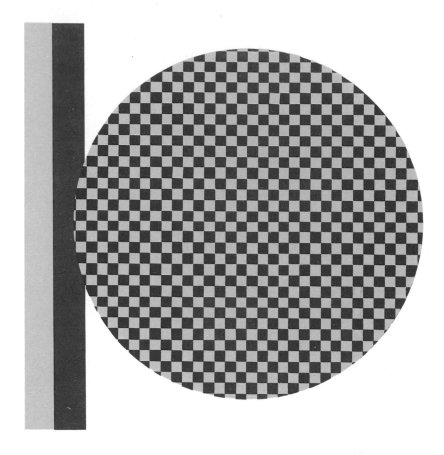

Fig. 8.10 The colors in the upper disk are different from the colors in the lower one. However, when the page is viewed from across the room under incandescent illumination, the two disks match, even if your vision is normal. This example of the color-blindness of normal vision is explained in the text.

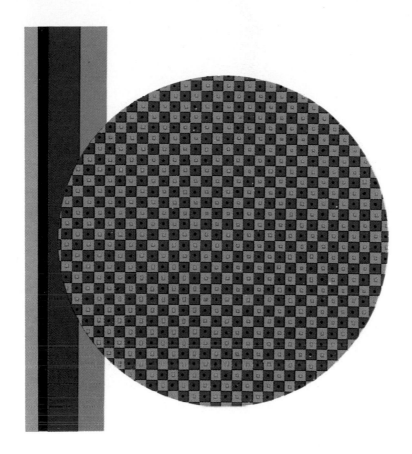

Fig. 8.21 **The upper disk contains four classes of small dots. When the page is illuminated by ordinary tungsten light, the lights reflected from these dots have about the same visual effects as monochromatic lights of 460, 540, and 620 nm, in the intensity relations depicted by the three vectors in Fig. 8.20. The mixture matches the color of grass, represented in the lower disk.**

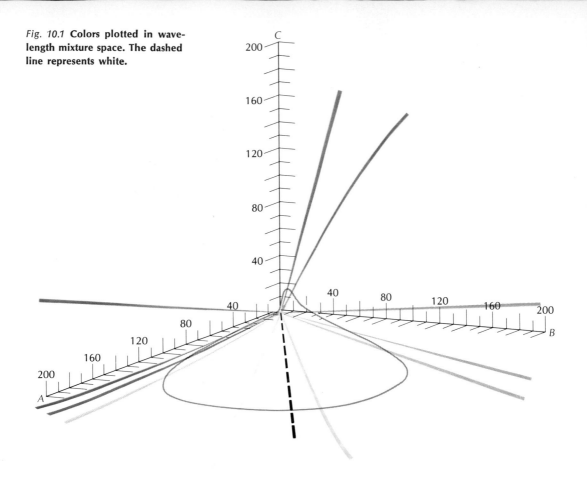

Fig. 10.1 Colors plotted in wavelength mixture space. The dashed line represents white.

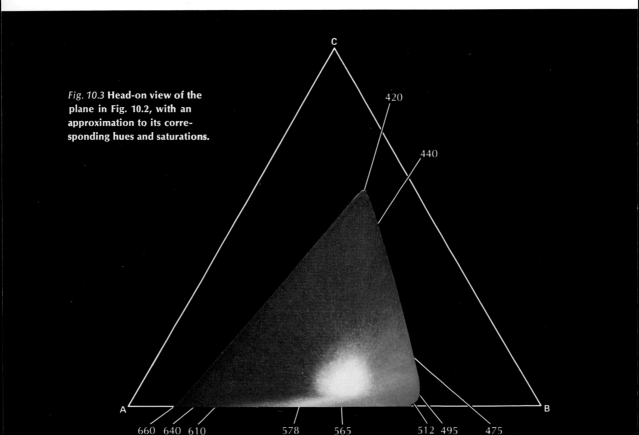

Fig. 10.3 Head-on view of the plane in Fig. 10.2, with an approximation to its corresponding hues and saturations.

connect points of equal hue. Note, first, that the hues of wavelengths near 575 nm (yellow) do not change much over the intensity range investigated. However, for wavelengths longer than about 575 nm the wavelength must be increased in order to maintain a constant hue as the intensity increases. Thus, the hue of any single wavelength longer than 575 nm becomes yellower as the intensity increases. For wavelengths shorter than about 575 nm, the hue also becomes yellower as the intensity increases.

The results are consistent with the theory under discussion and follow from the curves in Fig. 10.18, if Purdy's lowest intensity corresponds to an intensity greater than about -0.5 log units on the scale in Fig. 10.18, for the following reason: Choose any wavelength at an intensity of -0.5 or greater, note the corresponding Δ_{A-B}, and compare it with the Δ_{A-B} for the same wavelength at an intensity ten times greater (1.0 log unit greater). For all wavelengths (except 570 nm), the Δ_{A-B} is closer to that for yellow, that is, zero, at the higher intensity.

If Purdy's data are to be explained by the theory represented in Fig. 10.18, then it follows that if the intensity is lowered below Purdy's levels, the hues also ought to approach yellow. However, Purdy's lowest intensity was not more than a log unit or so above the cone threshold, and so it is possible that the reversal of Δ_{A-B} predicted by the theory would only occur below cone threshold, and therefore not be manifested in a reversal in hue.[14] Thus, the theory, that the physiological correlate of hue is that represented in Fig. 10.12, with the nonlinearity as in Eq. (1), is at least consistent with the available data.[15]

[14]Unfortunately, only one study has been published in which near-threshold intensities were investigated (Dagher et al., 1958), and hue shift data were tangential to the main aims of that study. As a result, the relevant findings are somewhat equivocal, but they seem to indicate that the hue shifts are largely in the same direction for near threshold stimuli as for the higher intensities studied by Purdy.

[15]An interesting point emerges from Fig. 10.18. Note that the curve for 570 nm is horizontal. That is not surprising since, at that wavelength, the A and B absorption spectra are equal, and therefore no matter what intensity is delivered to the eye, the difference in outputs of the A and B systems ought to be the same, i.e., zero (assuming that the K's for the A and B systems are equal). In fact, no matter what the nature of the nonlinearity, the hue of that wavelength should be invariant with intensity if hue is correlated with any measure of the relative outputs of the A and the B systems. Similarly, the hues of wavelengths near 570 nm do not change very strongly with intensity, even when the intensity changes over three or four log units. This is true despite the fact that the nonlinearity on which Fig. 10.18 is based approximates a logarithmic function over only one and a half log units. This illustrates an important point, but one that requires some explanation. It has already been shown that, if the nonlinearity in the visual system were perfectly logarithmic, (i.e., $A = K \cdot \log I$), and if the subsequent neural interactions that mediated the perception of hue simply subtracted the output of one color-system from another, then hue would change with wavelength, but would be completely independent of intensity over a very large range of intensities. (The hue of a given wavelength would only change when the ratio of the absorptions it produced in the three color-systems began to change, and that would occur only at extremely high intensities, where an appreciable fraction of the pigment is bleached.) Obviously, if the nonlinearity were almost logarithmic over some limited range of intensities, then it might be expected that hues would be approximately constant only over that range of intensities. Now the relationship $(K_1 \times I)/(K_2 + I)$ [Eq. (1)] is logarithmic only over a range of I of about

PHYSIOLOGICAL MEASURES OF WAVELENGTH- DEPENDENT RESPONSES The electrophysiology of color vision has been extensively studied in a large number of species, ranging from the bee to the monkey. There appear to be differences among the species (although there are striking similarities, for example, between the goldfish and the monkey), and since the physiology of the monkey is most likely to be similar to human physiology, only the work on the monkey will be discussed. Much of this work has been performed by DeValois and his co-workers.

Microelectrodes The technique to be discussed involves recording the activity of single neural units in the retinas and brains of anesthetized monkeys when their eyes are stimulated with lights of different wavelengths and intensities. If the entire optic nerve were laid across a pair of electrodes connected to an amplifier, the electrical activity that would be observed would be the sum of the activities of a very large number of separate neurons. If all units happened to operate in exactly the same way, this would provide no problem, but it is very clear that different optic nerve fibers do transmit different information about the retinal image. Therefore, there are many interesting problems, including the question of the physiological correlates of color vision, that cannot be answered by recording from large groups of neurons. The real answers must be deduced from records of the activity of single neurons.

Single mammalian neurons are extremely delicate; it is almost impossible to dissect a single nerve fiber out of, say, a mammalian optic nerve in order to record its activity. (Such a dissection procedure is commonly used on some animals, e.g., the horseshoe crab, in which the fibers are more resistant to damage.) In general, to record the activity of single neural units in the mammalian nervous system, extremely fine electrodes must be used, so fine that, when they are driven into a mass of neural tissue, they will be capable of recording the activity of

---

15:1, but the hues of most wavelengths do not change very much over a range of 10,000:1. Thus it might seem that Eq. (1) does not apply.

However, the plots in Fig. 10.18 are the result of assuming that Eq. (1) is applicable, and they show that, so long as the *ratio* of the two I's is not too large, the system is similar to a logarithmic one over any arbitrarily large intensity range. The relationship between an *input* and its *output* is approximately logarithmic only over a range of about 15:1, but when two inputs are held in a constant ratio, the *difference* between the two outputs is approximately logarithmic over any range of inputs so long as the *ratio* is not large. Thus the hues that are relatively invariant with intensity are those corresponding to wavelengths where the absorption spectra of the color systems are nearly the same in height.

This behavior of the expression $(K_1 \times I)/(K_2 + I)$ will be referred to again in later chapters, where it will be related to some crucial aspects of the perception of brightness (Weber's Law and brightness constancy).

only one or a few neurons. In fact, some electrodes are so small that they can be driven into a cell body without disturbing its normal activity.

An electrode is simply a device that provides a path by which electric current can flow between the neuron and a sensitive amplifying device. The amplifier drives some display device, usually an oscilloscope, that displays the amount of current flowing in the electrodes at each instant. Therefore, in order to record the activity of a single neuron, the electrode should provide a current path between one very tiny region of the animal and the amplifier. There are two general ways in which such electrodes, called microelectrodes, are made.

Metal electrodes are made by dipping a fine steel or tungsten wire in and out of a chemical solution while an electric current is driven through the wire and the solution. This procedure forms an extraordinarily fine point at the dipped end of the wire (the tip can be on the order of 1 μ, that is, 1/1000 mm across). If this super-sharp needle were used as an electrode, it would conduct current at its tip but also all along its length. To avoid this, so that current is collected from only the very tiny area at its tip, the electrode is coated with an insulating material everywhere except at the tip. This is usually accomplished by dipping the entire electrode in some form of varnish-like liquid, and then allowing the varnish to dry while the electrode is turned tip-upward. Gravity and surface tension make the varnish vanishingly thin at the tip, where the curvature of the surface is extreme, but leave the remainder of the electrode insulated (if the consistency of the varnish is exactly right, the electrode is very clean, the humidity and the confluence of the planets are favorable).

The other common technique for making electrodes involves drawing glass tubes out to very fine diameters, and filling them with a solution that conducts electricity. A hollow glass tube a few inches long and a millimeter or two in outside diameter is heated in the middle, and when the heated region is soft, the two ends of the tube are pulled

Fig. 10.20 **The result of heating a hollow glass tube in the middle and pulling it sharply. The tube has a very fine point and the hole runs all the way through.**

apart rapidly. (This can be done by hand, but is usually done by a machine designed for the purpose.) When it is done properly, the procedure results in two tubes like the one in Fig. 10.20. The hole down the middle of the tube extends all the way through the tip, no matter how fine the outside diameter is, and this outside diameter can be as small as a 0.1 μ — so small that the tip cannot be seen through the best optical microscope, and can only be observed with an electron microscope. The tube is then filled with a solution that conducts current, usually by submerging the tube in a salt solution and boiling. Next, a wire is inserted into the broad end of the electrode, and that wire is in turn connected to the amplifier. Thus, the electrode, which is called a micropipette, provides an electrical connection between the recording device and the very tiny region of tissue immediately adjacent to its tip.

The Preparation The term "preparation" refers to the animal that is to be recorded from, as well as his surgical treatment. The animal is anesthetized with one or a combination of anesthetics that are assumed not to disrupt the functioning of the neural elements to be tested. Since the region from which activity will be recorded is so small, the animals body is rigidly supported and movements are eliminated so far as it is possible to do so. If these movements are not limited, the electrode tip will move with respect to the tissue.[16] To restrict movement, the animal and all of the parts of the apparatus that hold the electrodes are usually mounted on a large, heavy table (made of concrete or marble), and the table is insulated as well as possible from the vibrations of the building. The animal's head is clamped rigidly to the table top, and muscle contractions are often eliminated by administering a form of curare, a drug that blocks transmission across neuromuscular junctions. The curare not only prevents the animal's skeletal muscles from contracting, but it also eliminates natural respiration, and therefore the animal must be artificially respirated by a mechanical respirator.

After all this preliminary preparation (and a lot more), the part of the nervous system to be recorded from is exposed as much as possible, and the microelectrode is positioned so that it can be driven down into the region of interest. Another, large, electrode, called the reference electrode, is placed somewhere else on the animal, so that it makes

[16]Techniques have been developed for microelectrode recording from awake and unrestricted animals, but because they are difficult and limited, they are not ordinarily used unless there is no alternative.

contact with the general body fluids. The wires from these two electrodes are connected to a special amplifier and display device so that any currents flowing between the two electrodes may be observed and recorded.

An optical system is also arranged to deliver stimuli (in this case, colored ones) to the animal's eye or eyes, which are sewn open. The cornea is sometimes kept moist and in good condition by a specially made contact lens.

The Measurements The next stage in the experimental procedure is to locate a single neuron to record from. This may be done in many different ways, and the choice of ways is extremely critical to the conclusions that can be drawn from the experiment (although this choice is rarely afforded much analysis or discussion in published reports of microelectrode work). The problem in locating a neuron to record from is, of course, that the neurons in most preparations cannot be seen, and even if they could be seen, the electrode tip cannot be. Therefore, the decision about whether or not the electrode tip is recording from a cell of interest must be based upon the electrical activity that it yields. (After an experiment is completed, the location of the electrode tip can sometimes be determined by special procedures. However, those procedures are so cumbersome that they have rarely been used in studies of color vision.) For example, one method commonly used is to drive the electrode down into the tissue until responses are recorded that seem clearly to be impulses coming from one or a few fibers. During this search, in some studies, the eye is in darkness. If so, the neurons that will be observed will be only those that produce spontaneous activity in the dark. In other studies, the search is made while the retina is dimly illuminated, and then the conclusions of the study pertain to those units that fire continuously under dim illumination.

The other search procedure that is used when recording from single fibers is to expose the retina continuously to stimuli to which it is believed the fibers are sensitive. For example, often one flash per second is delivered to the entire retina, or a line is swept back and forth, etc., while the electrode is driven into the tissue and the activity it detects is monitored. Obviously, each of these procedures may be biased in favor of a particular class of neurons, and one must therefore carefully consider the search procedure when attempting to evaluate the many statements in the literature concerning the proportion of nerve fibers that perform in some particular way. (In a rough sampling of published reports on single fiber recording, 100% of the reports devote at least two long paragraphs to a description of the apparatus, electrodes, anesthesia, etc., but only 10% of them say anything whatever about their search procedure.)

Once it has been established that the electrode is recording from one fiber (or a number of fibers small enough to allow the responses of single units to be selected out of the total record), the experimenter typically stimulates the retina with lights of various colors, intensities, shapes, etc., and notes the response of the fiber. Many fibers in the mammalian visual system display spontaneous activity, that is, they fire continuously even in the dark.[17] When this kind of fiber is stimulated, it may either increase or decrease its rate of firing. If the rate of firing is increased by a given stimulus, the stimulus is said to excite the fiber, and if the rate decreases, the stimulus is said to inhibit the fiber.

Both of these classes of response are found in the eye of the monkey when it is stimulated with lights of various wavelengths. If a unit does not display spontaneous activity, it can manifest an excitatory response to some particular stimulus by increasing its rate of firing (above zero), but inhibitory responses can only be observed if an excitatory stimulus is first identified, and then it is observed that a new stimulus, superimposed upon the excitatory one, reduces the response to the excitatory one.

The Results — Wavelength-Dependent Responses in the Brain of the Monkey

Virtually all of the published measurements of wavelength sensitivity in single fibers of the visual systems of primates have been made by DeValois and his co-workers, on the macaque monkey (DeValois *et al.*, 1966). These workers have, over many years, performed the extremely difficult task of determining, by psychophysical means, that the macaque is trichromatic, and appears to have color vision that is indistinguishable from that of the human. This fact lends considerable interest to their studies of the electrophysiology of the monkey's color vision, since it is a good bet that the human electrophysiology is similar.

All of the data that will be discussed here were taken from single fibers in the lateral geniculate nucleus (LGN), a part of the brain where

---

[17]Some workers have claimed that all fibers in the optic nerves of primates manifest spontaneous activity because they have never found one that did not. However, it is improper to make such an assertion, since there is no known search procedure that is guaranteed to be equally likely to sample every possible type of nerve fiber. No matter what set of stimuli are used while the electrode is being advanced into the tissue, there always might be units that respond only to some stimulus not in that set. In fact, many neurons in the visual cortex of the mammal respond only to very specific stimuli (see Chapter XV), stimuli so specific that these neurons were not detected during the first two decades of recording from single units in the brain.

many of the axons of the retinal ganglion cells (the optic nerve fibers) terminate. (There is evidence that recordings from the retinal ganglion cells themselves are substantially the same as those from the LGN with respect to wavelength sensitivity.) The data were obtained by driving a micropipette into the nucleus and stopping when spontaneous activity was recorded. (Thus the data pertain only to those cells that exhibit spontaneous activity. De Valois *et al.*, say, "In the absence of a stimulus, LGN cells are 'spontaneously' active . . ." [De Valois *et al.*, 1966, p. 968]. They do not say ". . . *some* LGN cells . . ." nor ". . . *all* LGN cells . . .," but imply the latter.)

The stimuli were flashes of light of various wavelengths delivered diffusely over the retina. Under these conditions, two classes of cells are evident. De Valois calls one class "spectrally opponent" cells and the other "nonopponent" cells. (These names are based upon the terminology used by Hurvich and Jamison in their extensive series of psychophysical studies of human color vision, e.g., see Jamison and Hurvich, 1961.) The opponent cells respond differently to lights of different wavelengths, being excited by some wavelengths and inhibited by others. The nonopponent cells respond in the same way to all wavelengths. About half of the nonopponent cells studied responded by increasing their firing rates to light of *any* wavelength while the other half decreased their rate.

Figure 10.21 shows typical spectral response curves for the nonopponent cells, and Fig. 10.22 is a sample of the variety of curves obtained from spectrally opponent units. It is easy to imagine that the responses of the various units in Figs. 10.21 are the results of combinations of excitations of the three classes of receptors. For example, suppose that a single unit in the LGN received excitation from all three of the kinds of cones in the retina. Its spectral response curve would, in general, have the shape displayed in Fig. 10.21a. Similarly, if it were inhibited by all three receptor types (or inhibited by a unit like that in Fig. 10.21a, or excited by a unit that was inhibited by all three receptor types), it would respond, in general, as in Fig. 10.21b. Qualitatively, the spectral response of a unit would also look like that in Fig. 10.21a if it were excited by only two of the cone types and unaffected by the other, or even if it were excited by only one cone type and unaffected by the other two.

Similarly the opponent cells in Fig. 10.22 appear to be excited by one or more and *inhibited* by the other cone type(s). DeValois was able to evaluate this possibility by measuring the spectral sensitivity curves of opponent cells after various chromatic adaptations. For the reasons discussed in Chapter IX, if a unit is excited (or inhibited) by only one cone type, the shape of its spectral response curve (its action

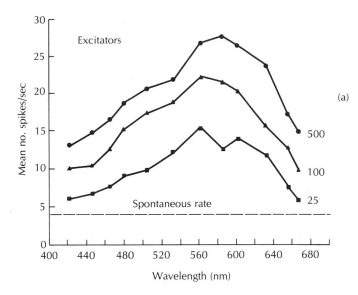

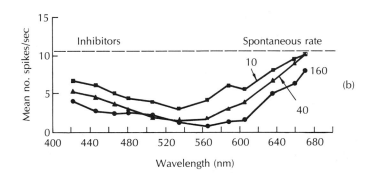

Fig. 10.21 **Average responses of non-opponent cells in the brain of the monkey. The units fire continuously at the rate labeled "spontaneous rate" until the eye is flooded with light of the wavelengths on the horizontal axis. The excitatory units in (a) respond to the stimulus by increasing their firing rates and the inhibitory units in (b) by reducing their firing rates. The three curves in each plot are three different intensity (energy) levels, in arbitrary units.** [*From DeValois et al. (1966).*]

spectrum) must be the same both before and after moderate light-adaptation regardless of the wavelength of the bleaching light. If, on the other hand, the shape of the curve after adaptation is different when the wavelength of bleaching light is changed, it must be true that the activity of the cell is affected by more than one class of receptor (the classes being defined by their action spectra).

From their measurements of the effect of bleaching by different wavelengths, DeValois and his co-workers (DeValois and Jacobs, 1968) have concluded that each of the opponent cells they examined was one of the following:

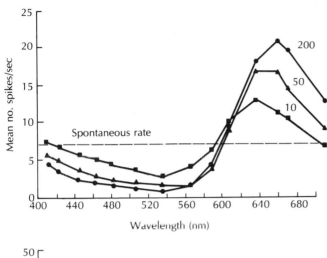

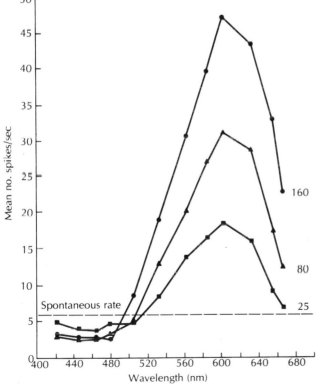

Fig. 10.22 **For a complete description of this figure, see the legend on the following page.**

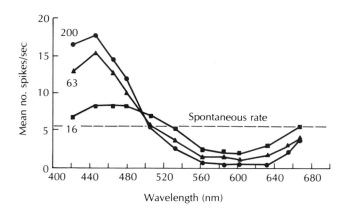

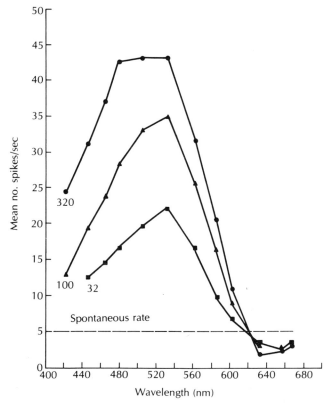

Fig. 10.22 **Average responses of various classes of spectrally opponent cells in the brain of the monkey. The three curves in each plot are three different intensity (energy) levels, in arbitrary units.** [*From DeValois et al. (1966).*]

(a) excited by the *A* and inhibited by the *B* system[18];
(b) inhibited by the *A* and excited by the *B* system;
(c) excited by the *A* and inhibited by the *C* system; or
(d) inhibited by the *A* and excited by the *C* system.

This does not mean that all of the responses of lateral geniculate cells normally fall into one of four distinct shapes. In fact, the curves, a few of which are shown in Fig. 10.22, actually seem to appear in all possible shapes. This is, evidently, the result of the fact that, while there are only four classes of inputs, the relative *strengths* of the inputs vary widely within each class. For example, some units are strongly excited by *A* and weakly inhibited by *B*, some are weakly excited by *A* and strongly inhibited by *B*, etc. However, after adaptation to lights whose wavelengths are chosen to suppress one of the inputs much more strongly than the other (e.g., an adapting light of 640 nm is absorbed 7.5 times as strongly by the *A* as by the *B* system), all of the units in the first two classes take on the same shape, that of the *B* system, while all of the remaining units take on the shape of the *C* system.

It is interesting to relate the four classes listed above to the model in Fig. 10.12, (p. 248). Types (a) and (b), above, are obviously redundant, in that the same information is carried by both types. Similarly, types (c) and (d) are redundant. However, a more subtle redundancy that might well have been expected is *not* in evidence. For example, if there were also units that were excited by *B* and inhibited by *C*, their information *about wavelength* would be redundant, in that the wavelength is already specified by just two channels, as shown in Fig. 10.12.

The third channel of information that is required in a trichromatic visual system presumably carries intensity information, and is manifested in the nonopponent units of Fig. 10.21.

---

[18]These color-system designations are from Fig. 8.9, p. 171. DeValois refers to them by their peak wavelengths; *A* peaks at 580 nm, *B* at 550 nm, and *C* at 435 nm.

XI ◇◇◇ THE PSYCHOPHYSIOLOGY OF BRIGHTNESS – I
SPATIAL INTERACTION IN THE VISUAL SYSTEM

IT is a reasonable assumption that the strength of the excitation produced when visual pigment molecules are isomerized is a monotonically increasing function of the *rate* of isomerization. (A monotonic
relationship means that for each value of one of the variables, there is
only one corresponding value of the other one. The assumption here
is that if the rate of isomerization is greater in one instance than another, then the strength of excitation will also be greater. That is, the
curve relating the rate of isomerization to the strength of excitation is
always rising, as in Fig. 11.1a, and does not level off or reverse its direction, as do the curves in Fig. 11.1b and c.) Some reasons for making
this assumption were discussed in detail in Chapter VI. Since the rate of
isomerization is certainly a monotonically increasing function of the
intensity of the light incident on the receptors, it is reasonable that the
strength of excitation of a receptor is a monotonically increasing function of the intensity (quanta per second) of the light falling on it. Furthermore, since the intensity of each point in the retinal image is di-

rectly proportional to the intensity of the corresponding point in the scene that the eye is viewing, the strength of excitation of any receptor ought to be a monotonically increasing function of the intensity of the point in space that is imaged on that receptor.

The *apparent brightness* of any point in the visual field also generally increases when the intensity of the light radiating from that point is increased. For example, when the current through a light bulb is raised, it radiates quanta at a greater rate and it also looks brighter. A white paper reflects more quanta per second than a black paper, and the white paper looks brighter. We have all observed such phenomena. Although most people are not aware of the physics of light nor of the photochemistry of visual excitation, we all tend implicitly to make an assumption like the one explicitly stated above, namely that the strength of visual excitation monotonically increases with the intensity of the light radiating from the object viewed. It follows from that very likely assumption and from the observation that objects which radiate more intensely look brighter, that the apparent brightness of an object is determined by the strength of excitation of the corresponding receptors. This conclusion can be restated as follows: The physiological correlate of the brightness of any point in the visual field is the strength of excitation of the receptors lying under the retinal image of that point. This conclusion is reasonable, but it is wrong. We are led to it not by faulty logic, but by imprecise perceptual data. In this chapter, evidence will be given that the brightness of a region depends strongly upon factors other than the intensity of light radiating from that region. A different physiological correlate of brightness, one consistent with accurate physiological and perceptual data will be presented.[1]

[1]The term "apparent brightness" will be shortened to "brightness" in this book. The term "brightness," then, will be used to refer to a *perceptual* dimension while "intensity" will refer to a *physical* dimension, for example, quanta per second per square millimeter.

Fig. 11.1 (a) A monotonic relationship between two variables; there is a unique value of one variable for each value of the other. In (b) and (c), that is not the case, and the relationships are nonmonotonic.

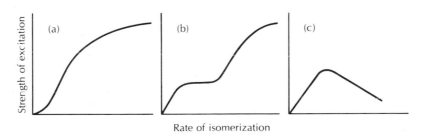

Strength of excitation

(a) (b) (c)

Rate of isomerization

DEMONSTRATIONS THAT BRIGHTNESS IS NOT A SIMPLE FUNCTION OF INTENSITY Figure 11.2a is a photograph of a black and white paper disk mounted on a motor in such a way that it can be spun. Figure 11.2b is a photograph of the pattern in Fig. 11.2a when it was spinning fast (fast enough to make many revolutions during the time that the camera shutter was open). The intensity distribution across any diameter of the spinning disk is plotted in Fig. 11.2c. It is generated in the following way: Consider any point in the inside disk of Fig. 11.2b. When the camera shutter was open, the corresponding point on the film was alternately illuminated by light from the black and then from the white area of the spinning pattern in Fig. 11.2a. About half of the time, the light falling on that point on the film was intense (when the white area was imaged on it) and half the time it was less intense (when the black area was imaged on it). That statement is true for every point within the central disk. Therefore, every point within the central disk will receive the same total amount of light during a long exposure, and the central disk will have a uniform intensity.

Now consider any point in the ring that surrounds the central disk in Fig. 11.2b. As the wheel spins, each corresponding point on the film will also be alternately stimulated by the black and white regions of of the pattern in Fig. 11.2a, but the white portion of the 360° of rotation is larger than the black portion. Therefore, while the shutter is open, the total amount of light falling on the film from every point in the ring is greater than the amount from the disk. The intensity distribution plotted in Fig. 11.2c illustrates the results.

The appearance of the pattern in Fig. 11.2b is not surprising. A disk at one intensity is surrounded by a ring at a somewhat higher intensity, and the figure looks like a disk surrounded by a somewhat brighter ring.

Now examine the pattern in Fig. 11.2d. In this pattern, the region near the center and the region near the outside of the disk both contain equal angular amounts of black and white, so that, when the spinning disk is photographed, the intensity at the center and the outside is identical, as shown in Fig. 11.2f. In the region between the two areas of equal intensity, the amounts of black and white vary in the particular way that gives rise to the overall intensity distribution plotted in Fig. 11.2f. However, the photograph of the spinning disk, Fig. 11.2e, looks virtually the same as the one in Fig. 11.2b. It looks like the disk is darker than the ring, even though the intensities over most of those two regions of Fig. 11.2e are identical. Here, then, is an instance in which two regions of identical intensity look different in brightness. Thus brightness is not always monotonically related to intensity.

Figure 11.3 is an example of the complementary case, where two areas have different intensities but the same brightness. The pattern in Fig. 11.3a, when spun, produces a disk of uniform intensity, as photographed in Fig. 11.3b and plotted in Fig. 11.3c. The pattern in Fig. 11.3d, when spun, produces a distribution like the one in Figs. 11.2a,b,c, except that the corners of the intensity distribution are rounded. Note that the spinning disk in Fig. 11.3e *looks* uniform even though the intensities of its inner and outer regions are different. In fact, the intensities in Fig. 11.3e are exactly the same as the corresponding intensities in Fig. 11.2b, where the difference in brightness between the regions is very evident.[2]

[2]If you do not believe that these pictures are honest, or even if you do, it is very easy to verify the phenomena without photography. Color wheel motors are available in almost every psychology laboratory. Borrow one and then simply cut out or paint the patterns and spin them.

The rules for construction of patterns are simple and logical. Out of moderately stiff white paper, cut a disk that is about ten inches in diameter. Find the center and punch a hole the proper size to fit the hub of the color wheel. Then draw a straight line from the center of the disk to the outside (i.e., the horizontal radii to the right of center in Figs. 11.2a and d). (You may wish to modify this step later, once you understand the procedure for constructing the patterns.)

Now you need to draw a second line from the center to the edge of the disk in such a way that the two lines will divide the disk into two areas, and when one of the areas is blackened while the other remains white, spinning the disk will produce the correct pattern.

Rules

(1) Any portion of a line that is radial, i.e., which, if extended, would intersect the center of the disk, will produce a corresponding region of uniform intensity in the spinning disk. For example, the two roughly horizontal line segments in Fig. 11.2a are each radial, and their corresponding regions are each uniform.

(2) Any portion of the line that is an arc concentric with the disk will produce an abrupt intensity difference. For example, the vertical steps that demarcate the inner boundaries of the rings in Figs. 11.2c and f are produced by arcs whose centers of curvature are the centers of the disks.

(3) Rules 1 and 2 are obviously special cases of the general rule that the average intensity at any given point in the spinning disk is directly proportional to the relative angular amounts of light and dark that are present at the radial distance of the point. More precisely, if you wish to produce any particular intensity distribution that has radial symmetry (that is the only kind that can be produced on a spinning color wheel), plot the desired distribution on polar coordinate paper, and then make a black and white pattern exactly like the one plotted.

To duplicate the effects in Figs. 11.2 and 11.3, the radial lines and arc should be drawn carefully, but the curved parts can be sketched in by hand.

The way in which intensity distributions can be formed by photographing these disks has already been discussed. Each point in the film integrates all of the light it absorbs during the exposure, and if, during the exposure, the disk revolves a large number of times (or any integral number of times), the photograph will then represent the average values of the intensities at each point.

When the disk is spun very fast (i.e., faster than about 3600 rpm) and when it is illuminated by daylight or tungsten light (not fluorescent light), it will look just the same to the naked eye as the photographs look. This is a result of the temporal summation in the visual system. When the spinning pattern is fixated, each receptor will alternately be illuminated brightly and dimly, as the image of the bright and the dark parts of the pattern sweep across it. The visual system essentially integrates the effects of all of the light falling on the retina over any period shorter than 10 or 15 msec, and this temporal summation of the visual system smooths out the alternations. The resulting excitation is the same as that which would result from a steady illumination, and therefore the pattern, if it is spun fast enough, looks steady, and, effectively, has the same intensity distribution as that on the photograph.

It is best to view the spinning patterns under sunlight, or under the light from a large incandescent lamp. When viewed under fluorescent lighting, the flicker of the light interacts with the rotation of the disk in such a way that patterns and colors not relevant to the demonstration will be produced. These patterns and colors may be of interest in their own right, but they are very distracting when the effects under discussion are to be demonstrated.

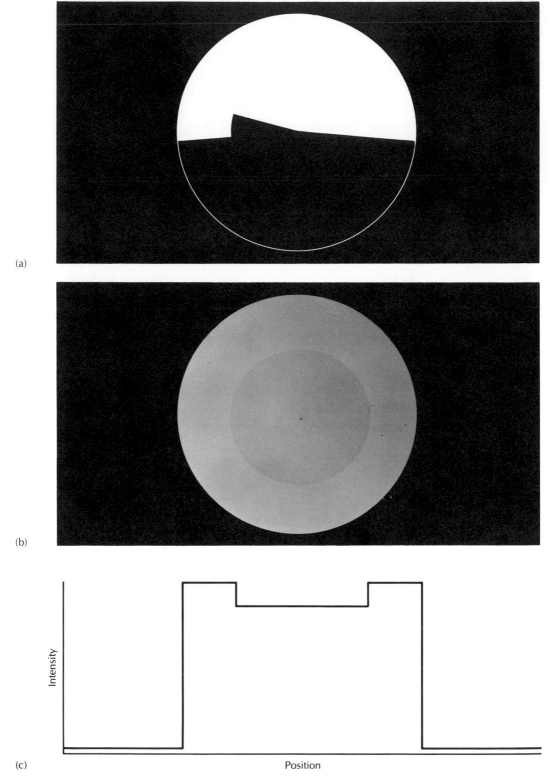

(a)

(b)

(c)

Intensity

Position

Fig. 11.2 **(a) A disk of black and white paper is mounted on a motor. (b) A photograph of the disk in (a) when it is spinning. The exposure in this photograph was long enough for the disk to make a large number of revolutions**

(d)

(e)

(f)

Intensity

Position

while the camera shutter was open. (c) The intensity distribution produced by
the spinning disk against its background is plotted. The illustrations in (d), (e),
and (f) are similar figures for a somewhat different intensity distribution.

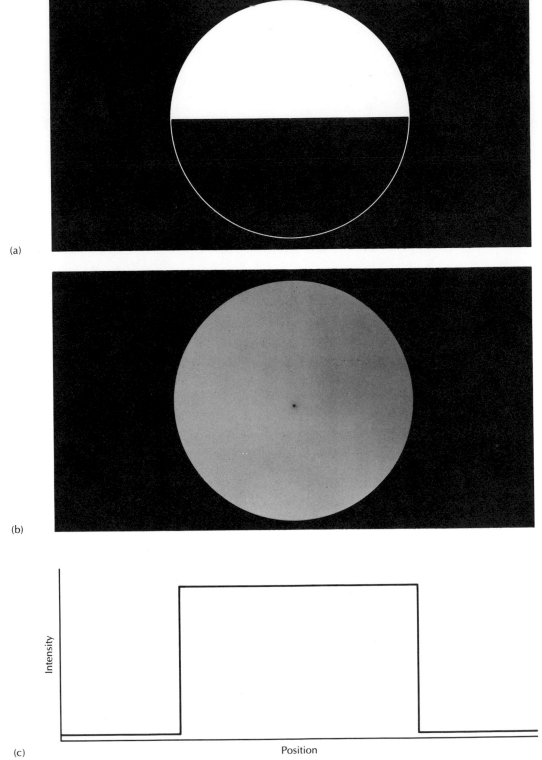

(a)

(b)

(c)

Position

Intensity

Fig. 11.3 **The disk in (a) produces a uniform intensity distribution when spun, while the disk in (d) produces a distribution in which the central region has a**

(d)

(e)

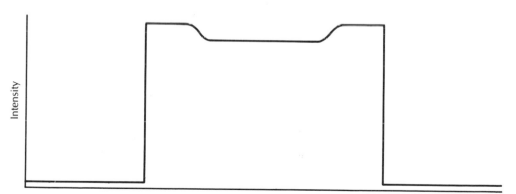

(f)

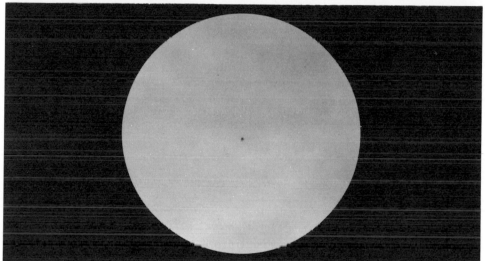

lower intensity than the outer region. Nevertheless, both disks appear uniform
in brightness.

(a)

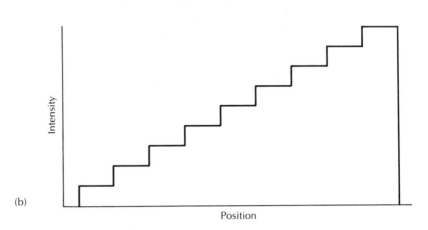

(b)

Position

Figure 11.4a is a striking example of the fact that areas that are identical in intensity can differ in brightness. The actual intensity distribution in this figure is plotted in Fig. 11.4b. While each strip in the pattern is uniform in physical intensity, the brightness distribution in the
pattern is strongly scalloped.

The pattern in Fig. 11.5a is called a Mach band pattern, after Ernst
Mach, who first described it in 1865. The intensity distribution is actually as plotted in Fig. 11.5b but the brightness distribution exhibits a
brighter stripe in the region marked *B* and a darker one at *D*. Here
again, the brightnesses at these regions, called Mach bands, do not
depend simply upon the intensities there.[3]

[3]The patterns in Figs. 11.4 and 11.5 can also be produced, with radial symmetry, on color wheels.
For example, Fig. 11.6 shows the Mach bands on a color wheel. Similarly, the patterns in Figs. 11.2
and 11.3 can be produced in a linear pattern, and the effects are essentially the same.

Fig. 11.5 **(a) A Mach band pattern and its intensity distribution. A bright band appears at** *B* **and a dark one at** *D*.

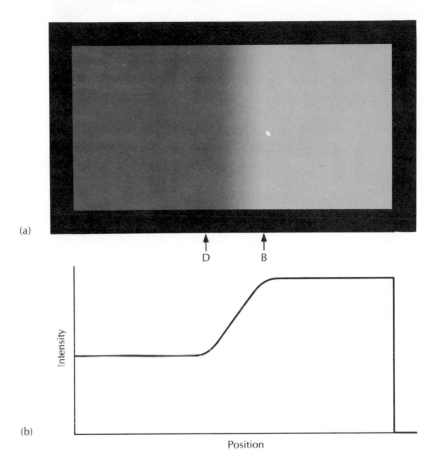

(a)

D   B

(b)

Intensity

Position

Contrast and Constancy The phenomenon called simultaneous contrast is a very commonly experienced example of the fact that the brightness of a region does not depend simply upon its intensity. Find a piece of gray or colored paper that is thick enough to be opaque. Look at it with one eye under any ordinary light and then hold it up at arm's length, between the eye you have chosen and the bright sky or a large light source. Note that the paper looks much darker when it is in front of the light source than it did when it was normally illuminated, even though the actual amount of light reflected from the paper is the same. In fact, if the background light is bright enough, the paper will look black when held in front of it. It is common experience to see objects or people silhouetted when they are strongly backlighted, even when the light actually reflected from them is more than ample to allow them to be seen when they are against a dark background.

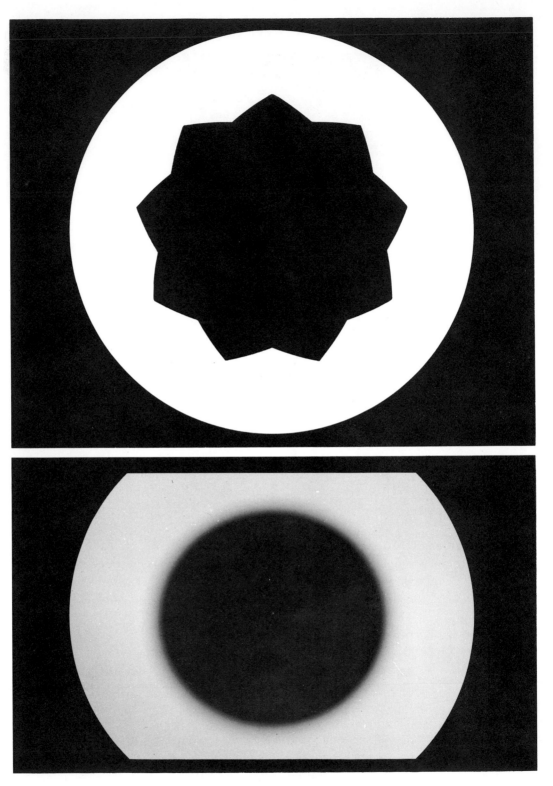

Fig. 11.6 **Mach bands produced on a color wheel.**

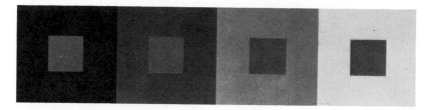

Fig. 11.7 **An example of simultaneous contrast. The small squares all have identical intensities, but their brightnesses are different because they lie on backgrounds that differ in intensity.**

This same phenomenon, brightness contrast, can be seen, although much less strongly, in Fig. 11.7. The intensities of the small squares are all identical, but their brightnesses are different because their backgrounds are of different intensities.

Brightness contrast is very closely related to another phenomenon; the brightness of any object remains fairly constant despite large changes in the illumination that falls on it. This is called *brightness constancy.* For example, a piece of ordinary white paper reflects about 90% of the incident light, while black paper reflects about 10%. When these papers are moved from ordinary room illumination into direct sunlight, the incident illumination, and therefore the reflected light intensity, may increase by 1000-fold; yet the papers still have about the same brightnesses as they had indoors. Furthermore, the black paper outside reflects $0.10 \times 1000 = 100$ relative units of intensity and the white paper inside reflects only $0.90 \times 1 = 0.9$ units; but the black paper outside still looks darker than the white paper inside.

Heinemann (1955) made an important study of brightness contrast and constancy that will be described in some detail here. He wanted to measure how the brightness of a patch of light was influenced by the

Fig. 11.8 **The stimulus configuration in most of Heinemann's experiments. The smaller disks (at intensities I_t and I_m) were 28′ in diameter, while the background (containing I_b) was 55′ in diameter. (The patterns on the left and right of the fixation point were actually presented one to each eye, but that is not important here.)** [*After Heinemann (1955).*]

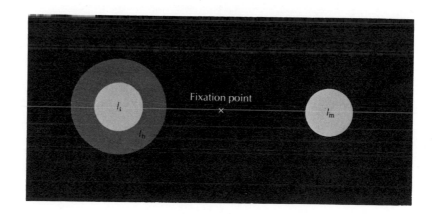

intensity of its background. To do this, he constructed an apparatus that presented the subject with a view like that illustrated in Fig. 11.8. His general procedure was to set the intensities of the "test" disk I_t and the background I_b at some predetermined levels and then ask the subject to adjust the intensity of the matching disk I_m until its brightness appeared equal to the test disk.

First, Heinemann set I_t at some value, say 100 intensity units, and then had the subject adjust I_m to make the two disks match, for a series of values of I_b. The results of such a set of measurements are shown in Fig. 11.9. When I_b is zero, the two disks match when $I_t = 100$ (except for so-called "constant errors," which are very small in relation to the effects being measured). Then as the intensity of the background I_b is gradually raised, the matching value I_m also rises slightly. This indicates that the brightness of the left-hand test disk increases slightly when the intensity of its background is raised. It is the opposite of a "contrast" effect.

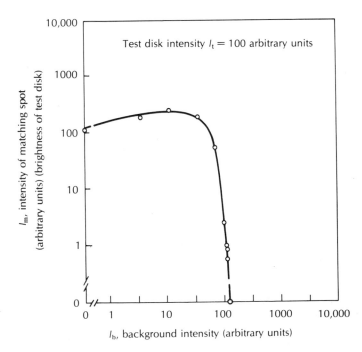

Fig. 11.9 **The effect upon the brightness of a disk of varying the intensity of its background. The vertical axis is actually the intensity of the matching spot when its brightness matched the brightness of the test spot. Thus, it is a measure of the brightness of the test spot.** [*After Heinemann (1955), Subject EGH.*]

As I_b continues to increase, the test disk brightness begins to *drop* until, when I_b is about 110 units, the subject sets I_m at zero, indicating that the test disk looks as dark as the dark background. This entire curve is a measure of brightness contrast: If the brightness of a region were independent of the intensity of its surroundings, the curve would be a horizontal line. The curve actually indicates the presence of a very strong contrast effect.

The entire curve in Fig. 11.9 was measured with the intensity of the test disk I_t set at a fixed level (100). Heinemann repeated these same measurements for a number of different I_t settings, and the results are shown in Fig. 11.10. Note that all the curves are essentially similar to the one in Fig. 10.9. As the background intensity increases from zero, there is a small increase in brightness, but when the background approaches the intensity of the disk, the brightness of the disk drops sharply.[4]

The curves in Fig. 11.10 represent a quantitative description of brightness contrast, but they also contain an extensive set of measurements of brightness *constancy*.

In order to understand this point, let us reexamine just what constancy is. In general, constancy refers to the fact that the brightness of an object tends to remain constant, independent of the illumination falling on it.

A procedure that is often used to measure brightness constancy helps to define it more precisely. A subject is seated in front of an array of patches of gray paper, ranging in shade from black to white. The illumination on this set of "matching" papers is held constant at all times. The subject is also shown a test patch that is simply another piece of gray paper, at some distance from him, and he is asked to pick out, from the series of grays in front of him, the one that looks the same as the test patch. The particular shade of the test patch can be varied from trial to trial, and the intensity of illumination on the test patch and its surroundings may also be varied.

So long as there are no extraordinary conditions, and in particular so long as the measurements are performed in an ordinary room that is normally lighted, the subject will almost always choose a matching

---

[4]For each curve, there is a value of background intensity that drives the brightness of the test disk just to zero. What would happen if the background intensity were increased beyond this level? Heinemann tried this. The subjects reported that the test disk looked darker than a patch with no light in it, and they therefore could not make a match. They were only able to make the match when Heinemann added a lighted background to the *matching disk* as well. Then both disks looked darker than an unlighted disk, and they could be matched.

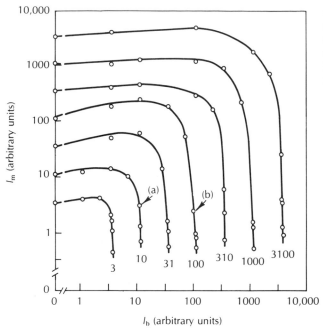

Fig. 11.10 **A set of curves like that in Fig. 11.9, for a number of different test disk intensities. The number below each curve gives** I_t **(in arbitrary units).** [*From Heinemann (1955), Subject EGH.*]

gray that is physically the same or nearly the same as the test gray. For example, if the test patch is a gray that reflects 50% of the incident light, he will say that it looks most like the matching patch that also reflects 50% of the light. He will do this even if the light falling on the test patch is 1000 times greater than that falling on the matching patches. The subject is essentially reporting that the shade of gray of the test patch stays the same regardless of the amount of light falling on it (even though the intensities of the retinal images of the test patch vary over 1000-fold).

When the subject's choices are of this kind, he is said to be exhibiting brightness constancy. If his judgments are completely independent of the illumination level, he is said to be exhibiting perfect constancy. On the other hand, if his choices indicate that the test patch looks lighter when its illumination increases, he is showing less than perfect or "under-constancy," and if it looks darker when the illumination is raised, that is "over-constancy."

Under ordinary conditions, most subjects show only minor departures from perfect constancy; in particular, perfect constancy obtains so long as the light from the source that is illuminating the test patch also falls on the regions surrounding the test patch. However, if the illumination is confined to the test patch alone (e.g., by projecting a spot of light exactly onto the test patch so that none of it spills on to the background), then the brightness of the test patch depends entirely upon the light falling on it, and no constancy is shown.

The significance of this phenomenon will be discussed at some length in Chapter XIII. Here, it is sufficient to explain the way in which Heinemann's data, shown in Fig. 11.10, do in fact constitute a set of quantitative measures of brightness constancy as well as contrast. We already know that when the light falling on a patch and its background is changed, constancy occurs and the patch continues to have the same brightness. Now consider just two points on the set of curves in Fig. 11.10, the points labeled (a) and (b). For the point labeled (a), the test spot intensity was 10 units and the background was 12 units. For the point labeled (b), the corresponding values are 100 and 120. That is, the difference between (a) and (b) is that the intensities of the test spot and its surround have both been multiplied by ten. Now, on the subject's retina, the change from (a) to (b) is exactly the same as that which would have occurred if he was looking at a gray piece of paper on a lighter gray background and the illumination on the entire scene was increased by ten-fold. His judgments of the brightness of the test patch under those two conditions are very similar (i.e., the values of I_m are almost the same). Thus the subject is, indeed, showing brightness constancy.

The points (a) and (b) were arbitrarily chosen from among the set of points for which the intensities of test spot and its surround are in a constant ratio. Heinemann examined such groups of points in some detail, and made a very important discovery. So long as the intensities of the test spot and its surround did not differ by more than about five-fold, the subjects showed very good constancy, even when the "illumination" was varied over a range of 1000:1. On the other hand, if the test spot was much more or much less intense than the background, then constancy began to break down. The general significance of the fact that constancy does occur under some conditions and breaks down under others will be discussed in detail in Chapter XIII. In the context of the present chapter, it is given as an example of the fact that the brightness of an object depends not upon the intensity of light falling on the retinal image of that point, but rather upon the relations among the intensities within the overall image.

All of the phenomena just described illustrate that the brightness at any point in the visual field is not always monotonically related to the intensity at that point. If the reasonable physiological assumption discussed at the beginning of this chapter is accepted, namely that receptor excitation is monotonically related to intensity, then these demonstrations disprove the hypothesis that the physiological correlate of the brightness at any point in the field is the strength of excitation of the corresponding receptors. All of these demonstrations do, however, illustrate that the brightness at any point depends on the relationships among the intensities in the visual field. That is, in every case the brightness at each point is determined by the intensity *distribution* in a region that includes the point in question and also includes some of the surrounding area. The excitatory effects of intensities at neighboring points evidently interact with each other, and the physiological correlate of the brightness at each point must be some function of the resulting postinteraction excitations.

There are a number of excellent physiological studies of the nature of spatial interactions in the visual systems of animals, and these studies are highly relevant to an understanding of the perception of brightness. Therefore, physiological evidence about spatial interactions in the visual system will be discussed now, and after that, we will return to a more detailed analysis of the related perceptual phenomena in an attempt to develop an adequate hypothesis for the physiological correlate of brightness.

EVIDENCE CONCERNING THE PHYSIOLOGICAL NATURE OF SPATIAL INTERACTION IN THE VISUAL SYSTEM

The Limulus

The animal shown in Fig. 11.11 is found on the shores of the East Coast of the United States, and is called the horseshoe crab (although it is not really a crab, but rather an arthropod), *Limulus*. The lateral eyes of this animal lend themselves to physiological analysis, and since preliminary studies indicated that many of the properties of this eye are similar to those of higher animals, including humans, it has been studied very extensively. Most of this work has been carried out in the laboratories of H. K. Hartline, first at the Johnson Foundation in Philadelphia and more recently at the Rockefeller University in New York. While it may seem that studies of so primitive an animal are unlikely to produce insights into human perception, these studies have, in fact, had an enormous influence upon current theories of the processes of human brightness perception. Furthermore, while it seems perfectly obvious that human visual processes are much more complicated than those of the *Limulus,* there is, as yet, no unequivocal evidence of any qualitative differences in the functioning of the human and the *Limulus* retinas that are relevant to human brightness perception. (There are almost certainly important differences with regard to the perception of motion and color, for example. Perhaps, however, the processes involved in the perception of brightness can be considered as very primitive properties of visual systems.)

The Preparation   *Limuli* are usually kept in a sandbox in a refrigerated room, where they bury themselves in the sea water-moistened sand. When an experiment is to be run, one of them is fished out and an eye removed. The equivalent of the cornea is a transparent part of the shell itself (see Fig. 11.11) and the retinal structures are attached to it. The optic nerve runs from the eye a few centimeters to the brain. Therefore, to remove the eye, a circle surrounding the eye is first sawed out of the shell. Then the optic nerve is severed as near to the brain as possible, and the eye, with a few centimeters of optic nerve attached, is lifted out. The eye is then mounted in such a way that the front is available for optic stimulation, while the neural tissue is kept moist. Electrodes may then be inserted into the neural tissue.

The eye of the *Limulus* is faceted (as the eye of the fly). In the human eye, there is a single optical system (the lens and cornea) that forms an image of the field on a mosaic of receptors, so that each receptor receives an amount of light proportional to the amount radiated or reflected from some particular region of the field. In the faceted eye of *Limulus,* there is a separate optical system for each facet, and the lens in each facet forms an image (although a very poor one) in the plane of the receptors contained in the facet. The characteristics of the lens, the shape of the facet, and the location of the visual pigment are such that light from a roughly circular area of the field falls on the visual pigment in each facet, and adjacent facets receive light from overlapping but somewhat displaced fields.

Comparing the optics of the *Limulus* eye to the optics of human eye, we can consider each facet in *Limulus* to be the rough analog of each receptor in the human. Each facet and each receptor receive light from a region of the field; the fields of different human receptors overlap because of diffraction, aberrations and scattered light, and the

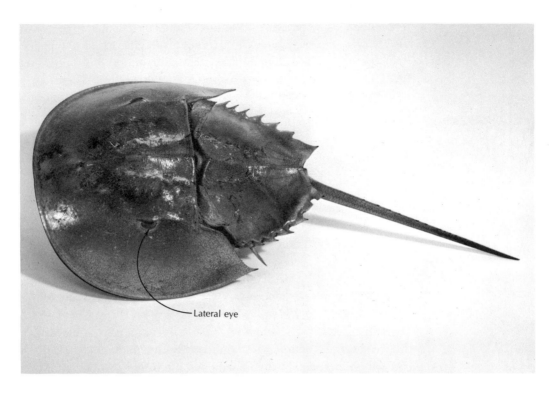

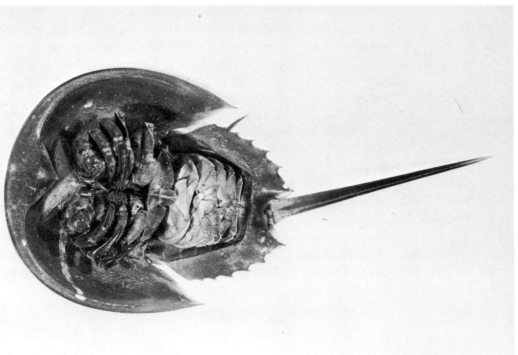

Lateral eye

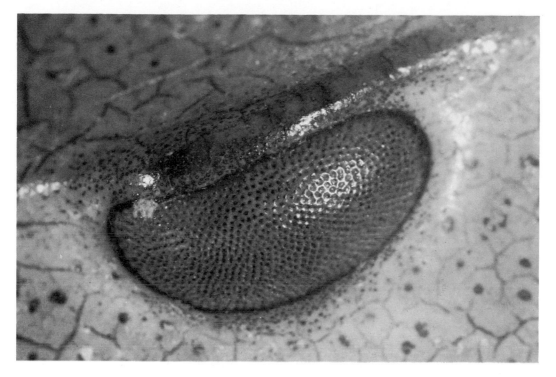

Fig. 11.11 **The arthropod** *Limulus,* **commonly called the horseshoe crab. At the left are top and bottom views; a close-up of the lateral eye is shown above.**

fields of different *Limulus* facets overlap because the angles between their axes are smaller than the angular extents of their fields.[5]

With skill and using a dissecting microscope, it is possible to tease a single nerve fiber out of the nerve of *Limulus,* and to drape the fiber over an electrode. When another electrode is then placed anywhere on the eye, and the two electrodes are connected to an amplifier and recording device, any nerve impulses that are conducted down that optic nerve fiber may be observed and recorded.

Recordings from   If the whole eye is illuminated, a series of nerve impulses will be re-
Single Facets   corded like those shown in Fig. 11.12. Suppose, now, that instead of

---

[5]Each facet contains several anatomically separate structures that contain visual pigment, and there is evidence that these structures, within one facet, may be able to act with a degree of independence, as if each facet were an eye containing a lens and several receptors. However, under the conditions to be discussed here, each facet will act as a single receptor. That is, only one output "channel" is being recorded from, and the facet is uniformly illuminated.

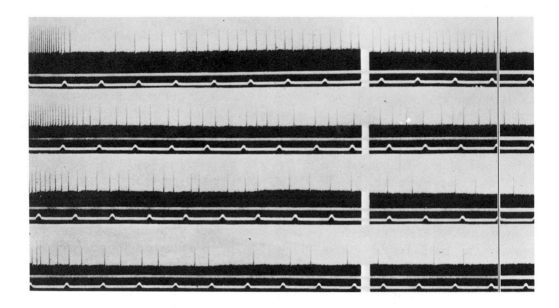

Onset of light   Extinction of light

Fig. 11.12 **Record of the electrical activity of a single fiber from the eye of** *Limulus*. **The spikes are nerve impulses and the regular deflections of the lower white line are time markers occurring every 0.2 sec. The intensity of stimulating light was reduced by a factor of ten for each successively lower record. The gap in each record represents an interval of a few seconds during which the light remained on.** [*From Hartline and Graham (1932).*]

lighting the entire eye, a spot of light smaller than the size of a facet were moved about over the eye, lighting only one facet at a time. Under these conditions, it is always found that the nerve fiber will respond *only* when one particular facet is illuminated. If the facets neighboring that particular one are illuminated, and care is taken to prevent light from scattering among facets, the nerve fiber will not respond. Thus it appears that the fiber being recorded from is excited by only a single facet, and that there is no spatial summation among facets. (Remember that if the analogous experiment were performed on a fiber connected to rods in the human retina, stimulation of any of a large group of rods would result in the firing of the axon. The excitations produced by many rods all add together, or summate, by the time they have reached the ganglion cells.)

If a different nerve fiber is placed over the electrode and the same procedure followed, it will always be found that a different facet must be illuminated in order to produce activity in the fiber. That is, each fiber in the optic nerve appears to be connected to a different facet (and it is also true that virtually every facet is connected to an optic nerve fiber).

Now, recording from a single fiber, a series of experiments may be performed. Figure 11.12 is an example of the activity recorded from such preparation for a number of different levels of intensity of the illumination, and Fig. 11.13 shows plots of these results. Figure 11.14 shows a series of measurements of the dark adaptation of a single facet of the *Limulus* eye. Although the time course of adaptation is different from human rods and cones, the general characteristics are clearly similar.

In general, every facet of the *Limulus* eye, when stimulated alone, responds in the way that one would expect from a general knowledge of human vision. However, the topic of interest in this chapter is the nature of the *interactions* that occur between receptors or facets.

The fact that no spatial summation in exhibited in the eye of *Limulus* has already been pointed out. However, *inhibitory* interaction among facets is a conspicuous feature of the action of the *Limulus* eye. For example, suppose that any facet, call it *A*, is illuminated steadily so that it is firing at a rate of 100 impulses per second. If, then, the light falling on *A* is unchanged, but light is added to a neighboring facet, *B*, the frequency of firing of *A* will *decrease*. That is, adding light to a

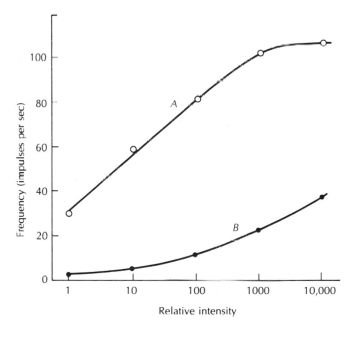

Fig. 11.13 **A plot of the records in Fig. 11.12 (plus one more point representing an intensity ten times greater than the greatest in Fig. 11.12). The curve labeled** *A* **is the rate of firing during the initial burst and** *B* **is the final equilibrium rate of firing.** [*After Hartline and Graham (1932).*]

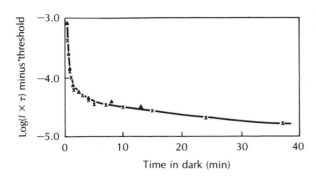

Fig. 11.14 **Dark-adaptation of a facet of the** *Limulus* **eye. The vertical axis represents the logarithm of the intensity of a flash just strong enough to cause the nerve fiber to fire one impulse.** [*From Hartline and McDonald (1947).*]

neighboring facet will reduce the activity in *A*; *B* may be said to be inhibiting *A*. In fact, the *only* form of interaction between facets that can be observed in the optic nerve of *Limulus* is inhibitory interaction. If any single facet if illuminated and recorded from, its activity will always either remain the same or decrease when light is added to any other single facet. The extent to which the activity is reduced is smaller if the illuminated facets are farther apart. When they are widely separated, illuminating one has no effect upon the activity of the other.

When these inhibitory interactions were first discovered, they were studied in a number of ways. For example, the magnitude of the inhibitory effect on a single facet was measured as a function of the intensity of light falling on a neighboring group of facets (Fig. 11.15a), as a function of the distance between the measured facet and the inhibiting region, (Fig. 11.15b), and as a function of the area of the inhibiting patch (Fig. 11.15c).[6]

The curves in Fig. 11.15 do not have simple shapes, and the results of these studies were very hard to interpret. They do not lead directly to an understanding of the processes involved. However, it is clear that inhibitory spatial interaction is present in the *Limulus* eye, and, since the eye is composed of separate facets, the shapes of these curves must somehow be determined by the interactions of each facet with each other one. For this reason, a different, and much more direct, study of the nature of the interactions was undertaken, and that study revealed that the underlying processes are remarkably simple.

Interactions among Individual Facets To clarify the nature of the inhibitory interactions among facets, the following procedure was followed: A single optic nerve fiber was dissected out and placed on an electrode. The eye was then explored

[6]The strength of inhibition is usually measured by illuminating the facet being recorded from, noting its rate of firing, then adding light to a neighboring (inhibiting) region, again noting the new rate of firing, and subtracting the second rate from the first.

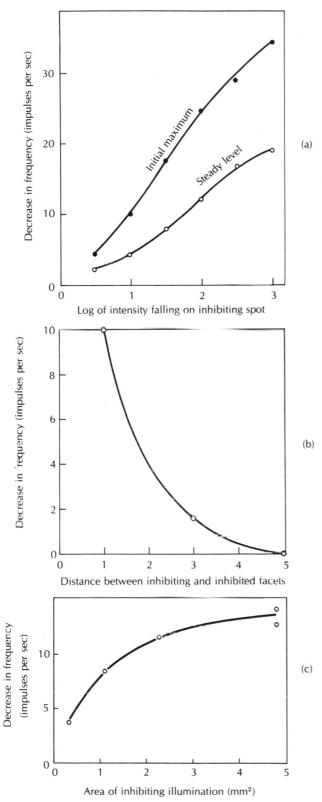

Fig. 11.15 **The effects of three variables upon the strength of inhibition in the eye of** *Limulus*. **The strength of inhibition (on the vertical axes) is the amount by which the presence of the inhibiting activity decreases the firing rate of the inhibited fiber. In (a), the strength of inhibition varies approximately logarithmically with the intensity of light falling on a region neighboring the facet recorded from. (The inhibitory effect is greatest when the inhibitory light is first turned on, and then falls to a steady level. The upper curve represents the initial inhibitory effect and the lower one, the equilibrium level.) In (b), the strength of inhibition varies strongly with the distance between the facet recorded from and the other illuminated region. (This particular function varies in different parts of the eye and in different directions. In (c), the inhibitory effect increases with the area of a spot of light falling on facets neighboring the one recorded from.** [*From Hartline et al. (1956); curve (b) is from the data described by Hartline on p. 664.*]

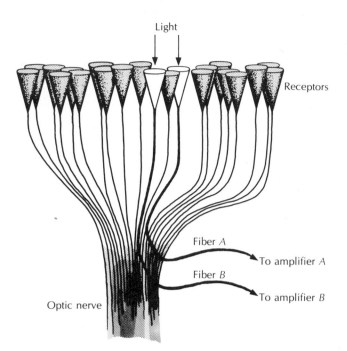

Light

Receptors

Fiber *A*

To amplifier *A*

Fiber *B*

To amplifier *B*

Optic nerve

Fig. 11.16 **Schematic representation of the procedure for recording from two neighboring facets simultaneously.**

with a small spot of light until the facet was found which, when illuminated by itself, caused the fiber to fire. Next, a search was made for another optic nerve fiber that was connected to a neighboring facet (i.e., one that fired when a neighboring facet was illuminated). When such a second fiber was found, recordings were taken from both of the fibers simultaneously, while their corresponding (two) facets were illuminated at various intensities. This is represented schematically in Fig. 11.16.

The curve in Fig. 11.17 shows one way of plotting the results. There is a curvilinear, and not very simple, relationship between the strength of inhibition exerted on a fiber and the logarithm of the intensity of the light falling on the inhibiting facet. (The function is strongly curved the other way if a linear intensity scale is used on the horizontal axis.) However, when the results of the experiment are plotted somewhat differently, a very simple relationship emerges. Such a plot is shown in Fig. 11.18a. The amount by which the firing of *A* is reduced when *B* is illuminated is a linear function of the *frequency of firing* of *B*. When *B* is illuminated very dimly, so that it is firing very slowly, it exerts no inhibition on *A* (as represented by the region to the left of the point labeled "inhibitory threshold" in the figure). As soon as the rate of firing of *B* is greater than this threshold frequency, the activity in *B* results in a reduction in the frequency of firing of A below the level that A would fire if B were dark. That is, B begins to inhibit A. When B is firing at a rate well above the inhibitory threshold, the amount of inhibition it exerts on A is linear with the frequency of firing of B. Once the inhibitory threshold is exceeded, it is as if some fixed proportion of the additional impulses fired by B were subtracted from the impulses fired by A. In this particular plot, 10% of the impulses fired by B over and above the inhibitory threshold are subtracted from A's impulses.

When both facets are illuminated and firing, B is effectively subtracting impulses from A, but at the same time, A is subtracting impulses from B, as shown in Fig. 11.18b. In other words, the two facets reciprocally inhibit each other in a simple linear way.

It is easy to write an equation that describes the relationship plotted in Fig. 11.18, and it will prove useful to do so.

Let F_a be the frequency of firing of A

          F_b be the frequency of firing of B

          e_a be the frequency at which A would fire if A alone were illuminated (i.e., B dark) (This "uninhibited" frequency might be called the level of excitation of A, and will be so referred to, hence the letter "e.")

          e_b be the excitation level of B

          K_{ab} be the coefficient representing the strength of the inhibition that A exerts on B

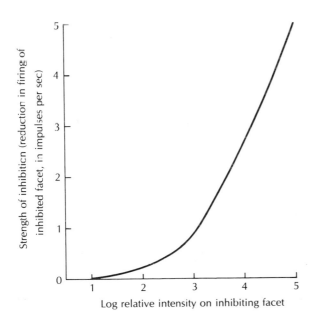

Fig. 11.17 **Plot of the relationship between the intensity of light falling on one facet and the extent to which it inhibits its neighbor.** [*Calculated from curve B in Fig. 11.13 and the curve in Fig. 11.18.*]

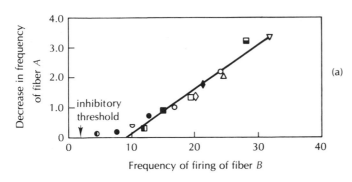

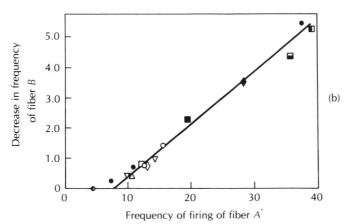

Fig. 11.18 **The relationship between the frequency of firing of a fiber and its inhibitory effect upon a neighboring fiber. When two facets** A **and** B **are both illuminated with varying intensities of light, each inhibits the other, as shown by these two graphs.** [From Hartline and Ratliff (1957).]

K_{ba} be the coefficient of inhibition that B exerts on A

θ_{ab} be the threshold of inhibition of A on B

θ_{ba} be the inhibitory threshold of B on A

Then:

$$F_a = e_a - K_{ba} (F_b - \theta_{ba}) \qquad \text{when} \quad F_b > \theta_{ba}, \qquad (1)$$

$$F_a = e_a \qquad\qquad\qquad\quad \text{when} \quad F_b < \theta_{ba}, \qquad (2)$$

and

$$F_b = e_b - K_{ab} (F_a - \theta_{ab}) \qquad \text{when} \quad F_a > \theta_{ab}, \qquad (3)$$

$$F_b = e_b \qquad\qquad\qquad\quad \text{when} \quad F_a < \theta_{ab}. \qquad (4)$$

Equation (1) may be read as follows: The frequency of firing of A equals the frequency that A would fire if it alone were illuminated (e_a) minus a fixed proportion (K_{ba}) of the rate at which B is firing over and above some threshold level. This equation only describes the system correctly so long as $F_b > \theta_{ba}$, that is, when the frequency of firing of the inhibiting facet equals or exceeds the inhibitory threshold.

When the frequency of B is lower than the inhibitory threshold ($F_b < \theta_{ba}$), the term $K_{ba}(F_b - \theta_{ba})$ in Eq. (1) is negative, and therefore, if Eq. (1) held, F_a would *increase* as F_b decreased from the inhibitory threshold to zero. However, from the data in Fig. 11.18, it is clear that this does not happen. Instead, when $F_b < \theta_{ba}$, $F_a = e_a$, as stated in Eq. (2).

Equations (3) and (4) can be read in exactly the same way, except that the facets are reversed in role.

It is probably easier to understand the equations, and to make sense of the additional data that will be presented, by referring to the schematic diagram in Fig. 11.19. This is a diagram of a simple system of neurons that would behave in the same way as the *Limulus* eye seems to behave. Light acts on some of the structures in a facet, causing the facet to output a certain excitation level e (which is roughly proportional to the logarithm of the light intensity). This excitation operates through an excitatory synapse to produce firing in the optic nerve fibers when the excitation exceeds the synaptic threshold. Whenever an optic nerve fiber fires, impulses are propagated down the fiber to the brain, but they also branch off and travel back along a collateral fiber to the neighboring region, where they inhibit the neighbor through an

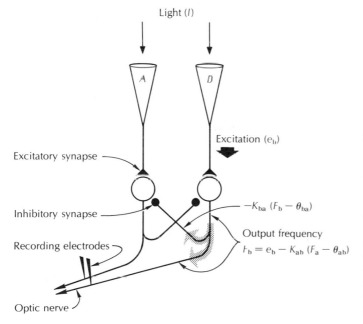

Light (I)

Excitation (e_b)

Excitatory synapse

Inhibitory synapse

$-K_{ba}(F_b - \theta_{ba})$

Output frequency

$F_b = e_b - K_{ab}(F_a - \theta_{ab})$

Recording electrodes

Optic nerve

Fig. 11.19 Schematic diagram of a set of neural connections that would behave as the retina in *Limulus* does. Light falls on the facets that contain photosensitive pigment. The effect of the light is to produce an excitation level e, which excites a synapse if the synaptic threshold is exceeded. Output impulses from the synapse travel down the optic nerve, but also branch off and inhibit the neighboring cell with a strength proportional to the strength of the output minus some threshold value. The system is symmetrical; each unit inhibits the other.

inhibitory synapse. If we assume that the synapses behave in a simple linear way, that is, that their outputs are proportional to the difference between the excitatory and inhibitory inputs, then each facet will inhibit the other by a fixed proportion of its own output.

This model manifests lateral, reciprocal, recurrent inhibition. It is lateral because it operates between regions that are separated spatially on the eye. It is reciprocal because each facet influences the other one. It is recurrent because the site where inhibition acts is earlier in the chain than the site from which it arises. That is, the inhibition, in addition to traveling laterally, also travels back toward the input end of the system. Such a recurrent arrangement is also called a negative feedback system.[7]

The line labeled B in Fig. 11.21 represents the inhibitory effect of a unit A on another unit B. If the same experiment is repeated when the inhibited unit C is farther from A, the plot changes as shown in Fig. 11.21. The farther apart are the two units being examined, the smaller is the slope (that is, the smaller is the inhibitory coefficient), and the greater is the inhibitory threshold, until, beyond a certain distance, one unit has no effect on the other.

It might be expected that the inhibitory effect of A on B, (K_{ab}) would be exactly the same as the inhibitory effect of B on A (K_{ba}) and, similar-

[7]The model in Fig. 11.19 is merely offered as an aid to remembering the equations and data to be presented here. It is certainly not the only plausible model that fits the data. For example, the data in Fig. 11.18 can also be fitted by a model in which the inhibition is nonrecurrent (Fig. 11.20). Data to be presented later can be fitted either by a single recurrent stage of inhibition or by more than one nonrecurrent stages, one following the other. The evidence strongly suggests that there is only one

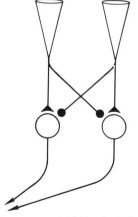

Fig. 11.20 A nonrecurrent lateral reciprocal inhibitory system. The inhibition acts at a site later in the chain than the site from which it originated. Thus the strength of inhibition is proportional not to the frequency of firing of the inhibiting unit, but rather to its excitation level.

"stage" in the *Limulus* eye, and that it therefore probably manifests recurrent inhibition. In the human, there are no data to discriminate between these possibilities, but the recurrent inhibitory model, being simpler than the model containing the appropriate set of nonrecurrent stages, will be used here. It should also be pointed out that there are many alternative ways of modeling recurrent inhibition. Again, the model in Fig. 11.19 is merely chosen because it is simple and convenient. It is not intended to represent the actual physiology of the *Limulus* eye.

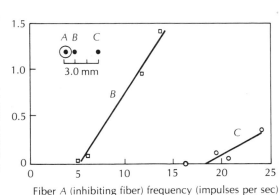

ly, that the inhibitory thresholds, (θ_{ab} and θ_{ba}) would be equal. In fact, there is some variation in the nature of the interconnections between facets that causes these values to differ for any given pair of facets. However, if a large group of receptors are all operating at the same time, as they almost always are under normal conditions, these statistical variations are effectively averaged out, and no serious error is made by considering that $K_{ab} = K_{ba}$ and $\theta_{ab} = \theta_{ba}$. Therefore, we can simplify Eqs. (1) and (3) by eliminating one set of subscripts:

$$F_a = e_a - K_{ab}(F_b - \theta_{ab}) \qquad \text{when} \quad F_b \gtrless \theta_{ab}, \tag{5}$$

$$F_b = e_b - K_{ab}(F_a - \theta_{ab}) \qquad \text{when} \quad F_a \gtrless \theta_{ab}. \tag{6}$$

So far, we have seen that, in the *Limulus* eye, each facet inhibits its neighbors by an amount proportional to its own frequency of firing, and that the strength of the interaction between facets decreases as the distance between the facets increases. Given only one more simple property of the system, all of the complicated curves in Fig. 11.15, and many features of great importance to the understanding of human vision, can be explained. The missing property is the way in which inhibitory influences add together.

To determine this property of the *Limulus* eye, three facets are recorded from in various combinations. Consider the relatively simple case in which the three facets are in a line as shown in Fig. 11.22. Suppose that the illumination on *B* is adjusted so that when it alone is stimulated, it will fire 100 impulses per second, as shown on the first line of the chart in Fig. 11.22. When *A* is also illuminated at some arbitrary level, it will inhibit *B*. In this example, assume that $K_{ab} = 0.1$

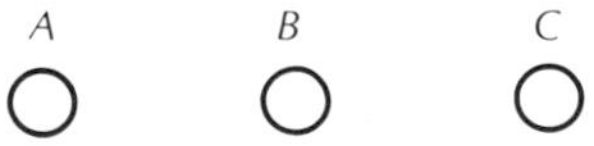

	A	B	C
	○	○	○

	Firing rates		
Stimulus	A	B	C
B alone	0	100	0
A and B	80	92	0
C and B	0	88	60
A and B and C	80	80	60

Fig. 11.22 **An example of the fact that the inhibitory effects of different facets add. When all three facets are illuminated, the total amount by which B is inhibited is simply the sum of the amounts by which it would be inhibited by A and by C each acting alone.**

and that $\theta_{ab} = 0$. Then, if A is illuminated strongly enough to fire 80 impulses per second, B will drop to 92 impulses per second. That is, B will be inhibited by 8 impulses per second (line 2 of the chart in Fig. 11.22). Then A is darkened and B and C are illuminated. If we assume that $K_{cb} = 0.2$ and $\theta_{cb} = 0$, and C is illuminated strongly enough to fire, say, 60 impulses per second, then C will inhibit B by 12 impulses per second, and B will fire 88 impulses per second (line 3 of Fig. 11.22). Now when all three facets are illuminated and the intensities of lights on A and C are adjusted so that they fire 80 and 60 impulses, respectively, B will undergo a total inhibition of 20 impulses per second, that is, simply the sum of the inhibitory effects of A and C (line 4, Fig. 11.22). In general, the total inhibition exerted on any facet is always simply the sum of all of the separate inhibitory influences on the facet.

Thus the equations that describe the frequencies of firing of three simultaneously stimulated units are[8]:

$$F_a = e_a - K_{ab}(F_b - \theta_{ab}) - K_{ac}(F_c - \theta_{ac})$$
$$\text{if} \quad F_b \geq \theta_{ab} \quad \text{and} \quad F_c \geq \theta_{ac},$$
$$F_b = e_b - K_{ab}(F_a - \theta_{ab}) - K_{bc}(F_c - \theta_{bc})$$
$$\text{if} \quad F_a \geq \theta_{ab} \quad \text{and} \quad F_c \geq \theta_{bc},$$
$$F_c = e_c - K_{ac}(F_a - \theta_{ac}) - K_{bc}(F_b - \theta_{bc})$$
$$\text{if} \quad F_a \geq \theta_{ac} \quad \text{and} \quad F_b \geq \theta_{bc}.$$

(The equations that hold when frequencies of firing are below inhibitory thresholds will be omitted for simplicity.) In general, for any number of interacting units, the expression for the frequency of firing of the ith unit is:

[8]Again assuming that $K_{ab} = K_{ba}$, etc.

$$F_i = e_i - \sum_{j=0}^{j=n} K_{ij} (F_j - \theta_{ij}). \tag{7}$$

That is, the frequency of any unit equals the excitation level minus the sum of all inhibitory influences.

Now let us examine the consequences of these interactions under some typical conditions. First, we will use two simplifying approximations: (1) the inhibitory coefficients between any pair of receptors (e.g., K_{ab} and K_{ba}) are equal (as discussed above), and (2) we will only consider examples in which the frequencies of firing are high compared with threshold; that is, where $F \gg \theta$, and we will therefore make the approximation that $\theta = 0$.

Then the equations for two units reduce to:

$$F_a = e_a - K F_b, \tag{8}$$
$$F_b = e_b - K F_a. \tag{9}$$

The general equation for any number of units is:

$$F_i = e_i - \sum_{j=0}^{j=n} K_{ij} F_j. \tag{10}$$

Now examine the series of conditions described in Fig. 11.23. The two facets are always illuminated strongly enough that, when illuminated alone, each would fire 100 impulses per second. That is, $e_a = 100$ and $e_b = 100$.

The figures in the chart are those calculated from Eq. (8) and (9), as in the sample calculation shown in the figure. Since the two units are equally stimulated ($e_a = e_b$) and since their inhibitory coefficients have

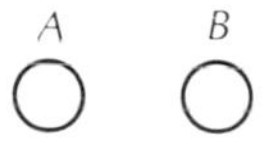

A   B

| Stimulus | K | \multicolumn{2}{c}{Frequency of Firing} |
		A	B
A alone	0.1	100	0
B alone	0.1	0	100
A and B	0.1	91	91
A and B	0.3	77	77
A and B	0.9	52.6	52.6

$F_a = e_a - KF_b$
$F_b = e_b - KF_a$
solving for F_a
$F_a = e_a - K(e_b - KF_a)$
$F_a = \dfrac{e_a - K \times e_b}{1 - K^2}$

therefore, when $K = 0.1$, $e_a = e_b = 100$
$F_a = \dfrac{100 - 10}{1 - 0.01} = 91$
$F_b = 100 - 0.1 \times 91$
$F_b = 91$

Fig. 11.23 The rates of firing of two facets that inhibit each other with various coefficients. As the inhibitory coefficient K increases, the rates of firing decrease. In this example, the two facets are illuminated with intensities such that their excitation levels, e, are equal.

been assumed to be equal ($K_{ab} = K_{ba}$), it is obvious that their outputs must also be equal. Note from the chart in Fig. 11.23 that if the inhibitory coefficient increases, the frequencies of firing decrease, as might be expected.

Now consider the case, illustrated in Fig. 11.24, in which the two units are not equally excited. Here, as a consequence of the inhibitory interaction, the difference in outputs is greater than it would be if there were no inhibition, and also the ratio of outputs is greater than it would be with no inhibition. Further, when the inhibitory coefficient is greater (as it would be, for example, if the two units were closer together), the difference between their firing rates increases. In fact, when the inhibitory coefficient is 0.5 or greater, the output of the less strongly illuminated unit is reduced to zero, and the other unit is thus uninhibited. This kind of interaction, then, can be said to be a contrast amplifier, in that the contrast between the two outputs is greater with inhibition than it would be without inhibition. We will return to this point later.

Suppose that the characteristics of a particular eye have been thoroughly investigated, and as a result, the following properties are known:

(1)   the relationship between the intensity of the stimulating light and the excitation level (e) of each receptor,

(2)   the inhibitory coefficients (K) that obtain between each pair of receptors, or the value of K as a function of the distance between receptors, and

(3)   the value of the inhibitory threshold (θ) as a function of the distance between receptors. (That value is assumed to be zero for this discussion.)

| Stimulus | K | Firing rates | |
		A	B
A alone	0.1	50	0
B alone	0.1	0	100
A and B	0.1	40.5	96
A and B	0.3	22	93.4
A and B	0.4	19	92.4
A and B $\geqq$ 0.5		0	100

Fig. 11.24 Firing rates of two mutually inhibitory facets that are unequally illuminated. The inhibitory interaction increases the difference between their outputs. Furthermore, when the inhibitory coefficient is 0.5 or greater, the output of the less strongly illuminated facet falls to zero and the more strongly illuminated one is thus uninhibited.

Given those parameters, the spatial distribution of output frequencies can be calculated for *any* given input intensity distribution, and so long as the values of K are not all zero, the output distributions will differ from the input distributions in some very interesting ways. For example, in the charts in Figs. 11.23 and 11.24, two receptors were illuminated, and the output frequencies were found by solving two equations in two unknowns (as in the sample calculation in Fig. 11.23). If five receptors are illuminated with any arbitrary pattern of light, the output distribution may be calculated by solving five equations in five unknowns. When the entire *Limulus* eye is illuminated with any pattern, the output distribution can be found by solving about 800 equations in 800 unknowns, since there are about 800 facets in the eye.

Obviously, finding the solution for that many equations by algebra is extraordinarily tedious (although *Limulus* does it one-eyed), and the resulting distribution may look quite complicated, but the processes that underlie these complicated transformations are themselves very simple. The curves in Fig. 11.15 are good examples. These plots represent the results of stimulating large numbers of facets in various spatial distributions. The curves themselves are moderately complicated, and do not provide very clear information about the nature of the spatial interaction in the eye. However, the plots could have been predicted exactly from a knowledge of Eq. (7) and the inhibitory coefficients, thresholds, and stimulation-to-excitation relationships in the eye.

Some of the results of the interactions between facets in *Limulus* have obvious implications for the understanding of human perception. For example, suppose that the intensity distribution in Fig. 11.5 is presented to the *Limulus* eye. That distribution is redrawn as the dashed line in Fig. 11.25. For most intensity distributions, it is virtually impossible to predict correctly the output distribution without actually solving the necessary equations, but for this particular pattern, a qualitatively correct prediction can be made from a general examination of the action of the visual system. Consider the facet labeled "1" in Fig. 11.25. It is being illuminated at an intensity indicated by the dashed line. If there were no inhibition in the eye, it would fire at some frequency, the excitation level, represented by the open circle above the receptor. In general, the excitation levels of the facets would be those plotted by the open circles in Fig. 11.25.

Now consider facet 1 again. Because inhibition is present in the eye, the actual output frequency of that facet will be lower than the dotted line ($F_1 < e_1$), that is, it is inhibited by its neighbors (which are all firing at some low level). (Assume, for convenience, that the pattern extends

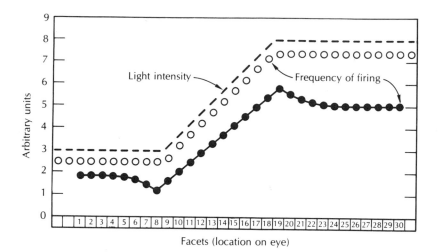

Fig. 11.25 **The rectangles along the horizontal axis represent a row of facets in the** Limulus **eye. When the intensity distribution shown by the dashed line is impressed on the eye, the activity levels of the receptors would be as indicated by the open circles if there were no inhibition; but with recurrent lateral inhibition, the output pattern of activity will have the shape represented by the solid line.**

Facets (location on eye)

indefinitely to the right and to the left.) The output frequency of facet 1 is indicated, then, by the solid circle above it. Similarly, facets 2 and 3 will be firing at about the same frequency, since they are equally excited and receive about the same amount of inhibition from their neighbors.

Now jump to the facet labeled 30. It is surrounded by facets that are firing more strongly than the facets surrounding facet 1, and therefore, it will receive more inhibition than facet 1. That is, the distance between the open circle and the solid circle is greater for facet 30 than for facet 1.

Now consider the output frequency of facets beginning with 1 and moving toward facet 8. All of these have the same excitation level, but the facets nearer the more intensely lighted region are nearer to facets that are more active, and therefore they will be more strongly inhibited. Thus facet 6 will have a lower output frequency than facet 5, 7 lower than 6, and 8 lower than 7, as plotted by solid circles in the figure. Moving from the right side of the figure toward the left, the units 30, 29, 28, etc. all are equally excited, but those nearer the darker side are nearer facets of lower activity. Hence the total inhibition exerted on 19 will be less than on 20, etc., and the output frequency of 19 will be higher than 20, 20 higher than 21, etc. In the sloping region between 8 and 19, the excitation and inhibition both increase smoothly.

Thus, when the intensity distribution represented by the dashed line falls on the eye of Limulus, the output distribution ought to have the shape indicated by the solid line. In general, if this light distribution falls on any retina that has this same kind of spatial interaction, the output distribution will have the general form of the solid line.

Drawing conclusions like the one above without actually solving the equations involved is a little hazardous. It is easy to be in error when so many mutually interacting elements are involved. As a check on the reasoning, Ratliff and Hartline (1959) performed an experiment on the *Limulus* eye in which they directly measured the output frequency distribution under these conditions, and the results of that experiment are shown in Fig. 11.26.

When the intensity distribution in Fig. 11.5 is presented to a human subject and he is asked to plot the *brightness* distribution, he will draw something that looks, at least qualitatively, just like the solid line in Fig. 11.25. If the human visual system manifests the same general kind of lateral inhibition that has been measured in the eye of *Limulus*, then it appears that his judgment of the brightness at each point in the pattern depends upon the output frequency of the corresponding part of the visual system. Thus, at least at a qualitative level, the hypothesis that there is such an inhibitory network in the human visual system provides a sufficient explanation for the perceptual phenomenon of Mach bands, given the further hypothesis that the physiological correlate of the brightness of any point is the frequency of firing of the spatially corresponding part of the visual system (after inhibition).

A similar qualitative analysis can be made for the pattern shown in Fig. 11.4. That input pattern, and the output pattern expected in a visual system with recurrent lateral inhibition, are plotted in Fig. 11.27. Note that the output pattern is qualitatively the same as that which a subject would draw if he were asked to plot the brightness distribution

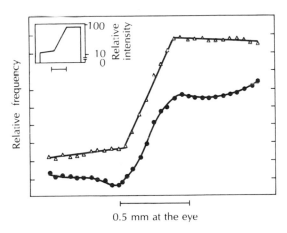

0.5 mm at the eye

Fig. 11.26 **Results of an actual measurement on the** *Limulus* **eye. The upper curve is taken without inhibition, and the lower one with inhibition. (For an explanation of how the data were obtained, see Ratliff and Hartline, 1959.) The light pattern was similar to that in Fig. 11.25, except that it did not extend indefinitely on each end, but instead, had real edges as indicated in the inset to this figure. These edges, and particularly the edge on the more intense side of the pattern, effect the output pattern just as they would be expected to do.** [*From Ratliff and Hartline (1959).*]

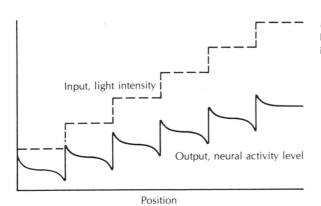

Fig. 11.27 **The output pattern (solid line) predicted for the dashed input intensity distribution.**

in Fig. 11.4. The appearance of most of the other distributions shown at the beginning of this chapter are also consistent with this theory of brightness perception. A more complete discussion of those patterns will be presented in the next chapter, where they will be analyzed quantitatively in relation to other data on the human visual system.

LATERAL INHIBITION IN THE RETINAS OF MAMMALS Electrophysiological experiments on the retinas of mammals, mostly cats and monkeys, also show clear evidence of lateral inhibitory interactions. To introduce these experiments, it is useful to reconsider the *Limulus* data. Suppose that the frequency of firing of a single facet in the *Limulus* eye is recorded while a spot of light much smaller than a single facet is moved over the surface of the eye. If the path of light were to pass through the right facet, the results of the experiment would be as plotted in Fig. 11.28a. The fiber would only fire when the spot of light fell within one particular facet. Let us call that facet the "excitatory facet," that is, the facet that excites the particular fiber being recorded from.

Now let the experiment be modified slightly, such that a dim light always falls on the excitatory facet and a brighter test spot is then moved across the eye as in the previous experiment. The results would be as plotted in Fig. 11.28b. The fiber would be firing constantly, since it is constantly illuminated, but as the moving spot approaches the excitatory facet it falls on facets that are closer and closer to the excited one, thus inhibiting that facet more and more strongly, reducing its firing rate. When the moving spot falls directly on the facet, however, the firing rate will increase to its maximum.

It is relatively easy to relate observations on the activity of the eye of *Limulus* to various hypotheses about the physiological nature of that eye. For example, the data presented above support the hypothesis that there are neural interconnections among facets that transmit inhibitory effects. The straightforwardness of such an interpretation is largely a consequence of the fact that the measurements were made very directly on individual facets and on small groups of interacting facets. Unfortunately, we cannot perform comparably clear experiments upon mammalian retinas, because it is not yet possible to illuminate *single* receptors. Optical aberrations in the eye and light scatter within the retinal tissues cause the smallest spot of light that can be projected on to the retina to spread over many receptors. Worse yet, it is almost impossible to determine precisely how large the stimulated group of receptors actually is.

Recall that the *Limulus* experiment represented in Fig. 11.28a was performed with a spot of light much smaller than a single facet. If the experiment were repeated with a spot whose diameter was, say, two facets wide, but containing the same total amount of light, the result

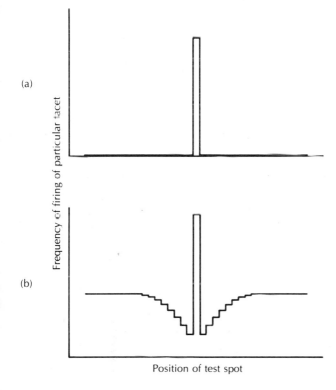

(a)

(b)

Frequency of firing of particular facet

Position of test spot

Fig. 11.28 The activity of a single facet as a test spot of light is moved across the eye in a path that crosses the facet. In (a), the eye is otherwise dark and activity occurs only when the test spot falls directly upon the facet. (The test spot is much smaller than the facet.) In (b), the excitatory facet is continuously illuminated while the test spot moves across the eye. Here, the approach of the test spot is signaled by a decrease in firing.

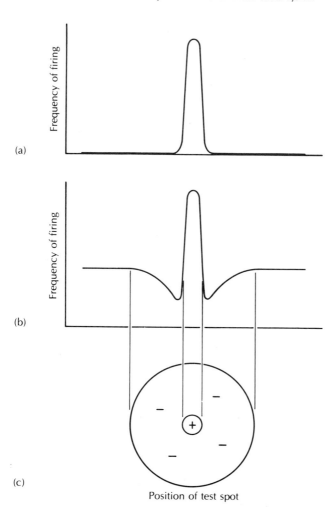

(a)

(b)

(c)

Position of test spot

Fig. 11.29 **The result of a pair of experiments identical to those in Fig. 11.28 except that the test spot has been enlarged to have a diameter twice that of the facets.**

would be as plotted in Fig. 11.29a. This result is different from the small-spot result in two ways. First, the width of the "excitatory" region is greater, and second, the corners are rounded. The reasons for both of these qualitative differences follow simply and directly from a careful consideration of the way in which the experiment is performed. It is very important that the reader work out these reasons for himself.

Similarly, if the experiment in Fig. 11.28b is repeated with a larger moving spot, the result will be as shown in Fig. 11.29b.

The diagram in Fig. 11.29c is an abbreviated way of representing some of the information contained in the plot in Fig. 11.29b. If recordings are made from a single facet while a spot of light is moved over the eye, there will be a small region, centered on the excitatory facet, in which the light will cause an increase in firing rate. This region is the disk in the center of Fig. 11.29c, and is labeled "+." When the spot falls anywhere in a surrounding region of the eye, its net effect on the facet being recorded from is inhibitory, as indicated by the ring labeled "−." When the spot falls even farther from the excitation facet, its effect will be below threshold, and it will not affect the excitatory facet.

The region included in this figure is called the receptive field of the fiber being recorded from, since it is that area of the eye in which light has an effect on the fiber. The size of the receptive field will depend upon the intensity of the stimulating light spot, as can readily be deduced from the data in Figs. 11.17 and 11.21. The receptive field size must also depend upon the size of the light spot being used to measure it (e.g., compare Figs. 11.28 and 11.29).

Furthermore, there is summation within the receptive field. Since inhibitory influences add to each other, two spots of light simultaneously falling within the inhibitory area will generally produce stronger inhibition than a single spot,[9] and the fiber will be most strongly inhibited if the entire inhibitory ring is illuminated. Similarly, two spots falling within the excitatory disk will produce stronger excitation than a single spot.

All of these properties are also manifested in the receptive fields of many ganglion cells in the retinas of monkeys and cats. In those retinas, most or all of the ganglion cells fire even when the eye is

---

[9]The only kind of interaction between facets that is ever observed under these conditions in the *Limulus* eye is inhibitory, and inhibitory effects always add. Nevertheless it is *not* always true that adding more light to neighboring facets will cause a decrease in the rate of firing of the facet being recorded from. If the conditions are correctly chosen, it is possible to add light to one region of the eye and observe an *increase* in the rate of firing of a facet in another region. For example, examine Fig. 11.30. When the facet being recorded from is illuminated and then the area labeled *B* is also illuminated, the frequency of firing will decrease, indicating that *B* is inhibiting *A*. Then if the shaded area *C* is also illuminated, but not so intensely as *B*, the frequency of firing of *A* will *increase*. What is

Fig. 11.30 **Configuration of stimuli such that the rate of firing of** *A* **is greater when** *C* **is illuminated that when** *C* **is dark.**

Facet being recorded from

happening is that the area *C*, being very close to *B*, will inhibit *B*, but because it is dimly illuminated and far from *A*, its effect on *A* will not exceed the inhibitory threshold, and it will not contribute inhibition to *A*. Since *C* inhibits *B*, and since the inhibitory effect of *B* on *A* depends upon the rate of firing of *B*, adding light to *C* will reduce the total inhibition acting upon *A*. Thus *A* will fire more rapidly when both *B* and *C* are illuminated than when *C* is dark. This effect has been given a special name, *disinhibition*, but it is not a special process. It is simply a necessary consequence of the inhibitory properties already discussed.

(a)

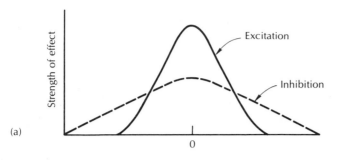

(b)

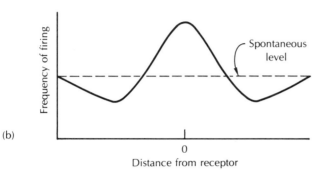

Distance from receptor

Fig. 11.31 **In (a), the solid line represents the spread of excitation from a
receptor located at zero, and the
dashed line represents the spread of
inhibition. The profile of the receptive
field of the neuron connected to such
a receptor would be as in (b). It would
be an "on-center" unit.**

in the dark. This activity is said to be spontaneous activity. If an
electrode is placed so as to record the activity in such a ganglion
cell, and then a small spot of light is presented at various positions on
the retina, the result is often just like that in Fig. 11.29c. That is, when
the spot falls anywhere in a small circular region, the rate of firing of
the fiber will increase, and when it falls anywhere in a ring immediately
surrounding that region, the rate will decrease (i.e., below the spontaneous rate). The receptive fields generally have the shape of that in
Fig. 11.29; their sizes depend upon the intensity and size of the
stimulating spot; and there is summation within the receptive field.

In the *Limulus* eye, every optic nerve fiber has exactly the kind of
receptive field in Fig. 11.29c. In the mammalian eye, many optic
nerve fibers manifest this kind of receptive field, but a roughly equal
number yield a field that is just the opposite, that is, in which light falling in the center inhibits firing and the surrounding ring has an
excitatory effect.

The first kind of field, called an on-center field, can be accounted for
by assuming a structure similar to that in the *Limulus*, in which each
receptor excites a ganglion cell and also sends inhibitory signals to its
neighbors. There are a number of different ways in which the off-cen-

ter receptive fields might occur. It may be that some receptors send a direct inhibitory signal to one ganglion cell and excitatory ones to surrounding cells. An alternative explanation is that there may be some ganglion cells whose only inputs are spontaneous activity and inhibition by on-center ganglion cells, thus yielding receptive fields of inverse polarity. At the present time, it is not clear whether either of these hypotheses is correct.

The sizes of the central disks of mammalian receptive fields are always appreciably larger than the diameters of individual mammalian receptors. As explained previously, this result would necessarily be obtained as a consequence of the fact that the stimulating spot is always larger than a receptor. However, it is quite possible that if the stimulating spot were to be made smaller than a receptor, the central disk of the receptive field would still be larger than one receptor diameter. (This is certainly true for rods.) Such a finding would indicate that interaction in the retina includes summation of excitatory as well as inhibitory signals.

For example, suppose that when a given receptor is excited by light, it radiates both excitation *and* inhibition to its neighbors, as indicated by the solid and dashed curves in Fig. 11.31a, respectively. The net

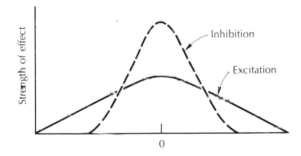

(a)

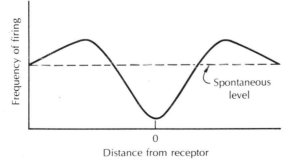

(b)

Fig. 11.32 **If the strength of the inhibitory effect of a receptor is greater than its excitatory effect, as in (a), the receptive field will be an "off-center" one, as in (b).**

result of these two opposing processes would be an on-center receptive field with a profile like that in Fig. 11.31b. Similarly, if the shapes of the excitatory and inhibitory spread functions were reversed as in Fig. 11.32a, the result would be an off-center receptive field as in Fig. 11.32b.

Since, at the present time, it is so difficult to determine the actual spread of light on a mammalian retina, there is no evidence that unequivocally permits a determination of whether the observed spread of excitation is neural or optical. However, we shall see in the following chapters that although the shape of the excitatory region of a receptive field has profound effects on perception, whether that shape is determined by the spread of light in the tissues, or the spread of excitation in the retinal neurons is probably not of great importance.

XII ◇◇◇ PSYCHOPHYSIOLOGY OF BRIGHTNESS—II
MODULATION TRANSFER FUNCTIONS

THE illustrations in the preceding chapter demonstrate that the brightness of any point in the visual field does not depend simply upon the intensity of light at that point. Instead, brightness seems to depend upon the relationships among intensities in the field. Knowledge of the precise relationship between brightness and the distribution of light would be useful in its own right; furthermore, such knowledge would provide powerful clues about the nature of the physiological processes that underlie perception.

To determine the relationship between brightness and the distribution of intensity, one might present subjects with visual displays consisting of every shape, intensity, size, etc., that one can think of, and catalog the resulting judgments of brightness. However, since there is no limit to the number of shapes, for example, that one can invent, the research and the catalog would never be completed. Obviously, it is necessary, instead, to try to find some relatively small set of relationships among the relevant variables that will describe all possible data. In the study of the *Limulus* discussed in the preceding chapter, that is exactly what was done. Measures of inhibition as a function of the shape of the inhibiting spot might have been made *ad infinitum*. Instead, having performed a few critical studies on interactions among individual units, Hartline and Ratliff were able to show that just three equations (one relating light intensity to excitation level, the other two relating the inhibitory coefficient and the inhibitory threshold to the distance between facets), are sufficient to predict accurately the results of *any* possible experiment in which an intensity distribution falls steadily upon the *Limulus* eye. (Temporal properties of the eye are not included in these equations, but will be discussed in Chapter XIV.)

In the following sections, a technique will be described that provides a way of predicting the response of the human visual system to any intensity distribution that conforms to certain restrictions. This technique has been applied for many years to the analysis of the temporal properties of systems such as telephones and high fidelity phonographs, and since the late 1950's it has been recognized as a powerful tool for the analysis of spatial properties of systems as well. The technique is called linear systems analysis, and the data it yields are called modulation transfer functions.

MODULATION TRANSFER FUNCTIONS

The pattern in Fig. 12.1a is usually called a grating. Its intensity distribution (plotted next to it) is a repetitive waveform called a square wave. The pattern in Fig. 12.1b has an intensity distribution that is called a sine wave, and it is consequently called a sine-wave grating. (The pattern in Fig. 12.1a should properly be called a square-wave grating.)

If two sine-wave gratings of different frequencies are superimposed upon each other, the resulting pattern of illumination can be found by adding the two sine waves together, point by point. For example, consider the sine-wave gratings in Figs. 12.2a and b. The grating in (b) contains twice as many stripes per inch as (a). When the two gratings are superimposed, the resulting light distribution is that in Fig. 12.2c. The intensity at each point along the horizontal axis is simply the sum of the two components, as shown in the plot. By adding together sine waves of various frequencies and amplitudes, it is possible to obtain distributions of many different shapes. In fact, Fourier's theorem,

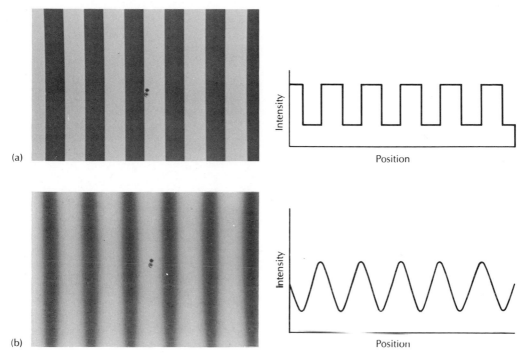

Fig. 12.1 **(a) The stripe pattern is called a square-wave grating. Its intensity distribution is plotted next to it. (b) This grating is called a sine-wave grating, because the intensity is a sinusoidal function of location.**

which is the foundation of the analytic technique under discussion, states that *any* wave form or distribution can be generated by summing the appropriate sine waves, and, as a corollary, any distribution can be completely described by specifying some particular set of sine waves (that set which, when added together, will reproduce the given distribution). The procedure for finding the waveform that is produced when a set of sine waves are added together is called Fourier synthesis. The procedure for finding the particular set of sine waves that must be added in order to obtain some given waveform is called Fourier analysis, and the sine-wave components thus obtained are called the Fourier components of the given wave.

For example, Fig. 12.3 illustrates that a square wave can be produced by adding together a particular set of sine waves. This figure shows that, as more and more of the appropriate waves are added together, the sum approaches a square wave more and more closely.[1]

---

[1] It is obvious that a square-wave grating in which the dark bars are *completely* dark, i.e., have zero intensity, cannot be produced by adding together sinusoidal distributions of ordinary light. If the light (Continued on p. 316.)

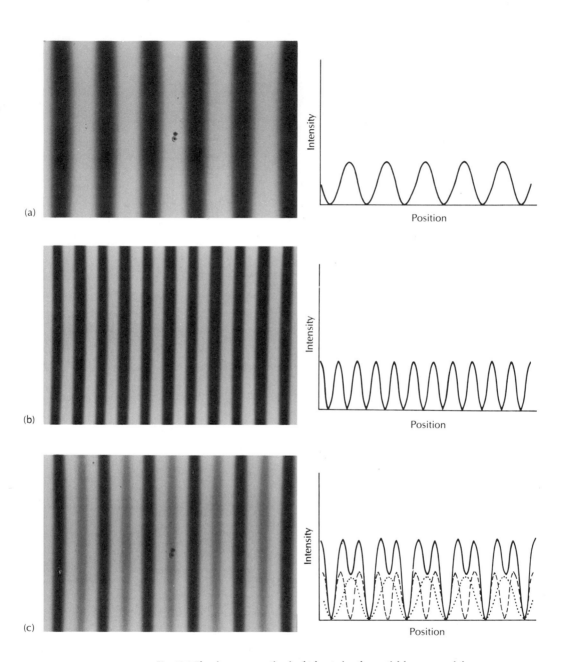

Fig. 12.2 **The sine-wave grating in (b) has twice the spatial frequency of the grating in (a). When the two light distributions are added together, the distribution in (c) results. The intensity at each point in (c) is simply the sum of the intensities in the corresponding points in (a) and (b).**

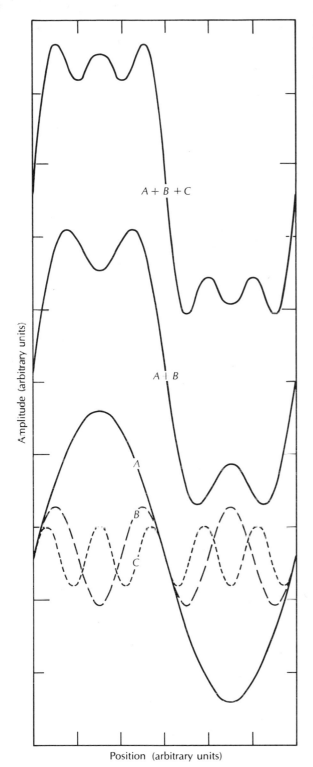

$A + B + C$

$A + B$

A

B

C

Amplitude (arbitrary units)

Position (arbitrary units)

Fig. 12.3 **The addition of sine waves to synthesize a square wave. When the frequencies of the sine waves are** F, $3F$, $5F$, $7F$, . . . , **and the corresponding amplitudes are** A, $\frac{1}{3}A$, $\frac{1}{5}A$, $\frac{1}{7}A$, . . . , **the sum of more and more such waves approaches a square wave more and more closely.**

(To reproduce *perfectly* any wave form that has sharp corners, as the square wave does, an infinite number of sine waves must be added together, but the relationship among those sine waves is often simple. To produce a square wave, one must begin with a sine wave that has the same frequency as the fundamental frequency of the square wave [*A* in Fig. 12.3] and add to it waves whose frequencies are 3×, 5×, 7×, . . . that of the fundamental frequency, and whose amplitudes are, respectively, 1/3, 1/5, 1/7, . . . of the fundamental frequency.)

Fourier analysis and synthesis may seem merely to be mathematical curiosities, but, in fact, they are the basis of an extraordinarily powerful tool to analyze the ways that systems respond to stimuli. Let us consider a very simple system, namely a lens, and apply Fourier analysis to the task of describing its behavior. We may perform the following experiment: We present the lens with a sine-wave grating object, and examine the image, that is, the intensity distribution in the image plane, as diagramed in Fig. 12.4. The distribution in the image plane will also be a sine wave, whose spatial frequency (lines per inch) depends on the magnification, and whose modulation amplitude (i.e., the difference between the intensities at the peaks and the troughs) depends upon the quality of the lens, as explained below. Suppose we begin with a target grating of very low frequency, and measure the modulation amplitude of the image distribution, say, by moving a small photocell across the image. The result of this measurement is plotted in Fig. 12.5 as point number 1. Then the target grating is exchanged for a new one that has the same amplitude as the first, but a higher spatial frequency, and the image distribution is measured again, resulting in point number 2. When this procedure is repeated for gratings whose amplitudes are all the same, but whose spatial frequencies vary, the result, for any real lens, will look like the plot in Fig. 12.5. As the frequency of the object (and therefore of the image) becomes greater and greater, the amplitude of modulation of the image distribution, that is the difference between the intensity at each bright part and at each dark part, becomes smaller and smaller. For extremely fine gratings, ones with very large numbers of lines per inch, the modula-

---

(*Continued from p. 313.*)

can have a negative effect, as with coherent light from a laser, for example, then a square wave, or any other pattern, can be perfectly reproduced. However, if the light being used is not coherent, and thus always has a positive effect, then the statement must be qualified by saying that some patterns can be reproduced exactly by the summation of the appropriate sine waves, and all remaining patterns can be reproduced exactly except for a uniform light covering the entire field. In other words, if we are allowed to add a uniform light of adjustable intensity to a given pattern, then the sum of the uniform light and the given pattern can be duplicated exactly by the sum of a set of sinusoidal components. We will see that this restriction is not important to the present discussion.

Fig. 12.4 **A lens forming an image of a sine-wave grating.**

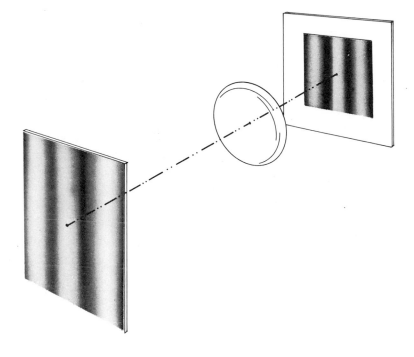

tion in the image becomes zero and the image plane contains a uniform intensity distribution.[2] This fact is commonly expressed in different terms, namely that a given lens cannot resolve very fine gratings, and "blurs them out."

The curve in Fig. 12.5 is a measure of the quality of the lens. A better lens will resolve finer gratings. That is, its curve will fall to zero at higher spatial frequencies.[3] This kind of curve is called the *transfer function* of the lens, because it describes the way in which the input (the intensity distribution in the object) is transferred, by the lens, to the output (the intensity distribution in the image); and it is called a *spatial modulation transfer function* (spatial MTF) because the property of the lens being measured is its ability to transfer spatial modulations of intensity from the object to the image.

---

[2]To anyone familiar with the behavior of electrical or mechanical filters in the time domain (e.g., high fidelity amplifier frequency response curves), the idea will seem strange that the output modulation actually goes to *zero* for some finite input frequency, but it really does. Certain aspects of the difference between the time and the space domains prevent responses from going to zero in the time domain but not in the spatial domain. The essential difference is that a real response can spread in any direction in space, but only in one direction in time.

[3]As a lens nears perfection, its high-frequency behavior comes to depend only upon diffraction, which, in turn, depends upon its diameter in relation to its focal length and the wavelength of the light forming the image. (See Chapter III.)

Obviously, the MTF of a lens is an indication of its ability to resolve gratings. However, when Fourier analysis and some other considerations are taken into account, this same MTF describes the behavior of the lens when the object is any intensity distribution whatever. That is, if the MTF is known, the exact intensity distribution of an image of *any* object can be calculated. Thus, the MTF completely describes what is essentially the stimulus–response relationship for that lens (neglecting phase shifts, as will be explained below).

Figure 12.6 contains a simple example of this operation. Here, a particular intensity distribution is taken as the object, and the task is to determine precisely what the image will be when it is formed by a given lens. The intensity distribution represented by the solid curve in Fig. 12.6a is the sum of the two sine-wave distributions that are dashed. Suppose that this is the intensity distribution of an "object" and that an image of it will be formed by a lens whose MTF is plotted in Fig. 12.6c. The intensity distribution of the image may be found as follows: First, the Fourier components of the input (the object) are found and plotted (Fig. 12.6b). This plot is called a spectrum, and is simply a representation of the amplitudes and frequencies contained in the object distribution. In this simple case, the spectrum of the object indicates that there are three Fourier components, or frequencies, in the object, at 0.0, 0.5, and 1.5 cycles per inch.

Fig. 12.5 **The relationship plotted here is called the** *modulation transfer function* **of a lens. When a lens forms an image of a sine-wave grating with some given modulation depth, the modulation depth of the image will depend upon the spatial frequency of the object grating. As the grating becomes very fine, that is, as the spatial frequency becomes very great, the image becomes a progressively poorer reproduction of the object, with the depth of modulation in the image becoming progressively smaller (for a fixed object-modulation depth).**

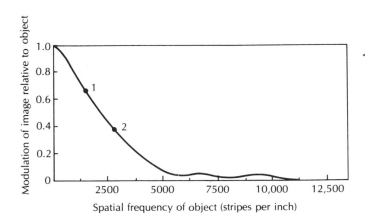

The sources of the 0.5- and 1.5-cycle components are obvious, but the zero frequency component requires explanation. A pure sine wave is symmetrical about zero, having equal positive and negative parts. A sine-wave grating that really contained only one Fourier component, say 0.5 cycles per inch, would exhibit bright regions alternating with regions of negative light. Thus, such a grating is a mathematical but not a physical possibility. The real sine-wave grating shown, for example, in Fig. 12.1b, is actually a mathematically correct sine wave added to a uniform field of light intense enough to raise the troughs of the sine wave up until they are positive.

Similarly, each of the two sine waves that are added together in Fig. 12.6a is actually the sum of a sine wave and a uniform field, and the total combination then, also contains a component that is really a uniform field. A uniform field has an infinite wavelength and thus a frequency of zero cycles per inch, and that is the Fourier component represented at zero frequency in Fig. 12.6b.

The three Fourier components in Fig. 12.6b are what the lens must transfer to the image plane. From the transfer function (Fig. 12.6c), it is clear that sine waves of zero frequency are transmitted at full amplitude; waves of 0.5 cycles per inch are transmitted at 95% of their input amplitudes; and frequencies of 1.5 at 25%. Therefore, the intensity distribution in the image plane will have the spectrum plotted in Fig. 12.6d, and will be as plotted in Fig. 12.6e (assuming negligible phase shifts, as explained below).

A somewhat more interesting example of the use of a transfer function is illustrated in Fig. 12.7. The intensity distribution chosen as the object is of a form that produces Mach bands (see Fig. 11.5). That distribution is plotted in Fig. 12.7a. Next, the pattern in Fig. 12.7a must be analyzed into its Fourier components, that is, the frequencies and amplitudes of the various sine waves that would have to be added together to reproduce the original distribution. The actual procedure required to extract the Fourier components is beyond the scope of this book, but the result of the Fourier analysis is as plotted in Fig. 12.7b. This plot means that the distribution in 12.7a contains sine waves at almost every frequency; i.e., a sine wave of frequency 0.5 cycles per degree at an amplitude of 110 units, another at frequency 1.5 cycles per degree, of amplitude 12 units, etc. If sine waves at each of those frequencies, and with the designated amplitudes, were all added together, the pattern in Fig. 12.7a would result.

The next step is to relate this plot, the amplitude spectrum of the object, to the transfer function of the lens, shown in Fig. 12.7c. Presenting the lens with the pattern in Fig. 12.7a is, in effect, presenting it

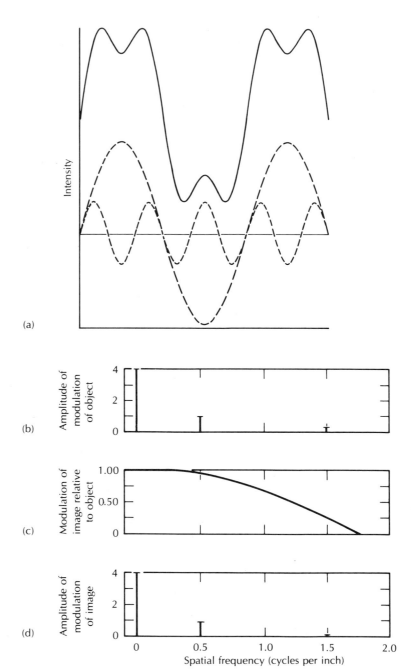

(a)

(b)

(c)

(d)

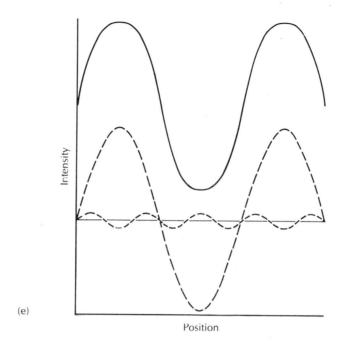

(e)

Fig. 12.6 Finding the intensity distribution in the image of a given object formed by a given lens. The object has the intensity distribution in (a), which is simply the sum of the two sinusoids. (These are the first two components of a square wave, as was illustrated in Fig. 12.3.) The plot in (b) indicates the sine-wave "content" of the object in (a). It is called the spectrum of the object, and shows that it contains three sine-wave components, one with a spatial frequency of 0.5 cycles per inch and an amplitude of 1.0 units, a second at a frequency of 1.5 cycles per inch, and an amplitude of 0.33 units, and a third with a spatial frequency of zero cycles per inch and an amplitude of 4 units. (The zero-frequency component represents a uniformly illuminated field.) The transfer function of the hypothetical lens is shown in (c), indicating that it transfers the lower frequencies with little attenuation, but attenuates the higher one by a factor of four. Therefore, the spectrum of the image will be as plotted in (d), and the three components represented in (d) are plotted and added together in (e). Thus, (e) is a plot of the intensity distribution of the image of the object in (a). (The spatial frequency is given here in units of cycles per inch. This unit implies that the object and image are always at fixed distances from the lens. The units of spatial frequency that are more generally applicable are angular units, e.g., cycles per degree, where the angle referred to is the angle between cycles of the object or image as subtended at the lens.)

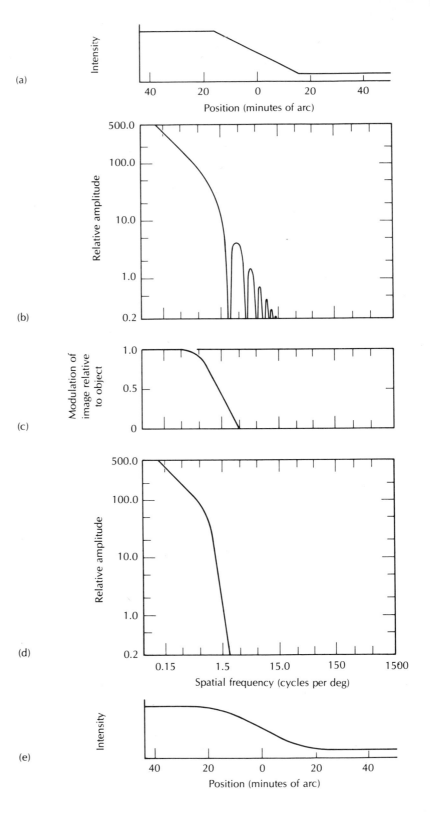

Fig. 12.7 **Finding the image of a Mach band pattern. The intensity distribution of the object is in (a). Its Fourier spectrum is plotted in (b), where it can be seen to contain an infinite number of sine-wave components. When this pattern is imaged by a lens that has the transfer function in (c), the spectrum of the image is that in (d), which is simply the product, at each frequency, of the heights of the plots in (b) and (c). When the sine-wave components in (d) are added together, they result in the intensity distribution in (e), which is the intensity distribution of the image of the object in (a).**

with the set of sine waves represented in Fig. 12.7b. The MTF says that the lens will attenuate the higher frequencies more and more. The plot in Fig. 12.7d is simply the result of multiplying the plot in Fig. 12.7b by the MTF. Each point is reduced in height by an amount depending upon the relative height of the MTF at its frequency. This plot, in Fig. 12.7d, is the amplitude spectrum of the *image*. That is, the image is the distribution that results from adding up the sine waves in Fig. 12.7d. This distribution can be found by Fourier synthesis, and comes out as plotted in Fig. 12.7e. It looks like the input distribution except that the corners are rounded off. In general, the high frequency Fourier components are what make sharp edges, and since all lenses have transfer functions that fall off at high spatial frequencies, the image of an object will always have edges that are less sharp than the edges in the object itself.

The procedure illustrated in Fig. 12.7 can be carried out for *any* input intensity distribution, and the resulting image can be calculated directly. Thus, to describe completely the behavior of a lens, it is not necessary to present it with every possible object and measure the images; it is only necessary to measure its responses to sine waves of various frequencies, and the result, the MTF, can be used to calculate the image of any object. The MTF is thus an extremely concise description of the behavior of the lens.[4]

In all of the discussion in this chapter, it is assumed that phase shifts are negligible, and that assumption is almost certainly correct. The concept of phase shift will be described briefly here, but will be treated in more detail in the discussion of the temporal properties of vision (Chapter XIV), where phase shifts are important. Suppose that a sinusoidal pattern is used as the object for a lens, and it is lined up so that one of the peaks of the sine wave, that is, one of the brightest parts, is exactly on the optic axis of the lens, as in Fig. 12.4. If simple geometrical optical principles are used to locate the image, it is clear that the image of that peak is also on the optic axis of the lens (where it intersects the image plane). However, if the lens manifested certain abberations, the image of the peak might not be in the line defined as the optic axis, but might be shifted to one side or the other. Such a shift is called a phase shift, because the part of the sine wave in the image that *does* fall on the optic axis will be a different phase of the sine wave than that to be expected.

[4]The MTF is not the only possible concise description, and intensity distributions other than sine waves can be used to perform analyses analogous to Fourier analysis. For example, if the light distribution in the image of a point object is known for a given lens, the image formed by that lens of any object may be calculated. However, the approach described in this chapter has advantages that have resulted in its being widely used in optics and vision.

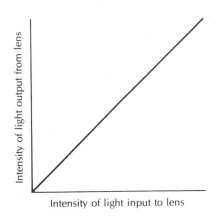

Intensity of light output from lens

Intensity of light input to lens

Fig. 12.8 **The linear relationship between the input and output intensities for any lens or combination of lenses.**

If a lens did produce phase shift, and if the shift were the same direction and *distance* at all frequencies (and therefore a shift in the *phase* of each wave that would be directly proportional to the frequency of the wave), it would merely mean that the entire image would be shifted sideways from the expected location. However, it is possible that the distance of the shift could be different for different frequencies. If so, then the MTF would not be sufficient to define the image of any object, since the relative positions of the various sine-wave components would not be known. Therefore, if there were a substantial phase shift that varied with frequency, both the MTF *and* the phase shift at each frequency would have to be known in order to predict the image correctly.

However, the phase shifts produced by most lenses, and by the optical system of the human eye, are relatively small near the optic axis (which, in the eye, is near the fovea), and only trivial errors are introduced by assuming that the phase shifts are zero.

At this point, it is probably obvious that Fourier techniques offer promise when applied to human vision. However, before exploring that possibility, it is important to understand some stringent conditions that must be met in order that Fourier techniques yield correct answers.

CONDITIONS NECESSARY FOR CORRECT USE OF THE MTF

Linearity

The use of the procedure illustrated in Fig. 12.7 depends upon the assumption that each of the Fourier components transferred through the lens adds to the others in a simple algebraic fashion in the image plane [that is, going from (d) to (e) in Fig. 12.7]. For any ordinary optical system, this assumption is certainly true. In general, if the intensity of the light radiated from the object to the lens is increased, the intensity of the image will be increased in direct proportion, since the only losses in light passing through a lens are from reflection at the surfaces and absorption within the glass, and both of these processes lose a constant proportion of the incident light. In other words, a plot relating the input intensity to the output intensity for a lens or system of lenses is linear, as in Fig. 12.8, and such a system is said to be a linear system.

More generally, a linear system is one that obeys the principle of superposition. Suppose an input that, by itself, yields an output value x, and another input that alone gives an output value y, are both impressed upon the system at the same time. A linear system, then, is one that will have an output $(x + y)$ regardless of the values of x and y. Furthermore, a system that is not linear for all values of input but does obey superposition over some limited range of inputs may be said to be linear over that range.

Fourier techniques only yield correct answers when applied to linear systems or to nonlinear systems that are operating in a linear range. They will yield incorrect results when applied to a system that is operating in a nonlinear way. For example, consider a visual system that acts as in the upper right plot of Fig. 12.9. If the intensity of stimulating light is below the threshold level, the output is zero; above that level,

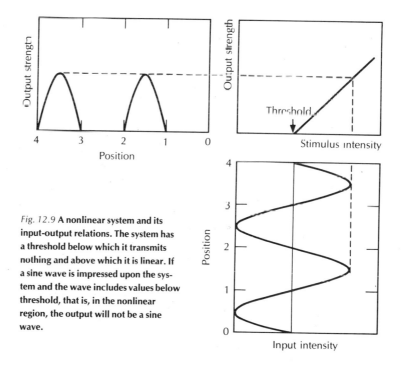

Fig. 12.9 **A nonlinear system and its input-output relations. The system has a threshold below which it transmits nothing and above which it is linear. If a sine wave is impressed upon the system and the wave includes values below threshold, that is, in the nonlinear region, the output will not be a sine wave.**

the output varies linearly with intensity. If a sine-wave intensity distribution were presented to a retina having this characteristic, and if the sine wave varied between zero and some value above threshold, as shown in Fig. 12.9, then any receptor on which the intensity was below the threshold would not be activated, but all receptors stimulated above threshold would respond in direct proportion to the intensity falling on them (since the curve is linear above threshold). Therefore, the output distribution—effectively the neural image—would be as plotted in Fig. 12.9. It would have pieces of sine wave interspersed between portions of equal (zero) amplitude.

The Fourier prediction for this system, if it were linear, is very simple. The spectrum of the input contains only two lines, one of them at zero frequency. That is, the input is the sum of a single sine wave and a uniform field. To obtain the Fourier prediction, these lines must then be multiplied by the heights of the MTF of the system at those frequencies. The result of this process will consist of two "output" components; a sine wave at the same frequency as the input sine wave (with an equal or smaller amplitude) and a uniform, or zero frequency, component. When these two components are added together to obtain the Fourier prediction for the output of the system in Fig. 12.9, the result will be a single sine wave on a uniform background. However, the *actual* output is a complicated wave form that contains some pieces of sine waves, but also contains Fourier components at many other frequencies. For example, the sharp corners in the output wave form indicate the presence of high-frequency components in the output that were not in the input.

In general, when any waveform is input to a *linear* system, the output is the sum of a set of sine waves whose frequencies are exactly the same as the frequencies of the sine-wave components of the input. The output is different from the input in that the *amplitudes* of the components are different. In a linear system, the spectrum of the output never contains any frequencies that were not present in the input spectrum. However, for a nonlinear system, the output will contain frequencies not present in the input. For example, the input and output spectra for the system in Fig. 12.9 are shown in Fig. 12.10. The nonlinearity introduces higher frequency components into the output.

If additional uniform light were added to the sine-wave input in Fig. 12.9, shifting the input wave so that it contained no intensities that were below threshold, then the system would be operating in its linear range, and the output would be a pure sine wave. Regardless of the wave form of the input, if any of it is below the threshold intensity, the output will not be correctly predicted by a Fourier procedure; but

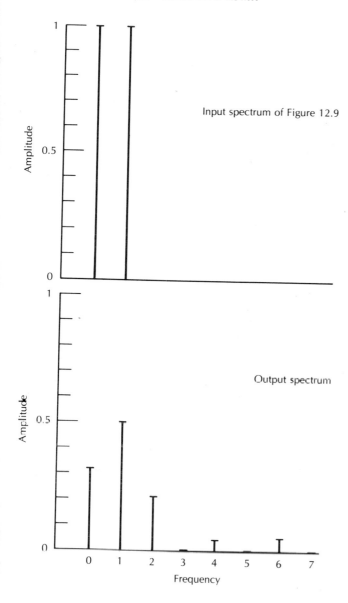

Input spectrum of Figure 12.9

Fig. 12.10 **The Fourier spectra of the input and the output from Fig. 12.9. The input spectrum contains only a uniform field (zero frequency) and a single sine wave, at an amplitude arbitrarily called 1.0. The nonlinearity of the system introduces other frequencies into the output.**

Output spectrum

when the input falls entirely within the linear part of the response curve, Fourier analysis will yield correct predictions.

The kind of nonlinearity just discussed is typical of biological systems, but biological systems frequently have another kind of nonlinearity as well, the one illustrated in Fig. 12.11. For example, in most visual systems, the neural response is roughly proportional to the logarithm of the input intensity. When a sine-wave intensity distribution is

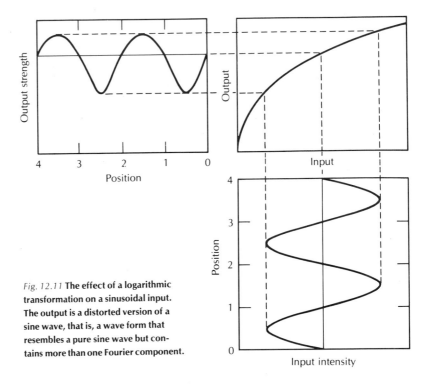

Fig. 12.11 **The effect of a logarithmic transformation on a sinusoidal input. The output is a distorted version of a sine wave, that is, a wave form that resembles a pure sine wave but contains more than one Fourier component.**

presented to a system with this characteristic, the output is a distorted form of the input, as illustrated in the figure. The output is not a single sine wave, but a mixture of many frequencies and amplitudes. Later, the implications of the nonlinearity in the human visual system will be examined in this context.

Homogeneity   A system is spatially homogeneous if its characteristics are the same in all locations. In particular, if a system is spatially homogeneous, then shifts in the location of the input pattern may cause shifts in the location of the output pattern, but the output pattern will not change except in position.

It is fairly obvious that, if an optical system is inhomogeneous, the MTF cannot be sufficient to define the image of any object, because the properties of the system differ with location, and the MTF contains no information about location.

The optical system of the human eye seems to be reasonably homogeneous near the optic axis, and thus, the MTF of the optical system may be used to find the properties of retinal images. However, there is ample evidence that the anatomy of the retina and visual pathways is markedly inhomogeneous. For example, the densities of rods and cones vary strongly with retinal position. Thus, caution must be used when applying Fourier techniques to the visual system as a whole.

To determine precisely the kinds and amounts of inhomogeneity that invalidate Fourier techniques is very difficult and requires sophisticated mathematical procedures, many of which have not yet been fully developed. However, there is evidence, to be discussed later, that Fourier techniques do permit correct predictions of human vision despite the known anatomical inhomogeneities. Whether this is the result of some self-homogenizing process [e.g., see Davidson (1968)], or of choosing test conditions that are insensitive to inhomogeneity is not yet known.

Isotropy   A system is isotropic if its characteristics are the same in all directions. For example, it is isotropic if the MTF measured with sinusoidal grating objects is the same regardless of whether the gratings are vertical, horizontal, or oblique (that is, regardless of their angular orientation with respect to the optic axis in the object plane). If a system is not isotropic, then a single MTF is not sufficient to describe the image of any object, but two MTF's measured at an angle to each other would be sufficient.

The optics of most human eyes show some astigmatism. That is, they behave in the same way as a combination of an ordinary, spherical lens and a cylindrical lens at some particular angular orientation. Phrased in a different way, the refractive strength of the eye is usually different for different angular orientations, so that the image of a point object will be elongated. For an eye that is prevented from changing its focus, the MTF measured with sine-wave gratings will extend to higher frequencies for some angular orientations of the grating than for others. Thus, the optics of the typical human eye are somewhat anisotropic. This kind of anisotropy, called astigmatism, is easily corrected by glasses (or contact lenses), and after such a correction, a single MTF can be used to find the retinal image of any object.

Even after the optics of the eye are corrected, there still remains some anisotropy; psychophysical MTF's (determined as explained below) for vertical and horizontal gratings extend to slightly higher frequencies than for oblique gratings. This anisotropy is probably attributable to the nervous system itself (although the possibility that it is a consequence of optical properties within the retina, such as anisotropic scatter of light, has not yet been ruled out). Thus, it restricts the use of a single MTF. However, many interesting conclusions about vision can be drawn solely from consideration of one-dimensional patterns (i.e., patterns such that intensity varies as a function of position in one direction but is constant in the perpendicular direction; e.g., sine-wave or square-wave gratings, linear Mach band patterns, etc.). Furthermore, the effects of this anisotropy are relatively small over much of the frequency range to which the eye is sensitive; e.g., at spatial frequencies equal to or less than 10 cycles per degree, the sensitivity to modulation is reduced by no more than about 15% by rotating the grating from vertical or horizontal to 45° (Campbell *et al.*, 1966). Therefore, after optical astigmatism has been corrected, the remaining anisotropy, in many instances, is small enough that a second MTF (at some other angle) is not necessary. (The effect of this anisotropy increases with frequency, so that, for example, the sensitivity to a grating of 30 lines per degree is only half as great when the grating is oriented at 45°.)

HUMAN VISUAL MODULATION TRANSFER FUNCTIONS There are several classes of experiments that are attempts to measure the MTF of the human visual system. These different classes require somewhat different interpretations, and they will, therefore, be treated separately.

"Direct" Measurements By direct analogy with the procedure used to measure the MTF of a lens, it would be desirable to be able to present a human subject with a series of sine-wave gratings all having the same amplitude but varying in frequency, and then obtain some measure of his perception of the patterns. In particular, we would like to know the *apparent* amplitude of each sine-wave pattern, that is, the difference between the brightness of the peaks and troughs of the wave, because the apparent amplitude is exactly an "output" of the human system. Thus a plot of the input frequency (for a fixed amplitude) against the apparent amplitude, would be exactly analogous to the plot of the MTF of a lens (e.g., Fig. 12.5). Given such a plot, and assuming that the human system is operating in a linear range (an assumption that will be discussed at length below) and that it is homogeneous and isotropic, we should be able to predict the appearance of any input pattern.

The drawing in Fig. 12.12 illustrates a way in which such measurements of apparent amplitude might be made. The subject is asked to

Fig. 12.12 **A stimulus arrangement that might be used to measure the MTF of the human visual system.** [*From Davidson (1966) p. 207.*]

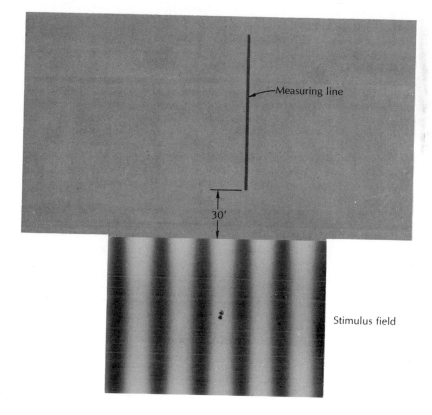

adjust the intensity of the measuring line until its brightness matches the brightness of the portion of the pattern directly below it. After he has made this match, the measuring line (or the pattern) is moved sideways, and a new reading is taken on a different part of the sine-wave pattern.[5]

If the human visual system were linear, and if the judgements involved no systematic errors, a plot of the resulting intensity settings as a function of the location along the sine-wave pattern would be a sine wave of the same frequency as the stimulus (input) pattern. However, the amplitude of this output sine wave would depend upon the spatial

---

[5]This arrangement was suggested by Davidson (1966), on the basis of his measures of the MTF, which will be discussed later. At this writing, no one has published any work using such a display. Lowry and DePalma (1961) used a similar display to derive a transfer function in a different way, but their measuring line extended all the way to the pattern being tested, and was against a dark background. Both of these factors exert appreciable influences on the brightnesses in the pattern itself, and thus seriously bias the measurements. Bryngdahl (1964) used a technique in which the entire field above the pattern was adjusted in intensity to match the brightness of some part of the pattern. This procedure also yields contaminated data because of the presence of the edge between the pattern and the measuring background. See Davidson (1966) for a quantification of this contamination.

frequency of the pattern. For example, since the MTF for any real lens has a shape generally like that shown earlier (Fig. 12.5), and since the human visual system contains such a lens, it might be expected that a very high frequency sine-wave pattern, that is, one with very fine and closely spaced lines, would tend to look uniform, and the intensity settings at different positions of the measuring line would all be almost the same. That is, the amplitude of the output wave would be very small when the input frequency was high. A plot of the amplitude of the subject's settings of the measuring line against the frequency of the stimulus pattern would then represent something like the MTF of the subject's visual system.

However, the human visual system is not linear. Therefore, when the input pattern is a sine wave, the output pattern will not be a pure sine wave, and there is no simple measure of the output amplitude that can be used in the same way as the corresponding plot for a linear system. The kind of plot in Fig. 12.5, of output amplitude versus input spatial frequency, can only properly be called a transfer function when it is a measure of a linear system. This kind of plot, when applied to nonlinear systems, will hereafter be called a *describing function*.

Threshold Measures The procedure just explained has not yet been used to measure the describing function of the human visual system, and it might, in fact, prove difficult to use. For example it seems possible that the judgment would be unreliable, since the comparison that the subject must make would seem to be a difficult one.

A procedure that has frequently been used because it appears to be straightforward, employs measurements of the thresholds for detecting sine-wave gratings. The subject is presented with a sine-wave grating of a particular spatial frequency, and the amplitude of the intensity variation is adjusted until he can just detect the presence of the grating, or just reliably distinguish it from a uniform field. When this procedure is repeated for a number of different spatial frequencies, the results take the form plotted as a solid line in Fig. 12.13. Now let us analyze what this plot means.

In order to interpret the plot, some assumption must be made about the relationships among the thresholds at different frequencies. The implicit assumption in most studies that use this procedure is that, whenever the amplitude of the input sine wave is just at the subject's threshold of detection, the "output" amplitude is some constant value. That is, it is assumed that the subject will always say he just sees the

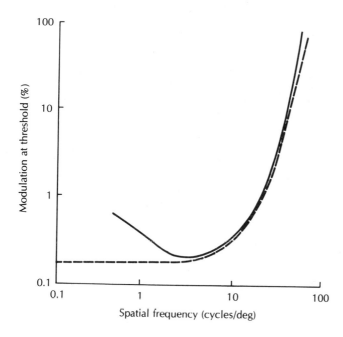

Fig. 12.13 **The solid curve is a describing function of the human visual system, obtained by measuring the threshold modulation at each spatial frequency. (100% modulation means that the troughs of the sine wave are completely dark.) The dashed curve is what would be expected for a lens under the same conditions of testing.** [*The solid curve is from Van Nes and Bouman (1965); λ = 525 nm, average intensity = 90 trolands.*]

pattern (within some statistical variation) when, somewhere in his system, there is an excitation pattern, called the output, that has some particular modulation depth that is identical for all spatial frequencies. It is assumed that the threshold for the amplitude of the "output" signal is the same regardless of the spatial frequency of the input. If this (questionable) assumption is accepted, then the function plotted in Fig. 12.13 means that, as the input frequency increases from a very low value, the amplitude needed to produce a constant *output* amplitude first decreases and then increases.

The relationship of this kind of plot to the transfer function of the lens that was plotted in Fig. 12.5 is a simple one. To obtain the plot in Fig. 12.5, sine waves of constant amplitude were input, and the output amplitudes were measured. If, instead, the amplitude of the input wave were adjusted to produce a constant *output* amplitude across the range of frequencies, the result would look like the dashed curve in Fig. 12.13.[6] (For any linear system, such as a lens, these two forms of the transfer function are equivalent, since, given one, the other can be easily calculated.)

A comparison between the dashed and solid curves in Fig. 12.13 reveals that the human visual system has properties that are substan-

---

[6]The dashed curve in Fig. 12.13 also differs from the MTF in Fig. 12.5 because the scales on the axes are linear in Fig. 12.5 and logarithmic in Fig. 12.13.

tially different from those of an ordinary optical system. In the human visual system, *low* spatial frequencies are attenuated as well as high ones.

The solid curve in Fig. 12.13 is a describing function of the human visual system, and it is a transfer function of the system if, under the conditions of measurement, the system is linear and homogeneous. While it is clear that the visual system is, in general, *not* a linear one, the following argument suggests that it may be essentially linear under these measuring conditions.

Suppose that the response of the visual system to changes in the input intensity is nonlinear, with a characteristic such as that plotted in Fig. 12.14. If the input amplitudes in the procedure under discussion were large, then the output would clearly be a nonlinear function of the input. In the actual conditions of measurement, however, the amplitudes of the input sine waves were usually very small. In fact, they were always small enough to ensure that the variations in intensity were at the threshold of detection and thus were actually large only near the extremes of detectable frequencies. In other words, the range of intensities presented in the test patterns usually covered only a small region of the curve in Fig. 12.14. Over any small range of intensities, the relationship between the input and the output is very nearly linear. (A technique will be discussed below in which the input range is, in essence, reduced to zero.)

To the extent that the visual system, under these conditions, is linear and homogeneous, and within the limits of our confidence in the assumption concerning the relationship among threshold values, the solid curve in Fig. 12.13 can be called a transfer function. However,

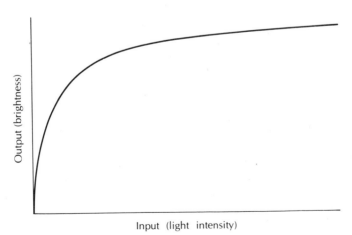

Fig. 12.14 **A hypothetical input-output characteristic for the human visual system, input being defined as the intensity of light falling on the retina and the output as the perceived brightness. The relationship is nonlinear. (It is actually the relationship discussed in Chapter X, and shown in Fig. 10.15.)**

Output (brightness)

Input (light intensity)

Fig. 12.15 **Typical pattern used for contrast matching. The pattern on the right contains a low spatial frequency at a high contrast and the one on the left a higher spatial frequency and a lower contrast.**

the threshold assumption is difficult to defend, and for this reason a third technique for measuring the MTF has been developed.

Contrast Matching Davidson (1966, 1968) developed the following procedure for measuring the MTF of the human visual system.

The subject fixates the center of a uniformly illuminated field. After enough time has passed for him to become photochemically light-adapted to this field, it is darkened for 1 sec, and a sine-wave grating is flashed on for a very brief time (0.5 msec). Then after another 1-sec period of darkness, a second grating is flashed, and he is asked to say which of the two gratings appeared to have the greater contrast; that is, in which of the two gratings did there appear to be a greater difference in brightness between the bright lines and the dark ones. The two gratings to be compared in this way are set at different spatial frequencies and amplitudes, as illustrated in Fig. 12.15. In a given series of trials, the spatial frequencies of the two gratings and the amplitude of one are held constant. The amplitude of the other is varied until it is such that for 50% of the trials the subject says one grating has more contrast and for the remaining 50% of the trials he says the other has. When the two amplitudes are so chosen, the subject, if asked, will say that the two patterns have different spacings (frequency) but the same apparent contrast. The frequency of one of the gratings is then changed, and the procedure repeated until every frequency has been compared with one standard frequency. The data from such a set of measurements are plotted in Fig. 12.16. (The vertical axis in this figure is a measure of *sensitivity*. It is thus reciprocally related to the threshold measure in Fig. 12.13.)

If we define the "output" of the human visual system as the subject's judgment of brightness (or more precisely, his judgment of relative brightness within each sine-wave pattern), then this curve gives, directly, the input amplitude necessary to produce a constant output amplitude, as a function of the input frequency. This definition of "output" is entirely appropriate, since the goal of the procedure is, at least in part, to describe concisely the relationship between any input intensity distribution and the resulting judgments of relative brightness.[7]

The curve in Fig. 12.16 may be used as a transfer function if the system is linear, homogeneous, and isotropic. The homogeneity and isotropy restrictions are the same here as they were for the threshold measurement technique. However, the linearity restriction is a different matter. The range of intensities that occur in the threshold technique are necessarily small (except at the extremes of frequency), and therefore it is reasonable to assume that the visual system is operating over a region that is essentially linear. However, when the matching procedure is used, the gratings are clearly visible, and the range of in-

[7]The relationship between threshold measurements of the MTF and matching measurements is somewhat paradoxical. There are procedures for measuring thresholds that yield unequivocal results, ones that we tend to describe as being unaffected by "subjective" factors. For example, on half of the trials, the field may be uniform and on the other half the grating is present. On each trial, the subject is forced to say whether or not the grating was present, and he is told whether he is right or wrong. The amplitude of the grating is then adjusted, from trial to trial, until an amplitude is found such that the subject is correct, say, 75% of the time. What this procedure unambiguously determines is the input amplitude necessary in order that the subject's visual system does not lose the information that a grating was present. It is not influenced by factors that are usually called "subjective," such as the subject's opinion about what a grating should look like (since he is essentially taught what a grating looks like by being told whether he is right or wrong). However, by the same token, this procedure cannot yield any information about the appearance of the stimulus. That is, it cannot, by itself, tell us anything about brightness or brightness differences. The perceptual bases upon which the subject is making his judgments are irrelevant. For example, he may be saying that a grating is present whenever the stimulus looks reddish, or seems to come on more slowly, etc.; the procedure itself neither asks about nor depends upon such perceptual phenomena. It only determines whether or not the information that a grating was present is transmitted from the subject's eyeballs to his mouth.

On the other hand, the procedure in which the subject matches two gratings so that they look alike in contrast, even though they may appear to be different in wavelength, is "subjective." It measures, directly, the relationship between the input intensity distribution and the resulting perceptual phenomena. While this "subjectivity" seems, superficially, to be undesirable (and is sometimes called unscientific), the subjective phenomenon is *exactly what we wish to measure*.

If the threshold procedure is to be used to make predictions about *brightness* distributions, an assumption must be made that links the threshold data with the subjective phenomenon called brightness. For example, the assumption is usually made, implicitly, that the difference in brightness between the brighter and the darker parts of a grating is always the same when the grating has a threshold amplitude, regardless of the wavelength of the grating. That assumption involves plenty of "subjectivity." Thus, the threshold measuring procedure begins with more "objective" measurements, but must be combined with "subjective" assumptions in order to permit predictions about brightness, while the matching procedure involves measurements which, themselves, are "subjective," but that require no further assumptions (of that kind) in order to be used to make predictions about brightness.

All of the preceding discussion is important to consider when we wish to use the MTF to describe brightness. However, another important purpose for measuring the visual MTF is to test theories about the physiological processes that operate in the visual system. Here, the relative merits of the threshold and matching procedures must be evaluated on somewhat different grounds. This will become evident later, when the physiological implications of the MTF are explained.

Fig. 12.16 **Describing function for the contrast-matching technique. The scale on the vertical axis bears an inverse relationship to that in Fig. 12.13. That is, higher values represent greater sensitivity or more apparent contrast.** [*The points at the three highest frequencies are extrapolated from the remaining points, which are from Davidson (1968), subject LF, 5.84 units contrast.*]

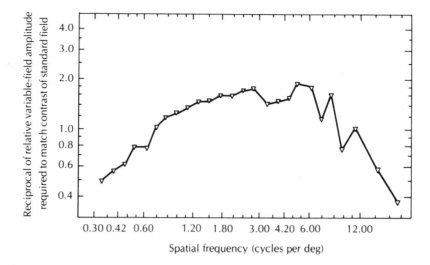

tensities within each stimulus field is, therefore, larger. Thus it is less likely that the system is operating over a linear range.

When a matching technique is used, the problem of linearity may be attacked by a procedure called small perturbation analysis. This procedure is really quite simple. We assume that, as the range of intensities in the stimulus approaches zero, that is, as the amplitude of the sine wave approaches zero, the system will be operating in a linear range. Several sets of measures of the describing function are taken. To take the measurements already described (those plotted in Fig. 12.16), a standard grating at some particular amplitude and frequency is compared with other gratings at different frequencies. The result, as plotted in Fig. 12.16, is a curve showing the amplitude at each frequency necessary to produce the same contrast as the standard grating. Then, all the measurements are repeated for several other standard gratings whose amplitudes differ.

Suppose the results came out as shown in Fig. 12.17. As the amplitude of the standard grating is made smaller and smaller, the curves change, approaching a limiting curve, the one labeled "extrapolated." This extrapolated curve is that which would be obtained if the amplitude of the standard were zero (assuming that the input versus output function of the system is not discontinuous). The extrapolated curve thus represents the action of the system when it is operating in a linear range.

Of course, the range of operation in this example is zero, and the transfer function so obtained can only be used to make correct predictions for patterns that have zero intensity modulation. Therefore, while

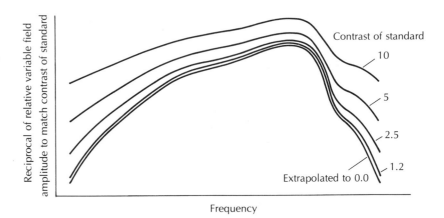

Fig. 12.17 **Hypothetical result of a contrast matching experiment at several different contrasts of the standard, for a strongly nonlinear system. The curve to be expected from a zero contrast standard has been extrapolated from the other curves.**

the procedure is logically proper, it does not seem to have much utility.

However, the example in Fig. 12.17 represents the results that would be obtained from a strongly nonlinear system. If the same procedure were carried out on a strictly linear system (e.g., a lens), all of the describing function curves would be identical and could be superimposed upon each other. If the procedure were carried out on a system that is linear over a given range and nonlinear beyond that range, all of the curves that were measured with signals falling within the linear range could be superimposed, and the other curves would be spread out, perhaps as in Fig. 12.17.

Evidence that the visual system is strongly nonlinear was discussed at length in Chapter X. However, it is quite possible that all or a large part of the nonlinearity manifested by the human visual system occurs very early, perhaps in the process by which isomerized photopigment molecules excite neural tissue. If this were true, that is, if the system were essentially linear after some initial nonlinearity, then it would be possible to extend greatly the usefulness of the MTF.

Let us assume that the nonlinearity *is* confined to stages that entirely precede interactions among spatially separated neurons, and that the nonlinearity is approximately logarithmic over small ranges of intensity. Now suppose that, instead of presenting the eye with a sine-wave grating test object, we present an exponential sine-wave grating. This is a target whose intensity distribution is such that, when its logarithm is taken, it is a sine wave, as illustrated in Fig. 12.18. When such a pattern is presented to a layer of receptors that have a logarithmic response, the output pattern of neural excitation, that is, the pattern that is input to the remainder of the visual system, is a sine-wave grating. Thus, if exponential sine waves (antilog sine waves) are presented instead of ordinary ones, the system might be "linearized."

That is, in fact, the procedure used by Davidson. The intensity distributions of his targets were not actually sine waves, but rather exponential sine waves. (For very small amplitudes, the difference between a sine wave and an exponential sine wave becomes vanishingly small.)

The result, when this procedure is applied to the human visual system, is shown in Fig. 12.19. All of the obtained curves are superimposed at frequencies below about 3 cycles per degree. The range of standard amplitudes employed in this experiment was about 5:1, and the data are thus consistent with the hypothesis that the visual system is essentially linear over a range of at least 5:1 for low spatial frequencies, once an initial logarithmic response has been compensated. (The

Fig. 12.18 The upper curve is a plot of the intensity distribution of an exponential (antilog) sine-wave grating. The lower plot is the output distribution that would result from putting the exponential sine wave through a logarithmic stage. It is a pure sine wave.

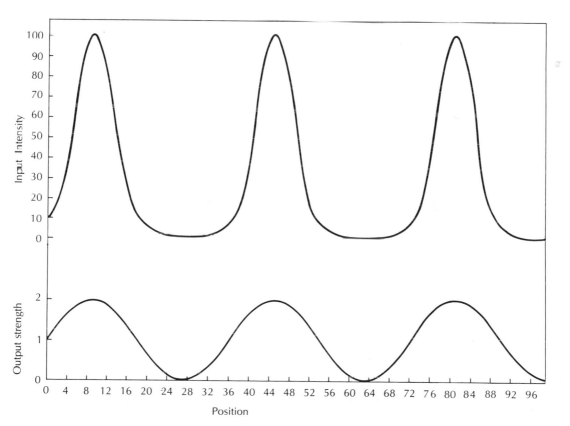

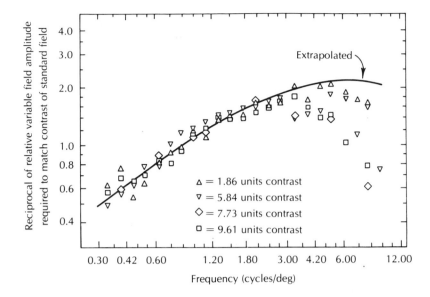

Fig. 12.19 **Actual data points collected from a contrast matching experiment, using exponential sine-wave targets. Standards of differing contrast were used, and a zero-contrast curve has been extrapolated. (The inverted triangles are the same as in Fig. 12.16, except that measurements were not made in this experiment at frequencies higher than 9 cycles per degree.)** [*From Davidson (1968) subject LF.*]

fact that the curves are superimposed does not *necessarily* mean that the system is linear over this range. Certain combinations of nonlinearities could also make the curves fall on one another. However, the most likely explanation of the fact that they are superimposed is that the system is close to linear over the range of intensities tested.)

Since all of the curves in Fig. 12.19 are superimposed for low spatial frequencies, it is very easy to extrapolate to the curve for zero amplitude. It is simply that same curve. At frequencies above 3 cycles per degree, the curves are not superimposed, and the extrapolation is a little more difficult.[8]

The extrapolated curve in Fig. 12.19 is the describing function that resulted when Davidson followed the procedures that have just been explained. This curve is *not* the describing function of the visual system. It is the describing function for the complete system measured by his experiment, and that system included the optical system that he constructed to present the stimuli. It is obviously important to be able to separate out the effects of the apparatus itself, and the principles of Fourier analysis provide a straightforward procedure for accomplishing this.

The logic is as follows: Suppose that a sine wave is input to one lin-

[8]Davidson makes a convincing argument that the lack of superposition at high frequencies is probably an artifact of his experimental equipment, rather than a manifestation of nonlinearity in the visual system (Davidson, 1966). Since he was not primarily interested in the high-frequency region of the curve, he did not explore this question further.

ear system, system *A,* and then the output of system *A* is input to another linear system, system *B.* The amplitude of the output of system *B* will be attenuated as the *product* of the attenuation in each system alone. For example, if, at the particular frequency of the sine wave being measured, the output of system *A* was reduced to ¹/₄ of the input amplitude, and system *B* attenuated sine waves of that frequency by ¹/₂, then the output of the combination of *A* and *B* would, obviously, be ¹/₈ of the input amplitude. In general, if the transfer functions of any number of linear systems are known (that is, if their attenuations at each frequency are known), then the transfer function of all of them in cascade is simply the product of their individual transfer functions.

Thus, the extrapolated curve in Fig. 12.19 is actually the product of the transfer function of the apparatus (the apparatus was known to be linear), and the transfer function of the visual system (assuming it is linearized). Therefore, Davidson measured the transfer function of his experimental apparatus, by a procedure like that previously described for measuring the MTF of a lens. He then divided the curve in Fig. 12.19 by the apparatus MTF.

The result of this operation is the curve in Fig. 12.20. Assuming homogeneity and isotropy, we shall then call this curve a transfer function for the human visual system.

At the time of this writing, this kind of curve has only been obtained under one restricted and arbitrarily chosen set of conditions [i.e., a mean intensity of 740 foot lamberts, fields flashed for 0.5 msec, white light, etc.] However, it will be shown in the next section that even for this limited set of conditions, the results yield important insights into perceptual phenomena and their physiological bases. Fur-

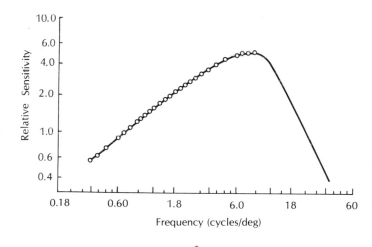

Fig. 12.20 **Describing function for the human visual system after correction for the transfer function of the experimental apparatus. The circles are extrapolated data points.** [*From Davidson (1968) subject LF.*] **The region without data points is an estimate of the high-frequency portion of the curve based upon threshold measurements by Campbell and Green (1965).**

thermore, the curve in Fig. 12.20 is quite similar to the functions obtained by threshold techniques under somewhat different conditions (e.g., Fig. 12.13), and so it is reasonable to go on and examine the implications of this relationship.

PERCEPTUAL PHENOMENA RELATED TO THE TRANSFER FUNCTION   Let us begin by examining the direct meaning of the transfer function. Suppose that two sine-wave gratings were being examined, one at a spatial frequency of 6 lines per degree of arc and the other at 25 lines per degree, both having the same amplitude. The curve in Fig. 12.20 is higher at 6 than at 25 lines per degree, and therefore the 6 cycle-per-degree grating would appear to the subject to have more contrast. That result is consistent with common experience. Very finely spaced gratings are hard to resolve. In addition, however, the curve in Fig. 12.20 shows that very *coarse* gratings, that is, ones with very long wavelengths, also appear to have less contrast than gratings of intermediate spacing.

These perceptual phenomena are directly apparent in Fig. 12.21. This is a photograph of the face of a cathode ray tube (similar to a television picture tube) on which a special pattern has been imposed. Any line drawn horizontally across the picture would intersect sinusoidal changes in intensity whose amplitude is constant but whose frequency increases from left to right. Moving vertically downward on the picture, the *amplitude* of the waves decreases. If you hold this photograph at arm's length (then the frequency scale is approximately correct), you will note that there is a sort of triangular appearance to the border formed by the visible parts of the stripes. For example, if you do not need glasses, or if your glasses are properly corrected for a target at arm's length, the line at about 6 cycles per degree will be visible over more of its length than the other lines. The lines at higher and at lower frequencies will appear to be progressively shorter.[9]

The meanings of the threshold measures (Fig. 12.13) and the measures of apparent contrast (Fig. 12.20), and the differences between them are also nicely illustrated in Fig. 12.21. The stripes at high and low frequencies are only visible when their amplitudés are relatively high (that is, those stripes do not appear to extend very far downward) while the stripe at about 6 cycles per degree is still visible when its am-

---

[9]If you move farther away from Fig. 12.21, the peak wavelength will shift toward the left, because the stripe that now has a frequency of 6 cycles per degree is farther to the left. (That is, the retinal image of the figure is smaller, and therefore, a larger stripe in the picture is needed to produce the same size stripe on the retina.)

plitude is very low. Thus, the curve traced out by the apparent bottoms of the lines provides a visualization of the *threshold* measurements. A visualization of the *contrast* measures is also apparent in Fig. 12.21, although it is not so striking. The apparent contrast along any single horizontal line cutting across the pattern is low at both high and low frequencies, and is greatest at about 6 cycles per degree.

The MTF in Fig. 12.20 was measured under a restricted set of conditions, namely when the target was briefly flashed and when the contrasts were not too great. The measurements represented in Fig. 12.13 are similar, and were also for low contrast targets, although those targets were viewed steadily, not flashed. Taking these restrictions into account, the demonstrations illustrated in Chapter XI are consistent with MTF, and, in fact, could have been predicted from it.

Consider, first, the demonstration of Mach bands in Fig. 11.5. A Mach band intensity distribution is plotted again in Fig. 12.22a. Going through the steps in Fig. 12.22b–e, it is evident that the "output" pattern predicted from the MTF is very similar to the pattern that a subject would draw if he were asked to plot the brightness distribution in the pattern. Thus Mach bands may be a special case of the general characteristic represented by the MTF.

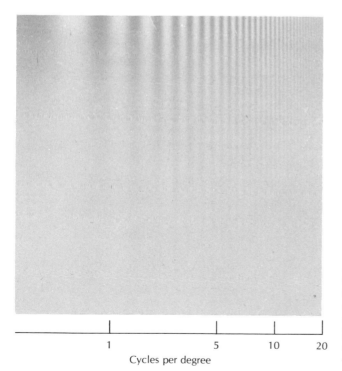

1   5   10   20

Cycles per degree

Fig. 12.21 **A demonstration of the transfer function of your visual system. It is explained in the text. The frequency scale is approximately correct when the figure is held at arm's length.** [*Photograph furnished by F. Campbell and J. Robson, unpublished.*]

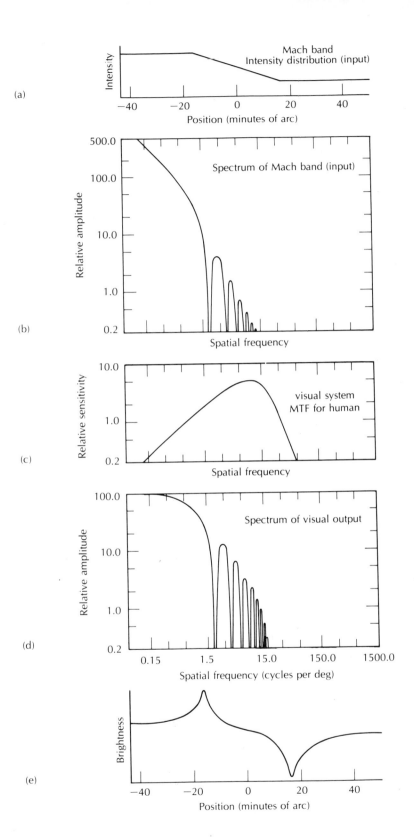

Fig. 12.22 **Calculation of the (perceptual) brightness distribution for a Mach band pattern predicted from the human MTF. The input intensity distribution is shown in (a). The Fourier spectrum of this pattern is given in (b). The transfer function in (c) is that in Fig. 12.20. Multiplying the input spectrum by this MTF results in the spectrum shown in (d), which yields, by Fourier synthesis, the output or brightness pattern in (e).** [*The curves in (a), (c), and (e) are from Davidson (1966) subject LF; a linear system is assumed.*]

(a)

Mach band
Intensity distribution (input)

(b)

Spectrum of Mach band (input)

(c)

visual system
MTF for human

(d)

Spectrum of visual output

(e)

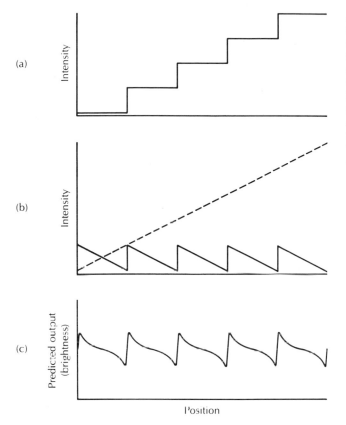

(a)

(b)

(c)

Position

Fig. 12.23 **The staircase intensity distribution in (a) may be considered as the sum of the two intensity distributions in (b). Since the visual system attenuates low frequencies, it will attenuate that component represented by the straight line in (b), and it will also attenuate the very high frequencies associated with the sharp corners in (b). The expected result is shown in (c). The actual appearance of this pattern was shown in Fig. 11.4.**

Let us examine this point more closely. The data from which the MTF in Fig. 12.20 was derived were obtained by a matching procedure. The subject was presented with pairs of sine-wave gratings and was asked to equate the brightness differences between their bright and dark regions. The subjects actually reported that the task was less ambiguous than it sounded, because when a pair of gratings matched, they matched not only in contrast but also in absolute brightness. That is, the bright bars in each grating were equally bright, and so were the dark bars. Therefore it is quite clear that the MTF in Fig. 12.20 is a measure of the transfer between physical (intensity) units at the input and perceptual units, brightness, at the output. Thus the units of "output," such as in the plot in Fig. 12.22e, are really brightness units, and knowing the input intensity distribution, it should be possible to make correct predictions about the apparent brightness distribution. In other words, we should expect that when a subject is shown the distribution in Fig. 12.22a, he will report that the field appears to contain a bright

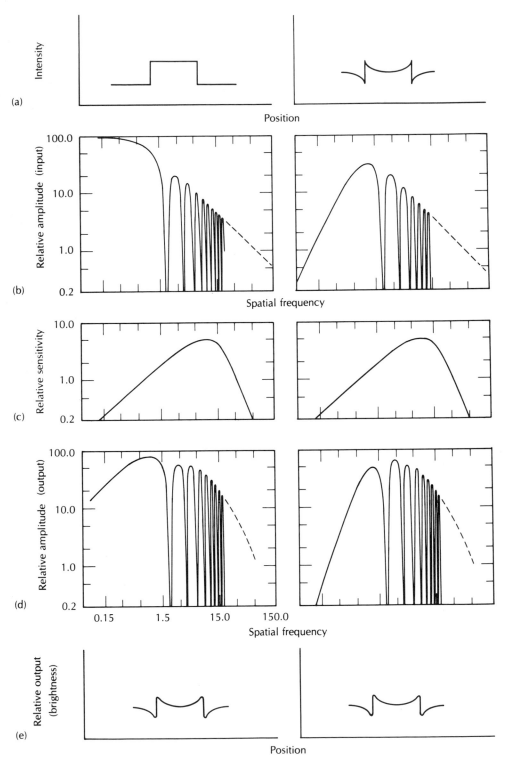

and a dark band, roughly centered on the parts of the field where the discontinuities in intensity are found.[10]

The intensity distribution in Fig. 11.4 is replotted in Fig. 12.23a. A Fourier analysis could be carried out on this figure, just as in Fig. 12.22, but much of the analysis can be cut short by noting a particular feature of this distribution, namely that it is the sum of the two intensity distributions plotted in Fig. 12.23b. In any wave form (or intensity profile), sharp corners and regions containing curves with relatively small radii of curvature are represented by high frequencies in the Fourier spectrum, while regions with large radii of curvature are represented by low frequencies. Thus the Fourier spectrum of the straight-line component in Fig. 12.23b has all its energy at very low frequencies (its radius of curvature is infinite), and as a consequence, that component will be strongly attenuated by the visual system. On the other hand, the spectrum of the saw-tooth component has its energy in the moderate and high frequency range. The moderate frequencies will be transmitted well, and the very high ones attenuated. Thus, the expected output is as plotted in Fig. 12.3c, and that is approximately what the brightness distribution looks like.

Now consider the pair of patterns shown in Fig. 11.2. Their intensity distributions are replotted in Fig. 12.24a, and their spectra in Fig. 12.24b. The spectra (remember) represent the amplitudes of the Fourier components that must be added together to produce the patterns. Note that the only difference between the two spectra in Fig. 12.24b is in the low frequency region. The high frequency parts are virtually identical. This fact can be described verbally as follows: The two distributions in Fig. 12.24a are identical with respect to their "corners." The only way in which they are different is that the one on the right has regions of very gradual change (large radii of curvature) while the corresponding regions in the one on the left exhibit no change (infinite radius of curvature).

The output curves for these two distributions can be constructed by Fourier techniques as represented in Figs. 12.24b-e. The two output curves in Fig. 12.24c are very similar, and the reason for the similarity is clear. The only difference between the two input distributions is in

---

[10]If a hypothetical logarithmic transformation is taken into account, the predicted brightness distribution fits that which is observed very accurately (Davidson, 1966).

Fig. 12.24 **Fourier prediction of the brightness distributions that should result from the intensity distributions in (a). Photographs possessing these distributions were shown in Fig. 11.2.**

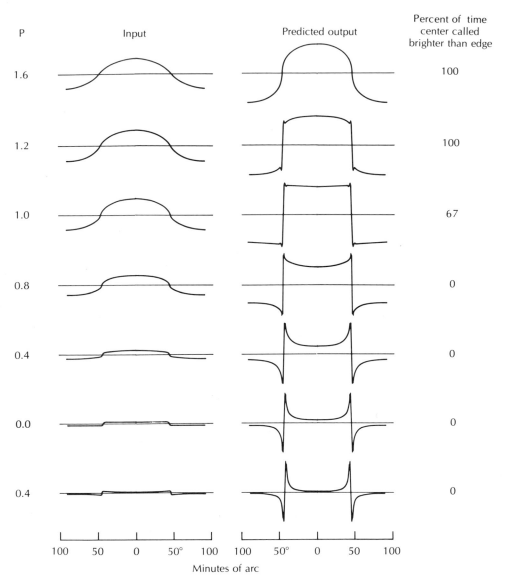

Fig. 12.25 **Diagram of an experiment to measure carefully the brightness distributions for the intensity distributions is shown in Fig. 12.24a. The numbers in the left-hand column represent a parameter of the shape of the "input" curves. The curves in the "input" column are intensity distributions that were presented to the subjects in brief flashes at relatively low contrast. The curves in the "calculated output" column are the output curves predicted by Fourier analysis, using the MTF from Fig. 12.20. (The input curve for *P* = 0 is the step on the left in Fig. 12.24a, and the output distribution is the corresponding one in Fig. 12.24e.) The last column contains the subjects' judgments. The input distribution whose predicted output was closest to a step (*P* = 1.0) was about equally likely to be judged brighter and darker in the middle (when the subjects were forced to call it one or the other), and the input pattern that was really a step (*P* = 0) was always judged as predicted.** [*From Davidson (1966).*]

their low-frequency components, and the visual system strongly attenuates low-frequency components. Therefore, the properties of the visual system attenuate the differences between these two patterns, and
the resulting outputs are very similar. That is, the two patterns look
alike.

The use of the MTF leads to the prediction that these two patterns
should look alike, and they do. However, if a subject were asked to
plot the *apparent* intensity distribution (i.e. the brightness distribution)
of each, he would probably make two plots that both look like the *left*
plot in Fig. 12.24a, while the preceding analysis predicts that they both
ought to look like the plot on the *right*. How can this inconsistency be
accounted for? There is very good evidence that the discrepancy does
not reflect an inadequacy in the application of Fourier techniques to
human vision. It is much more likely a result of the difference between
the conditions of measurement of the MTF and the conditions for
viewing the pattern in Fig. 12.24.

Remember that the MTF used in Fig. 12.24 was measured by
presenting a subject with briefly flashed, low-contrast patterns
and asking him to match them in apparent contrast, while the pattern in Fig. 12.24a is presented steadily and the subject is asked
what the distribution appears to be. Any one or combination of
these differences in conditions might account for the discrepancy.
An experiment performed by Davidson (1966) provides partial
clarification of this question. In preliminary work, he presented subjects with the intensity distribution at the left in Fig. 12.24a (in the form
of a long stripe that was brighter than its background), when the contrast was low and the exposure was brief. When the subjects were
simply asked to say what they saw, they described a light stripe on a
slightly less bright background. When asked whether the stripe was
uniform in brightness, they said yes (at first). However, upon *careful*
psychophysical measurement, which will be described below, it be-
came evident that the stripe did not appear to be of uniform intensity,
and in fact, its brightness distribution was just that which would be
predicted from the MTF.

Davidson constructed a series of stripe test patterns whose distributions are shown in the "input" column of Fig. 12.25. These patterns
were constructed in such a way that the output patterns predicted on
the basis of the MTF were those shown in the "calculated output" col
umn of Fig. 12.25. Note, in particular, two special cases. The input
pattern for $p = 0.0$ is the pattern already under discussion. It is simply a
uniform stripe. The output pattern is the same as that on the left in Fig.

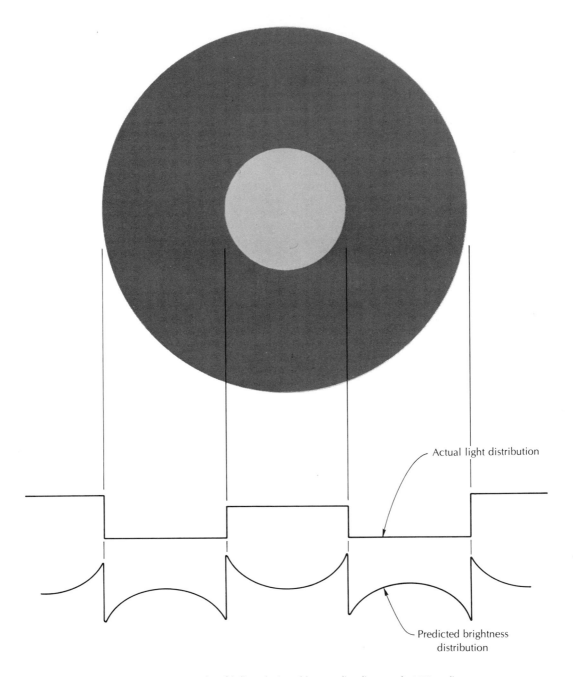

Actual light distribution

Predicted brightness distribution

Fig. 12.26 **When this figure is viewed from reading distance, the MTF prediction is that the center of the central disk should have almost the same brightness as the middle region of the dark ring. That is clearly not the case.**

12.24e. The input pattern for $P = 1.0$ is rounded just enough that its predicted output pattern is as close to rectangular as it can be.[11]

Subjects were shown these various targets, individually in brief flashes, and were asked to judge whether the center of the stripe was brighter or darker than the edge of the stripe. Their responses were recorded without any comment about whether they were right or wrong. This procedure was performed repeatedly for all of the patterns. The results are shown in the righthand column. The physically uniform stripe ($P = 0.0$) always appeared brighter at its edges, and the stripe that appeared uniform was $P = 1.0$ or one close to it.

These results clearly agree with the predictions made on the basis of the MTF. Furthermore, after the subjects had been exposed to the various members of this series of stimuli, their verbal descriptions of the appearance of the patterns changed. The pattern for $P = 0.0$, originally called a "uniform stripe," was described in a strikingly different way. The brightness at the center of the bright stripe was judged to be about the same as the brightness of the *background* at some distance from the stripe. This, too, agrees well with the MTF prediction.

It can be concluded that, when a subject is shown a uniform stripe and asked to describe it, he will call it a uniform stripe, but if he is given the opportunity to choose among alternatives rather than simply to use the language he brings with him to the experiment, his results will be consistent with the MTF. In general, then, the MTF and Fourier techniques may not be sufficient to predict a subject's responses when he is asked to describe what he sees, particularly if what he sees fits some common set of words reasonably well. However, when his responses are disengaged from his common language by a careful psychophysical technique, the predictive power of the MTF is manifested.

Comparable measurements have not been made for patterns under steady viewing conditions and moderately high contrasts, but certainly the center of the disk in Fig. 12.26 does not appear to have the same brightness as the middle of its dark background, even though the MTF leads to that prediction. (It may well be, however, that careful measurement would reveal that the edges of the disk are brighter than its center.) Thus it is apparent that the MTF predictions break down under many ordinary viewing conditions. Since the MTF's measured by Davidson and independently by Campbell (and by many others) all agree

---

[11]There is no way to produce an input distribution, to be viewed normally by the eye, that can overcome a slight rounding of the corners in its output pattern, but since the phenomena of interest here are primarily those involving low spatial frequencies, the rounding of corners is of no consequence.

Fig. 12.27 The intensity distribution in the contrast demonstration of Fig. 11.7 is plotted in (a), and the predicted output (brightness) distribution is plotted in (b). The regions corresponding to the small squares have been shaded in these plots. Notice that, while their intensities are all identical, their predicted brightnesses depend upon the intensities of their backgrounds.

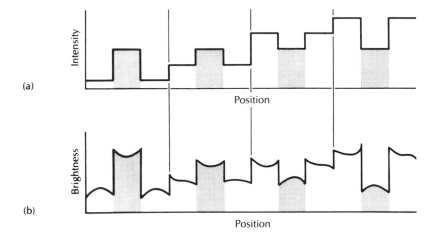

(a)

(b)

in general form, and since Campbell's were measured under normal viewing conditions (the subject simply looked at the pattern and made judgments), the breakdown in MTF predictions is probably not a result of the time factor in the viewing conditions. It is much more likely that the errors in prediction are caused by high target contrasts. Certainly a high-contrast breakdown should be expected, since the visual system is not linear, and since both Campbell's and Davidson's MTF's were measured for low contrasts.

Since the MTF seems to be a very promising way of describing the relationship between the distribution of light in the retinal image and the distribution of brightness, an important next step in this research is the evaluation of the nonlinearity in the visual system. If the nonlinearity is fully understood, it may well be possible to make accurate predictions, on the basis of the MTF or a similar measure, that will hold for patterns with high contrast as well as low.

The contrast phenomenon illustrated in Fig. 11.7 can also be predicted from the MTF. The intensity distributions for the various parts of this figure are plotted in Fig. 12.27a. The output distributions predicted from the MTF are plotted in 12.27b. Note that at the input (Fig. 12.27a) the small squares (represented by the shaded regions of Fig. 12.27) are all at the same level while the background level is changing, but at output, the shaded regions change. This is consistent with the perceptual phenomenon; the small squares themselves appear darker when they are presented against more intense backgrounds. However, here, as in the preceding example, the brightness distribution within each small square seems more uniform than the MTF prediction.

Now consider the MTF prediction for the cases illustrated in Fig.

12.28. The only difference between the two patterns is that an intensity of 90 units has been added to the entire pattern on the right. If the visual system were linear, the MTF would lead to the prediction that the outputs from the two small spots would be very similar; the only difference between the two patterns is a uniform field, and the visual system is very insensitive to a uniform (low spatial frequency) field.[12]

This prediction is clearly wrong. The contrast in the pattern on the right appears to be much smaller. (If the light added to the field were great enough, the contrast would be so small that the disk would not be discernable. This fact is closely related to Weber's law.)

However, this example is clearly one in which the intensity differences are too large to expect the system to approximate a linear one. If we make the assumption that the nonlinearity is simply a logarithmic transformation at the receptor level, then the prediction is consistent with the MTF, as illustrated in Fig. 12.29.

Now consider the important case called brightness constancy. This is illustrated in Fig. 12.30a, where the intensities in the right-hand figure are all the same multiple of those on the left (as explained on pp. 282–283). When an early logarithmic transformation is again assumed, the inputs to the rest of the system, Fig. 12.30b, differ only by a uniform field, and the two outputs should be very similar. In other words, a combination of a logarithmic transformation and the measured MTF lead to the prediction that brightness constancy should occur. (This discussion of brightness constancy will be greatly enlarged in Chapter XIII.)

[12]Since these patterns are not infinitely large, the field added to the pattern on the right is not of zero frequency. High-frequency components are manifested near its edges. Therefore, the MTF prediction only applies to the central regions of the patterns.

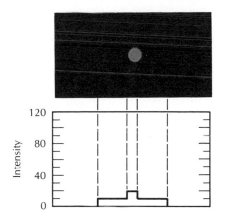 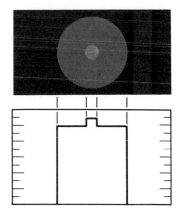

Fig. 12.28 The pattern on the left is identical with the one on the right except that 90 (arbitrary) units of intensity have been added uniformly over it, as plotted below. If linearity is assumed, the MTF prediction is that the two small spots will look identical, since low spatial frequencies are attenuated.

PHYSIOLOGICAL IMPLICATIONS OF THE MODULATION TRANSFER FUNCTION

The transfer functions shown in Figs, 12.13 and 12.20 are consistent with reasonable hypotheses about the physiology of the human visual system.

The High-Frequency Region

Examine the region of the MTF in Fig. 12.20 that extends from the peak to the right, that is, the region in which the sensitivity decreases as the frequency increases. The decreasing sensitivity in this part of the curve is characteristic of any ordinary optical system, and is often used as a measure of the quality of optical systems. The characteristics of this region of the MTF are determined in part by the optics of the eye. However, there is good evidence that the optical properties of the lens and cornea are not the only factors that limit high-frequency sensitivity; the properties of the retina itself play an important role in determining the shape of the transfer function for high spatial frequencies. That evidence is obtained as follows.

If two narrow slits are placed in front of the pupil of the eye, as in Fig. 12.31, and light with a particular property called coherence is made to pass through them (such light is produced by a laser, or by passing monochromatic light through a very small aperture), an intensity distribution will be produced on the retina that closely approximates a sine-wave grating, and the characteristics of that grating will be almost completely independent of the refractive properties of the

Fig. 12.29 **If it is assumed that a logarithmic transformation occurs at a stage preceding the spatial interaction in the visual system, then the patterns of light intensity falling on the retina in Fig. 12.28 will yield the excitation patterns plotted here at the input to the spatial interaction system. After the low-frequency difference between the patterns is removed, they differ in that the small disk on the left yields a larger output. Thus when a logarithmic transformation or something like it is assumed, the prediction agrees with the appearance of the pattern.**

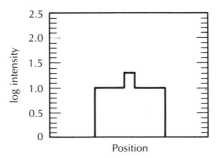

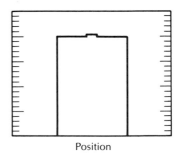

Fig. 12.30 **The paradigm for brightness constancy. The distribution on the right in (a) has an intensity that is the same as that on the left except that it is multiplied, everywhere, by 6. After a logarithmic transformation, the two patterns are identical except for a zero-frequency component (i.e., the right-hand pattern in (b) is identical to the left-hand pattern except that it is about 0.8 units higher everywhere ($\log_{10} 6 = 0.78$).**

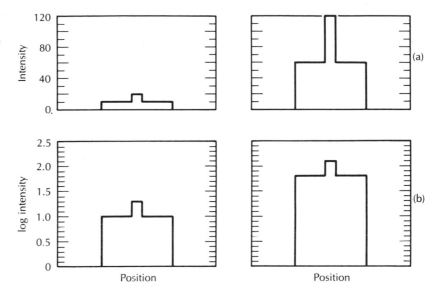

cornea or lens of the eye. Campbell and Green (1965) have measured the MTF using test patterns produced in this way, and it is essentially the same as that measured during normal viewing of a sine-wave target through a 2.5 mm pupil.[13] Therefore, the drop in sensitivity at high frequencies cannot depend importantly upon the properties of the cornea and lens, and must, thus, be a manifestation of some retinal property or properties. (For large pupils, the aberations of the eye probably are primarily responsible for the loss of high-frequency sensitivity.)

Exactly what the crucial retinal properties are is not yet known, but there are three obvious possibilities. A first is the finite size of the individual receptors. This factor has been given extensive attention in the literature, but there is no convincing evidence that the size of the receptors plays any part in limiting visual functioning, and there is ample evidence that this factor is negligible under many conditions. However, since the receptor mosaic might appear to be an important factor, and since it has appeared so to many authors, it will be discussed briefly here.

Figure 12.32 is a photograph of the retinal mosaic at the fovea. The

---

[13]The spatial frequency of the grating on the retina can be varied by changing the separation between the two slits, and its modulation depth by superimposing upon it a uniform field of adjustable intensity. (The intensities of the light forming the grating and that forming the uniform field must be covaried if the average intensity, that is, the adaptation level, is to be held constant despite changes in the modulation depth.) To obtain their MTF, Campbell and Green found the threshold modulation depth for each of a number of spatial frequencies.

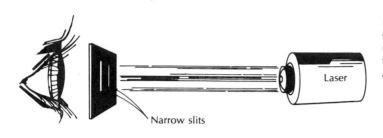

Fig. 12.31 **Sketch of an apparatus to obtain a sine-wave grating on the retina that is relatively independent of the optical properties of the cornea and lens.**

Narrow slits

diameters of the cones and the distance between cone centers is about 3 μ, or 35 seconds of arc (35″) (This dimension may become as small as 20″ at the very center of the fovea.) If we make the very reasonable assumption that each cone acts as a unit, that is, that the output of any particular cone depends only upon the total amount of light absorbed by all of the pigment in it, then it is obvious that the dimensions of the cones would impose some limit on visual functioning if no other factors set higher limits. For example, a visual system with these dimensions could not discriminate between a single point of light and a pair of points if the stimuli were placed on the retina in such a way that both members of the pair of points always fell on a single receptor. (For simplicity, assume that each member of the pair was half as intense as the single point.) This is a clear instance in which the retinal mosaic would limit acuity. However, under the very best conditions, the human visual system does not even approach that limit. Two points must be 1′ apart, that is, two or three cone-diameters apart, in order that they be discriminated from a single point under optimal conditions, and those conditions rarely occur. (They did not obtain in either of the MTF determinations under discussion.)

A fine, dark line on a bright background can be detected when it is only one second of arc wide. This fact has puzzled many writers, since it seems to be irreconcilable with the size of the retinal mosaic. However, upon closer examination, it is clear that this perceptual phenomenon has nothing to do with the retinal mosaic. Theoretically, a visual system limited only by the size of its receptors should be able to detect the presence of any object, no matter how small. A dark point 1″ in diameter will cause one receptor to be stimulated less strongly than the others, even if the receptors are 1 ft in diameter.

In fact, a human cannot see a dark dot 1″ in diameter; because of the optical properties of the eye, which spread the light, a dot that small does not produce a large enough change in intensity on any receptor. A dark dot must be about 1′ in diameter to be seen, and a line 1″ wide must be more than about 30′ *long* to be detected. In other words, the change in intensity on the retina that results from the presence of the line is distributed over some 60 or 70 cones.

In general, it is clear that, while the size of the cones could theoretically limit certain visual tasks, the limits of human vision at high spatial frequencies are actually set by other factors.

A factor that is much more likely to have a real effect on the transfer function is as follows: Light scatters somewhat when it strikes the retina. This scatter effectively reduces the amplitude of modulation of *any* grating, but it reduces the amplitude of high-frequency gratings more strongly than low ones. If you present a subject with a small bright spot of light and examine his retinal image with an ophthalmoscope (see Appendix III), you will see very clearly the spreading of the light when it strikes the retina. It is similar to the way the light spreads when a small spot is projected onto your hand. The Stiles-Crawford effect (p. 140) certainly reduces the deleterious effects of this spreading (that is, light entering the cones from the sides is probably less likely to be absorbed by the visual pigment), but scatter may still be the factor that sets the limit of resolution at high spatial frequencies.

Another factor that might affect the behavior of the visual system at high spatial frequencies is neural summation. Spatial summation in the rod system has already been discussed (Chapter II), and it was pointed out in that discussion that the visual acuity in the rod system was poor.

Fig. 12.32 **Photomicrograph of human foveal cones, seen end-on. These areas are near but not at the center of the fovea.** [From Polyak (1957). Copyright © 1957 by the University of Chicago Press.]

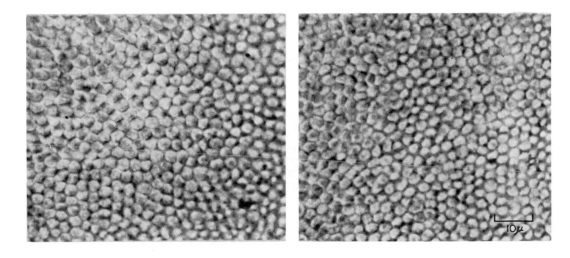

In general, if many neighboring receptors all contribute excitation to the same ganglion cell and there are fewer ganglion cells than receptors, spatial resolution suffers. In the extreme case, suppose that all receptors were connected only to one huge ganglion cell and optic nerve fiber. The signals sent from the eye, then, could contain no information about the spatial distribution of the light on the retina, but only about the total amount of light falling on all receptors.

If the signals among neighboring receptors were additive, then resolution for high spatial frequencies would suffer, but sine-wave components with wavelengths long compared with the distance over which summation occurred would not be so strongly affected. In fact, such neural summation produces results that are essentially like those produced by scattering of the light within the retinal surface. At the present time, there is no evidence by which the relative parts played by neural summation and by light scattering can be evaluated in the human eye.

The Low Frequency End of the Transfer Function The sensitivity of the visual system drops for gratings of low spatial frequency as well as for the high frequencies. There seems to be only one plausible explanation of this low frequency attenuation: The drop in sensitivity at low frequencies is exactly what would be expected if there were lateral inhibitory interactions in the human visual system. An examination of Fig. 12.33 should indicate, at least in a rough way, why this should be. Curves like those in the middle of Fig. 12.33 have already been explained (see pp. 301–303). The presence of lateral inhibition produces output peaks near regions where the input intensity changes rapidly. Tracing up and down the series of plots in Fig. 12.33, it is clear that the height of the output peaks depends upon the spatial rate of change of intensity at the input; the more gradual the intensity change, the smaller the output. The peaks are a consequence of the fact that receptors just on the bright side of the input edge are receiving relatively less inhibition because they are near a dimly lit area. Similarly, the troughs on the dark side are caused by the increased inhibition coming from the more intensely lighted area. (If this is not clear, reread pp. 301–303, where it is explained more fully.) When the input change becomes more gradual, the peaks and troughs are reduced in amplitude because the differences between neighboring receptors are smaller, both in their excitations and in the inhibition impressed upon them.

Since sine-wave gratings of lower frequencies have more gradual changes in intensity, a system with lateral inhibitory interaction that

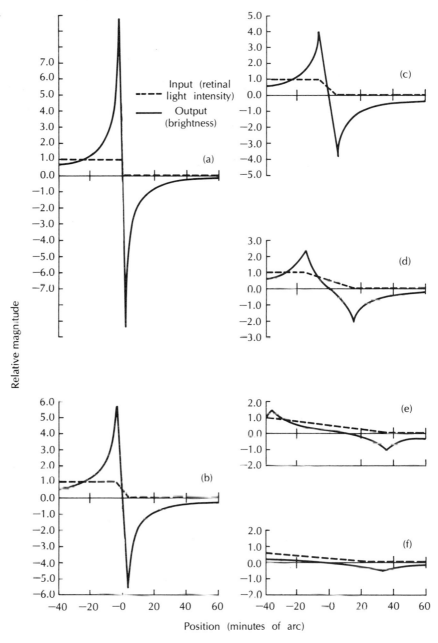

Fig. 12.33 **Retinal light distributions and the corresponding brightness predictions, based upon the MTF measured by Davidson.** [*From Davidson (1966).*]

decreases with distance will attenuate low-frequency sine-wave gratings more strongly than higher frequency gratings. Conversely, by analyzing the shape of the transfer function, certain characteristics of the spatial interactions in the visual system can be determined. For example, if there is only a single stage or level in the human visual system that manifests recurrent inhibitory interaction, then, for the subject whose MTF is shown in Fig. 12.20, the strength of inhibition radiated from an excited point is simply inversely proportional to the distance from the point (Davidson, 1966).[14]

There are a number of reasonable physiological theories specifying the manner in which inhibitory interaction operates in the human eye. One of these theories, a very simple one and one that is consistent with the facts gathered so far, is diagramed in Fig. 12.34. Each receptor excites a neuron, which in turn excites an optic nerve fiber, as well as a set of fibers that travel laterally through the retina. These lateral fibers do not branch, their properties are constant throughout their length, and their distribution is random in the lateral layer. During maturation or experience with light, or both, synapses are formed between the cell bodies that lie in the lateral layer and whatever lateral fibers happen to be near them, and these synapses are inhibitory. Furthermore, inhibitory influences add, as in *Limulus*.

Thus, each receptor excites one optic nerve fiber, and also sends recurrent inhibitory signals in all directions. Furthermore, each receptor unit collects inhibition from many of its neighbors. The probability that an inhibitory fiber originating at any one receptor will synapse with any other receptor unit is, then, inversely proportional to the distance between the two units; consequently, the number of inhibitory synapses between any two receptor units will vary inversely with the distance between them. Since we have assumed that the fibers have uniform properties throughout their lengths, the inhibitory coefficient (K in the *Limulus* equations of Chapter XI) will thus be inversely proportional to the distance between units.

Assuming a model of this kind, the curves in Fig. 12.35 represent the retinal state when a subject looks at a point of light. The spread of light resulting from aberations, diffraction, scatter in the retina, etc., result in a light distribution on the retina as represented by the curve labeled "excitation" while the resulting inhibition (which depends upon the distribution of light) contributes a negative component, as diagramed. The net effect of these two influences is the "output" in Fig. 12.36. A point of light in space thus produces, on the retina, a central region in which excitation predominates, surrounded by a region in which inhibition predominates.

---

[14]This is the only "distance function" that is consistent with the "single recurrent stage" assumption and with the MTF for this subject. The shape for this subject is a remarkably simple one; the data from Davidson's other subject yielded a similar, but somewhat more complicated curve and thus a more complex distance function. Furthermore, it is possible that, under different experimental conditions, a different MTF might be obtained, and a different distance function calculated. That is, the distance function may depend upon the state of the eye.

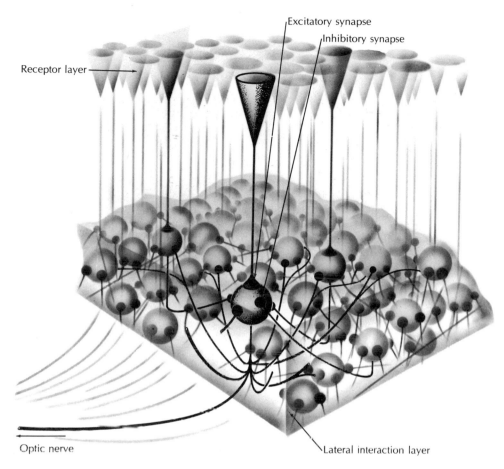

Excitatory synapse

Inhibitory synapse

Receptor layer

Optic nerve

Lateral interaction layer

Fig. 12.34 A simple model of a set of neural interconnections that is quantitatively consistent with the MTF in Fig. 12.20. Each receptor excites a single
cell body, which in turn sends impulses up the optic nerve and also along col-
laterals that spread over the retina. Wherever a collateral comes near to a cell
body, an inhibitory synapse is formed.

From this diagram it is possible to predict the result of a hypothetical
physiological experiment. Suppose that a microelectrode were inserted into the human optic nerve in such a way that the electrode recorded the activity in a single nerve fiber of the cone system. Let us further assume either that the fiber has some spontaneous activity in the
dark, or, if not, that the corresponding retinal region is dimly illuminated at such a level that the fiber fires continuously at a low rate. Now
suppose the receptive field of this fiber were mapped. That is, suppose
that a point of light were moved about in the visual field, and its effect

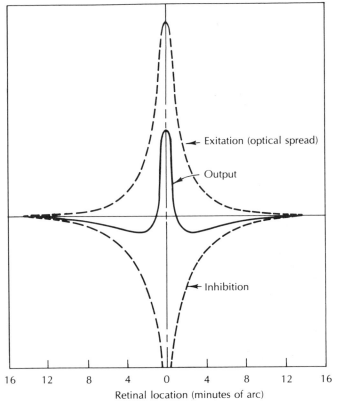

Exitation (optical spread)

Output

Inhibition

16   12   8   4   0   4   8   12   16

Retinal location (minutes of arc)

Fig. 12.35 **The effects of a point of light upon the visual system, as calculated from the MTF in Fig. 12.20 combined with independent measures of the optical properties of the eye. The geometrical image of a point of light is at zero. Diffraction, aberrations, etc., spread the light to give the distribution labeled "excitation," while inhibition spreads from each point with a strength that is inversely proportional to distance. The resulting output distribution is the solid line.** [*After Davidson (1966)*.]

on the firing rate in that fiber were recorded at each position. (There would be important temporal effects in such an experiment, but their description will be delayed until Chapter XIV.) A plot of the receptive field would be as in Fig. 12.36. Whenever the image of the light was centered on the receptor that excited the fiber, the excitatory effects would be stronger than the inhibitory ones and there would be an increase in firing rate. If the spot were moved slightly to the side, the fiber would still be excited, though less strongly, and would also be inhibited (less strongly), but the net effect would be an excitatory one. As the stimulating point is moved farther from the center, a point will be reached at which the excitation and inhibition are equal, and when the light is moved even farther, there will be a reduction in the firing rate. Thus the receptive fields of fibers with this kind of interconnection will be concentrically organized, center-on types.

The plots in Fig. 12.35, are not chosen haphazardly. The solid curve in Fig. 12.35 is the result of calculating, on the basis of Davidson's MTF, what the brightness distribution must be for a single luminous point on a less intense background. In other words, to the extent that the system is linear, isotropic, and homogenous, the plot in Fig. 12.35 must be the shape of the brightness distribution resulting when Davidson's subject LF looked at a bright point. The "excitatory" curve in Fig. 12.35 is an estimate of the actual retinal light distribution in the image of a point (resulting from diffraction, aberations, and scatter). The "inhibitory" curve is simply the algebraic difference between the output curve and the excitation one. (This procedure is based on the assumption that excitation and inhibition simply add algebraically in the eye.) Thus the MTF measurements yield a receptive-field plot for the human visual system that is entirely consistent with receptive fields measured directly in cat and monkey retinas, and is also consistent with the theory that there is lateral inhibition in the human visual system with properties qualitatively similar to those in *Limulus*.

Now suppose that we make a slight change in the retinal model in Fig. 12.34, interposing another stage between the receptors and the optic nerve such that whenever the input to this stage increases in activity, the output decreases, and vice-versa. The MTF of such a model would be identical with the old one, except that the phase would be shifted 180°. That is, wherever there was a more intense band in the input, there would be a region of *lower* activity in the output. This model is also completely consistent with the experimental results. Superficially, a model of this type would seem to predict inverted brightness patterns, but there is nothing that requires us to believe that the subject will see something as brighter when the output is greater.

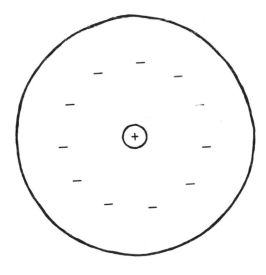

Fig. 12.36 **The expected receptive field of a single foveal human optic-nerve fiber. It corresponds to the solid curve in Fig. 12.35.**

We have only hypothesized that brightness depends monotonically on output. *A priori*, it is just as reasonable to assume that a greater output correlates with *decreased* brightness.

The point of this discussion is that the MTF also fits a model in which the results of a physiological experiment would be exactly reversed, that is, in which the receptive fields would be concentrically organized, center-off units. (In cats and monkeys, center-off units are just as common as center-on ones.) Therefore, we conclude either that all of the optic nerve fibers involved in judgments of brightness have concentrically organized receptive fields of the same polarity (e.g., center-on), or else that a mixture of on-center and off-center fields determines the perception of brightness, but with one type predominating. In the latter case, the output plot in Fig. 12.35 is the average receptive field.

Note that this entire discussion refers only to those parts of the visual apparatus that contribute to the perception of brightness. It is likely that there are other forms of interaction in the visual system as well. Such outputs may parallel the outputs described above, and mediate other perceptual dimensions. For example, the perception of motion may well be governed by neurons whose patterns of connections are quite different from those that govern brightness.

XIII ◇◇◇ BRIGHTNESS AND COLOR CONSTANCY

IS ALL THIS PERCEPTION? TO many people who study perceptual phenomena, the material discussed so far seems to have little to do with what they would like to call "perception." These scientists, along with many philosophers, try to draw a distinction between "sensation," which is similar to what has been discussed in this book, and "perception," which involves more of the psyche. If there is any real difference between the meanings of these two words, it is not important for the present purposes.

This book presents some of what is known about seeing and its relations to physical and physiological events. Virtually nothing will be said here about the influence of such factors as suggestion, knowledge, emotion, etc., on what we see. One reason for this omission is that, for all of the perceptual phenomena discussed so far, the influences of these "psychological" factors are vanishingly small when compared with the influences of physical and known physiological parameters.

The literature dealing with perceptual phenomena is preponderantly preoccupied with the effects of "psychological" factors, while often completely neglecting analyses of physical conditions that account for 99.9% of the magnitude of the phenomena.[1]

The perceptual phenomenon called brightness constancy is very interesting in this respect. Brightness constancy has already been described in Chapter XI. One way that it has been studied in the classical literature is as follows: A subject is presented with a piece of grey cardboard hanging from the ceiling, say 10 ft in front of him in a room, and he is also given a box with a window in it through which he can see a series of pieces of paper graded in brightness from black through many shades of gray to white. There is also a light in the box that illuminates the set of grays. These conditions are shown in Fig. 13.1. He is asked to say which of the shades of gray (call these the comparison grays) is the same as the big piece that is out in front of him (call this the standard). If the intensity of the light falling on the standard cardboard is the same as that falling on the comparison grays, it is not surprising that the subject will pick out the comparison gray that is physically the same as the standard gray, or very close to it. That is, he will pick out a comparison gray that has the same reflectance (ratio of reflected to incident light) as the standard gray, and this is to be expected, since those two grays reflect equal intensities of light to the eye.

Now, suppose the intensity of the room lights is cut in half (while the light falling on the comparison grays remains the same) and the experiment is repeated. If the subject were making his matches purely on the basis of the physical intensities of the retinal images of the standard and comparison patches, he would now choose a comparison gray whose reflectance was half that of the standard. However, typically he will again choose the one that is physically identical to the standard, that is, that has the *same* reflectance as the standard. In general, the subject will always pick that same comparison gray, or one very close to it, regardless of changes in the illumination falling on the standard cardboard. In other words, the subject's responses indicate that the brightness of the standard seems constant regardless of the illumination falling on it. That is why the phenomenon is called "brightness constancy."

Note that the subject acts as though he were somehow responding to the reflectance of the cardboard rather than to the *amount of light* it

[1]For example, by manipulating a subject's motivation, it is possible to change the value of his dark-adapted visual threshold by about 15% (Swets, 1964, p. 53), while his threshold can be changed by 10,000,000% by light-adapting him (Rushton, 1962b), and the brightness of a patch of light can be changed by more than 1,000,000% by presenting it against a bright background (Heinemann, 1955).

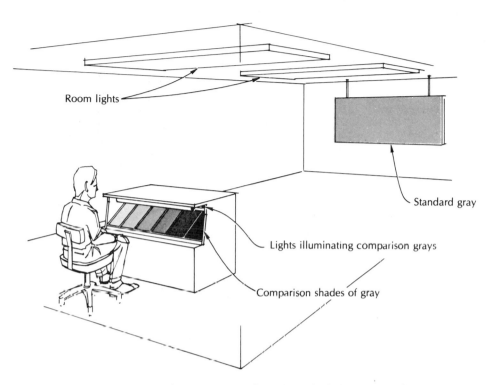

Fig. 13.1 **Sketch of a classical experimental setup for the measurement of brightness constancy. The subject sees a "standard" gray target illuminated by the room lights and is asked to choose the one from a set of different shades of gray, the "comparison grays," that appears to be the same as the standard. The comparison grays are seen through a window in a box that prevents the room illumination from falling on them, but that provides illumination of its own.**

actually reflected. That is, it appears that he is seeing some property of the object itself, independent of the intensity of the retinal image of that object. This rather striking observation both demanded and suggested an explanation. The explanation that permeates the psychological literature is either meaningless or absurd, depending upon how one interprets it, but it is evidently very captivating. Basically, it goes like this. We certainly do not want to suppose that a subject can sense directly the physical properties of an object (e.g., its reflectance). His information about the object must come either from the light reflected from the object, or from his past experience with the object, or from some combination of both. Now the demonstration of constancy described above works perfectly well when the subject has no prior knowledge of the cardboards used, so past experience with the particular stimuli is not necessary. What the subject must be doing, then, is

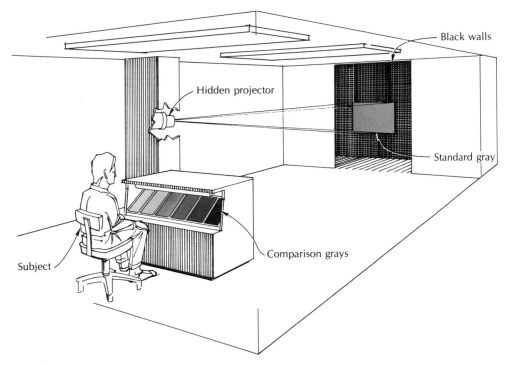

Fig. 13.2 **A modification of the setup in Fig. 13.1, allowing the standard target to be lighted both by the room illumination and by an extra, hidden, light source. The hidden source is a slide projector that illuminates only the region of the standard target. Furthermore, any light that might happen to miss the target is trapped in the black chamber behind the standard and cannot be seen by the subject.**

observing the intensities of the retinal images of the objects, and also estimating the intensity of the illumination on each object, and he must be responding to the ratio of those two values. Or put more crudely, the subject must be estimating the intensity of the illumination and compensating for it. Otherwise, how could he match the two (differently illuminated) cardboards in *reflectance*?

This "explanation" can be tested in several clear ways. Conditions can be constructed such that the subject's estimates of the illumination will be mistaken, and he will then give judgments that differ accordingly. For example, in Fig. 13.2, a projector is arranged so that it is hidden from the subject and projects light onto the standard cardboard *only*. The subject has no way of knowing that the projector is there, and therefore ought to misjudge the illumination on the standard, not realizing it is as high as it really is. Consequently, we would predict that he will make the wrong compensation for the illumination, and will judge the reflectance as greater than it really is.

This experiment works very well. The subject does exactly what is predicted. Under these conditions, the cardboard looks much brighter than it did before the projector was turned on. Furthermore, if the presence of the extra, hidden, illumination is then revealed to the subject by placing a piece of white paper partly in front of the standard, so that the paper catches part of the projected light, or by causing the projected light to fall onto the background as well as the standard, the standard will suddenly appear much darker.

The converse can also be easily demonstrated. If a hidden shadow caster is arranged so that it casts a shadow just on the standard but nowhere else, the subject will be led to overestimate the illumination on the standard, and should therefore judge it as darker than he would if the shadow revealed its presence by falling at least partly on the background as well as the standard. This prediction is also clearly verified by the data.

Now let us examine this explanation of brightness constancy a little more closely. First of all, it is clear that the cognitive connotations of the explanation are wrong. The subject is not aware of "estimating" the illumination. The term "estimate," then, is not used in its usual meaning. Similarly, any "compensation for the illumination" is not a conscious one. In fact, the phenomenon is completely independent of whether or not the subject actually knows the true lighting conditions, or even if he has a gross misconception about what they are. If the presence of the projector is revealed to the subject by simply saying, "Voila, there is a projector that you didn't know about before," the revelation will have no effect on the judgments at all. Moreover, the demonstration is just as impressive to the experimenter as it is to the subject. Therefore, it is clear that conscious awareness of the presence of the projector and knowledge of the fact that there really is extra illumination falling on the cardboard are irrelevant to the phenomenon. Thus, those aspects of the explanation are erroneous that imply the operation of cognitive factors.

Now, how can the subject unconsciously estimate the illumination? What information could he have that would allow him to make a correct estimate? There are only two kinds of information available to him. One is the cognitive information that there are, for example, fourteen 40-watt lamps in the room. We know that this information is irrelevant to the phenomenon. The only other information available to him is the set of intensities of the retinal images of all the various objects in the room. One of those objects is the standard itself, but the purpose of the explanation is to account for the fact that the subject does *not* base his judgments upon this intensity. All that is left is the set of intensities of the retinal images of the other objects in view, and some writers have asserted that the subject derives his estimate of illumination from *these*. The intensity of the retinal image of an object or any collection of objects cannot provide information about the illumination on the object(s) unless the reflectance of the object(s) is *already* known; and the explanation under discussion states that the reflectance is sensed by estimating the illumination. Thus the "explanation" is circular.

To get out of this bind, it has been suggested that the subject estimates the illumination by taking an average of the retinal-image intensities of all the objects in the field. It is a little harder to reject this suggestion because the suggestion is a little more complicated. However, the average retinal intensity carries no more information about the incident illumination than does the intensity of any part of the retinal image.

Another modification of this explanation is that the subject's judgment of brightness is based upon the ratio of the retinal-image intensity of the object to a weighted mean of the intensities of all the other objects in the field. This "explanation" is indeed consistent with all of the data if the weighting factors are adjusted for each situation, but then it really ceases to be an explanation. It is essentially a restatement of the phenomenon itself. The important questions still remain: How does the subject find this weighted mean and what determines the weightings in each situation?

While the kinds of explanation just discussed were in vogue, no one questioned the fact that brightness constancy was a perceptual phenomenon. However, it will be shown here that brightness constancy can be accounted for if the physiological properties of the visual system are such that it produces a logarithmic transformation followed by strong lateral inhibition. When the nature of the explanation of constancy changes from one involving judgments and estimates (even though they may be unconscious) to one involving quanta of light and neural interactions, the phenomenon itself is often regarded as having somehow changed from a perceptual one to a "sensory" one. In general, it seems that any phenomenon for which a physiological explanation is discovered will be excluded from the ranks of psychological or perceptual phenomena. Since it is likely that every phenomenon has a discoverable physiological basis, psychology and perception, when defined in that way, are on their way out.

Now we can discuss the question, "Is all this perception?" Almost all of the topics discussed in this book are ones having known or plausible physiological explanations. A definition of the term "perception" that does not include these topics is one that is self-eliminating, since the number of topics included in such a definition approaches zero as science progresses.

A PHYSIOLOGICAL EXPLANATION OF BRIGHTNESS CONSTANCY The contrast modulation transfer functions discussed in the preceding chapter indicate that the response of the visual system diminishes for very low spatial frequencies. In fact, by extrapolation, sensitivity is close to zero when the spatial frequency is zero. (If a field has zero spatial frequency, it is a perfectly uniform field, homogeneous in intensity and infinite in extent.) The fact that visual modulation sensitivity is close to zero for such a field means that, should two uniform (zero frequency) fields be shown in succession, one more intense than the other, the resulting brightnesses would be almost identical.[2]

It is clearly impossible to test this prediction directly. It is impossible to produce uniform visual fields of infinite extent, because the receptor surface is of finite extent. Further, the inhomogeneities in the eyeball (stray blood corpuscles floating near the retina, the retinal blood vessels themselves, etc.) prevent the field from being truly homogeneous. Nevertheless such fields (called *ganzvelts*) have been approximated in several ways. One procedure is for the subject to wear a contact lens made of a translucent plastic. Another is to cut a ping-pong ball in half and fit it over the eye. Still another procedure is to place the subject in the center of a large sphere that is evenly illuminated. The results of all of these techniques are similar. It seems to be true that, as the field approaches more and more closely to perfect uniformity, differences in the intensities and even the colors of successively presented fields become harder and harder to detect. That is, all such fields look alike so long as they are above the cone intensity threshold.

This insensitivity to zero spatial-frequency can be explained in terms of the physiological properties of the visual system that have already been discussed. Each stimulated point receives inhibition from its neighbors. If the separate inhibitions are very strong, or if the total number of inhibiting neighbors is very large, then the total inhibition acting on each stimulated point will be large. For such a system, the

---

[2]This prediction cannot be expected to hold at very low intensities. The MTF data were taken under conditions such that no part of the relevant visual field had a very low intensity or looked dark, and it is well known that the visual system changes fundamentally at low intensities, when the rod system predominates. The discussion here applies only to conditions in which the cone system predominates.

excitatory effect of any increase in intensity of a uniform field will almost be canceled out by the inhibitory effect, and, in general, increasing the intensity of a uniform field will produce almost no change in the output of the system. (Temporal effects will be neglected in all of the present discussion. That is, we will ignore any transient changes in brightness that might occur when a uniform field is uniformly incremented. Such temporal effects will be discussed in Chapter XIV.)

For the same reason, the presence of strong lateral inhibition tends to nullify the response to a uniform increment in a nonuniform field. That is, if a constant amount of excitation is added everywhere to a nonuniform input pattern, the output pattern will not change very much.

The relationship between these phenomena and brightness constancy was briefly explained in the preceding chapter. However, it is important enough that it will be discussed again, in more detail, here. As explained above, brightness should be constant when the illumination falling on a uniform field of infinite extent is changed. In brightness constancy, a *non*uniform field (e.g., one containing a standard object) is uniformly changed in *illumination* and the brightness of the object does not change. When the illumination on a nonuniform field is increased, the intensities of the retinal images of the various objects do not all increase by the same *amount,* because objects reflect fixed *proportions* of the incident light (as explained in Chapter III). For example, suppose that the illumination were 1000 units and were then changed to 2000 units. The retinal image of an object of 10% reflectance would change 100 units (from 100 to 200 units), while an object of 80% reflectance would change 800 units (from 800 to 1600). Thus, when the illumination on a scene is uniformly increased, the intensities of the images of the various objects may change by different amounts; but the *ratios* of the intensities of their images remain constant. When the ratios do remain constant, brightness constancy holds, that is, the brightnesses of the objects remain approximately constant.

Now let us reconsider the physiology of the visual system. It is almost certainly true that there is a transformation very early in the visual system that is roughly logarithmic (as discussed on pp. 249–253). It is reasonable to suppose that this transformation occurs earlier than the stage or stages that involve lateral inhibition. Consider the consequences of such a supposition. The scene described above, illuminated at 1000 units of intensity, contains two objects reflecting 100 and 800 units of intensity. The signals input to the lateral inhibitory system will be proportional to the *logarithms* of these intensities. That is:

$$e = k \log(IR),$$

where e is the excitation input to the lateral inhibitory system, k is a constant of proportionality, I is the intensity of the incident illumination, and R is the reflectance of the object.

Then

$$e_1 = k \log(1000 \times 0.10) = 2.0k,$$

$$e_2 = k \log(1000 \times 0.80) = 2.9k.$$

Now, when the illumination is doubled:

$$e_1 = k \log(200) = 2.3k,$$

$$e_2 = k \log(1600) = 3.2k.$$

In other words, when the illumination is increased, the effect upon the excitation levels after a logarithmic transformation is simply to add an equal amount of excitation to all points ($0.3k$ in the example above). Adding a uniform increment to the input of a system with strong lateral inhibition results in a negligible change in the output. Thus, brightness constancy may be explained by combining the likely assumption that a transformation approximating a logarithmic one occurs early in the visual system with another reasonable assumption, that lateral inhibition occurs at a subsequent stage or stages.[3]

Now we may reconsider briefly the breakdown of constancy caused by the "hidden projector" in Fig. 13.2. The only respect in which the projector must be "hidden" is that its light must fall only on the target and not on the background. That condition must obviously cause a "breakdown of constancy" unless the subject can somehow actually sense the *reflectance* of the target, and he cannot do that. When the light is restricted to the target, the target looks brighter than it would if perfect constancy held, because the target intensity is increased *relative* to its surroundings.

When the concealment of the projector is abandoned by allowing some of its light to fall on the background (e.g., by placing a piece of paper behind the target and in the projected beam), the target suddenly darkens, as it should when the intensity of its background is increased while its intensity is not changed.

---

[3]It should be noted that two different kinds of nonlinearity may be present in the human visual system. The kind discussed above may be taken into account by applying the appropriate correction. That is, to predict what an output distribution will be, each point in the intensity distribution must be corrected (e.g., by taking its logarithm), and then this transformed distribution is taken as the input to

THE LIMITS OF BRIGHTNESS CONSTANCY

Constancy holds reasonably well over an extremely wide range of illumination levels. That is, the brightness of a target is judged to be almost constant when the illumination falling on it and its surroundings is varied over wide limits.[4] Furthermore, the "background" need not be very large. As long as the illumination that is varied falls on a region contiguous with the target and extending about one half a degree or more beyond its edges, the brightness of the target will be constant. The fact that the surround need not be large is consistent with the MTF, as demonstrated in Fig. 13.3. The output curves in this figure are calculated from the transfer function in Fig. 12.20. Note that the increase in the size of the annular "background" between Figs. 13.3a and b scarcely affects the output distribution of the target.

Constancy, however, breaks down when the intensities of the retinal images of the target and its surround differ strongly. The relationship between constancy and the intensities of the target and its surround has been studied extensively by Heinemann (1955). His results were discussed in Chapter XI, but they are reproduced in a somewhat different form in Fig. 13.4, where it is clear that the greater the ratio of intensities, the poorer the constancy.

The discussion of nonlinearity in Chapter X may be very relevant to the fact that constancy holds over a huge range of illumination intensities, but only when the ratio of intensities of the object and its background is not too large. If the visual system can be correctly characterized as beginning with a nonlinear stage followed by a stage with strong lateral inhibition, and if the nonlinearity is strictly logarithmic, then constancy should hold for *any* intensity ratio. This was explained in the preceding section. However, if the nonlinearity were not exactly logarithmic, constancy *should* break down when the object and its background differ strongly. For example, consider the result to be expected if the nonlinear relationship between the input and output of an early stage in the visual system were of the form discussed in Chapter X, i.e.,

---

a linear inhibitory system. However, there is another class of possible nonlinearities that cannot be handled so easily. If the lateral interaction system is itself nonlinear, then no simple corrections exist that will permit the use of the transfer function for predicting output distributions when the input differences are large. At the time of this writing, the actual nature of the nonlinearities in the visual system is unknown.

[4]Constancy can obviously be demonstrated equally well by changing the reflectances of the target and its surround but keeping them in the same ratio. Since the visual system has available to it only the information in the light coming from the field, changing all the reflectances in a fixed ratio is identical, visually, with changing the incident illumination. Similarly, the illumination falling on the target can be different from that falling on the surround and constancy will still hold as long as the ratio of those two levels is constant. A classic experiment on constancy was performed in this way (Wallach, 1948).

$$\text{output} = \frac{K_1 \times \text{input}}{K_2 + \text{input}}$$

and that this stage is followed by one exhibiting strong lateral inhibition.

In Chapter X, that form of nonlinearity, together with strong inhibition (i.e., subtraction between color systems), was shown to provide a possible explanation of the ways that the hues of monochromatic lights change with intensity, and the conditions for brightness constancy are perfectly analogous. When a patch of monochromatic light illuminates the retina, it excites the three color-systems in some particular set of ratios, depending upon its wavelength. When its intensity is increased, the ratios remain the same. It was explained in Chapter X that a perfectly logarithmic transformation followed by inhibition (subtraction) would result in a constant hue as the intensity changed, but that the nonlinearity shown above would produce certain changes in hue. In particular, the amount and direction of the change in hue should depend upon the values of the ratios of excitations, a ratio of 1:0 yielding no hue shift, and larger or smaller ratios yielding correspondingly larger shifts. This relationship was shown quantitatively in Fig. 10.18, p. 256.

Similarly, under the conditions where brightness constancy occurs, an object and its background are illuminated by a common source so that, when the illumination is increased, the ratio of the excitations corresponding to the object and its background is constant. If the nonlinearity were perfectly logarithmic, the resulting brightnesses would be perfectly constant; but if, instead, the nonlinearity is of the form above, then the degree of brightness constancy (the analog of the "hue constancy" in Chapter X) should depend upon the ratio of the excitations corresponding to the object and its background. The more strongly that ratio departs from 1:0, the greater should be the departures from perfect brightness constancy.

(The plot in Fig. 10.18 may also be applied to brightness constancy. Each curve now represents a particular ratio of the intensities of a test patch and its background. If the difference between their outputs, i.e., the vertical axis in Fig. 10.18, does not change with changing illumination, then, with strong lateral inhibition, the brightness should not change. That is, the flatter the curve, the greater the predicted amount of constancy.)

Thus the breakdown in constancy for large intensity ratios may result from the same processes that cause hues to change with intensity.

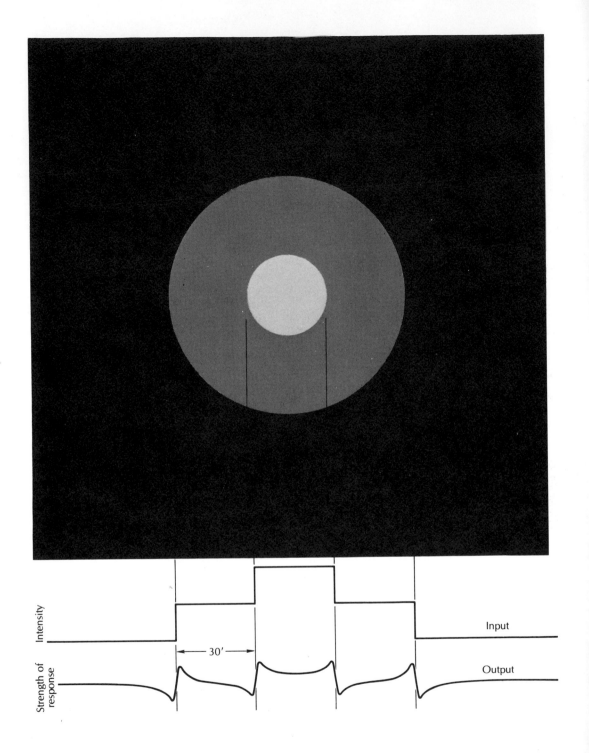

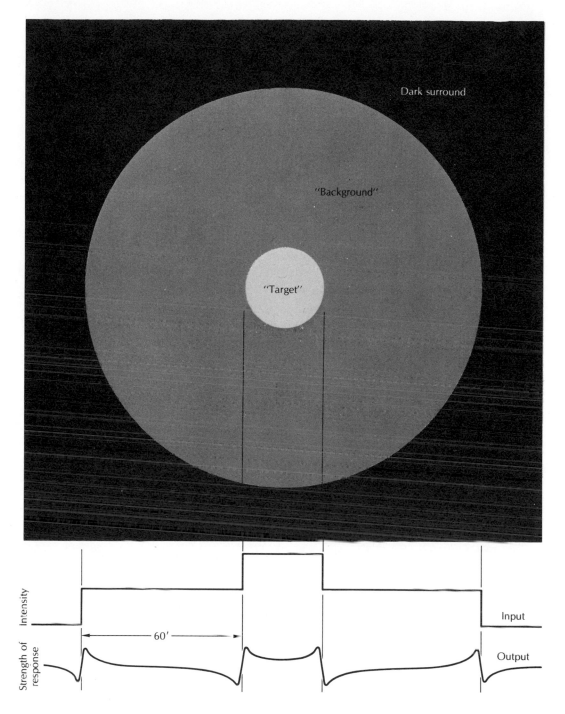

Fig. 13.3 **The effect of a background on the brightness of a target does not depend upon the size of the background, so long as the background is larger than about 30′. The output curves are calculated from the MTF in Fig. 12.20. The output pattern corresponding to the target is essentially the same for the two examples in (a) (left) and (b) (above).**

Both hue and brightness are fairly constant over extremely large changes in intensity, so long as the ratio of the excitations of the interacting systems (color systems; regions of the retina underlying the image of the object and its background) is not too different from 1.0.

The maximum ratio of reflectances of typical objects is about nine or ten to one. That is, the reflectance of ordinary white objects is about 90% (e.g., paper) and of ordinary black objects is about 10%. Thus constancy will hold reasonably well for most ordinary objects. It is only when extra illumination is added to a region, or when the region is self-luminous, that constancy breaks down badly.

Since most of our experience is, thus, with objects that are in the constancy range, it is possible that the mechanisms that produce constancy are developed as a consequence of experience with objects.

Fig. 13.4 **Brightness constancy is best when the intensities reflected from the object and its background are similar. A value of 1.0 on the vertical axis represents perfect constancy, that is, when the brightness of a target is independent of its intensity. A value of zero means that the brightness of the target changes just as fast, with a change in intensity, as does the brightness of a target against a completely dark background. The points are derived from the data of Heinemann (1955), as explained below, and the curve is fitted by eye, to asymptote at a constancy of zero.**
The value for the "amount of constancy" of each point was obtained by measuring the slopes of one set of Heinemann's curves (his Fig. 4, subject EGH) at a number of different points that represent different ratios of test spot to background intensity. The slopes of these curves are measures of the rates at which the brightness changes as a function of intensity.

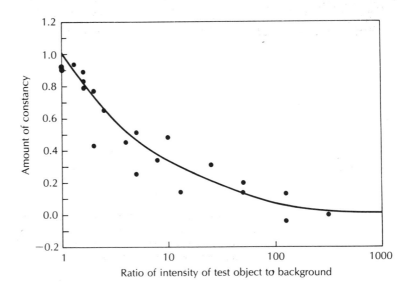

Ratio of intensity of test object to background

Perhaps if we were raised in an environment with a much greater or smaller range of contrasts (e.g., in outer space or under the sea), the range over which constancy holds would be correspondingly different. (For some reason that is hard to understand, most people implicitly assume that if a phenomenon has a physiological explanation, the phenomenon is independent of the subject's experience. That is almost certainly a fallacious assumption, since it is very likely that every behavior and percept, regardless of its precursors, has physiological correlates, and many behaviors and percepts are obviously dependent upon past experience. Thus it is perfectly possible, for example, that the lateral inhibitory network in the human retina can only develop if patterns of light fall on the retina.)

It seems likely that the mechanisms mediating constancy are the result of evolutionary selection. That possibility implies that constancy is a phenomenon that has survival value, and many glib discussions of that thesis have been published. It is said, for example, that if it were not for brightness constancy, every object would look different each time a cloud passed across the sun, and we would therefore have a harder time recognizing that any given object was the same object at different times. Put another way, the perceptual phenomenon of constancy makes our experience agree with the "fact" that objects really are constant. The question of whether or not that is really a "fact," and the other metaphysical questions stimulated by this consideration, are not relevant to the present book.

It is relevant, however, to point out that brightness constancy is a manifestation of a *loss* of information by the visual system. No information about the world is gained by constancy. It is merely that absolute intensity information is largely lost. Loss of information, per se, cannot have survival value, but a mechanism that loses any particular class of information may have survival value if it is properly related to other aspects of the organism. For example, when a rock is seen approaching the head at high velocity, the natural response is to close the eyelids and duck. This response results in a severe loss of information, and its survival value rests completely upon the fact that the corneas and head are liable to damage by rocks. When the subject is wearing a strong space helmet and running over rough terrain, the same response can be maladaptive.

Similarly, if the neural circuits in the brain are only capable of processing a limited amount of information, then it may be adaptive to reject, at the periphery, that information which is less important for survival, thereby making the entire central capacity available for the more important information; and it seems quite reasonable that information about relative intensities is more important for human survival than information about absolute intensities. It does not matter very much to a human what the absolute light level is (unless he is a photographer, and then he needs a light meter to regain the information his visual system has lost), but it is important for him to distinguish among different objects. It is also convenient that, with constancy, our perceptions are correlated with a property of objects themselves (i.e., their reflectances) rather than with the incident illumination. If absolute intensity information were not lost, we would have to take the general level of illumination into account every time we wished to identify an object by its reflectance. (If our skins were filled with chlorophyl and we received an important part of our nutrients directly from sunlight, then our visual systems might well have developed in such a way as to throw away information about relative intensities in order to retain and process absolute intensity information.)

HUE CONTRAST AND HUE CONSTANCY   In general, if an achromatic target is surrounded by a background of a particular hue, the target takes on a hue complementary to the surround. That is, it takes on the hue of that particular wavelength or mixture of wavelengths which, when mixed with the background in the proper proportions, would make the background achromatic. If a target that is already colored is surrounded by a background of a different hue, the hue of the target will be a mixture of its original hue and the hue complementary to that of the background. (See Appendix IV for instructions on setting up a really striking demonstration of this phenomenon.)

This is commonly called color contrast, but, in keeping with the terminology of Chapter X, it will be called hue contrast here. Hue contrast bears an obvious similarity to the brightness contrast that was discussed in Chapters XI and XII.

A Physiological Mechanism for Hue Contrast   At the time of this writing, there is no unequivocal physiological evidence to support any particular physiological explanation of hue contrast. However, there is one explanation that is fairly simple and plausible. In Chapter XI, evidence was presented indicating that each retinal receptor and its associated cells inhibits its neighbors. It was implicit in that discussion that the strength of the inhibitory interaction between any pair of receptors depended only upon the distance between the units, but it would be entirely consistent with all known evidence if like receptors inhibited each other more strongly than unlike ones. That is, it is quite possible that a given red-sensitive receptor (and its associated cells) inhibits other red-sensitive cells more strongly than it inhibits green-sensitive and blue-sensitive cells; that green-sensitive units inhibit other green-sensitive cells more strongly than red or blue ones, etc.

That hypothesis is not unreasonable. The different classes of receptors are chemically different, and, since there is some evidence that neural connections may be guided in their embryological development by chemical signals, it is quite possible that the inhibitory connections between like cells are more extensive than among unlike cells. It is also possible, if inhibitory connections develop as a consequence of retinal stimulation, that like units may become more strongly connected because they are more likely to be excited simultaneously.

If lateral inhibition were stronger among like receptors than among unlike ones, then the phenomenon of hue contrast would result for the following reasons: First, let us assume that the hue of any given region of the spectrum depends upon the relative strengths of the outputs of three neural channels somewhere after lateral inhibition has operated. For example, the subject may see yellow if the outputs of a green-sensitive and a red-sensitive channel bear some particular ratio or difference. (This kind of consideration was discussed in detail in Chapter X.) Similarly, the subject would see white, if, for example, the outputs of all channels were equal. (It is important to note that the *particular* relationships among the channels that correspond to "white," "yellow," etc., are irrelevant to this general argument. All that is necessary is that the perceived hues are correlated with *some* aspect of the relationship among the channels.)

Suppose that the subject looks at a gray target on a dark surround. The activities produced by the target are, say, equal in all three channels. Now let the surround be changed from black to white. The white surround would stimulate all three channels equally, thus equally inhibiting all three channels in the region of the target, and the target would appear as a darker gray. (That phenomenon was discussed extensively in Chapter XI.) If the surround were changed to red, then the surround would stimulate the red-sensitive channel most strongly, and the red-sensitive channel within the retinal image of the target would thus be more strongly inhibited than the other channels. Since, with a colorless surround, all three channels in the target were assumed to be equally active, the red surround would produce, in the target, an activity level in the red channel that would be lower than that of the green and blue channels. The target would thus have a hue different from gray; it would have the same hue as a patch (on a dark background) that was originally white and then had some long wavelength energy removed from it, and the hue of such a patch would be bluish-green.

Obviously, if the long wavelength (red) light that had been removed from an initially white patch were added back to it, the patch would look white again. Therefore, by definition, the wavelength mixture remaining in the patch after the red was removed is complimentary to that which was removed. Similarly, then, if inhibition among like receptors is stronger than among unlike ones, the hue induced into a gray target by a colored surround will be the hue of that wavelength or mixture of wavelengths that is the complement of the surround.

Hue Constancy   Most of the energy in the visible light radiated from a common incandescent bulb is in the red end of the spectrum, while the light from a cloudless sky is stronger in the blue end. If two patches of light, one from each of these sources, fell side by side on an ordinary piece of paper, the patch illuminated by incandescent light would look yellow while the sky-lighted patch would look blue. If, however, the entire paper and its background were illuminated with incandescent light alone, or with skylight alone, it would look white. A piece of paper viewed during the day in a room with a skylight looks essentially the same as when it is viewed at night and the room is illuminated with incandescent light, even though the spectral compositions of the lights reflected from the paper under the two conditions are so different that they can easily be distinguished when seen side by side.

In general, the hue of any object remains relatively constant even when the hue of the illumination, and therefore the actual spectral composition of the light reflected from the object, is changed over fairly wide limits. (This is true only so long as the illuminant falls on the background as well as the object, just as in brightness constancy.) This phenomenon is commonly called color constancy, but it will be called hue constancy here. It is obviously very similar to brightness constancy; and just as brightness constancy would necessarily occur if the visual system contained a logarithmic transformation and strong lateral inhibition, hue constancy would be expected if the same properties were present and if inhibition were stronger among like receptors than among unlike ones. Then differences in wavelength composition presented side by side will be transmitted (just as differences in intensity, side by side are transmitted). However, such a system suppresses signals related to the absolute wavelength-composition of the field, just as information about absolute intensity information is suppressed. For example, if a red light is added uniformly over a field, the red-sensitive receptors will undergo almost no change in output (just as adding intensity uniformly to an achromatic field will not appreciably change the output of the system). Thus, moderate changes in the wavelength composition of the light that illuminates a scene do not change the relative outputs of the three color-systems, and hence do not change the perceived hues of objects. (Hue constancy obviously breaks down when the wavelength composition of the illumination is changed sufficiently to alter appreciably the spectral composition of the light reflected from an object *relative* to its background.)

XIV ◇◇◇ TEMPORAL PROPERTIES OF THE VISUAL SYSTEM

CHAPTER XII contained an extensive discussion of the application of Fourier techniques to the analysis of spatial interactions in the visual system. The principal reason for using such techniques is that a single function, the transfer function, provides a concise description of the behavior of the system for any input distribution whatever, providing that the necessary conditions (e.g., linearity) are met. Fourier techniques have been applied to the spatial domain only very recently, but for 150 years they have been used for the analysis of temporal events. For example, the so-called frequency-response curve of a high-fidelity amplifier or loud speaker is, in fact, a temporal transfer function. It is obtained by feeding *temporal* sine waves of fixed amplitude and varying frequency into the amplifier or loudspeaker, and measuring the amplitudes of the corresponding output waves.

A typical frequency-response curve, or temporal modulation trans-

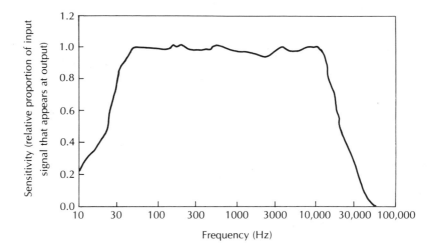

Fig. 14.1 **The temporal modulation transfer function (frequency-response curve) of a typical public address system.**

fer function, for a public address system is shown in Fig. 14.1. The system passes all frequencies in the range from 50 to 10,000 cycles per second (or hertz, abbreviated Hz) about equally well, and attenuates frequencies above and below those levels. Now the signals to be transmitted through a public address system represent sounds, and sounds are complex wave forms that can be analyzed into Fourier components. For example, the wave form of the sound of a piano playing the C below middle C is reproduced in Fig. 14.2. This wave form, and therefore this sound, can be reproduced exactly by the proper combination of the set of sine waves indicated in the spectrum of Fig. 14.2. Since the Fourier components that make up the sound are all within the frequency range of 50 to 10,000 Hz, when a piano plays C at the microphone end of the public address system, the sound will be reproduced at the loudspeaker end with high fidelity, that is, it will be a faithful replica of the original. However, if some of the Fourier components of the sound were outside that frequency range, those components would be relatively attenuated at the output, and the output sound would not be a faithful copy of the input sound. (Ideally, a public address system should have a transfer function that is flat from zero to an infinite frequency. However, it is very difficult, technically, to construct microphones and loudspeakers that operate well at very low and very high frequencies. Furthermore, since the corresponding transfer function for hearing in even the best human ear falls virtually to zero above 20,000 Hz, there is no need to build a public address system with a good frequency response above that value.)

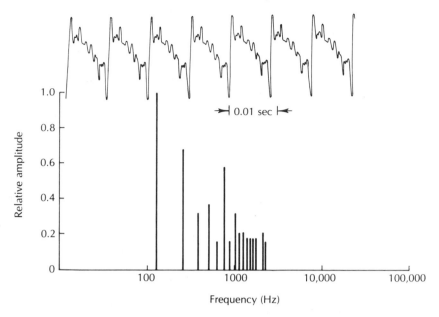

Fig. 14.3 **The effect of phase upon the addition of Fourier components. The
component waves F_1 and F_2 are identical in (a) and (b), but the phase of F_2
has been shifted with respect to F_1. The wave that is the sum of the two
components changes its shape when the phases of its components change.**

(a)   (b)

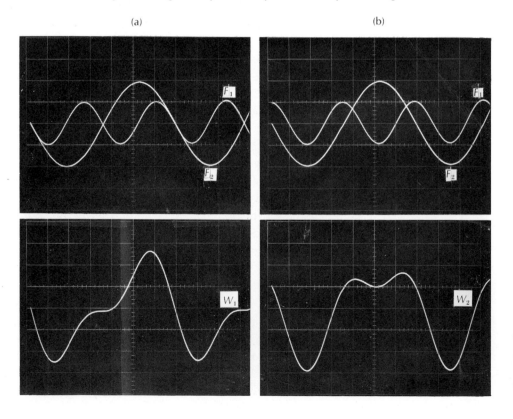

PHASE The logic by which a time-varying output function can be determined for any input (given the temporal transfer function of the system) is almost identical to that given for spatial interactions described in Chapter XII. There is only one important difference. The relative phases of the Fourier components were neglected in Chapter XII because the shifts in phase that occur in the optical system of the eye are generally negligible (except possibly in the far periphery of the retina, where their effects on vision are negligible), and there is no reason to suspect that there are phase shifts introduced into spatial patterns by any of the other elements of the visual system. But the situation is quite different with respect to the temporal properties of the visual system. It is certain that neural elements introduce temporal phase shifts that vary with frequency, and these phase shifts must, therefore, be taken into account if Fourier techniques are to be fully utilized.[1]

Despite the clear importance of temporal phase shifts in vision, no one has yet devised a method to measure them unequivocally.[2]

Although there is an absence of clear information on phase shifts, we will see in the following discussion that Fourier techniques are already of great usefulness in the study of temporal effects in vision.

THE TEMPORAL MODULATION TRANSFER FUNCTION Temporal frequency-response curves have been obtained for the human visual system in ways analogous to those used to determine the spatial transfer function, and to the extent that the visual system is linear, these curves may be used as transfer functions to predict the response to any kind of temporal change in light intensity (if the phase shifts are known or assumed).

An extensive set of measurements of the temporal frequency re-

---

[1]The term "phase," and its effects on Fourier synthesis, are illustrated in Fig. 14.3. In Fig. 14.3a, two sine waves of different frequencies F_1 and F_2 are added together to form the complex wave W_1. In Fig. 14.3b, the same two wave forms are added together, except that F_2 has been shifted along the time axis with respect F_1; that is, the phase between the waves has been changed. Note that the new complex wave W_2 is different from W_1. Thus, in general, to synthesize any given wave form, the frequencies, amplitudes, *and phases* of its Fourier components must be known.

[2]A very interesting attempt was reported by Veringa (1964). He stimulated the human eye with sinusoidally varying illumination and, simultaneously, passed an electric current through the eye whose intensity varied sinusoidally at the same frequency. He found that the perceptibility of the resulting flicker sensation varied as the phase of the electrical stimulation was varied with respect to the light modulation.

By determining the phase difference between the two stimulations that produced minimal flicker over a range of frequencies, he was able to infer the magnitudes of the phase shifts that occurred between the sites of photic and of electrical stimulation. However, the site of electrical stimulation, while not yet known for certain, is surely retinal, and therefore Veringa's technique measured only a small part of the overall phase shift in the visual system.

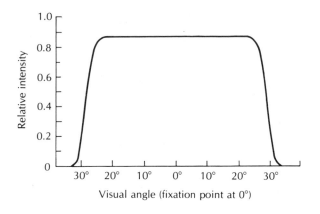

(a)

Fig. 14.4 (a) **The intensity profile of Kelly's stimulus field. The field was a large light disk, vignetted or blurred at the edges. (b) The intensity of the disk shown in (a) was varied sinusoidally with time, and the subject adjusted the modulation amplitude until the flicker was just barely noticeable.** [*From Kelly (1961a).*]

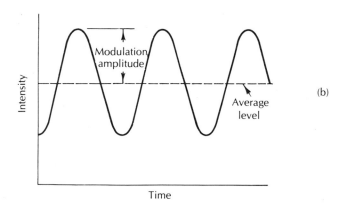

(b)

sponse of the eye has been carried out by Kelly (1961a). Kelly presented his subjects with a very large, uniformly illuminated disk, about 60° in diameter, whose edges were blurred as diagramed in Fig. 14.4a. (The reason for the large size and blurred edges will be explained below.) The disk was always uniformly illuminated (except for the edges), but the intensity could be varied sinusoidally in time, as diagramed in Fig. 14.4b, over a range of frequencies and amplitudes. The subject looked at this disk while its intensity was being varied sinusoidally at some particular frequency, and he adjusted the amplitude until the variation was just barely visible, that is, until the variation was just big enough that the field did not look steady in brightness. Throughout the measurement, the average level was held constant. Such an amplitude threshold was determined at each of a number of

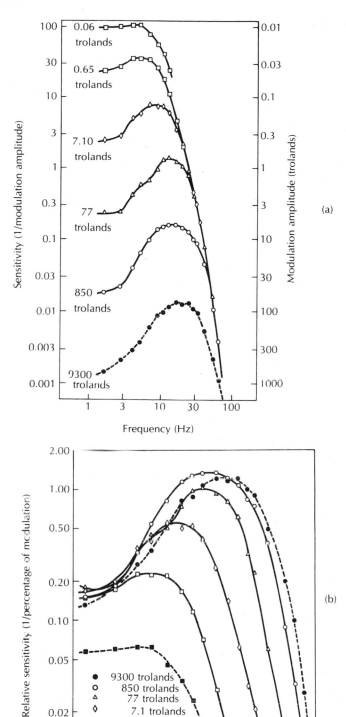

(a)

(b)

Fig. 14.5 **The results of Kelly's experiment, plotted in two different ways. The separate curves are for different average levels (in units called trolands, that are a measure of the intensity of light falling on the retina).** [*From Kelly (1961a).*]

different frequencies, and for several different average levels. The results are represented in two different ways in Fig. 14.5.

Except for the lowest average intensities, these curves are generally similar in shape to the spatial transfer functions presented in Chapter XII. The visual system is maximally sensitive to frequencies between about 10 and 30 Hz. Consider, first the set of curves in Fig. 14.5a. Each of these curves was obtained at a different average intensity. The scale on the vertical axis is a measure of the sensitivity to the intensity modulation. An important feature of these curves is that they all form a common envelope at high frequencies. This means that at any given high frequency, the subject will just be able to detect an intensity modulation of a certain amplitude, regardless of its average value. In other words, if a light is sinusoidally modulated just strongly enough to appear to flicker, and then a steady light is added to it, it will still be just at the threshold for flicker. What determines whether or not the fluctuation will be seen is the absolute amplitude of the fluctuation, not the level around which it is fluctuating. Note, however, that this holds only for the high-frequency region of the curves. Different average intensities produce different curves at low modulation frequencies.

Figure 14.5b is another plot of the same data. Here, the scale on the vertical axis has been changed to illustrate a different point. The vertical axis now represents the sensitivity not to the actual amplitude of the modulation, but rather to the *percentage of* modulation, that is, the ratio of the modulation amplitude to the average level (multiplied by 100). When the data are plotted in *this* way, the curves are coincident at *low* frequencies and separate at high ones. If low-frequency modulation is set just at the threshold amplitude and then a steady light is added to it, the modulation will no longer be noticeable. It will become noticeable again when the amplitude is increased until the *percentage of* modulation is the same as it used to be. (This behavior is an instance of the operation of Weber's Law.)

If a system is linear, then a given modulation amplitude at the input will produce an output modulation that is independent of the absolute level of the input. This can be seen from Fig. 14.6a. The straight line represents a linear relation between input and output. Now suppose the input is varied sinusoidally as a function of time, between a peak of b and a trough of d. This variation can be represented by plotting the sine wave as a function of time and (input) amplitude, as the curve labeled A. Each input value ($a,b,c,. . .$) produces some corresponding output value, and these outputs (a', b', c' . . .) can be read from the

Fig. 14.6 **The output that results from impressing a sine wave upon the input of a linear system (a) and a nonlinear system (b). Note that the amplitude of modulation at the output is independent of the average level of the input for a linear system, but depends strongly upon the average level of the input for a nonlinear system. In (b), the input amplitudes waves** A **and** B **are equal, but, because the average level of** B **is twice that of** A, **the corresponding output amplitude of** B' **is smaller than** A'. **The particular nonlinearity shown here is logarithmic. As a consequence, since the average level of** B **(and** C**) is twice that of** A, **the output amplitudes of** A **and** C **will be equal when the input amplitude of** C **is twice that of** A. **That is, for any given output amplitude, the input amplitude must be a fixed** *proportion* **of the average level.**

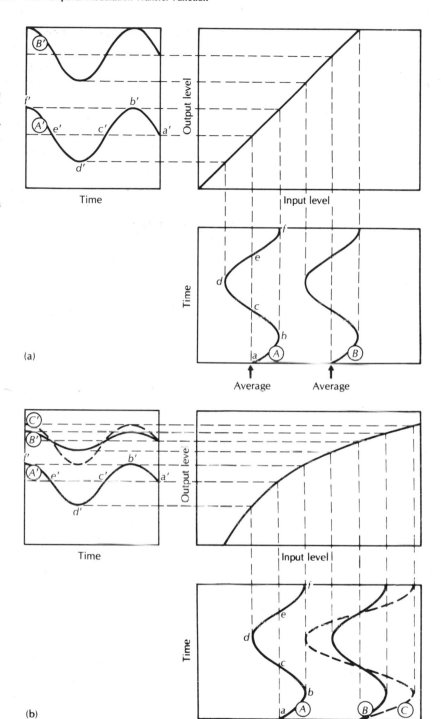

(a)

(b)

input–output characteristic; the output wave form can thus be plotted as the curve A'. In this linear case, when the input is a sine wave, the output is also a sine wave. Now, if a sine wave of the same amplitude but a different average value were input (as the wave labeled B), the output would have the same amplitude (curve B'). In general, for a linear system, the output amplitude is independent of the average level of the input.

The corresponding behavior for a nonlinear system is illustrated in Fig. 14.6b. Here it is evident that a sine wave at the input produces a distorted wave at the output (that is, the output contains Fourier components that are higher harmonics of input frequency), and that the output amplitude depends upon the average value of the input as well as its amplitude.

Now let us apply these considerations to the curves in Fig. 14.5. It is reasonable to describe part of the visual system by saying that there is some stage, let us call it a "decision" stage, whose output is of one kind when a light is seen to flicker and of another kind when it is not seen to flicker. Furthermore, we may say that this stage acts as though it had a threshold, in the sense that when the input variation is less than some amount, it says "no flicker," and when the input is greater, it says "flicker." (It should be understood that this threshold is not necessarily at some fixed level, but may depend upon stochastic processes and vary randomly. That possibility is not relevant to the present discussion.)

At some given frequency, a particular modulation amplitude can be found that will just produce enough modulation at the input to the decision stage to be at its threshold. If the visual system preceding the decision stage is linear, then that same amplitude ought to be the threshold modulation regardless of the average value. That is just the way the visual system behaves at high frequencies. Within very wide limits, the visual system acts as though it is linear when it is presented with high-frequency temporal intensity modulation of near threshold amplitude.

On the other hand, at low temporal frequencies, the visual system is clearly not linear. However, its behavior is consistent with the theory described in several of the preceding chapters, namely that there is an approximately logarithmic transformation between light intensity and neural excitation. In fact, the particular nonlinearity illustrated in Fig. 14.6b is a logarithmic one. Note that the average level of the input labeled B is twice that of A, and in order that the amplitude of the corresponding output wave be equal to the amplitude of A', the input amplitude must be doubled (waves C and C').

The Visual Response to High Temporal Frequencies

Bloch's Law

The left-hand column of graphs in Fig. 14.7 represents a set of flashes of varying durations and amplitudes. The areas under all of these graphs are equal. For example, the uppermost flash has an intensity of 40 units and a duration of 2 msec, the second has an intensity of 20 units and a duration of 4 msec, etc. This means that the total number of quanta delivered in all of these flashes is the same. In the middle column in Fig. 14.7 are plotted the Fourier spectra of these flashes, and in the last column, these spectra have been multiplied by the frequency response curve for 7.1 trolands in Fig. 14.5. If it is assumed that the visual system is linear, then this third column should also represent the Fourier components of the outputs of the visual system.

The first four plots in the output column are virtually identical. The application of Fourier techniques thus leads to the prediction that the first four flashes should all look alike to a subject. That prediction is in good agreement with the facts. When a flash is presented to an eye that is adapted to a moderate illumination level (e.g., 7.1 trolands), the total number of quanta required to detect the flash is constant for all equal quantum flashes shorter than about 30 msec (Barlow, 1958). Thirty milliseconds is said to be the critical duration. That all flashes shorter than some critical duration cause equal effects is called Bloch's Law.

The reason that the output spectra for all short flashes are virtually the same becomes evident from a comparison of the MTF for 7.1 trolands in Fig. 14.5 and the spectra in Fig. 14.7. The spectra of short flashes are almost identical for frequencies below 40 Hz, and the light-adapted visual system is very insensitive to frequencies higher than that. Now, however, examine the remaining curves in Fig. 14.5 and note that as the average intensity is lowered, the high-frequency sensitivity is also lowered. Thus, Fourier analysis leads to the prediction that the more dark-adapted is the eye, the longer will be the critical duration, and there is ample evidence to verify that prediction.

Critical Fusion Frequency

When a light is flashing slowly, the individual flashes are distinguishable, but if the same light flashes at a very high rate, the light will be indistinguishable from a steady light of the same average intensity. If the frequency of flashing of a light is gradually increased from a low rate, there will be some frequency for which the light will just look steady (the flashes will just "fuse"), and this is called the critical fusion frequency, or CFF.

Several thousands of studies of the factors that influence the CFF have been published, and in almost all of them, the stimulus is a light that is turned on and off, that is, a square-wave intensity modulation. Kelly's experiments also contain measures of the CFF, but for lights

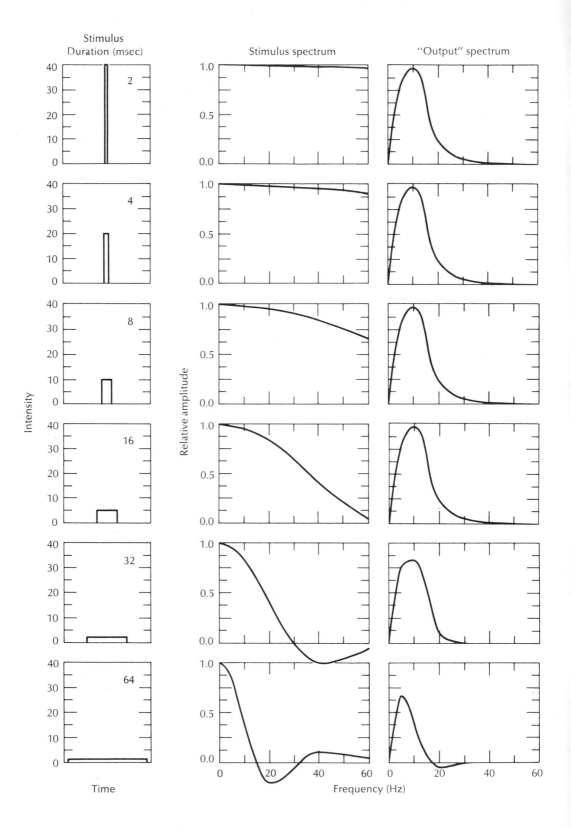

Stimulus
Duration (msec)

Stimulus spectrum

"Output" spectrum

Intensity

Time

Relative amplitude

Frequency (Hz)

whose intensity is changing sinusoidally. Suppose, for example, that Kelly's subjects were shown a field whose intensity was sinusoidally varying with a fixed amplitude, and the frequency was gradually increased until they said that they no longer detected the intensity variation. Such an experiment is diagramed in Fig. 14.8, superimposed upon one of Kelly's curves. The horizontal dashed line represents a stimulus of fixed amplitude (5% modulation) and variable frequency. If the frequency at which this stimulus was first presented were in the middle range, say, at 10 Hz and were gradually increased, the subject would say that the field appeared steady when the frequency reached 19 Hz. That is, 19 Hz is his CFF when the modulation is 5%. (Note that there is another CFF at a low frequency when measured this way [3 Hz in Fig. 14.8].)

When the modulation amplitude is made as large as possible (i.e., when the intensity is zero at the trough of the wave — the modulation is 100%), the CFF, for this mean intensity level, is 40 Hz. Thus Kelly's experiment does contain measures of the CFF for sinusoidal stimuli.

Kelly's experiment also provides measures of the CFF for square wave flicker, when Fourier techniques are brought to bear on his data. Figure 14.9 represents an analysis of a typical determination of the CFF using flashing lights. The plots in the column on the left represent a stimulus flashing on and off with a so-called light/dark ratio of 1. (That is, the light is on half the time and off half the time.) In the typical CFF measurement, the frequency of this square wave is increased (as repre-

Fig. 14.7 **Fourier technique applied to the perception of short flashes of light. The column on the left is a set of plots of intensity as a function of time for six kinds of flash. Descending the column, the flashes double in duration and halve in intensity, so that the total number of quanta delivered by each of the flashes is the same. The Fourier spectra of these flashes are plotted in the middle column. These spectra actually extend to infinite frequency, but as will be evident, the components with frequencies above about 60 Hz are not relevant to this analysis, and have been omitted from these plots. (Some of the values in the plots of the longer flashes are negative. This merely means that, when they are added together with the other components to reproduce the original flash, they must be added in with a one-half-cycle phase shift with respect to the positive components.) The right column contains plots of the input (or stimulus) spectra multiplied by the sensitivity at each frequency, as measured by the MTF in Fig. 14.5, the curve for 7.1 trolands. To the extent that the visual system is linear under these conditions, these are then the plots of the Fourier spectra of the outputs corresponding to each of the inputs in the left-most column. Note that the output spectra for all flashes of durations of 16 msec and shorter are virtually identical, but the 32- and 64-msec flashes give different output spectra. This would lead to the prediction that all flashes of 16-msec duration and shorter should look alike at an adaptation level of 7.1 trolands, and they do.**

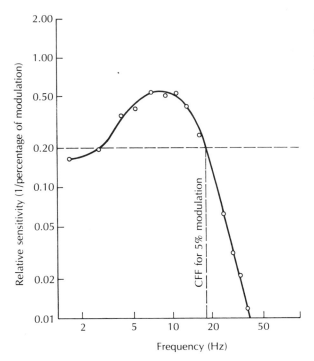

Fig. 14.8 **Diagram of a CFF measurement using sinusoidal intensity modulation. The curve is the same as that for 7.1 trolands in Fig. 14.5. The CFF for a modulation of 5% is 19 Hz, (and 3 Hz at low frequency), and it rises to 40 Hz at a modulation amplitude of 100%.**

sented by moving downward in the left column of Fig. 14.9) until the subject says that the field no longer appears to flicker. The Fourier components of these various stimuli are shown in the second column of plots. As the frequency of the flashes increases, the frequencies of the Fourier components also increase. When these components are transmitted through the visual system, the resulting (output) Fourier components are as plotted in the third column (using the MTF in Fig. 14.5). As the frequency of the flashes increases, the amplitude of the output modulation decreases until, at the CFF, the output modulation is at the threshold level.

Note that, at all but the lowest frequency in Fig. 14.9, the output is essentially a pure sine wave (i.e., there is only one Fourier component) even though the input is square. The reason for this is clear. The Fourier components of a square wave are: a sine wave with a frequency equal to the repetition rate of the square wave (this is called the fundamental frequency, or the first harmonic), a sine wave of frequency three times the fundamental (the third harmonic), another at five times the fundamental, another at seven times, etc. The MTF drops steeply at high frequencies, and therefore when the fundamental frequency is anywhere near the CFF, the visual system is so insensitive to the other Fourier components that their contributions are negligible. (This effect is made even stronger by the fact that the amplitudes of the higher harmonics are smaller at the input, as shown in the second column of

Fig. 14.9 **Analysis of a typical CFF measurement with square-wave intensity modulation. The left column contains plots of intensity versus time for a set of flicker stimuli. The frequency increases going down the column. The Fourier components of these stimuli are plotted in the next column, labeled "input spectra." (The zero frequency components, the average levels, have been neglected because they are the same for all input waves. Furthermore, the components higher than 120 Hz have been omitted for reasons that are obvious from an examination of the "output spectra" column.) When these components are multiplied by the relative sensitivities of the visual system to sine waves at those frequencies, as read from the curve in Fig. 14.5, the output spectra in the right column result. (Here, the zero frequency component and all others whose amplitudes are smaller than 1% of the maximum component have been omitted.)**

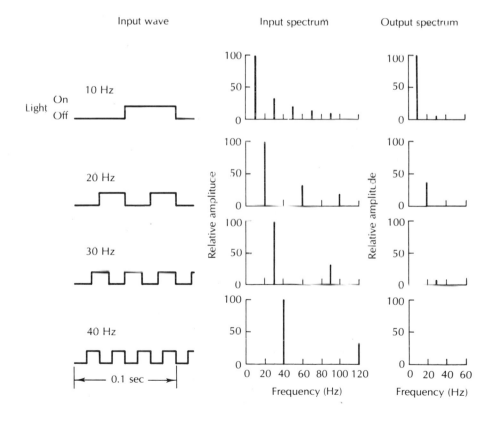

Fig. 14.9.) It follows that the CFF for a square wave ought to be the same as that for a sine wave of equivalent modulation depth, and that is exactly what is found.[3]

(On the other hand, it is also clear from this analysis that square waves with low repetition rates will yield outputs that are very different from sine waves of the same frequency. For square waves of very low repetition rates, the perceptual consequence will be determined primarily by the higher harmonics.)

The crucial point to be extracted from this discussion is that the curve that all of the separate curves form where they join at high frequencies in Fig. 14.5 appears to be a complete description of the threshold behavior of the human visual system to high-frequency modulation of light stimuli. The visual system seems to respond linearly to all high-frequency modulation. It is quite possible to devise any number of experiments that measure the threshold for some new temporal wave form or different kind of flash, and such experiments are constantly being reported, but as long as the stimuli contain only high-frequency Fourier components or as long as the different stimuli to be compared differ only in their high-frequency components, then the experiments are simply special-case repetitions of the MTF measurements. For example, several studies have been reported in which the CFF for pulses of light was measured as a function of the light/dark ratio. Kelly has clearly shown that the results of these studies can be deduced directly from his MTF's (Kelly, 1961b).

The Visual Response to Low Temporal Frequencies   The frequency-response curves plotted in Fig. 14.5 do not extend below 2 Hz; Kelly's apparatus did not permit him to make measurements at still lower frequencies; but there is excellent reason to believe that, as the frequency approaches zero, the sensitivity also approaches zero or very close to it. That is, if the field of view were homogeneously illuminated, of infinite extent (to avoid bias that might enter if the field has *spatial* frequencies), and if its intensity were to change extremely slowly, the subject would not be able to tell that it was changing, no matter how large the total change. This is essentially the same as the conclusion that was reached in the discussion of the spatial MTF in Chapter XII. Even when the field of view is not homogeneously illumi-

---

[3]The modulation amplitude of the fundamental Fourier component of a square wave is larger than the amplitude of the square wave itself. (The reason for this should be clear from a reexamination of Fig. 12.3.) Thus, if square-wave flicker is produced by alternately turning a light on and off, there is no way to produce a real sine-wave flicker of "equivalent" modulation. To compare correctly the CFF for square-wave and for sine-wave modulation, the CFF for the square wave must be measured when the intensity of the square wave alternates between two levels neither of which is zero.

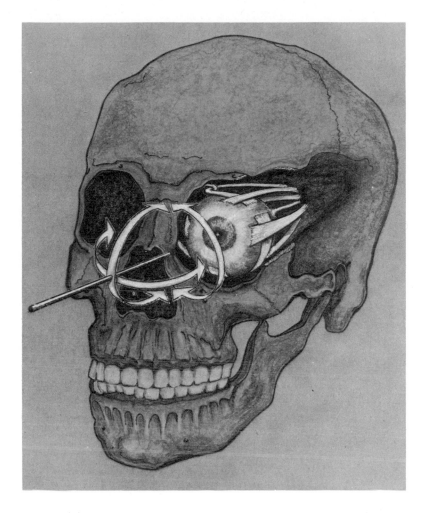

Fig. 14.10 **The eyeball with its attached muscles, which can cause the eye to rotate in its socket in any of the directions indicated, or in any combination of those directions.**

nated, if the intensity of light falling on each point in the retina is perfectly constant, the sensitivity of the visual system evidently falls close to zero. This evidence is derived from experiments on "stabilized" retinal images.

Stabilized Retinal Images Your eyes are always in motion. That motion is obvious when you look around the room, or when you visually follow a moving object, but even when you try to fixate a point as steadily as you can, your eyes are in continual motion. This motion is extremely small, but its effects on the visual system are profound.

The eye can move in and out, sideways, and up and down in its socket, and can also rotate horizontally, vertically, and tortionally (that is, it can twist a little about the line of sight as an axis). The rotary components are diagramed in Fig. 14.10.

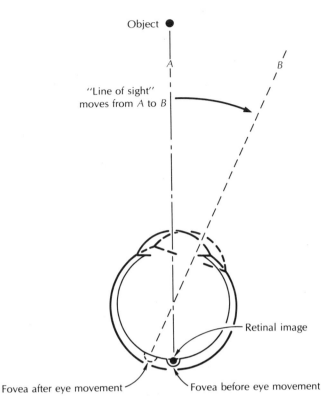

Object ●

A

B

"Line of sight" moves from A to B

Fig. 14.11 **Diagram showing that when the eye rotates in its socket, the retina slides beneath the retinal image.**

Retinal image

Fovea after eye movement

Fovea before eye movement

When the eye rotates, the retinal image stays essentially in the same place, but the retina slides underneath it, as diagramed in Fig. 14.11. This is the mechanism by which we can look at one object or another. If you look at this mark * , what you have done is rotated your eyes until your foveas are located under the images of the mark. If you look at *this* mark * , then the image of the first mark is falling on peripheral retina, and if you then shift back to the first * you rotate your eyes such that your foveas lie under the image of the first mark again (and the second mark now falls on peripheral retina).

Even if you try to fixate a mark as steadily as possible, very small rotary motions continue to occur, and they are called involuntary eye movements. Figure 14.12 is a segment of a typical record of the horizontal component of involuntary eye movements. An extremely small tremor is just barely visible in the figure. It almost certainly has negligible visual significance. The important characteristics in this record are the drifts and the abrupt movements. The abrupt movements are called saccadic eye movements, or saccades. The drifts are partly a consequence of instability in the neuromuscular system of the eyes and, on the average, during ordinary fixation, they cause the image of the fixated object to drift away from the center of the fovea. As the image drifts farther and farther from the center of the fovea, a saccadic movement is more and more likely to occur, and when it does, it will, on the average, reduce the error introduced by the drift (Cornsweet, 1956).[4]

The average drift rate is a few minutes of arc per second, and the average saccade size about 10′, although these values differ among individuals and also depend to some degree upon the type of target being fixated. Because of these movements, the retinal image is constantly shifting with respect to the retina, across distances that are large

[4]The drift also contains a component that tends to correct errors and whose strength depends upon the conditions of viewing (Steinman et al., 1967).

Fig. 14.12 **Segment of a typical record of the horizontal rotations of a subject's eye as he tries to fixate steadily. The fine time lines occur every 0.1 sec. To understand the meaning of this record, imagine that the film is moved vertically downward at a rate of ten time-lines per second, while the subject tries to fixate a point. The trace then represents the horizontal displacements of his line of sight. A record of the vertical components of the movement taken at the same time would look similar.**

⊢—⊣ ⊢—10 minutes of arc

compared with the sizes of receptors (the foveal cone diameter is about 1/2 to 1/3 of a minute of arc). The retinal image movements are also large compared with the optical line-spread function, which is about 4 or 5' wide (width for half-amplitude) under typical conditions (Westheimer and Campbell, 1962).[5]

Once the existence of these involuntary eye movements was discovered, there was a considerable amount of speculation about their effects on vision. Two viewpoints developed. According to one, motions of the retinal image reduce the subject's visual acuity just as movement of a camera during the exposure time blurs the picture. The opposite point of view, that movement of the retinal image enhances acuity, was also very popular, although the reasoning that leads to that statement was not clear in its original presentation (Marshall and Talbot, 1942), nor has it ever been made very clear since.[6]

In order to obtain precise measurements of involuntary eye movements, Ratliff and Riggs developed a technique that is now widely used (Ratliff and Riggs, 1950). The subject wears a tightly fitting contact lens (not one of the tiny lenses that are in common use, but a larger, specially fitted one) on which a plane mirror is mounted. Light is reflected from the mirror, as shown in Fig. 14.13, and onto a continuously moving photographic film. Rotations of the eye about an axis perpendicular to the plane of the figure will cause the image of the filament to move across the film, and a record like the one in Fig. 14.12 will result. While the movements are being recorded, the subject looks at a fixation target through the eye that is wearing the lens.

If you were a subject in this kind of experiment, you might notice that while you are fixating the target, the filament image, moving over the film, is visible off to one side. If it were not too far in the periphery, you would even be able to see that when you deliberately move your eye a little to the right, the filament image also moves to the right, and vice versa. It was probably this kind of observation that led workers in two independent laboratories, virtually simultaneously, to develop a procedure for determining the effects of eye movements on vision. Both Riggs and his students at Brown University, and Ditchburn and

---

[5]When a subject looks at an infinitesimally narrow bright line, the retinal image is not infinitesimal, but spreads on the retina. (This spread is called the line-spread function, as explained in Chapters III and XII.)

[6]This whole question is somewhat confounded by semantic problems (e.g., defining "acuity" and "improvement") but within reasonable definitions of those words, movements of the eye could increase visual acuity through a limited number of complicated and implausible mechanisms. They are not worth elaborating here because the experimental results, to be discussed below, clearly indicate that acuity is not improved by eye movements.

Fig. 14.13 **Top view diagram of a device for recording small eye movements. Light from the filament passes through a lens, is reflected from a mirror imbedded in the contact lens, and then passes through another lens that forms an image of the filament in the plane of a moving strip of film. The subject fixates a target, using the eye that wears the contact lens. When his eye rotates, say, to the right, the mirror rotates to the right, and the filament image thus moves to the right across the film. (To obtain a record of side-to-side movement not contaminated by up-and-down movement, a lamp with a long vertical filament is used, and a cylindrical lens or a slit with its long axis horizontal is placed just in front of the film.)**

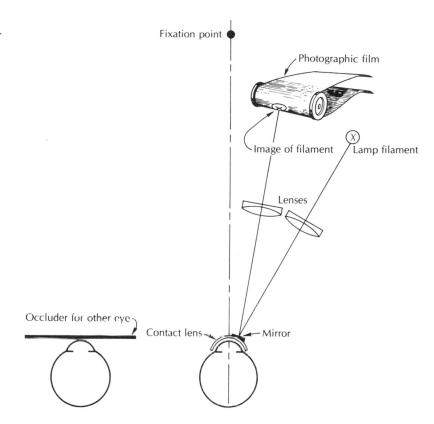

Fixation point

Photographic film

Image of filament   Lamp filament

Lenses

Occluder for other eye

Contact lens   Mirror

his students at the University of Reading, England, were recording eye movements by the contact lens technique, and both published very surprising findings within a few months of each other (Ditchburn and Ginsburg, 1952; Riggs et al., 1953).

The procedure they used to test the effects of eye movements on vision was one that permits the eye to move normally, but prevents the retinal image from shifting with respect to the retina. In principle, an easy way to do this would be to attach a small slide projector to a contact lens, and let the subject look through the lens at the projected picture. Then, whenever his eye moved, say, one degree to the right, the picture would also move one degree to the right. That is, if the retina were to slide one degree to the left, the projected picture would move one degree to the right, the retinal image would thus move the same distance to the left, and there would be no motion of the retinal image with respect to the retina. If the subject were looking at a particular part of the projected picture, he would continue to "look at" that part regardless of how he moved his eye.

Fig. 14.14 **Apparatus to provide a retinal image that is motionless with respect to the retina. Light from the projector is reflected from the contact-lens mirror to a screen, where it forms an image of the slide. The subject views that image through an optical path, containing four mirrors, whose length is exactly twice the distance from the eye to the screen. When the eye rotates one degree, the image moves two degrees across the screen, and this motion appears as a one degree movement through the viewing path. Thus, although the eye is free to move, the retinal image always moves through the same distance as the retina, and the image is "stabilized" on the retina.** [*After Riggs et al. (1953).*]

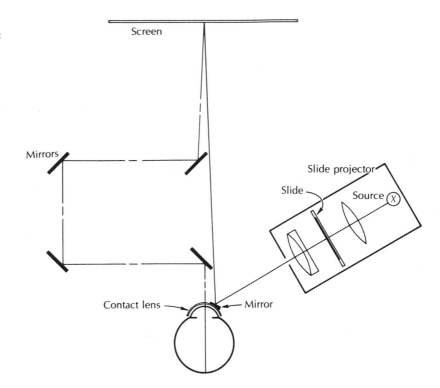

When light from an ordinary slide projector is reflected from a mirror mounted on a contact lens and onto a screen, the projected picture will also move in direct proportion to the movement of the eye that wears the lens. However, with that simple arrangement, the image will not be stationary with respect to the retina. When a mirror is rotated through an angle α, the reflected light is rotated through an angle 2α. (The angle of rotation α is added both to the angle of incidence and the angle of reflection.) Therefore, if a subject simply viewed a pattern reflected from his contact lens onto a screen, then when his eye moved, say one degree to the right, the target would move *two* degrees to the right, instead of the one degree movement that is desired. To overcome this problem, the optical arrangement in Fig. 14.14 may be used. The screen is viewed through a path consisting of four reflecting surfaces. This viewing path is exactly twice as long as the direct distance between the eye and the screen. Therefore when the eye moves one degree, the image moves two degrees on the screen, but only one degree at the retina. The result is the elimination of relative motion between the retina and the retinal image. Such an image is called a stabilized image.

When a subject looks at a stabilized image, he reports that the target, when first turned on, looks very sharp and clear, but then it rapidly fades out and disappears and the field looks uniformly gray. Stabilized patterns disappear within seconds, or even fractions of a second, after being presented. After the image has disappeared, if it is moved across the retina (e.g., by shifting the slide in its holder or by kicking the apparatus), it will reappear and then quickly disappear again. Similarly, if the intensity of the image is changed, it will reappear temporarily. In general, when a stabilized image is first presented or moved, it is seen with normal or supernormal acuity, but it soon disappears.

Normally, eye movements cause the retinal image to move across the retina, and this motion causes the intensity of the light falling on receptors near edges to change. In a stabilized image, however, the temporal frequency is zero and the target disappears. The stabilized image is, thus, essentially an extrapolation of Kelly's experiment to zero temporal frequency, and the sensitivity there is close to zero.

It is now clear why Kelly used such a large field in his experiments, and why he tapered the intensity at its borders. If he had used a small field with sharp edges, eye movements would have produced temporal frequencies in the receptors that would have been unpredictable and difficult to take into account. Each time the eye moved, receptors near the edge of the retinal image of the bright field would have undergone changes in intensity over and above those that Kelly deliberately introduced in his experimental procedure. However, when the field is very large, the regions where these changes occur are presumably far removed from the parts of the visual system that mediate the subject's judgment and it may be assumed that they do not appreciably influence the judgments. Furthermore, when the intensity at the edges of the field is tapered, a given size of eye movement produces a smaller intensity change on any receptor near the edge.

Figure 14.15 shows two sets of MTF measurements. One was carried out with a small, sharp-edged stimulus field (dashed curve), and the other with a field of the same size but having blurred edges. It is clear that the sharp edges of the small field raise the low-frequency region of the curve. This finding is consistent with the argument presented above. When the field has sharp edges, small eye movements introduce high temporal-frequency signals into the visual system. These signals have a negligible effect when the modulation frequency is already high, but when the intended modulation frequency is low, eye movements make the actual frequency high, and the threshold stays at its high-frequency level.[7]

[7]Kelly has recently shown that, while the difference between the results for sharp and blurred fields may be explained by the effects of eye movements (and the arguments given above are, in fact, the

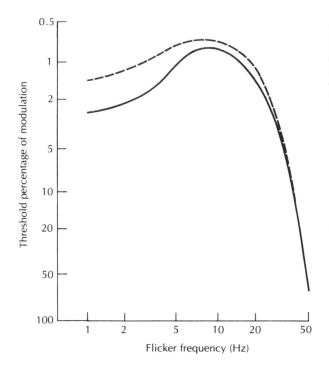

Fig. 14.15 **Temporal modulation transfer functions for small flickering fields against a nonflickering background whose intensity is the same as the average of the flickering field. The dashed curve is for a field with sharp edges and the solid one for a field with blurred edges.** [*From Kelly (1969).*]

It is not necessary to wear a contact lens in order to see, or not see, a stabilized image. One stabilized "image" that none of us can see every day is the light distribution produced by the shadows of our retinal blood vessels. Figure 6.2 (color insert) is a photograph of the back of the normal human eye, as seen through the pupil. Between the cornea and the receptor layer is an extensive network of blood vessels, that cast extremely sharp and contrasting shadows on the retina. If you look at a uniformly illuminated wall, these strong shadows ought to be clearly visible, but they are not. The reason is evidently that the blood vessels are attached to the retina and move with it, so that their shadows are stabilized and disappear. If you are observant and a late riser, you may be able to see these shadows fleetingly when you first open your eyes in the morning and look at a light wall or ceiling. Open just one eye at a time, and briefly. The shadows immediately disappear, but you can reinstate them a few times by closing your eye very

reasons he originally chose to use a field with blurred edges), these differences would also be expected, even in the absence of eye movements if the inhibitory pathways in the retina had certain simple temporal properties (Kelly, 1969). Thus it may well turn out that the difference between the sharp and the blurred field shown in Fig. 14.15 will remain even when the retinal image is stabilized on the retina.

quickly after they disappear, and then reopening and closing the eye repeatedly.

The shadows of the retinal blood vessels remain invisible because they are ordinarily stationary with respect to the retina. However, the vessels actually lie in a layer that is a few tenths of a millimeter in front of the receptors, and thus there are a few simple procedures that can be used to make the shadows move across the retina, rendering them clearly visible. The simplest technique is to shine a small, moving spot of light on the sclera. For example, in a darkened room, look toward your nose, place the bulb of a penlight right next to your sclera, and continuously move it around. The light will pass through the sclera and illuminate the retina on the opposite side of your eyeball. Then, when the light moves around, the source of illumination, as seen from the opposite side of the eyeball, moves through a fairly large angle and this causes the shadows of the vessels to move across the retina. When you do this, you will see a very large pattern of shadows that look as if they were projected onto whatever you are looking at. As long as you keep the light moving, the shadows will remain visible.

With a little more trouble, you can see a very striking view of the very small capillaries in your eye. Get a small diameter (e.g., 1/16 in.) incoherent fiber optic bundle. (They can be obtained for a few dollars from Edmund Scientific Co., Barrington, N.J.) Also get a narrow-band interference filter that transmits light very close to 415 nm. (You will probably have to order this specially made, for about $50.) Now illuminate one end of the fiber optic bundle with the 415 nm light, from as intense a source as possible, hold the other end of the bundle a few mm from your cornea, look directly into it, and continuously move it around. You will see a fine pattern of blood vessels that form a mesh-work everywhere except in the very center of your visual field (there are no capillaries in the central fovea) that disappears as soon as you stop moving the source. The fiber optic bundle should have a small diameter so that the source will be small and thus the shadows will be sharp, and the light should be from a narrow band at 415 nm because blood has a very sharp and strong absorption band at this wavelength, yielding high contrast between the vessels and their background.

Another, related, phenomenon can also be seen with this setup. When you stop moving the fiber optic bundle, you will see a large, relatively uniform, light blue field. However, if you look carefully, you will soon begin to see that the whole field is filled with small specks that seem to move jerkily over random paths. The specks are either the shadows of individual blood corpuscles traveling down the capillaries, or else they are the spaces between groups of corpuscles. Note that, while the specks appear to follow random paths, the paths do not change, but have fixed locations in the field. Furthermore, while the timing of the motion of the specks seems haphazard at first, careful observation will show that their movement is perfectly correlated with your pulse. (Once you have practiced with this demonstration, or perhaps even if you have not, you may be able to see these specks when you stare monocularly at a clear blue sky.[8])

Figure 14.16 is a demonstration of the insensitivity of the human visual system to low-frequency stimuli, that is, stimuli so designed that no parts of the retina undergo rapid changes in illumination. Hold your hand over one eye and stare with the other eye as steadily as you can at the dot in the middle of the blurred disk in Fig. 14.16. The disk soon fades and disappears. If you close the seeing eye for a few seconds and then open it, the disk will reappear, and then fade again. Now fixate the dot until the disk fades, and then shift your gaze to the X. Again you will see that the disk reappears, and it will reappear each time you shift your eyes between the dot and X.

There are two factors that contribute to the disappearance of the disk. First, since the disk has blurred edges, its *spatial* frequency con-

---

[8]When an image is stabilized by the use of a contact lens, it is usually observed that the image fades out and disappears, but then, from time to time, "spontaneously" reappears. Such reappearances are less frequent when the contact lens fits very tightly. They do not occur at all with such perfectly stabilized patterns as the shadows of the retinal blood vessels. Furthermore, the amount of slippage that does occur with even the best-fitting contact lenses is certainly sufficient to cause reappearance of most targets (Cornsweet, 1966). For these reasons and a variety of others, this writer believes that reappearances of a stabilized image are a consequence of the slippage of the contact lens and the resulting displacement of the retinal image.

Several authors have suggested that reappearance is not a consequence of uncontrolled retinal image motion. They say, instead, that some internal process causes the reappearance, and that by studying the appearance of the restored image, they can study the nature of this process [e.g., Pritchard *et al.* (1960)]. When stabilized images reappear, they are often fragmented and these fragments frequently are described as simple or meaningful units, rather than simply as a random selection of elements from the original figure. Such reports have been interpreted as providing support for the contention that reappearance is not a consequence of contact-lens slippage.

However, both the simplicity and the meaningfulness of these forms would be expected even if the reappearance were entirely due to uncontrolled retina image motion. When a contact lens slips, it does so in some particular direction. Those components of the target that are lines or edges perpendicular to the direction of slippage will be most strongly affected by the slippage, and thus are more likely to reappear. This introduces "simplicity" or "systematization" into the appearance of the regenerated picture. Furthermore, when a subject is presented with a series of random and nonrandom shapes under ordinary viewing conditions and is later asked to describe them, his report is very likely to contain more meaningful than nonmeaningful shapes, and more simple than complex ones.

The strongest evidence in support of spontaneous reappearance of stabilized images is the fact that afterimages, which are certainly stabilized "images," do reappear from time to time. However, afterimages are not perfectly stabilized, since they continuously decrease in intensity with dark-adaptation and also evidently spread somewhat within the retina as time passes (Brindley, 1963), and they may also be quite sensitive to small changes in the retinal blood supply, such as would result from changes in the pressure exerted upon the eyeball by the eyelid.

Until there is meaningful evidence that the reappearance of stabilized images is not a consequence of poor stabilization, there seems to be no need to speculate upon more subtle internal organizing processes.

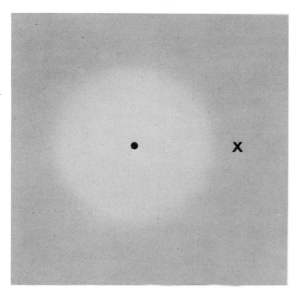

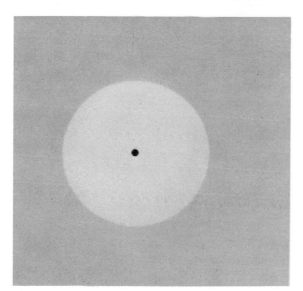

Fig. 14.16 **A demonstration of the insensitivity of the visual system to low-
frequency targets. If you fixate the dot
steadily, the blurred disk will disappear,
but it will reappear if you close and
then open your eye, or if you shift your
fixation from the dot to the X. The sharp
disk does not disappear when steadily
fixated (unless you are a very steady
fixator).** [*From Cornsweet (1969).*]

tent is low, and the visual system attenuates low spatial frequencies, as
discussed in Chapter XII. Second, the blurring of the disk reduces the
temporal effects of eye movements. The sharply focused disk in Fig.
14.16 does not disappear, because each involuntary eye movement
produces a large change in the intensity falling on the receptors near
the edge of its retinal image, as illustrated in Fig. 14.17a. When the
disk is blurred, however, the same movement produces only a small

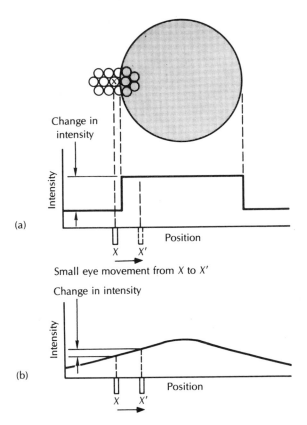

Fig. 14.17 **Involuntary eye movements produce strong intensity changes on the retina when a sharply defined pattern is fixated, as shown in (a), but a movement of the same size produces only a very small change in intensity on any receptor when a blurred target (b) is fixated.** [*From Cornsweet (1969).*]

change in illumination, as in Fig. 14.17b. A large change, such as that resulting from a large eye movement or from closing and opening the eye, is necessary to restore the visibility of the blurred disk.

PHYSIOLOGICAL CORRELATES OF TEMPORAL EVENTS In preceding chapters, we presented an extensive discussion of the lateral inhibitory interactions that occur in visual systems. These interactions have great explanatory power with respect to certain classes of perceptual phenomena that depend upon *spatial* intensity distributions. A further examination of the necessary *temporal* consequences of exactly the same machinery reveals that lateral recurrent inhibition may also account for many of the temporal perceptual phenomena described in this chapter. In fact, any visual system in which recurrent inhibition is strong will necessarily manifest many of the temporal properties discussed here.

Figure 14.18a is a schematic representation of a set of visual elements that manifest recurrent inhibition. If all the elements are essentially identical, and if the illuminations falling on each of them are equal, then the behavior of the set of all of them may be completely described by the behavior of a single unit that possesses self-inhibition, as in Fig. 14.18b.[9] This equivalence is useful, because it is less awk-

[9]The single unit is only exactly equivalent to the set of three when the three inhibitory paths are all of equal length, i.e., the delays in arrival of inhibition, to be discussed soon, are all equal.

Fig. 14.18 **(a) (left) Schematic representation of a set of three receptors that manifest mutual recurrent inhibition. If the properties of the three (or any other number of) receptors are all identical and they are all illuminated equally, then they will behave, as a group, in exactly the same way as a single receptor with self-inhibition, as diagramed in (b) (right).**

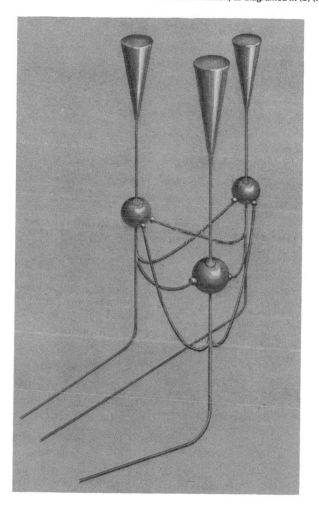

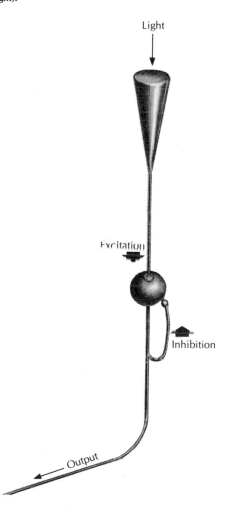

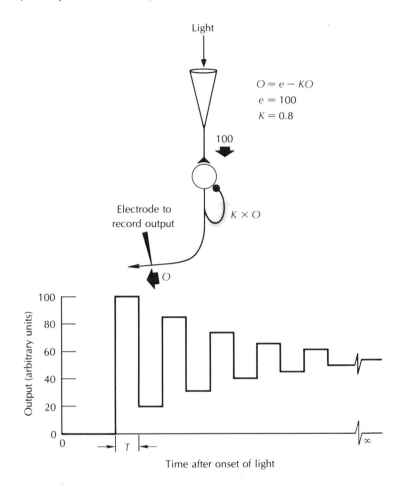

Fig. 14.19 **The behavior of a receptor with self-inhibition (or any group of identical mutually inhibitory receptors) when suddenly illuminated at time zero. After an initial delay, the output undergoes a damped oscillation, as explained in the text.**

ward to describe the behavior of a single element than the behavior of three or more, and the remainder of this discussion will therefore describe the equivalent unit shown in Fig. 14.18b.

The temporal behavior of the unit when it is suddenly illuminated is shown in Fig. 14.19. For this example, the excitation level, that is, the output level that would obtain in the absence of inhibition, has been taken as 100, and the inhibitory coefficient as 0.8. When the illumination is turned on, the activity in the system that precedes the synapse will be 100 and it will remain 100 so long as the illumination remains on (neglecting photochemical adaptation). This activity travels down the system, passing through the excitatory synapse. It branches at the origin of the inhibitory collateral, where $0.8 \times 100 = 80$ units head back toward the inhibitory synapse while 100 units continue on until they pass the electrode. Therefore, after an initial delay, the time necessary for the activity to begin in the receptor and to pass from there to the electrode site, the electrode will begin to record a level of 100.

Meanwhile, the inhibitory signal is traveling along its collateral, and after a delay determined by the conduction velocity in the inhibitory collateral and its length, the inhibition will arrive at the synapse, where it will reduce the output at that point to $100 - 80 = 20$. This new level (20) will pass down the system and arrive at the electrode some time later, as plotted. The time T is the time required for the activity to travel from the excitatory synapse down to the point where the inhibitory collateral branches off and then back up the collateral and across the inhibitory synapse.

Now the output is only 20, and the inhibitory signal will therefore fall to $20 \times 0.8 = 16$. Thus the output will rise to $100 - 16 = 84$. This will cause a subsequent increase in inhibition to $84 \times 0.8 = 67.2$, and the output will drop to $100 - 67.2 = 32.8$, etc. The output thus oscillates with a frequency determined by the conduction time around the inhibitory loop, and it is a damped oscillation (that is, one whose amplitude steadily decreases), approaching an asympotic value of:

$$O = e - KO,$$

$$O = \frac{e}{1 + K} = \frac{100}{1.8},$$

$$O = 55.6$$

The oscillation plotted in Fig. 14.19 has square corners, but it is obvious that any real system, and particularly any physiological system, will contain properties, not included in the schematic model, that tend to round the corners. That is, any physiological system will have features that attenuate high frequencies. Thus an output curve for a real system with recurrent inhibition might look like that in Fig. 14.20, which is a plot of the activity of a single fiber in the eye of the *Limulus* as a function of time after the onset of a light that illuminates it and its neighbors.

When the intensity of a stimulus is suddenly reduced, the output of a system with recurrent inhibition will be as plotted in Fig. 14.21. Just after the intensity is reduced, the excitation input is reduced but the inhibition is still at the initial, high level, and the output drops strongly. Then a damped oscillation proceeds, just as it does when the light is increased.

It is easy to rough out the general shape of the temporal modulation transfer function for such a system. Suppose that the transfer function were found by stimulating with light whose intensity varied sinus-

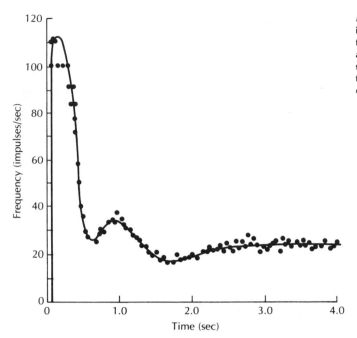

Fig. 14.20 **An actual plot of the output, in impulses per second, of a single facet in the eye of the horseshoe crab as a function of the time after the onset of a stimulus that illuminated the facet and its neighbors.** [*From Ratliff et al.(1963).*]

oidally in time with a fixed amplitude and average value, and the output was recorded. If the system is linear (we will assume that the experiment is performed with small signals and that the system is linear under these conditions), then the output will also undergo sinusoidal oscillations. When the input frequency is extremely low, the level of inhibition will never be far out of step with the excitation level, and the output will have some particular amplitude. In the extreme case where the inhibitory coefficient is very large, the output will be very small and the modulation amplitude will thus also be small. However,

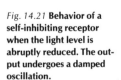

Fig. 14.21 **Behavior of a self-inhibiting receptor when the light level is abruptly reduced. The output undergoes a damped oscillation.**

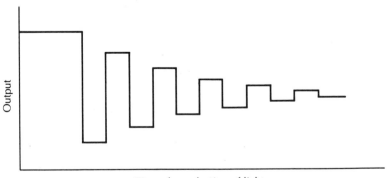

Time after reduction of light

as the input frequency is increased, the excitatory and inhibitory effects will begin to get out of phase with each other; when the intensity increases, the increase in inhibition will lag behind, allowing more excitation to get through; when the intensity decreases, the decrease in inhibition will lag behind, causing the output to be *lower* than it would be if there were no lag. In general, then, as the modulation frequency increases from zero, the amplitude of the output modulation will increase. However, this increase will not continue indefinitely as the input frequency rises. The output modulation will be at a peak when the frequency is such that the input excitation at the synapse is at a maximum just when the inhibition is at a minimum and vice versa. (That condition occurs when the time per light cycle equals exactly twice the time required for signals to travel around the inhibitory loop.)

At high frequencies, the input intensity will undergo many cycles during the time the inhibitory signals are traveling around their loop, and the output modulation will be smaller than at its peak. Furthermore, at high frequencies various factors such as the inertia of the ionic processes involved prevent these inhibitory signals from following the input modulation, and the output modulation will approach zero.[10] The net result of these factors is a transfer function with a shape generally like that in Fig. 14.5. Therefore, recurrent inhibition in combination with ordinary inertia and related effects are sufficient to explain, qualitatively, all of the phenomena that are consistent with Kelly's transfer function.

It is certainly true that the assumption of linearity, necessary to predict responses from the transfer function, is invalid under many conditions. However, it is also true that some and possibly a great many of the nonlinearities can be treated without changing the basic principles described here. For example, if it is assumed that a logarithmic transformation occurs prior to the inhibitory interaction, the *interactions* may still be treated as a linear system, and the behavior of the system as a whole may still be predicted from the transfer function after the nonlinearity is taken into account. The next important step in this kind of research will undoubtedly be the evaluation of the nonlinearities in the visual system.

The matter of nonlinearity may be restated in different terms, as fol-

[10]The transfer function for a perfect self-inhibitory system with no elements other than those diagrammed in Fig. 14.18 has a complex shape that dips to zero repeatedly as the frequency increases. However, any real system includes elements, not represented in Fig. 14.18, that slow down the responses and yield a smooth transfer function like that in Fig. 14.5. In addition to obvious dampeners such as chemicals that must flow from one place to another, structural characteristics smooth the responses. For example, if the lengths of the inhibitory interconnections among units vary, then the arrival of inhibition will be spread in time, and the system as a whole will behave more sluggishly.

lows. The simple recurrent inhibition system diagramed in Fig. 14.18 is certainly not sufficient to account for all temporal perceptual phenomena, but if the further assumption is made that the excitation level is a nonlinear function of the light intensity (an assumption for which there is excellent evidence in *Limulus* and fair evidence in mammals), then the model does remarkably well.

Modes of Firing of Mammalian Retinal Ganglion Cells

Figure 14.22a is a plot of the rate of firing of a single fiber from the eye of *Limulus* during a change in stimulus intensity. It follows from the preceding discussion (and that in Chapters XI and XII) that the result would be as in Fig. 14.22b if the strength of inhibitory interaction were much greater.

When an entire mammalian eye is flooded with light and the activity of a single ganglion cell or optic nerve fiber is recorded, the result always takes on one of the three forms shown in Fig. 14.22c, d, and e. (No other types of optic nerve fiber activity have yet been described when the entire eye is illuminated. However, the procedures by which such measurements are taken require that only a sample of the optic nerve fiber population be studied, and it is possible that the sample is biased. For example, very small fibers are unlikely to be recorded from, and fibers that do not respond continuously in the dark or that do not respond to large flashes of light are likely to be missed. Therefore, the types of activity described may not be the only types present in the optic nerve.)

The type of activity shown in Fig. 14.22c is called "on" activity. It is just like that recorded from every facet in the *Limulus* eye, except that it is superimposed upon a steady background level of activity, and the inhibitory effects may be stronger. The presence of this kind of activity in the eye of the cat, the monkey, and all other mammals studied, suggests that inhibition is a prominent factor in mammalian vision.

A second form of activity in mammalian optic nerve fibers is called the "off" response, as shown in Fig. 14.22d. The fiber stops firing when the light is increased, and fires strongly just after the light is decreased. This response is the inverse of the "on" response.

A third type is the "on-off" pattern, illustrated in Fig. 14.22e. There is an increase in activity both at the onset and the turn-off of the stimulus. This type of response, while common and relatively stable in some lower animals such as the frog, is less common in mammals, and seems to be much more ephemeral, its presence depending upon the

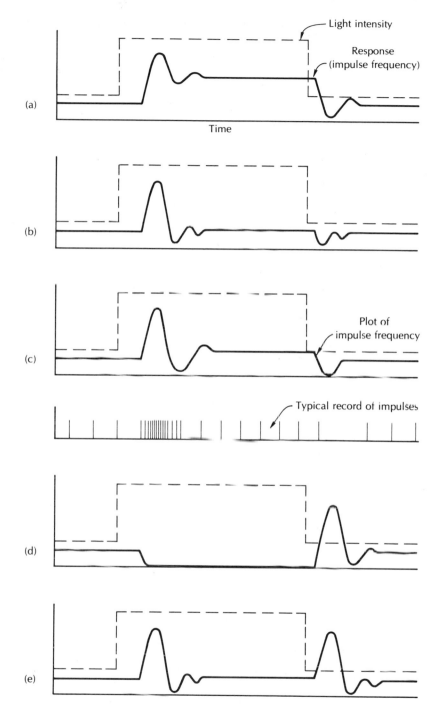

Fig. 14.22 **Plots of the outputs (impulse frequencies) of various visual units when the illumination on the entire eye is first increased and then decreased. Every unit in the eye of the horseshoe crab responds as in (a). If the inhibitory strength were greatly increased, the response would be as in (b). The plots in (c), (d), and (e) are those obtained from different single optic nerve fibers in the eye of a mammal when the entire retina is illuminated. Note that the smooth solid curves are all plots of rates of firing. The actual records from which such plots may be derived look like that in (c), consisting of a series of spikes whose spacing varies.**

condition of the retina, the state of light-adaptation, and other similar factors.

These three types of single fiber activity are found when the entire eye is illuminated, but when the stimulating spot is reduced to a small point, a fiber that gave an "on" response will be found to be one with an "on-center" receptive field, and an "off" fiber can be shown to have an "off-center" characteristic. (These classes of receptive fields were discussed at length in Chapter XI.) Thus the characteristic response of a fiber can be changed from "on" to "off" by changing the distribution or the location of the light falling on the retina, and these categorizations of responses in terms of their temporal characteristics are really reflections of the same neural interconnections as those responsible for the spatial characteristics of receptive fields.

XV ◇◇◇ STIMULUS GENERALIZATION

IN common language, attributing some characteristic to a variety of different people or situations is called generalizing. In psychology texts, a more formal definition is often given: stimulus generalization has occurred if two or more physically different stimuli elicit the same response. These two definitions, the scientific and common language ones, are really the same. If one makes the generalization that all men are rational (a generalization need not be correct), he is attributing the same property, that is, he is making the same response, to many physically different stimuli.

There is a large class of phenomena that fit the definition of generalization, but that are usually considered trivial examples. For instance, a human will give the same response to two stimuli of differing wavelengths when the wavelengths are extremely close to each other. He will call stimuli at 650.00 nm and at 650.01 nm by the same name.

(It can be argued convincingly that, given the right procedure and a very large number of trials, a statistically significant difference between the response to 650.00 and 650.01 nm could be observed. However, for the purposes of this argument, we will assume a relatively small number of trials.) This is clearly a case of generalization, as defined above, but it seems trivial. It is very important to understand why it is *not* trivial. Measurements of the difference in wavelength required for a subject to discriminate, that is, the difference required to prevent generalization, provide important data with which color vision may be studied. Why is it that a difference of 5 nm can be discriminated while one of 0.01 nm cannot? The answer to that question must reveal important characteristics of the visual system.

The literature contains extensive discussions of the perceptual and physiological mechanisms within us that cause us to generalize among quantities that differ physically by very small amounts. These mechanisms are usually called threshold mechanisms, but any theory attempting to explain thresholds (e.g., signal detection theories, neural threshold models, etc.) is also a theory about stimulus generalization (among stimuli that differ by small amounts).

In another form of stimulus generalization, two stimuli that are very different, physically, are judged to be identical. An example that, at first, appears trivial is the fact that a subject will give identical responses to 1000 quanta at 1 nm and 1,000,000 quanta at 1 nm, and the same response, again, to 1,000,000 quanta at 10 nm, etc. (The visible spectrum runs from about 400 to 800 nm.) All of these stimuli are indistinguishable from each other and from zero quanta. This is clearly a case of generalization, and it is an important one because it is exactly the kind of measurement that must be made in order to determine the physical characteristics of the stimuli that *do* affect the visual system.

A set of examples of this class of generalization that is obviously nontrivial are the data of wavelength mixture matches. For example, to a trichromat, a particular mixture of wavelengths can be made to look identical with another mixture containing a completely different set of wavelengths. Most of the content of the chapters on color vision in this book is concerned with exactly this form of generalization. The physiological theories of the visual system discussed in the color vision chapters were developed to explain color mixture data, and they may thus be considered as theories of the machinery of generalization. The inputs to the machinery are different but the outputs are identical; and that *is* generalization.

However, neither of the kinds of generalization just described really seem to fit what is usually meant by the word "generalization." When a subject is said to have generalized two stimuli, it is implicit that the stimuli are, in fact, distinguishable, but that the subject gives them the same response anyway. When a large and a small square are both called "square," even though the size difference is obvious, *that* is called generalization. In fact, the word "all" in the generalization paradigm "all ——— are ——— (e.g., all redheads are temperamental) inherently expresses the idea that the elements are distinguishable. If there were no way at all of distinguishing one redhead from another, the statement would simply be "the redhead is temperamental."

In this form of generalization, the stimuli are different, and there are at least two responses available, one of which is identical for all generalized stimuli and the other is different for the individual stimuli. For example, suppose that a subject is shown two patches, one containing 1,000,000 quanta per sec at 575 nm and the other 10,000,000 quanta per sec at 575 nm, and he is asked to give each a color name. He will say "yellow" to each stimulus If those are the only responses that the subject makes, it is impossible to distinguish this kind of generalization from the kinds just discussed in which the two stimuli are completely indistinguishable.[1] We might conclude that when these two physically different stimuli are presented as inputs to the subject, the outputs are identical; we would then begin to ask interesting questions, such as, what kind of a system would give identical outputs when these two stimuli are input.

However, if we were to go one step further in this experiment and determine whether or not the subject could tell the stimuli apart, we would immediately find that he was able to. He could discriminate reliably between them, and if asked, would say that the patch delivering 10,000,000 quanta per sec was brighter. The fact that he is capable of discriminating between the stimuli is positive evidence that the difference between the two stimuli has not been completely lost by his visual system. However, since, under some conditions he generalizes between them while under others he discriminates, there seem to be at least two physiological channels through which information about the lights flows, one of which has lost information about the difference between them (the "hue" channel) while the other, performing different operations on the input, retains the difference (the "brightness" channel).

---

[1] The subject *might* say "yellow" to both stimuli, but say it differently for the two. For example, he might always say "yellow" louder when presented with the more intense stimulus. For this discussion, we will assume either that there are no reliable differences between his responses, or that the discussion refers only to those aspects of his responses that really *are* identical. Or, to use an extreme case, suppose that the subject has a set of switches in front of him, each labeled with a different color name. He responds by closing one of the switches, and the experimenter only records which switch was closed on each trial (not the latencies, switch pressure, etc.)

If the information that two inputs are different is lost during the very first stage of reception (e.g., information about the wavelength of a quantum is lost when it is absorbed by a visual pigment molecule), then the two inputs must *always* result in identical responses. Conversely, even if a subject gives some identical responses to two different stimuli, if it is *possible* for him to give different responses reliably, then the information that the inputs are different cannot have been lost at the initial stage in the system.

It is useful to describe the visual system as a set of channels leading to different kinds of responses (e.g., hue, brightness, size, etc.), all of which are fed by the initial reception stage (or stages when, for example, there are three classes of cones). Each channel, then, is so constructed that it loses information about certain kinds of differences between inputs while transmitting information about other kinds. A simple example, already discussed in Chapter X, is shown in Fig. 15.1.

Fig. 15.1 **Example of a model of a perceptual system containing parallel channels. Light of a given wavelength falls on three classes of receptors that differ in their absorption spectra. The outputs of the receptors are proportional to the logarithms of their rates of quantal absorption. The left-most channel is excited by B and inhibited by A; therefore, assuming algebraic summation of excitation and inhibition, the output of that channel will be proportional to the ratio of the rates of quantal absorption of channels A and B. Similarly, the output of the middle channel will be proportional to the ratio of C to A. The outputs of these two channels will thus be dependent upon the wavelength and independent of the intensity of the illumination. The remaining channel is excited by all three receptor types, and its output will thus vary with intensity as well as wavelength. (Obviously, the channel that retains intensity information need not be excited by all three receptors. Any one would be sufficient.)**

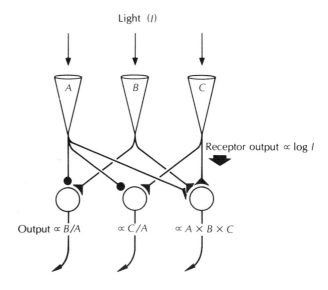

Light (I)

Receptor output $\propto \log I$

Output $\propto B/A$ $\propto C/A$ $\propto A \times B \times C$

Two of the output channels carry information about the ratios of excitations of the three types of cones; therefore the signals that they carry do not retain information about stimulus intensity. For example, when 1,000,000 and 10,000,000 quanta at 575 nm are the two stimuli, the outputs of the ratio channels will be identical for both stimuli; the outputs of these ratio channels depend only on wavelength, and are independent of the intensities of the stimuli (so long as they are not so extraordinarily intense that they bleach appreciable proportions of the pigments). These outputs presumably determine the subject's perception of hue.

If these channels were the only ones through which information could be transmitted from the retina to the effectors, then the two patches would be indistinguishable; since they are not indistinguishable, another channel must be postulated. One possible channel that retains intensity information is shown in Fig. 15.1. It simply transmits the sum of the signals from the three types of cones,[2] and this quantity depends upon the intensity of the stimulus. Such a channel would then transmit information with which the subject could discriminate between the patches, and to which quantity he might attach the name "brightness."

THE GENERALIZATION OF VISUAL SHAPES When two shapes both subtend extremely small angles at the subject's eye (e.g., two stars of different sizes or even shapes), generalization will occur. That is, the subject will say they both have the same size and shape. Furthermore, if their intensities are properly adjusted and their spectral compositions are the same, they will be indistinguishable. The processes that cause the loss of information about the differences between the two shapes have been discussed in Chapters III and XII. Briefly, the optics of the eye are such that the shapes of the retinal intensity distributions of all very small objects are identical and, therefore, by adjusting the intensity of the light from one of the two objects, the two retinal images can be made completely identical.[3] Thus the mechanisms that lose "shape" information for very small objects, and therefore the mechanisms that account for this type of generalization, are known. They are diffraction, aberations, light scatter, etc.

[2] With the postulated logarithmic transformation, the output of this stage is proportional to the product of the three quantal-absorption rates.

[3] The differences between the shapes of small objects are completely contained in their high-frequency spatial sine-wave content, and the optics of the eye (and possibly neural summation) limit the transmission of high frequencies.

Now, suppose a subject is shown two squares, one clearly larger than the other, and he says that he sees two squares, one larger than the other. He is generalizing when he calls them both squares, and discriminating when he says they differ in size. The subject can be said to be generalizing, categorizing, abstracting, or demonstrating a concept; in this context, those terms are all equivalent. Since he can do both of these things at the same time, it is useful to conceive of at least two parallel channels within him; one generalizes between the two stimuli and the other does not. The channel that generalizes loses the information that the squares are different, while the other channel (or channels) transmits that information.

There are two classes of models that have been developed to explain shape generalization. One class depends heavily upon learning while the other depends more upon genetically determined structures. The learning model will be presented first, the genetic one second, and then some physiological evidence relevant to both will be discussed.

A Model that Learns Shape Generalization To simplify the following discussion, we will use a straight line as an example of a "form"; a subject will call long and short straight lines by the same name, "straight line," and will distinguish such lines from crooked ones. Now let us consider a prototypic model of a machine (or nervous system) that will exhibit shape generalization (or, to use another term, shape recognition). That is, we wish to design a machine, representing a hypothesis about the nature of a part of the human nervous system, that will say "straight line" whenever it is shown one and will not say "straight line" when it is shown any other form. To simplify the discussion further, we will restrict the possible visual forms to those that can be represented on a 4 × 4 checkerboard by making each square either black or white. Two such forms are illustrated in Fig. 15.2. Further, let us assume that most human subjects would identify a form of this kind as a straight line if at least two squares are white and if all white squares are adjacent to each other and lie in either the same row or the same column.[4] We may then define "straight line" as any figure having these properties, as, for example, the shape in Fig. 15.2b. Now the problem is to design a machine out of elements whose properties are similar to the properties of neurons, and that will say "straight" when shown a straight line.

[4]For further simplicity, we shall consider only white lines on a black background.

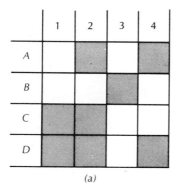

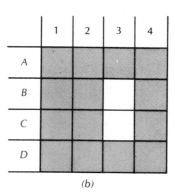

(a)   (b)

At the input end, it is obviously sensible to provide the machine with a 4 × 4 matrix of photosensors, corresponding to the possible stimulus array, and we will assume a mechanism (e.g., a lens) that places the stimulus array on the sensor array.

A general form of machine to satisfy the requirements for generalizing "straight" is represented in Fig. 15.3. There are a total of 120 possible figures[5] that can be presented on a 4 × 4 matrix, and in the model there is a separate layer for every one of these possibilities. Each layer contains the connections between photosensors that correspond to one possible figure. Suppose, for example, that the stimulus figure presented to the machine illuminates only photosensors A1 and A3. Their signals travel through all of the layers, resulting the excitation of one output neuron, the one labeled (A1, A3).

Initially, there are no connections to the response machinery. Now suppose we say to the machine, "tell us whenever you see a straight line." When shown the pattern (A1, A3), it will give no response, and it has thus performed correctly. We now proceed to present the machine with various other input patterns, just as they might occur in the ordinary experience of an infant. At some time, the stimulus will be one that we have defined as a straight line. For example, suppose that the input pattern is (A1, B1). The machine, when this is first presented, will obviously generalize; that is, it will give the same response (no response) to this form as it did to all the others previously presented. However, the teacher (parent?) now tells the machine that this was really "straight," and he will do so in this model simply by making a connection between the active output neuron and the response device, as indicated by the dashed line. The response device says

[5]We will define "figure" as one in which at least two squares are light.

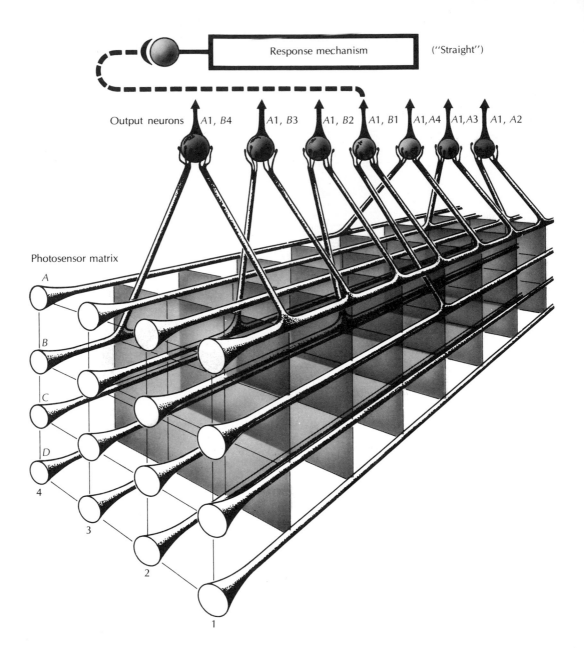

Output neurons

A1, B4   *A1, B3*   *A1, B2*   *A1, B1*   *A1,A4*   *A1,A3*   *A1, A2*

Response mechanism   ("Straight")

Photosensor matrix

A

B

C

D

4

3

2

1

Fig. 15.3 **Schematic diagram of a small part (the sensing array and seven layers out of a total of 120 layers) of a class of machines that learn to generalize shapes. Each layer makes the connections among one of the 120 possible combinations of photosensors, and the synapses to the output neurons have thresholds such that an output neuron will fire if and only if *all* of the input neurons are active. Thus, each output neuron uniquely signals one particular illumination pattern. A response mechanism is also provided that says "straight" whenever it is activated. Initially, there are no connections between output neurons and the response mechanism, and the machine is taught to call "straight" all figures that we have defined as "straight," by making a connection between the active output neuron and the response mechanism every time a pattern we define as straight is presented and the machine does not respond.**

"straight" when it is activated. Thus, the next time that this particular pattern (A1, B1) appears, the machine will correctly call it straight.

If this procedure is carried out for a long enough time that all possible straight lines have been presented and reinforced, the machine will thereafter perform perfectly. It can be said to generalize, giving the same response to many different inputs; it can also be said to "recognize" straight lines, in that it identifies each straight line as such and does not call other figures straight lines; it can be said to "abstract" the property "straightness"; it can also be said to have the "concept" of "straightness."

This model achieves shape generalization through an extended learning period. In fact, it must learn every single figure that it calls a straight line. It is important to note that the same machine could obviously have been taught to call any arbitrary collection of shapes "straight." There is nothing in the *untrained* device that categorizes shapes.[6]

A Model with Built-in Generalization It is certainly true that some of the generalization that occurs in humans does not require learning. For example, the fact that all very small shapes are seen as the same shape depends upon the optical properties of the eye. Therefore, the type of model described above cannot account for all human generalization. Going to the other extreme, it is easy, now, to conceive of a shape-generalization model that does not require any learning at all.

In the preceding section, a model was developed that learned to generalize. To devise a model that does not require teaching, all we need to do is to take that model, before it is taught anything, and pre wire all of the connections that would have been made as a consequence of learning. That is, we need only to postulate that, in the ge-

---

[6]Although "shape" is not built in, the machine does contain a fairly elaborate structure. Therefore, its transmission from parent to child would require appreciable genetic direction. That is, an instruction manual on how, exactly, to construct the machine so that every possible configuration of inputs is represented by an output neuron would be a fairly large document.

However, a machine that would perform almost as well could be constructed by following a much simpler set of directions, in the following way: The receptor array is the same as that in the machine described above, and there are a large number of layers as well. However, the instruction for building the machine is simply that each layer will connect a *random* selection of the inputs to an output neuron. Obviously, if there were an infinite number of layers, all possible input configurations would be represented (some many times), and the machine could then perform just as well as the more orderly one described above. As the number of layers is reduced, the possibility of unlearnable shapes increases. Thus, while the second machine would make many errors unless it were much larger than the first, the genetic information required to grow the second machine is much smaller than the corresponding requirement for the first.

netic code for the organism, there are instructions to connect together the output neurons from all the layers that correspond to what we have called straight lines. Then we have a device that is indistinguishable from the educated learning device.

The fact that these two models are identical in final form illustrates an important point. There are two independent questions that may be asked about the physiological correlates of any behavior or experience. One question asks about the nature of the correlates and of the structure that generates them. The other, *independent* question asks about conditions (i.e., genetic and environmental) that are necessary in order that the correlates develop. While the fact that these questions are independent may seem obvious, it evidently is not. For example, many writers have contrasted what they consider to be two mutually exclusive classes of theories of brightness constancy, i.e., physiological theories and learning theories. The kind of theory described in Chapter XIII, where it is suggested that brightness constancy is a consequence of a logarithmic transformation and strong lateral inhibition, is thought to be in conflict with the class of theories that claim constancy is a result of experience with real objects (whose reflectances are constant despite changes in illumination). It should be obvious that the two theories are not contradictory. It is perfectly possible that lateral inhibitory connections cannot form in the eye unless certain sets of environmental conditions are met. That is, these connections may be "learned."

In psychology, there is a long history of vigorous but remarkably confused debate between those who believe that perception is learned and those who maintain that it is a consequence of the structure of the organism. There is no logical conflict between these views unless one believes that those perceptual phenomena that are learned have no physical or physiological correlates in the organism; very few modern scientists hold that belief.

PHYSIOLOGICAL EVIDENCE FOR MAMMALIAN GENERALIZATION MECHANISMS

All of the processes in the visual system that lose information are mechanisms of generalization, and discussions of these processes are distributed throughout this book. The optical properties of the eye result in generalization among shapes that differ by very small amounts. Spatial summation among rods produces generalization of the same kind. The fact that wavelength information is lost when a quantum is absorbed by a visual pigment molecule accounts for generalization among all wavelengths in the monochromat, and, in combination with the fact that the number of types of visual pigment is limited, provides a mechanism by which different mixtures of wavelengths are generalized by the normal visual system (i.e., color mixture data). Strong lateral inhibition in the visual system accounts for generalization among different levels of illumination (brightness constancy).

Recently, Hubel and Wiesel have published a series of experiments revealing the physiological nature of a set of mechanisms that generalize shapes (Hubel and Wiesel, 1959, 1965). These remarkable studies give evidence of a mechanism surprisingly similar to the straight-line generalizer described above.

Hubel and Wiesel performed most of their experiments on the visual systems of cats. They recorded the activity in single nerve cells at three stages along the visual pathways, the optic nerve, the lateral geniculate body, and the visual cortex, and related the nature of the recorded activity to the position of a stimulus pattern moved about in the visual field.

The animals were anesthetized, their heads were held rigid in a head holder, one eye was sewn open and fitted with a contact lens to prevent it from drying, and eye movements were eliminated by drugs. An optical system provided spots of light and patterns that could be moved over the retina. Electrodes were inserted into the visual pathway to record the activity of single cells, and the relationships between the activity and the position of the spot of light on the screen were studied.[7]

When the electrode was placed in the optic nerve, thus recording the output of the retinal ganglion cells, Hubel and Weisel's procedure yielded results like those already discussed in Chapter XI; maps of the receptive fields of the retinal ganglion cells generally appear as in Fig. 15.4a. They consist of a central disk where light will have one effect upon the cell (either an increase or a decrease in firing rate) and a concentric ring in which light will have the opposite effect.

Within the receptive field of a fiber, there is spatial summation. For example, two small spots within the excitatory region will be more effective than one, the most effective stimulus being one that just fills the central disk or the ring. When areas of both the ring and disk are illuminated at the same time, the effect is smaller than when only one region is illuminated.

The optic nerve fibers terminate in a region of the brain called the

---

[7]When a spot of light is stationary on the mammalian retina and its intensity is constant, the spot soon ceases to affect the neural activity. The maximum effect of a light stimulus occurs when it goes on and off, as discussed in Chapter XIV. Therefore, Hubel and Wiesel continuously flickered their stimuli at 1 Hz.

Fig. 15.4 **Maps of the receptive fields of individual retinal ganglion cells and cells in the lateral geniculate nucleus of the cat are shown in (a). Such fields were discussed extensively in Chapter XI. The "+" signs indicate that a spot of light falling in that area causes the firing rate to increase, and a "−" indicates that light causes a decrease in firing rate. The maps in (b) are taken from single cells in the visual cortex (area 17) as a spot is moved over the retina. These are representative of what Hubel and Wiesel call "simple" cortical cells. The long axis of any such cell may be in any angular orientation.** [*After Hubel and Wiesel (1962).*]

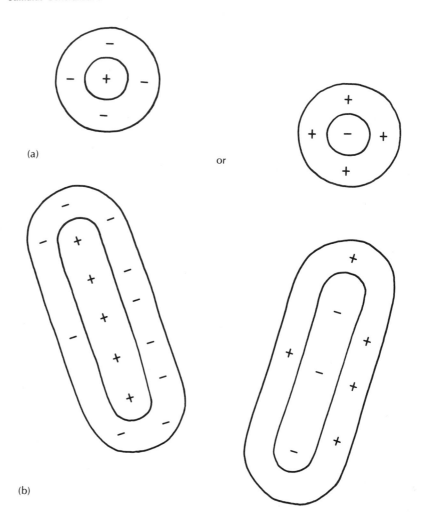

(a)   or

(b)

lateral geniculate body where they synapse with other neurons that terminate in the visual cortex. When Hubel and Wiesel introduced their electrodes into the lateral geniculate, they found receptive fields that had essentially the same maps as those of the ganglion cells. (There are some important differences between the responses of the retinal ganglion cells and the geniculate units but those differences are not relevant to the present discussion.) However, when electrodes were introduced into what is almost certainly the next level of the visual pathways, area 17 of the cerebral cortex, the receptive fields differed from those of the optic nerve and lateral geniculate units in interesting ways. For convenience, Hubel and Wiesel divided these receptive fields into two classes, simple and complex. The simple fields may be mapped by following the same procedure as for the receptive fields of the ganglion cells, but the receptive fields of the complex units cannot be mapped in the same way.

The simple cortical receptive fields in area 17 are mostly of the form illustrated in Fig. 15.4b. They are essentially identical to the fields of retinal ganglion cells, except that they are elongated.[8] Any given simple cortical cell will respond to spots of light anywhere within an elongated area whose long axis may have any particular angular orientation, and it may be of the center-on or the center-off type. There is summation within a given receptive field, so that a maximal response (either a maximal increase or a maximal decrease) will occur when the central area is entirely illuminated, or when the surrounding annulus is entirely illuminated; but when both regions are illuminated at the same time, the response will be very small, or even nonexistent. For example, if the entire retina is illuminated, such a unit will give, at most, a very weak response, and many units give no response at all. However, if the stimulation is restricted to a small spot somewhere in the receptive field, the response will be vigorous.

Because there is summation within the receptive fields, these units respond most strongly to a line in just the right place and orientation, but the line may be either a light line on a dark field or a dark one on a bright field. (Obviously, the sign of the response will be opposite in these two cases.) If such a line is slightly tilted with respect to the axis of the receptive field, the response will be greatly reduced, because areas from both of the antagonistic parts of the field will be activated.

A set of neural connections that may be responsible for the shapes of the receptive fields of retinal ganglion cells was discussed in Chapter XI. Hubel and Wiesel have proposed a very simple addition to this model that would account for the kinds of simple cortical receptive fields just described. The geniculate fibers sending inputs into the visual cortex have circular receptive fields, as shown in Fig. 15.4a. Hubel and Wiesel propose that each simple cortical cell has as its inputs a set of geniculate fibers whose receptive fields are all in a row. This scheme is diagramed in Fig. 15.5.

The other type of units that Hubel and Wiesel reported in area 17 have more complicated receptive fields. For example, some of these units respond to lines at a particular orientation, just as do the simple units, but while a simple unit would respond only to a line at some particular tilt *and in some particular location*, the corresponding com-

---

[8]Remember that these receptive field maps are maps of the retina, *not* the cortex. Each map represents the various locations on the retina where a spot of light will affect a particular cortical cell.

plex unit responds to a line at a particular tilt regardless of where it is located within a fairly broad area of the retina (typically about 5°). When this complex cortical unit fires, it means that there is a line, somewhere in a region of the field, that is tilted at some particular angle. If a different complex cell fires, it means that there is a line at some other angle. In other words, outputs of these cells contain information about slant, and have lost information about location in space. The set of connections from the retina to these units is thus a system that abstracts "slant," or that generalizes among all stimuli of the same slant, regardless of their locations (within broad limits).

Hubel and Wiesel have suggested a very simple addition to the neural model in Fig. 15.5 that will account for the behavior of these complex units. They propose that the inputs to each complex unit are the outputs from a group of simple cortical units, all of whose (elongated) receptive fields are parallel and adjacent. Thus an extremely simple set of neural connections (lateral inhibition at the retina

Fig. 15.5 **Semischematic diagram of a set of neural connections suggested by Hubel and Wiesel to explain the receptive fields of their "simple" cortical cells in the brain of the cat. Two simple cells are shown, each of which collects inputs from cells in the geniculate whose receptive fields are all in a row (and of like sign, e.g., on-center). The simple cells fire if any one or more of their input neurons are firing. The receptive field of the simple cell will thus be like that of Fig. 14.4b.**

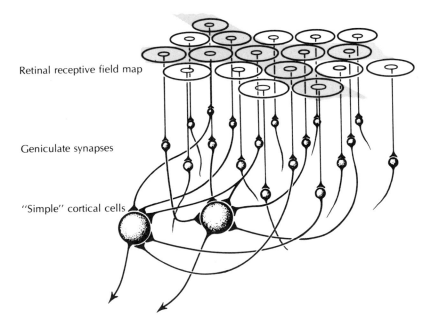

Retinal receptive field map

Geniculate synapses

"Simple" cortical cells

and two stages of directional lateral summation in the cortex) can produce a brain cell whose activity abstracts "slant."

Hubel and Wiesel have also collected some very interesting evidence concerning the ontogenic development of cortical receptive fields. Briefly, they found both simple and complex receptive fields in the brains of kittens so young that their eyes had not yet opened. However, such units were greatly reduced in number in kittens that had been deprived of pattern vision (e.g., by milky contact lenses) during their first three months of life. Thus, slant-abstracting units develop on the basis of genetic instructions, but they evidently require patterned stimulation in order to remain viable.

It is relatively easy to imagine additions to the neural model in Fig. 15.5 that abstract more complex stimulus features. For example, if all complex units whose fields were either parallel to a given line or perpendicular to it summated on another unit, that unit would be a "corner detector." [And while that sounds rather far-fetched, Hubel and Wiesel (1965) have reported the presence of units that respond just that way in secondary cortical areas of the cat brain.]

Probably the most active area in current sensory physiology is the electrophysiological measurement of receptive fields in the visual systems of animals. The preceding discussion presented only a small sample of Hubel and Wiesel's work. Extensive research is also being carried out by them and in other laboratories, for example, on units that respond when a target moves in one direction and do not respond when it moves in the opposite direction (Barlow and Levick, 1965). Only a general introduction to this mushrooming field has been presented here, because it is too early to be confident about the directions it will take. However, it is already very clear that we are close to an understanding of the neurophysiology of some processes that abstract, or generalize, some very complex properties of the visual environment.

XVI ◇◇◇ SPECULATIONS ON "HIGHER PROCESSES"

WHY DID INHIBITION EVOLVE? THE presence of strong lateral inhibition in the visual system profoundly influences what we see. Its primary effect is to suppress signals carrying information about steady states. For example, it is probably inhibition that is responsible for the disappearance of stabilized retinal images, and for our relative insensitivity to absolute illumination levels. Both of these phenomena, and in fact all of the consequences of inhibition, represent losses in sensitivity or information.[1] A loss in sensitivity hardly seems to be advantageous to an organism, but our ideas of evolution lead us to the supposition that any feature that has successfully established itself must provide some net increase in its possessors' probability of survival. How, then, does inhibition fit our concept of evolution? Why did inhibition evolve?

[1] Lateral inhibition, per se, does not cause a loss of information; it only causes a reduction in the level of activity of certain neurons. However, the nervous system also contains sources of "noise,"

434

The most prevalent answer to this question is seriously misleading. Many writers have compared the shape of an input distribution, such as the light distribution in the retinal image of an edge, with the output pattern resulting from lateral inhibition, and noted that the output distribution has somewhat sharper corners. In general, abrupt differences in input intensity will be enhanced relative to less abrupt differences and steady levels. These writers have drawn the conclusion that the lateral inhibitory network "enhances" edges and contours, and, since edges seem to be the parts of the field that carry the most important visual information, inhibition is adaptive.

However, inhibition does not enhance edges. It just suppresses signals corresponding to edges less strongly than it suppresses the rest of the signals. (If lateral inhibition could be turned off suddenly, the outputs corresponding to any pattern would all *increase*. None would decrease.) There is no way in which neural processing, no matter how elaborate or of what kind, can increase the amount of information about a visual object beyond the amount that is present in the retinal image. The very best that neural processing can do is *not* to *lose* information. Then why has inhibition evolved?

Inhibition does, indeed, result in certain losses in sensitivity, but those very losses serve a vital function in the neural mechanisms that abstract properties of the visual environment. We usually think of the process of abstracting, or of forming concepts, as a creative process, and in many respects it is. From an information processing standpoint, however, the formation of a concept represents a *loss* in information. A device that successfully identifies all rectangles with equal sides as "squares," regardless of their sizes, orientations, colors, etc., obviously loses vast amounts of information, and it *must* do so if it is to perform its function. Other devices that detect those lost properties may well be present, in parallel with the "square" abstractor, but that abstractor, itself, loses information in the very process of abstracting. Similarly, when an engineer tries to design a machine that abstracts some property of the environment, he must figure out how to construct it so that it will lose certain classes of information (without losing the property of interest), and when he has figured that out, the problem is solved.

The fact that inhibition plays a crucial role in neural abstraction mechanisms is clearly illustrated in an analysis of the data of Hubel

---

that is, more or less random fluctuations in firing rates, and when a lower firing rate is fed into a system with a fixed amount of "noise," the signal is more likely to be confused with the noise; the effective information content is therefore lowered.

and Wiesel. Figure 16.1 is a map of the receptive field of one of Hubel and Wiesel's "simple" cortical cells, as discussed in Chapter XV. This cell increases its response rate when a small spot of light falls anywhere within the central oblong area and decreases its response for any spot falling in the surrounding region. Furthermore, there is summation among all the regions of this receptive field, so that two spots falling in the center will cause a greater excitation than one, two falling in the periphery will cause more inhibition than one, and if one spot falls in the center and another on the surround, their effects will tend to cancel. Thus the cell will respond most strongly when a line of light falls on the retina in such a way that it just fills the excitatory center. If the line is then tilted a little, some of it may still fall on the excitatory center of the field, but more of it will fall on the inhibitory surround, and the response of the cell will be nullified.

As Hubel and Wiesel suggested, their "complex" cortical cells may be excited by the outputs of many simple cells, all of whose receptive fields are oriented in parallel and near each other (Hubel and Weisel, 1959). Such a cell would fire whenever a line of the proper tilt was present anywhere within a broad region, regardless of the exact location of the line, and the cell would not fire if a line at some other tilt were present. The unit can then be described as a "line at 14° from the vertical" detector or abstractor.

The essential requirement of this or any other feature abstractor is a dual one; it must respond when a given feature is present and not re-

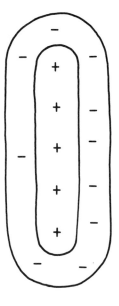

Fig. 16.1 **Map of the receptive field of a "simple" cortical unit. The "+" signs denote the region in which light causes an increase in firing rate and the "−" signs denote a decrease. Other cells may have inhibitory centers and excitatory surrounds, and the orientation of the oblong varies from one cell to another.** [*After Hubel and Wiesel (1959).*]

spond when it is not. The slant detector just described would respond just as strongly (actually more strongly) to a line of the correct tilt if no inhibition were present, but it would also respond to lines of all other tilts. Inhibition is what causes it *not* to fire when the proper feature is *not* present. Similarly, inhibition that spreads differently in different directions is probably responsible for the fact that retinal motion detectors do not respond when a target is moved in one direction [while they do when it is moved in other directions (Barlow and Levick, 1965)]. Thus, inhibition plays a critical role in the functioning of feature detectors.

Feature detectors, themselves, seem to have obvious biological value. While an extensive consideration of the significance of feature detectors is beyond the scope of this book, it is clear that there are varieties of stimuli for which the same response is appropriate (e.g., run, whether it is an old lion or a young one) and feature detectors provide an efficient means for accomplishing this.

To review then, inhibition does result in the loss of some kinds of information, but it is those very losses that provide biological utility.

The fact that stabilized retinal images disappear is probably a consequence of inhibition. That consequence apparently has little evolutionary significance for man, since his normal eye movements preclude the natural occurrence of stabilized retinal images. However, the late Gordon Walls, who made extensive and fascinating comparisons among the visual systems of vertebrates (Walls, 1963), put forth the following interesting observation (in a personal communication, not in his book). Most birds have very underdeveloped external eye muscles. Many birds, when searching for food, seem to assume frozen postures between abrupt movements, while others are in constant motion when they feed, pecking, hopping, and flying. Walls suggested that the relatively motionless birds have no involuntary eye movements and hold themselves rigid enough to experience stabilized retinal images. If that is right, then inhibition suppresses all the retinal signals except those from moving objects, thus making every receptor a "moving object" detector. He further suggested that these are birds that feed on moving prey, while the moving birds feed on berries and seeds.

Another consequence of inhibition is our extreme insensitivity to illumination level. The fact that we exhibit a high degree of brightness constancy means that we are very poor at judging the intensity of illumination of the visual scene. (The relationship between inhibition and insensitivity to illumination levels was explained in Chapters XII and XIII.)

It is compelling to try to find the biological benefit of this loss of information, but this is probably the wrong approach. Instead, consider the following argument: Just because a particular neural circuit loses some information, the organism as a whole does not necessarily lose that information. Certainly we have no difficulty in distinguishing a red circle from a red square even though there almost certainly are units in our nervous systems that fire identically for both. While a particular system may lose information, that information can still be retained by some other system that is in parallel with the first.

Now, let us acknowledge that the loss of absolute intensity information is a consequence of an inhibitory system that probably has other reasons for its existence. Then we are in a position to ask a new question. Instead of asking why evolution has caused absolute intensity information to be lost, we can ask why a system has not evolved that runs in parallel with the system containing inhibition, and that preserves the absolute intensity information that is certainly present in the receptors. Apparently, either the necessary mutations just haven't happened yet, or else the survival value of retaining absolute intensity information is not great enough to outweigh the disadvantages that would accrue from the required increase in complexity of genetic material and neural structure.

"HIGHER" PROCESSES

It is pleasing, at least to this writer, to consider the possibility that the human nervous system, despite its obvious overall complexity, is really composed of a very large number of repetitions and slight variations of a few simple mechanisms (just as our most advanced computers are constructed of a few kinds of simple building blocks). Regardless of one's esthetic or moral views, it seems useful to assume that this is true in the absence of strong evidence to the contrary. This approach provides a basis (or maybe just a rationalization) for explaining another large set of human behaviors by a direct extrapolation of the physiological mechanisms of recurrent inhibition.

Our nervous systems contain many mechanisms that are capable of learning. To any system that learns and remembers, information about steady states is redundant. Any given condition always began (or the organism first came into its presence) as a transient event, by definition. Once it has begun, if the organism has memory, it need not be continuously reminded of the condition. If the condition stops, that, too, is a transient that will be transmitted.

Thus inhibition, which suppresses signals from stimuli that are unchanging, would seem to perform an adaptive function. However, the mere fact that some information is redundant, by itself, does not explain why there is any advantage in suppressing it. If there *is* advantage in suppressing redundant information, there must be some *dis*advantage in transmitting it.

The amount of information impinging upon our array of receptors at every instant is virtually infinite—differences in light intensity and wavelength, sound, temperature, the touch of our clothes, the tensions in our muscles, etc. If our nervous systems were capable of processing all that information, then any mechanisms that lost some of it would be undesirable; but our nervous systems are certainly not capable of processing all the information available to our senses, nor even a small fraction of it, and *that* must be a crucial factor in the evolution of the nervous system. Suppose, for example, that the brain could only process and store or make use of 1% of the information output by our receptors at any instant. Then there would be no way for the individual to avoid losing 99% of the information. It would obviously be more adaptive to *select* the 1% that will be processed, rather than simply to lose some and process the rest on a haphazard or first come, first served basis.

It would be very adaptive to analyze in detail each bit of input information and decide whether to throw it away or process it, but that would already involve a processing capacity that we do not have. The best that the system can do is to put all the input information through some relatively primitive processors that select, from all the inputs, those classes that generally contain the most *useful* information. Let us consider a few examples of processes that select useful information.

Aftereffects If you stare for a minute or two at a field that contains objects continuously moving in one direction, and then the motion is stopped, the field appears to move in the opposite direction. This phenomenon, called the aftereffect of motion, is often demonstrated with a spiral that is slowly turned. If it appears to expand while turning, it will seem to contract when stopped, and vice versa. The same phenomenon is commonly experienced when a traveler has been looking out of a side window while the car or train is in motion; when the vehicle stops, the scene out the window seems to move forward (opposite to the direction it moved during travel).

Motion aftereffects are easy to demonstrate at home. Just mistune the "vertical hold" control of your television set so that the picture drifts vertically at a rate of one or two frames per second, and stare at the screen for a few minutes. Then abruptly retune the set, or look at any stationary object, and it will seem to drift in the opposite direction.

This motion aftereffect is just one example of what seems to be a very general rule in human perception. If any form of stimulation is continued for a long time and then is terminated, the subject experiences the opposite condition for a while. Thus, if you try to lift your arm against a restraining force for a minute and then remove the restraining force, the arm seems to be buoyed up by an opposite force. If you wear rose-colored glasses, the world is green when you take them off. If you stare at a field of tilted lines for a few minutes, a vertical one looks tilted the opposite way (Gibson and Radner, 1937). If you look through prisms that give color fringes to all vertical edges, then when these prisms are removed, you see color fringes of the opposite polarity [i.e., if the fringes were originally red through violet from left to right, they appear to be violet through red, left to right, when the prisms are removed. (Held, 1954)[2]]

In all of these examples, when careful measurements are made it becomes evident that, all during the original exposure to the stimulus, the perception grows weaker, or to phrase the same phenomenon in a different way, the subject adapts to it. Then, when the original stimulus is removed, the reversed perception occurs.

A very simple physiological explanation of these phenomena is as follows: Note, first, that the sequence of events for, say, a motion aftereffect is very similar to the simple example discussed extensively in Chapter XIV in which light falls on a set of receptors and associated neurons that manifest strong lateral inhibition. In the dark, the units maintain a spontaneous firing rate. When a light is first turned on, the firing rate increases, but then, when inhibition begins to operate, the firing rate drops, approaching an equilibrium rate that is closer to the spontaneous rate (see Figs. 14.20 and 14.22). When the light is extinguished, the excitation stops before the inhibition has decayed away, and the firing rate, therefore, undergoes a momentary reduction below the spontaneous rate. This sequence of responses is just the same as that for aftereffects of more complicated stimuli, and a simple recurrent inhibition network is sufficient to explain it.

How might such an explanation be extended to, say, the aftereffect of vertical motion? Let us first assume that there is some neuron or set of neurons somewhere in the visual system that abstracts downward

---

[2]This effect is not strong enough to be seen easily, but when careful measures are taken, it reliably appears. For example, if, after prism removal, the subject is asked to adjust a variable prism until there are no color fringes, we will set the variable prism to have a nonzero power (Held, 1954).

motion. That is, assume that the neural interactions intervening between the receptors and this particular neuron are such that the neuron fires most strongly when patterns move downward on the retina, and is inhibited when the motion is upward. [Barlow and Levick (1965) have reported just such units in the rabbit retina.] Let us now postulate that the output of this unit feeds a circuit that manifests recurrent inhibition, and that the output of *that* system is the physiological correlate of our perception of motion in the vertical direction. This is diagramed in Fig. 16.2.

Then, when a vertically moving field is steadily viewed, the perceived motion will be strongest at first, and then progressively weaker as inhibition reduces the output. When the motion is stopped, the motion detector will stop exciting the recurrent inhibition circuit before the inhibition decays, thus driving the output of the unit below its resting level. That is the same as the output that would have occurred if the visual object were actually moving upward, and thus the subject should see movement in the upward direction.

It is easy to imagine similar neural machinery that would account for any aftereffects. In general, two things are required. One is some set of interactions that abstracts the particular feature in such a way that activities of opposite sign are the correlates of perceptions of opposite conditions. The other is recurrent inhibition in the output path.

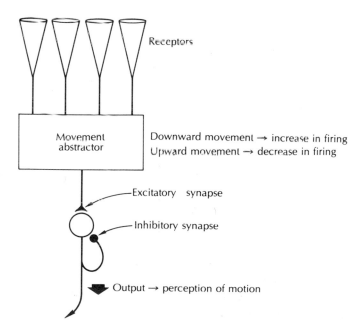

Fig. 16.2 **Schematic diagram of a neural system that exhibits a motion aftereffect. The receptor outputs are processed by a "movement detector," the output of the movement detector undergoes recurrent inhibition, and the final output is the correlate of the perception of movement.**

Attention   Stop reading for a moment at the end of this sentence and listen to the sounds that surround you. Maybe a clock is ticking or an air-conditioning unit hums. Before you stopped to listen, it is unlikely that you were hearing those sounds, although you may continue to hear them now. Certainly if the sounds are steady and not overpoweringly loud, you will stop hearing them pretty soon.

A closely related phenomenon is that if we have stopped hearing some continuous sound and then the sound goes off, we notice the cessation. In fact, when a clock stops ticking, it seems as though we hear the last few ticks. (An old story illustrates an extreme case. At 11:46 in the evening, an electrical failure disabled Big Ben's chimes so that they could not sound. At 12:00 sharp, the man who lived next door leapt out of bed and shouted: "What was that?")

This phenomenon bears a strong resemblance to the aftereffects described above. In fact, it is not easy to distinguish between these two classes of phenomena. We can easily extend the aftereffect explanation to cover the kind of example where we stop hearing a clock, if we hypothesize that, during the initial time when we did hear it, a set of neural interactions was developed that abstracts the relevant property (two ticks per second), and that the output of that mechanism undergoes recurrent inhibition. That is, we must postulate some machinery that *learns* and has inhibition in its output. The conditions that are required if learning is to occur have been the subject of intensive study for many years, and will not be discussed here. It is perfectly clear, however, that animals can learn quickly, and therefore, the explanation offered here for adaptation to ticking clocks is no less plausible than that for motion aftereffects.

One interesting conclusion that follows from this hypothesis concerns what happens when the clock stops ticking. The hypothesis suggests that what we hear then is not the last few ticks, but rather a couple of antiticks. That is, if a neural assemblage has been formed in such a way that it generates an output when there are "two ticks per second" at its input, and if we stop hearing the ticks because this output is reduced by recurrent inhibition, then the sudden removal of the input will cause the output to go negative for a brief time, and *that* is what we hear.

This whole discussion about not hearing clocks that are ticking is really a discussion of one aspect of attention. We say that we stopped hearing the clock because we stopped paying attention to it, or we were attending to something else. The process is certainly a very general one. We stop noticing the picture hanging in the front hall or the paint we mean to scrape off the window. These processes, too, may be explained by the same mechanism, given only that we have within us neural aggregates capable of "learning" the picture and the paint, and we obviously do.[3]

The process we call attention is usually considered a reflection of a very high level of consciousness, and it doesn't seem fitting to try to explain part of it in terms of something so drab as neural circuitry. It is, however, hard to imagine that attention is not a manifestation of neural circuitry. It seems more reasonable to think that the neural circuits that learn pictures and that inhibit themselves *are* high-level systems. Even the edge detectors of Hubel and Wiesel appear to be the result of a large number of different interactions, and any circuit that learns a picture must have as inputs an enormous number of edge detectors, color detectors, etc., besides having the capacity for learning. So while it may be possible to describe the overall functioning of such a circuit in simple words, and while the components that contribute to the circuit may themselves all be simple, the circuit is still exceedingly complex; it fits any definition of a high-level system.

Regardless of any particular theory about the mechanism of attention, the result of this mechanism is a loss of information. Therefore, it is again interesting to ask why a mechanism that loses information would have evolved, and one plausible answer to that question is similar in essence to the one given for recurrent inhibition. The attention mechanism can be conceived of as a high-level feature detector, the feature being "change." Only things that are changing are transmitted by this mechanism. The steady-state conditions of the world around us are not transmitted through the attention mechanism and into the rest of our brains. They would be redundant to a system that can learn.

---

[3]Another, at least equally important, aspect of what we call attention is characterized by the fact that we seem only to be able to pay attention to one thing at a time. "Attention" seems to consist of two processes, one of which suppresses steady states, and the other that chooses among those transient events that are transmitted by the first mechanism, perhaps making a guess, on some primitive basis, about which of all these remaining inputs contains the most useful information.

APPENDIX I ◇◇◇ VISUAL ANGLE

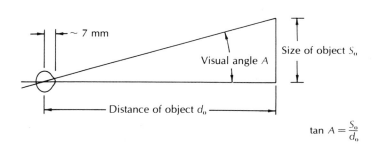

$$\tan A = \frac{S_o}{d_o}$$

The apex is approximately 7 mm behind the foremost point of the cornea.

Table of Visual Angles of Common Objects[a]

Object	Distance d_0	Visual angle A
Sun	93,000,000 mi	30′
Moon	240,000 mi	30′
Quarter	Arm's length (70 cm)	2°
Quarter	90 yd	1′
Quarter	3 mi	1″
Lowercase pica type letter	Reading distance (40 cm)	13′

[a]1° (degree) = 60′ (minutes of arc); 1′ = 60″ (seconds of arc); tan 1″ = 0.0000048; tan 1′ = 0.00029. For small angles, the tangent of an angle varies linearly with the size of the angle (e.g., tan 10′ = 10 × tan 1′).

APPENDIX II ◇◇◇ FILTER TRANSMISSION VERSUS DENSITY

Density	Transmission (%)[a]	Density	Transmission (%)[a]
0.0	100	1.0	10
0.1	79	1.1	7.9
0.2	63	1.2	6.3
0.3	50	1.3	5.0
0.4	40		etc.
0.5	32		
0.6	25	2.0	1.0
0.7	20	2.1	0.79
0.8	16	2.3	0.63
0.9	13		etc.

[a]Percentage of Transmission $= 100 \times \dfrac{1}{10^d}$

APPENDIX III ◇◇◇ HOW TO BUILD AN OPHTHALMOSCOPE

The device diagramed in Fig. IIIa can be constructed cheaply, and will provide an excellent view of the retina. A description of its principles of operation will be given first, followed by specific directions for construction and alignment. However, the description and directions are intimately related; i.e., it will be easier to understand the principles when you actually start to build the opthalmoscope, and vice versa.

THEORY OF OPERATION Light from a source is imaged by lens L_1 on to an aperture A_1 after passing through a heat-absorbing filter. The aperture is just a hole in an opaque plate with an opaque bar across it, e.g., a piece of wire. The light passing through A_1 passes through two lenses, L_2 and L_3, and then strikes an ordinary piece of glass, which serves as a beam splitter. Most

447

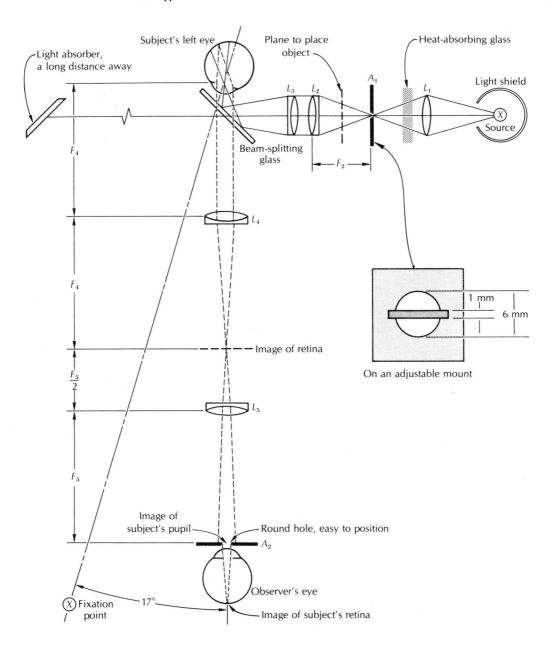

Light absorber,
a long distance away

Subject's left eye

Plane to place
object

Heat-absorbing glass

L_3 L_2

A_1

L_1

Light shield

X Source

F_4

Beam-splitting
glass

F_2

L_4

F_4

1 mm

6 mm

Image of retina

On an adjustable mount

$\frac{F_5}{2}$

L_5

F_5

Image of
subject's pupil

Round hole, easy to position

A_2

Observer's eye

X Fixation
point

17°

Image of subject's retina

Fig. IIIa

of the light, (about 90% of it) passes through the glass and falls on a black surface, as far away as possible, and angled so that as little as possible of the light that hits it will be reflected back to the beam-splitter. The roughly 10% of the light that is reflected from the glass goes on to enter the subject's eye. The lenses L_2 and L_3 form an image of the hole in A_1 in the plane of the subject's pupil, and the light then goes on into the eye to illuminate a circular area of the retina.

Now, consider any one point on the retina. That point will diffusely reflect some of the incident light, and some of that reflected light will emerge from the pupil. If the subject is focused on the fixation point, a long distance away, then the rays from any one point that emerge from his eye will be almost parallel, as shown by the dashed lines in the diagram. About 10% of those rays will be reflected from the beam splitter and be lost, but the remaining 90% will pass through the beam splitter and strike lens L_4. Since the rays from the retina are almost parallel as they strike L_4, they will form an image of the retina about in the focal plane of L_4, as shown in the figure. The light then passes through lens L_5, which makes the rays from the retina diverge less strongly (so that it is as if the image of the retina were farther away from L_5). The rays then pass through a round-hole aperture A_2, and enter the observer's eye, which he has placed just behind the hole. The rays from the subject's retina are diverging slightly when they enter the observer's eye, and therefore, if the observer is focused for moderate distance, the optics of his eye will form an image of the subject's retina on the observer's retina. That is, he will see the subject's retina in sharp focus.

It is probably obvious by now that this optical system is much more complicated than it need be in order to do the things just described. The reason for this complexity is that, without it, the light reflected from the subject's cornea and iris would obscure the view of his retina. These extra reflections are eliminated in the following way.

Aperture A_1 is imaged on the cornea, and the opaque bar across the middle of it, when it is lined up right on the optic axis, eliminates just that light that would otherwise have been reflected from the cornea into L_4. That is, there is only a fairly small region of the cornea over which reflected light would travel in just the directions that would cause it to enter L_4, and the opaque bar in A_1 prevents light from falling on that region. All of the light that does enter the eye and illuminates the retina, passes through those regions of the cornea that are angled strongly enough so that the reflected light misses L_4. Thus, the corneal reflection does not obscure the retina image.

Furthermore, L_4 is at its focal distance from the eye, so that it renders the light from the iris parallel. Therefore, an image of the iris is formed in the focal plane of lens L_5, where A_2 is. The hole in A_2 is smaller than the image of the subject's pupil. Thus, when the device is lined up correctly, any light reflected from the subject's iris forms an image of the iris on the opaque part of A_2, and cannot enter the observer's eye to obscure the view of the retina.

SPECIFIC
CONSTRUCTION
DETAILS

The light source can be any ordinary incandescent lamp that is not frosted. A slide projector of one or two hundred watts, with the lenses removed will do very well.

All of the lenses except L_1 ought to be of reasonably good quality. The focal lengths of all the lenses except L_1 should be about 200 mm and the diameters about 40 mm but none of the focal lengths or diameters given here are critical. They can vary by 50% without serious difficulty. Reasonably good lenses, called "achromats," can be purchased from Edmund Scientific Co., Barrington, New Jersey, for a few dollars each. (Lens L_1 need not be an achromat.)

Lens L_1 can be any lens that forms an image of the filament on the hole in A_1 at some convenient distance from the source. It should be of at least ¾ in. diameter.

Heat-absorbing glass can be purchased from Edmund Scientific Company, or, if you are using a slide projector as a source, there may already be some in it.

Lenses L_2 and L_3 are identical, and should be placed with their more convex sides facing each other, as indicated, to form the best image of A_1 in the plane of the subject's pupil.

The beam-splitting glass can be any piece of reasonably flat glass. A microscope slide is a convenient beam splitter.

The light absorber can be any black surface, set as far from the optics as possible, and angled to minimize reflection. Any light reflected from the absorber and back to the beam-splitter will be superimposed on the view of the retina, reducing its contrast.

It is very important, if the device is to work well, that the subject's head be fixed firmly so that his eye does not move around very much. This can easily be accomplished by purchasing a box of dental impression compound (or begging one from your dentist) of the kind that softens in hot water (e.g., Kerr Impression Compound, type 1, working temperature 132°F, Kerr Manufacturing Company, Detroit, Michigan). Soften a stick of the compound in hot water, mold it onto a metal plate about two inches wide and any length, and then, while the compound is soft, have the subject bite into it firmly enough to leave an impression of his teeth. Figure IIIb shows two such bite bars. Then clamp the plate rigidly to the table on which the optics will be assembled. Try to

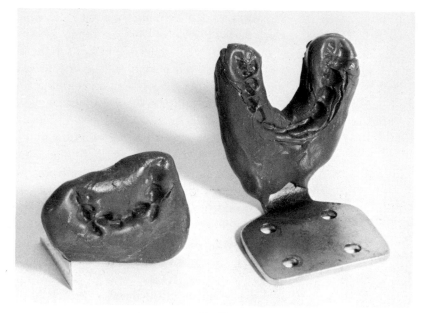

Fig. IIIb

clamp it at a height and angle such that the subject will be comfortable when he is biting on it.

With the subject biting on the bite bar and looking at the fixation point, try to position the optics so that the image of A_1 is exactly centered on his iris and in focus in that plane. (The light will look bright to the subject, but so long as the source is not more than one or two hundred watts and there is heat-absorbing glass in the path, it will do him no harm. If you want to make sure, look briefly and then see how long the after-image lasts. If it is clearly noticeable for longer than about 5 min, the light *is* too bright.)

Now put L_4 in place, about its focal length away from the eye, and L_5 in line, so that the distance between L_4 and L_5 is about equal to the focal length of L_4 plus half the focal length of L_5.

Now get one more lens (not shown in the diagram), a short focal-length eyepiece (e.g., 1-in. focal length achromat). Put this lens right up to your eye and look at your finger through it. You will see your finger, or any other object, clearly when it is about 1 in. away from the lens. Now in the plane of A_2, there is an image of the subject's pupil. Use the eyepiece to find this image by holding it right up to your eye and moving around and in and out about an inch behind where A_2 will be. (A_2 is not yet in place.) When you get in the right position, you will see a magnified image of the subject's iris and pupil, and, if things are close to proper alignment, his pupil will be pink, illuminated from the back by light reflected from the retina. There will probably also be a small, round, bright reflection in focus in the plane of the pupil. This is formed by light reflected from the cornea, and will cast a haze over the view of the retina if it is not eliminated. It may be removed by moving A_1 up or down until the shadow of the bar across it is centered on the cornea.

Once the stop A_1 is positioned correctly and the pupil looks pink through the eyepiece, put stop A_2 in place. It should be placed in the plane of the image of the pupil (i.e., the edges of the hole should be in focus through the eyepiece when the iris is in focus) and should be moved sideways and up and down until it is centered on the image of the pupil. In that position, it will prevent the light reflected from the iris from obscuring the view of the retina. Now put your eye right up to the hole in A_2 (without the eyepiece), and you should see the subject's retina.

If the retina seems to have a haze of light superimposed upon it, check to make sure that the corneal reflection is really eliminated, by looking at the hole in A_2 with the eyepiece. When you have a good view of the retina, move the fixation point around a little and have the subject follow it. When it is in just the right place, about at the angle indicated in Fig. IIIa and at about the same height as the optics, you should be able to see the optic disk (the blindspot). (When the fixation point is changed, you will probably have to realign A_2 a little.)

In Fig. IIIa, a plane is indicated between L_2 and A_1. If an object is placed in this plane, an image of it will be in good focus on the subject's retina, and it will be visible when his retina is visible. Try putting your finger or a transparency or slide in that plane, and you will be able to see, directly, the subject's retinal image of it.

Appendix IV ◇◇◇ Demonstration of Color Contrast (Colored Shadows)

FIND two slide projectors of any kind whatever, place them a few feet apart, and point them so that their projected spots of light overlap each other more or less completely. (No slides should be in the projectors, and they should be focused, or defocused, so that each simply throws a diffuse blotch of light on the wall.) The room should be dimly illuminated or dark, except for the projectors. Now place a piece of colored glass, cellophane, or anthing else that is transparent but colored, so that it interrupts all of the light from the brighter of the two projectors. (Red usually does not work very well, but green, blue, yellow, or purple all give strong effects.) The light falling on the wall, now a mixture of white and the color of the filter (say green), should appear as a very desaturated green. If the mixture is strongly

453

colored, try desaturating it by putting the filter over the other projector instead.

Now place your hand somewhere between the projectors and the wall, and examine the colors in its shadows.

There will be one dark region that is illuminated only by stray light in the room (if your hand is close enough to the wall), another region illuminated only by green light, a third only by white light, and the surround illuminated by the mixture of green and white. The region illuminated only by white light will take on the hue complementary to the hue of the color filter.

REFERENCES

Baker, H. D. (1953). Instantaneous thresholds and early dark adaptation. *J. Opt. Soc. Am.* **43**, 798-803.

Barlow, H. B. (1958). Temporal and spatial summation in human vision at different background intensities. *J. Physiol. (London)* **141**, 337-350.

Barlow, H. B., and Levick, W. (1965). The mechanism of directionally sensitive units in the rabbit's retina. *J. Physiol. (London)* **178**, 477-504.

Bongard, M. M., Smirnov, M. S., and Friedrich, L. (1957). The four-dimensional colour space of the extra-foveal retinal area of the human eye. *In* "Visual Problems of Colour," Vol. 1, p. 325. N.P.L. Symp. No. 8, London. Her Majesty's Stationery Office.

Bouman, M. A. (1955). Absolute threshold conditions for visual perception. *J. Opt. Soc. Am.* **45**, 36-43.

Boynton, R. M., and Gordon, J. (1965). "Bezold-Bruke hue shift measured by color-naming technique. *J. Opt. Soc. Am.* **55**, 78-86.

Brindley, G. S. (1959). The discrimination of after-images. *J. Physiol. (London)* **147**, 194-203.

Brindley, G. S. (1960). "Physiology of the Retina and the Visual Pathway," Arnold, London.

Brindley, G. S. (1962). The site of electrical excitation of the human eye. *J. Physiol. (London)* **164**, 189-200.

Brindley, G. S. (1963). Afterimages. *Scientific American* **209**, October, 84-93.

Brindley, G. S., and Rushton, W. A. H. (1959). The colour of monochromatic light when passed into the human retina from behind. *J. Physiol. (London)* **147**, 204-208.

Brown, K. T., Watanabe, K., and Murakami, M. (1965). Early and Late Receptor Potentials of Monkey Cones and Rods. *Cold Spring Harbor Symposia on Quantitative Biology,* Vol. XXX, Cold Spring Harbor Laboratory of Quantitative Biology, Cold Spring Harbor, L.I., New York.

Brown, P. K., and Wald, G. (1964). Visual pigment in single rods and cones of the human retina. *Science* **144**, 45-52.

Bryngdahl, O. (1964). Characteristics of the visual system: psychological measurements of the response to spatial sine-wave stimuli in the mesopic region. *J. Opt. Soc. Am.* **54**, 1152-1160.

Campbell, F. W., and Green, D. G. (1965). Optical and retinal factors affecting visual resolution. *J. Physiol. (London)* **181**, 576-593.

Campbell, F. W., Kulikowski, J. J., and Levinson, J. (1966). The effect of orientation on the visual resolution of gratings. *J. Physiol. (London)* **187**, 427-436.

Campbell, F. W., and Rushton, W. A. H. (1955). Measurement of the scotopic pigment in the living human eye. *J. Physiol. (London)* **130**, 131-147.

Cone, R. A. (1965). The early receptor potential of the vertebrate eye. *Cold Spring Harbor Symposia on Quantitative Biology,* Vol. XXX, Cold Spring Harbor Laboratory of Quantitative Biology, Cold Spring Harbor, L.I., New York.

Cornsweet, T. N. (1956). Determination of the stimuli for involuntary drifts and saccadic eye movements. *J. Opt. Soc. Am.* **46**, 987-993.

Cornsweet, T. N. (1962). Changes in the appearance of stimuli of very high luminance. *Psychol. Rev.* **69**, 257-273.

Cornsweet, T. N. (1966). Stabilized image techniques. *Recent Develop. Vision Res.* M. A. Whitcomb (ed.) NAS-NRC Publication No. 1272.

Cornsweet, T. N. (1969). Information processing in human visual systems. *SRI J.* Feature issue no. 5, January, 1969.

Cornsweet, T. N., and Pinsker, H. M. (1965). Luminance discrimination of brief flashes under various conditions of adaptation. *J. Physiol. (London)* **176**, 294-310.

Dagher, M., Cruz, A., and Plaza, L. (1958). Colour thresholds with monochromatic stimuli in the spectral region 530-630 mμ. "Visual Problems of Colour," Vol. II, National Physical Laboratory Symposium No. 8, pp. 387-398, H. M. Stationery Office, London.

Davidson, M. L. (1966). "A Perturbation Analysis of Spatial Brightness Interaction in Flashed Visual Fields," Ph.D. Thesis, Univ. of California, Berkeley.

Davidson, M. L. (1968). Perturbation approach to spatial brightness interaction in human vision. *J. Opt. Soc. Am.* **58**, 1300-1309.

Davson, H. (1949). "The Physiology of the Eye," McGraw-Hill (Blakiston), New York.

DeValois, R. L., Abromov, I., and Jacobs, G. H. (1966). Analysis of response patterns of LGN cells. *J. Opt. Soc. Am.* **56**, 966-977.

DeValois, R. L., and Jacobs, G. H. (1968). Primate color vision. *Science* **162**, 533-540.

Ditchburn, R. W., and Ginsborg, B. L. (1952). Vision with a stabilized retinal image. *Nature* **170**, 36-37.

Dowling, J. E. (1965). Foveal receptors of the monkey retina: fine structure. *Science* **147**, 57-59.

Dowling, J. E., and Boycott, B. B. (1966). Organization of the primate retina: electron microscopy. *Proc. Roy. Soc. (London) Ser. B.* **166**, 80-111.

Duke-Elder, Sir Stewart (1958). "The Eye in Evolution; System of Ophthalmology," Vol. 1. Mosby, St. Louis, Missouri.

Enoch, J. M., and Fry, G. A. (1958). Characteristics of a model retinal receptor studied at microwave frequencies. *J. Opt. Soc. Am.* **48**, 899-911.

Fletcher, H. (1929). "Speech and Hearing," Van Nostrand, Princeton, New Jersey.

Fuortes, M. G. F. (1959). Initiation of impulses in the visual cells of *Limulus. J. Physiol. (London)* **148**, 14-28.

Gibson, J. J., and Radner, M. (1937). Adaptation, aftereffect, and contrast in the perception of tilted lines. I. qualitative studies. *J. Exptl. Psychol.* **20**, 453-467.

Graham, C. H., and Margaria, R. (1935). Area and the intensity-time relation in the peripheral retina. *Am. J. Physiol.* **113**, 299-305.

Greeff, Z. (1900). Graefe-Saemisch Hb. ges. augenheilk., II, **1**, Kap. 5.

Hagins, W. A. (1955). The quantum efficiency of bleaching of rhodopsin *in situ. J. Physiol. (London)* **129**, 22P-23P.

Hartline, H. K., and Graham, C. H. (1932). Nerve impulses from single receptors in the eye. *J. Cell. Comp. Physiol.* **1**, 277-295.

Hartline, H. K., and McDonald, P. R. (1947). Light and dark adaptation of single photoreceptor elements in the eye of *Limulus. J. Cell. Comp. Physiol.* **30**, 225-253.

Hartline, H. K., and Ratliff, F. (1957). Inhibitory interaction of receptor units in the eye of *Limulus. J. Genl. Physiol,* **40**, 357-376.

Hartline, H. K., Wagner, H. G., and MacNichol, E. F. (1952). The Peripheral Origin of Nervous Activity in the Visual System. *Cold Spring Harbor Symposia on Quantitative Biology,* Vol. 17, pp. 125-141, Cold Spring Harbor Laboratory of Quantitative Biology, Cold Spring Harbor, L. I., New York.

Hartline, H. K., Wagner, H. G., and Ratliff, F. (1956). Inhibition in the Eye of *Limulus. J. Gen. Physiol.* **39**, 651-673.

Hecht, S., Schlaer, S., and Pirenne, M. H. (1942). Energy, quanta, and vision. *J. Gen. Physiol.* **25**, 819-840.

Heinemann, E. G. (1955). Simultaneous brightness induction as a function of inducing- and test-field luminance. *J. Exptl. Psychol.* **50**, 89-96.

Held, R. (1954). Visual adaptation to chromatic dispersion. Presented to Meeting of Eastern Psychological Association.

Hodgkin, A. L. (1948). The local electric changes associated with repetitive action in a non-modulated axon. *J. Physiol. (London)* **107**, 165-181.

Hubel, D. H., and Wiesel, T. N. (1959). Receptive fields of single neurones in the cat's striate cortex. *J. Physiol. (London)* **148**, 574-591.

Hubel, D. H., and Wiesel, T. N. (1962). Receptive fields, binocular interaction, and functional architecture in the cat's visual cortex. *J. Physiol. (London)* **160**, 106-154.

Hubel, D. H., and Wiesel, T. N. (1965). Receptive fields and functional architecture in two nonstriate visual areas (18 and 19) of the cat. *J. Neurophysiol.* **28**, 228-289.

Ivanoff, A. (1956). About the spherical aberration of the eye. *J. Opt. Soc. Am.* **46**, 901-903.

Jameson, D., and Hurvich, L. M. (1961). Opponent chromatic induction: experimental evaluation and theoretical account. *J. Opt. Soc. Am.* **51**, 46-53.

Kelly, D. H. (1961a). Visual responses to time-dependent stimuli. I. amplitude sensitivity measurements. *J. Opt. Soc. Am.* **51**, 422-429.

Kelly, D. H. (1961b). Flicker fusion and harmonic analysis. *J. Opt. Soc. Am.* **51**, 917-918.

Kelly, D. H. (1969). Flickering patterns and lateral inhibition. *J. Opt. Soc. Am.* **59**, 1361-1370.

Kohlrausch, A. (1931). "Handbuch der normalen und pathologischen-Physiologie," Vol. 12/2, p. 1499. Springer, Berlin.

Krinov, E. L. (1947). "Izadeltel' styo Akad. Nauk." USSR (Curve obtained from Wyszecki and Stiles, 1967).

Kropf, A., and Hubbard, R. (1958). The mechanism of bleaching rhodopsin. *Ann. N. Y. Acad. Sci.* **74**, 266-280.

Lowry, E. M., and DePalma, J. J. (1961). Sine-wave response of the visual system. I. the Mach phenomenon. *J. Opt. Soc. Am.,* **51**, 740-746.

Ludvigh, E., and McCarthy, E. F. (1938). Absorption of visible light by the refractive media of the human eye. *Arch. Ophthal.* **20**, 37-51.

Luria, S. M. and Schwartz, I. (1960). Visual Acuity Under Red vs. White Illumination, U. S. Nav. Med. Res. Lab., Rept. No. 19, Groton, Conn.

MacAdam, D. L. (1965). Analytical approximations for color metric coefficients, IV. smoothed modifications of Friele's formulas, *J. Opt. Soc. Am.* **55**, 91-95.

Marks, W. B., Dobell W. H., and MacNichol, J. R. (1964). Visual pigments of single primate cones. *Science* **143**, 1181-1183.

Marshall, W. H., and Talbot, S. A. (1942). Recent evidence for neural mechanisms in vision leading to a general theory of sensory acuity, *in* H. Klüver (ed). "Visual Mechanisms." *Biol. Symp.* **7**, 117-164. Lancaster, Pennsylvania, Jacques Cattell.

Maxwell, J. C. (1861). On the theory of three primary colours. Lecture delivered in 1861. W. D. Nevin (ed.), *Sci. Papers* **1**, Cambridge Univ. Press, London, 1890, 445–450.

Moon, P. (1940). Proposed standard solar-radiation curves for engineering use. *J. Franklin Inst.* **230**, 583.

O'Brien, B. (1951). Vision and resolution in the central retina. *J. Opt. Soc. Am.* **41**, 882–894.

Osterberg, G. (1935). Topography of the layer of rods and cones in the human retina. *Acta. Ophthal. Suppl.* 6

Pirenne, M. H. (1967). "Vision and the Eye," 2nd ed., Associated Book Publishers, London.

Pitt, F. H. G. (1944). The nature of normal trichromatic and dichromatic vision. *Proc. Roy. Soc. (London) Ser. B* **132**, 101–117.

Polyak, S. (1957). "The Vertebrate Visual System," Univ. of Chicago Press, Chicago.

Pritchard, R. M., Heron, W., and Hebb, D. O. (1960). Visual perception approached by the method of stabilized images. *Can. J. Psychol.* **14**, 67.

Purdy, D. M. (1931). Spectral hue as a function of intensity. *Am. J. Psychol.* **43**, 541.

Purdy, D. M. (1937). The Bezold–Brucke phenomenon and contours for constant hue. *Am. J. Psychol.* **49**, 313–315.

Purkinje, Johann. (1825). Beobachtungen und Versuche zur Physiologie der Sinne. *Zweites Bändchen.* pp. 192. G. Reimer, Berlin.

Ratliff, F., and Hartline, H. K. (1959). The responses of *Limulus* optic nerve fibers to patterns of illumination on the retinal mosaic. *J. Gen. Physiol.* **42**, 1241–1255.

Ratliff, F., Hartline, H. K., and Miller, W. H. (1963). Spatial and temporal aspects of retinal inhibitory interaction. *J. Opt. Soc. Am.* **53**, 110–120.

Ratliff, F., and Riggs, L. A. (1950). Involuntary motions of the eye during monocular fixation. *J. Exptl. Psychol.* **40**, 687–701.

Riggs, L. A., Ratliff, F., Cornsweet, J. C., and Cornsweet, T. N. (1953). The disappearance of steadily fixated visual test objects. *J. Opt. Soc. Am.* **43**, 495–501.

Rushton, W. A. H. (1958a). Kinetics of cone pigments measured objectively on the living human fovea. *Ann. N.Y. Acad. Sci.* **74**, 291–304.

Rushton, W. A. H. (1958b). Visual pigments in the colour blind. *Nature* **182**, 690–692.

Rushton, W. A. H. (1961). Peripheral coding in the nervous system, in "Sensory Communication," W. A. Rosenblith (ed.), Mass. Inst. Technol. Press, Cambridge, Massachusetts.

Rushton, W. A. H. (1962a). Visual pigments in man in "The Sherrington Lectures," Vol. VI, Thomas, Springfield, Ill.

Rushton, W. A. H. (1963a). A cone pigment in the protanope. *J. Physiol. (London)* **168**, 345–359.

Rushton, W. A. H. (1963b). Cone pigment kinetics in the protanope. *J. Physiol. (London)* **168**, 374–388.

Rushton, W. A. H. (1964). Colour blindness and cone pigments. *Am. J. Optom. and Arch. Am. Acad. Optom.* Prentice Lecture, **41**, 265-282.

Rushton, W. A. H. (1965). The Ferrier lecture. Visual adaptation. *Proc. Roy. Soc. (London) Ser. B.* **162**, 20-46.

Safir, A., and Hyams, L. A. (1969). Distribution of cone orientations as an explanation of the Stiles-Crawford effect. *J. Opt. Soc. Am.* **59**, 757-766.

Schultze, M. (1866). Zur anatomie und physiologie der Retina. *Arch. Mikr. Anat.,* **2**, 175-286.

Sinden, R. H. (1923). Studies based on spectral complementaries. *J. Opt. Soc. Am.* **7**, 1123-1153.

Steinman, R. M., Cunitz, R. J., Timberlake, G. T., and Herman, M. (1967). Voluntary control of microsaccades during maintained monocular fixation. *Science* **155**, 1577-1579.

Stiles, W. S., and Crawford, B. H. (1933). The luminous efficiency of rays entering the eye pupil at different points. *Proc. Roy. Soc. (London) Ser. B* **112**, 428-450.

Swets, J. A. (1964). "Signal Detection and Recognition by Human Observers," Wiley, New York.

van den Brink, G. (1962). Measurement of the geometrical aberrations of the eye. *Vision Res.* **2**, 233.

Van Nes, F. L., and Bouman, M. A. (1965). The effects of wavelength and luminance on visual modulation transfer. *Excerpta, Medica, Intern. Congr. Ser. No. 125.* "Performance of the Eye at Low Luminance." Proc. of the Symposium, Delft.

Veringa, F. (1964). Electro-optical stimulation of the human retina as a research technique. *in* "Flicker," (Henkes, H. E., and van der Tweel, L. H., eds.) Dr. W. Junk Publishers, The Hague, pp. 72-82.

von Bekesy, G. (1949). On the resonance curve and the decay period at various points on the cochlear partition, *J. Acoust. Soc. Am.* **21**, 245-254.

Wald, G. (1945). Human vision and the spectrum. *Science* **101**, 653-658.

Wald, G. (1964). The receptors for human color vision. *Science* **145**, 1007-1017.

Wald, G., and Brown, P. K. (1965). Human color vision and color blindness. Symposia on Quantitative Biology, Vol. XXX, pp. 345-359, The Cold Spring Harbor Laboratory of Quantitative Biology; Cold Springs Harbor, New York.

Wald, G., Brown, P. K., and Gibbons, I. R. (1963). The problem of visual excitation. *J. Opt. Soc. Am.* **53**, 20-35.

Wald, G., Brown, P. K., and Smith, P. H. (1955). Iodopsin. *J. Gen. Physiol.* **38**, 623-681.

Wallach, H. (1948). Brightness constancy and the nature of achromatic colors. *J. Exptl. Psychol.* **38**, 310-324.

Walls, G. L. (1963). "The Vertebrate Eye and Its Adaptive Radiation." Hafner, New York.

Walraven, P. L. (1961). On the Bezold-Brucke phenomenon. *J. Opt. Soc. Am.* **51**, 1113-1116.

Walters, H. V., and Wright, W. D. (1943). The spectral sensitivity of the fovea and extrafovea in the Purkinje range. *Proc. Roy. Soc. (London) Ser. B* **131**, 340-361.

Weale, R. A. (1965). Vision and fundus reflectometry: a review. *Photochem. Photobiol.* **4**, 67-87.

Weisskopf, V. F. (1968). How light interacts with matter. *Scientific American* **219**, No. 3, 60-71.

Westheimer, G. (1967). Dependence of the magnitude of the Stiles-Crawford effect on retinal location. *J. Physiol. (London)* **192**, 309-315.

Westheimer, G., and Campbell, F. W. (1962). Light distribution in the image formed by the living human eye. *J. Opt. Soc. Am.* **52**, 1040-1045.

Wolken, J. J. (1966). "Vision," Thomas, Springfield, Illinois.

Wyszecki, G., and Stiles, W. S. (1967). "Color Science," Wiley, New York.

Zegers, R. T. (1959). Photo-sensitization in relation to mean and standard deviation values. *Psychol. Monogr.* **73**, 1-25.

SUGGESTED GENERAL READINGS

This is a very small sampling of the many excellent books covering various topics related to vision. They were selected for their particular relevance to the topics discussed in this text.

1. Monk, G. S. (1963). "Light," 2nd ed. Boulder, New York. This is a clearly written and fairly elementary coverage of physical and geometrical optics.

2. Stevens, C. F. (1966). "Neurophysiology: A Primer," Wiley, New York. An excellent elementary introduction to the actions of the nervous system.

3. Brindley, G. S. (1960). "Physiology of the Retina and the Visual Pathway," Arnold, London. This is a superb analysis of certain topics in the electrophysiology, psychophysics, and psychophysiology of vision. However, it is extremely difficult reading.

4. Ratliff, F. (1965). "Mach Bands: Quantitative Studies on Neural Networks in the Retina," Holden-Day, San Francisco. In addition to translations of some early papers of Ernst Mach on the perception of brightness, this book contains a very well written review of spatial interactions in the visual system, relying heavily upon work on the eye of *Limulus*.

5. Wyszecki, G. W., and Stiles, W. S. (1967). "Color Science, Concepts and Methods, Quantitative Data and Formulas," Wiley, New York. This is an extraordinarily complete work on color vision and topics related to color vision.

6. Graham, C. H. (ed.) (1965). "Vision and Visual Perception," Wiley, New York. This book contains, within a single volume, a large amount of information about almost all the fundamental topics in visual perception.

7. Davson, H. (ed.) (1962). "The Eye," 4 Vols. Academic Press, New York. This set of books gives comprehensive coverage to the physiology and optics of the eyeball, and of many topics in visual perception.

AUTHOR INDEX

SUBJECT INDEX